Think tank traditions

Published in our
centenary year
~ **2004** ~
MANCHESTER
UNIVERSITY
PRESS

Think tank traditions

Policy research and the politics of ideas

edited by Diane Stone
and Andrew Denham

Manchester University Press

Copyright © Manchester University Press 2004

While copyright in the volume as a whole is vested in Manchester University Press, copyright in individual chapters belongs to their respective authors, and no chapter may be reproduced wholly or in part without the express permission in writing of both author and publisher.

www.manchesteruniversitypress.co.uk

British Library Cataloguing-in-Publication Data
A catalogue record for this book is available from the British Library

Library of Congress Cataloging-in-Publication Data applied for

ISBN 0 7190 6478 3 *hardback*
     0 7190 6479 1 *paperback*

First published 2004

11 10 09 08 07 06 05 04   10 9 8 7 6 5 4 3 2 1

Typeset in Sabon with Gill Sans display
by Action Publishing Technology Ltd, Gloucester

Contents

List of tables and figures	page vii
Acknowledgements	viii
List of contributors	ix
List of abbreviations	xiii

1 Introduction: think tanks, policy advice and governance
   Diane Stone   1

I The international dimension

2 Institutes of international affairs: their roles in foreign policy-making, opinion mobilization and unofficial diplomacy
   Inderjeet Parmar   19

3 Think tanks beyond nation-states   *Diane Stone*   34

4 European Union think tanks: generating ideas, analysis and debate   *Heidi Ullrich*   51

II European think tank traditions

5 Think tanks in Germany   *Martin Thunert*   71

6 Italy: think tanks and the political system   *Sonia Lucarelli and Claudio M. Radaelli*   89

7 French think tanks in comparative perspective
   Catherine Fieschi and John Gaffney   105

8 Think tanks, post communism and democracy in Russia and Central and Eastern Europe   *Mark Sandle*   121

III Think tanks in democratic development and economic transition

9 The Chinese tradition of policy research institutes
  Ming-Chen Shai with Diane Stone 141

10 Think tanks in Japan: a new alternative *Makiko Ueno* 163

11 Think tanks and Malaysian development *Su-ming Khoo* 179

12 Think tanks in developing countries: lessons from Argentina
  Miguel Braun, Antonio Cicioni and Nicolas J. Ducote 198

IV The Anglo-American tradition

13 The business of ideas: the think tank industry in the USA
  Donald E. Abelson 215

14 A 'hollowed-out' tradition? British think tanks in the twenty-first century *Andrew Denham and Mark Garnett* 232

15 Australian think tanks *Ian Marsh and Diane Stone* 247

16 Three decades of Canadian think tanks: evolving institutions, conditions and strategies *Evert A. Lindquist* 264

Afterword: soft power, global agendas *William Wallace* 281

Appendix: think tanks and their web sites Diane Stone 291
Bibliography 299
Index 317

List of tables and figures

Tables

4.1	Selected EU think tanks: a typology	page 54
5.1	Types of think tanks in Germany	72
5.2	German political foundations	79
5.3	(Estimated) policy impact of think tanks	85
7.1	Sample of French think tanks	108
12.1	Classification of think tanks in Argentina by organizational form	203
13.1	Selected profile of American think tanks	222
14.1	Selection of British think tanks	233
14.2	Categories of British think tanks	244
15.1	Selected Australian think tanks	251
16.1	Selected Canadian policy think tanks	268

Figures

12.1	Research versus implementation orientation of Argentine think tanks	204

Acknowledgements

At the invitation of our publishers, Manchester University Press, we were cajoled into producing another volume on think tanks to follow on the developments that had occurred in this sector since the publication of *Think tanks across nations* in 1998. We owe a great debt to our contributors, who went well beyond updating their chapters to rewrite and reconceptualize their analyses substantially. Our nine new contributors have helped us greatly in our efforts to expand the remit of this volume and develop a stronger focus on the international activities of think tanks.

Several chapters in this volume appeared in their first guise at the 1995, 1996, 1997 and 2001 annual conferences of the Political Studies Association at the Universities of York, Glasgow, Ulster and Manchester respectively. One paper was presented at the 2000 Global Development Network annual conference in Tokyo. We are very grateful for the lively discussion that ensued from participants at all these meetings.

Among the many individuals who helped us in this enterprise, we would like to extend our thanks again to Tony Mason and Richard Delahunty at Manchester University Press for their patience and commitment to this project. Additionally, the book would never have been completed without the assistance of Marc Schelhase at the University of Warwick, who knocked the final manuscript into shape. Finally, we wish to thank the members of our families and promise them that we will not do this again.

List of contributors

Donald E. Abelson is professor of the Department of Political Science, University of Western Ontario, where he teaches courses on American politics and international relations. He is the author of several publications on think tanks, including *Do Think Tanks Matter? Assessing the Impact of Public Policy Institutes* (2002). dabelson@uwo.ca.

Miguel Braun holds a BA in economics from Universidad de San Andrés and a PhD in economics from Harvard University. He is co-founder and director of fiscal policy, CIPPEC. Additionally, he is invited professor, Universidad de San Andrés, and a consultant for IDB, United Nations/ECLAC. Recent work includes 'Fiscal Rules for Subnational Governments: Some Organizing Principles and Latin American Experiences' (joint conference paper with Mariano Tommasi), and *Political Institutions for Fiscal Solvency* (2002). braunmi@yahoo.com.

Antonio Cicioni holds a BA in political science from the Universidad de San Andrés and a Masters degree in education from Harvard University. He is co-founder and former director of education policy, CIPPEC. He is also the founder and president of Foro Vecinal de Vicente López, a locally based political party in Buenos Aires. He is the author of several articles on education, transparency and government reinvention. ac@cippec.org.

Andrew Denham is reader in government at the University of Nottingham. He is the author of *Think Tanks of the New Right* (1996) and co-author (with Mark Garnett) of *British Think Tanks and the Climate of Opinion* (1998), *Keith Joseph* (2001) and several articles on the role and influence of British think tanks. Andrew.Denham@nottingham.ac.uk.

Nicolas J. Ducote holds a BA in international affairs from the Universidad de San Andrés and a Masters in public policy from the JFK School of Government, Harvard University. He is co-founder and executive director of CIPPEC. A former director of the National School of Government, and a former board member of INAP, he is currently serving on the National Council Monitoring Political Reform. He has also been an international consultant for the United Nations, Transparency International, CEPAL, World Economic Forum, and Kissinger McLarty Associates, among others. nd@cippec.org.

Catherine Fieschi's interests are in European comparative politics. Her research has focused on institutional approaches to the theory of ideologies and more particularly ideologies of the far right in France. She has published on the French and European extreme right, on populism as well as on institutions. Her other interests include comparative politics and comparative methods, institutional and organizational analysis, and theories of citizenship and national identity formation. She is book reviews editor for the journal *French Politics* and director of the Centre for the Study of European Governance. Forthcoming publications include *Populism in the French Fifth Republic* and a co-edited book with Colin Hay, *Ideational Institutionalism and the New Europe*. catherine.fieschi@nottingham.ac.uk.

John Gaffney is professor of French government at Aston University. He is author of *The French Left and the Fifth Republic* (1989) and *The Language of Political Leadership in Contemporary Britain* (1996). He has also edited six books on French and on European politics. He has a particular interest in political rhetoric and political leadership. He is currently engaged in two book projects, one on French politics and one on political leadership. He is the series editor for the new Cassell series 'Contemporary European Politics, Culture, and Society'. j.gaffney@aston.ac.uk.

Mark Garnett is the author of several books on British politics, including *Principles and Politics in Contemporary Britain* (1996) and (with Andrew Denham) *British Think Tanks and the Climate of Opinion* (1998) and *Keith Joseph* (2001). He has taught politics at the universities of Bristol and Leicester. ma_garnett@hotmail.com.

Su-ming Khoo is a lecturer in the Department of Political Science and Sociology, National University of Galway. Her research areas include the sociology of development, cultural theory and the sociology of globalization, with particular interest in alternative development and issues of democratization. s.khoo@nuigalway.ie.

Evert A. Lindquist is director of the School of Public Administration at the University of Victoria in Canada. Previously he worked at the University of Toronto. He is the author of numerous articles on think tanks and on central government agencies, and has been chair of the Research Committee of the Institute of Public Administration of Canada. evert@uvic.ca.

Sonia Lucarelli is an adjoint professor of international relations at the University of Bologna at Forlì. Her areas of interest include IR theory, European security and EU foreign policy. Among her recent publications are *Europe and the Breakup of Yugoslavia: A Political Failure in Search of a Scholarly Explanation* (2000), *La polis europea: L'Unione europea oltre l'euro* (ed., 2002), and *Studi internazionali: i luoghi del sapere in Italia* (with Roberto Menotti, eds, 2002). She is also the author of articles and book chapters on the areas of interest mentioned above. lucarell@tiscalinet.it.

Ian Marsh is a senior fellow in the Political Science Program, Research School of Social Sciences, Australian National University. Recent publications include *Democracy, Governance and Economic Performance, East and Southeast Asia* (with Takashi Inoguchi and Jean Blondel, 1999) and *Beyond the Two Party*

List of contributors   xi

System: Political Representation, Economic Competitiveness and Australian Politics (1999). imarsh@coombs.anu.edu.au.

Inderjeet Parmar is senior lecturer in government in the Centre for International Politics, Department of Government, at the University of Manchester. He has published a book, *Special Interests, the State and the Anglo-American Alliance, 1939–1945* (1995), and several journal articles on US and British foreign policy elites and organizations. He is currently writing a book comparing the roles and influence of Chatham House and the Council on Foreign Relations, 1939–45. Msrgsip@fs1.ec.man.ac.uk.

Claudio M. Radaelli is professor of public policy analysis at Bradford University and co-director of the 2002–03 European Forum of the EUI, Florence. He is the author of *The Politics of Corporate Taxation in the European Union: Knowledge and International Policy Agendas* (1997), *Technocracy in the European Union* (1999) and *The Future of Tax Policy in the EU* (2000). Recent publications include *The Politics of Europeanisation* (with Kevin Featherstone, eds, 2003) and *Governing Regulation: Regulatory Impact Analysis in the OECD Countries and the EU* (ed., 2001). Claudio.Radaelli@IUE.it; c.radaelli@bradford.ac.uk.

Mark Sandle is principal lecturer in Russian and Soviet history at De Montfort University, Leicester. He has published two books, *A Short History of Soviet Socialism* (1999) and *Brezhnev Reconsidered* (with Edwin Bacon, eds, 2002). His research interests lie in the field of ideology and the intelligentsia in the post-Stalin period of Soviet history. He is currently working on a monograph on Gorbachev. masandle@dmu.ac.uk.

Ming-Chen Shai is an assistant professor of public affairs management at Hsuan Chuang University in Taiwan. In 2001, he obtained a PhD in politics and international studies from the University of Warwick. His current research interests focus on the impact of think tanks on policy process, think tanks and political signaling, and electronic government. mshai722@ms59.hinet.net.

Diane Stone is reader in politics and international studies at the University of Warwick and a consultant to the Center for Policy Studies at the Central European University. Her research interests include knowledge institutions; the political economy of higher education; conceptual developments in the study of policy networks; and the political process of policy transfer. Recent articles are to be found in *Global Governance* (2003), *Compare* (2002), *Global Networks* (2002), *Global Social Policy* (2001), *Global Society* (2000) and *Governance* (2000), and she has written and edited books on think tanks. She sits on the governing bodies of the Overseas Development Institute and the Global Development Network. Diane.Stone@warwick.ac.uk.

Martin Thunert has worked at the University of Hamburg and the University of Mannheim and is now visiting associate professor of political science at the University of Michigan. He received his MA from Goethe-University, Frankfurt, and his DPhil. from the University of Augsburg, both in Germany. His areas of teaching and research are comparative politics and public policy. His work has focused on West European as well as North American politics. He has completed a comparative study on the role of think tanks in modern societies focusing on recent developments in the United States, Canada, Britain, Germany and other European countries. His most recent publications in English are 'Players Beyond Borders? German Think Tanks as Catalysts of Internationalisation' (2000) and 'Germany' (2001). martin.thunert@t-online.de; thunert@umich.edu.

Makiko Ueno received her doctoral degree in engineering from the University of Tokyo. Since 1986, she has been working as a research associate at a leading American think tank, the Urban Institute, in Washington, DC. Her research and efforts have expanded from analysing housing policy to bridging the gap in the ideas and concepts of the American and Japanese non-profit sector, think tanks, policy institutions and democratic civil societies. Her publications include *Think Tanks of the World: Linking Knowledge With Public Policy* (with Takahiro Suzuki, 1993), *A Japanese Think Tank: Exploring Alternative Models* (with Raymond Struyk and Takahiro Suzuki, eds, 1993) and its Japanese edition, *Seisaku Keisei to Nihongata Sinku Tanku* (ed. and trans., 1994), and *Think Tanks in a Democratic Society: An Alternative Voice* (with Jeffrey Telgarsky, 1996). MUeno@ui.urban.org.

Heidi Ullrich is currently visiting lecturer at the London School of Economics, where she has also taught a summer school course on the European Union since 1997. Previously she served as senior trade policy officer with Consumers International, lectured on EU integration at the University of Southampton, and held research positions with the US Mission to the WTO and a member of the European Parliament. She has published on topics including the G8's relations with the EU, the G8 in global economic governance, and the WTO and civil society relations. Her writings have appeared in the *Journal of European Public Policy* and *G8 Governance*. H.K.Ullrich@lse.ac.uk.

William Wallace is professor of international relations at the London School of Economics. He was director of studies at the Royal Institute of International Affairs in London 1978–90, and has participated in a wide range of transnational think tank activities in Europe, North America and East Asia. W.Wallace@lse.ac.uk.

List of abbreviations

Abbreviations and acronyms for think tanks are given in the appendix.

ACOSS	Australian Council on Social Services
AKAR	Angkatan Keadilan Rakyat (Malaysia)
ALP	Australian Labor Party
APEC	Asia Pacific Economic Cooperation
ASEAN	Association of Southeast Asian Nations
BN	Barisan Nasional (Malaysia)
CBO	Congressional Budget Office (US)
CCP	Chinese Communist Party
CDU	Christian Democratic Party (Germany)
CEE	Central and Eastern Europe
CIPE	Center for International Private Enterprise
CPSU	Soviet Communist Party
CSU	Christian Social Union in Bavaria
DAP	Democratic Action Party (Malaysia)
DEA	Department of External Affairs
DGB	German Federation of Trade Unions
EMU	European Monetary Union
EUI	European University Institute
FDP	Free Democratic Party – Liberals (Germany)
GDR	German Democratic Republic
IAI	Independent Administrative Institutions
IIA	institutes of international affairs
IMF	International Monetary Fund
IR	international relations
LDP	Liberal Democratic Party (Japan)
LPA	Liberal Party of Australia
LSE	London School of Economics
LUTH	Islamic Bank and Pilgrim Savings Fund (Malaysia)
MCA	Malaysian Chinese Association
METI	Ministry of Economy, Trade and Industry (Japan)
MIC	Malayan Indian Congress
MLIT	Ministry of Land, Infrastructure and Transport (Japan)

MOF	Ministry of Finance (Japan)
NECC	National Economic Consultative Committee (Malaysia)
NEP	New Economic Policy (Malaysia)
NGO	non-governmental organization
OECD	Organization for Economic Co-operation and Development
OPEC	Organization of Petroleum Exporting Countries
OSCE	Organization for Security and Co-operation in Europe
PAS	Islamic Party (Malaysia)
PBS	Parti Bersatu Sabah (Malaysia)
PDS	Party of Democratic Socialism (Germany)
PLA	People's Liberation Army (China)
PSU	Unified Socialist Party (France)
SDP	Social Democratic Party (UK)
SPD	Social Democratic Party (Germany)
UIA	International Islamic University (Malaysia)
UMNO	United Malays Nationalist Organization
USAID	United States Agency for International Development
USSR	Union of Soviet Socialist Republics
WBI	World Bank Institute
WTO	World Trade Organization

I   Diane Stone[1]

Introduction: think tanks, policy advice and governance

The think tank is ubiquitous. This type of organization and activity has spread into most countries. In *Think tanks across nations* (1998), we claimed that until the 1990s, policy research institutes had been accorded little scholarly investigation. In the five years between that volume and this one, think tanks have increased in prominence and number throughout the world. So too have academic analyses.

Where discussion of think tanks was once limited almost exclusively to Anglo-American systems[2], interest has expanded to other Organization for Economic Co-operation and Development (OECD) nations. Wider disciplinary interest has resulted from scholars working on comparative politics and public policy (see Stone, 2000d, 2002; Weaver and Stares, 2001) to include international relations and security studies specialists (Parmar, 1999a, 1999b; Wallace, 1994) as well as a greater array of anthropologists, economists and sociologists writing in this field. Since 2000, a number of doctoral studies of the think tank phenomenon have been completed.[3] Current research trends are increasingly focused on think tank development in the developing world (McGann and Weaver, 2000) and post-communist transition countries (see Goodwin and Nacht, 1995; Krastev, 2000b; Quigley, 1997; Struyk, 1999). These studies come not only in the wake of an explosion of think tank numbers but also in response to the increasing activity of other organizations seeking policy advice and promoting think tank growth. Private foundations, corporations and other non-state actors are demanding high-quality research, policy analysis and ideological argumentation. Governments and international organizations often regard think tanks as a means to extend policy analytic capacities, aid civil society development or promote human capital development (ODC, 1999). Consequently, the study of think tanks has moved from being a social science 'cottage industry' and is now maturing with the emergence of a small transnational research community of think tank analysts.

Analysis of think tanks has fallen into two broad schools. Those focused on the organizational form – such as Weaver (1989) with McGann (McGann and Weaver, 2000) and Smith (1991) – were interested in explaining why and how think tanks have emerged and why some are influential. These analyses distinguished independent public policy institutes from academic research centres, government research units or lobbyists. They were focused on the organizational ingredients of what makes a think tank successful, how think tanks are managed, who funds them, who quotes them and whom they try to influence.

Writers in the second school of analysis (many included in this volume) view think tanks as a vehicle for broader questions about the policy process and the role of ideas and expertise in decision-making. Often, they have employed network approaches such as 'policy community', 'advocacy coalitions' and 'epistemic communities' to explain why ideas matter in the broader context of changing political coalitions and power arrangements. Alternatively, contributors have identified changes in the architecture of the state or its functions to explain why windows of opportunity open or close for think tanks. These studies cut to a central issue in the analysis of think tanks: policy influence and political impact, addressed at the end of this introduction.

The dilemmas of definition

Think tanks vary considerably in size, structure, policy ambit and significance. As a consequence of this diversity, alongside cultural variations in comprehending the role of these organizations, there are considerable difficulties in defining 'think tank'. Virtually all of our contributors point to this dilemma. As chapters 6, 7 and 9 on Italy, France and China indicate, adopting an Anglo-American definition of 'think tank' is problematic. In particular, the notion that a think tank requires independence or autonomy from the state in order to be 'free-thinking' is a peculiar Anglo-American predilection that does not travel well into other cultures. For instance, the line between both French and Chinese policy intellectuals and the state is blurred to such an extent that to talk of independence as a defining characteristic of think tanks makes little sense in their respective cultural contexts; the same is true in other countries.

'Think tank' is a slippery term. It has been applied haphazardly to any organization undertaking policy-related, technical or scientific research and analysis. Such organizations may operate within government (this is evident in the case of most Russian and Chinese think tanks), or be independent non-profit organizations, or be attached to a profit-making corporate entity (as is often the case in Japan). The Anglo-American understanding is of relatively autonomous organizations engaged in the analysis of policy issues independently of government, political parties and pressure groups. It is a *'relative* autonomy', as think tanks are often in resource-dependent relationships with these organizations. Funding may come from government sources, but these institutes attempt to maintain their research freedom and at least claim not to be beholden to any specific interest. They try to influence or inform policy through intellectual argument and analysis rather than direct lobbying. They are engaged in the rigorous analysis of policy issues and are concerned with the ideas and concepts that underpin policy. Towards this end, think tanks collect, synthesize and create a range of information products, often directed towards a political or bureaucratic audience, but sometimes also for the benefit of the media, interest groups, business, international civil society and the general public of a nation.

The degree of overlap between think tanks and other organizations in society prevents a precise, clear-cut boundary between think tanks and other entities. However, they differ sufficiently to justify separate categorisation. They have been described as 'universities without students' (Weaver, 1989: 564). The difference is that think tanks are not normally involved in teaching as degree-granting institutions (there are a few exceptions, notably Research and Development (RAND) in the USA). It would be convenient to treat think tanks as more intellectual variants of pressure groups, but again this is not a satisfactory categorization. There are important differences between think tank and pressure group activity – for example, think tanks do not engage in public demonstrations or political lobbying. Think tanks tend to address multiple policy areas (notwithstanding specialization) rather than focus on a single issue or interest as do many pressure groups. Private and public philanthropic foundations are also distinct entitities. Foundations are usually research benefactors providing funding for research rather than undertaking it. However, there are exceptions. With their huge endowments, the Russell Sage Foundation and the Carnegie Endowment for International Peace (CEIP) function as think tanks with in-house researchers. In Italy, the Fondazione Agnelli is also an 'operating foundation', producing policy-relevant research. The more commercial think tanks could be said to be functioning in the same way as consultancy firms, financial institutions or legal offices that provide advice and analysis. However, while a number of think tanks provide advice or analysis on a fee-for-service basis, such services often represent a minor part of their overall activities, whereas for a consultancy it is the main operation. Banks and law firms are primarily engaged in other, considerably more profitable activities than policy research. In sum, there are some important differences.

As think tanks have proliferated in other regions, the think tank idea has been stretched. In tandem with this development, our concept of 'think tank' has loosened since *Think tanks across nations*. While the term 'think tank' has often been adopted in its English wording, with all its cultural connotations (Krastev, 2000b), in some countries, and especially Central and Eastern Europe (CEE), it has been applied to government research units that lack autonomy from political interests. Increasingly, 'think tank' is equated with a policy research *function* and set of analytic or policy advisory practices rather than a specific legal *organizational structure* as a non-profit or private sector body.

Alongside this conceptual stretching, the lexical currency has been debased. Not only is there is considerable scholarly difference over how to identify these organizations, but in some countries the directors and senior scholars of these organizations often make bold distinctions between what is a 'research institute' and a 'think tank'. Usually, such disputes revolve around the role of advocacy or publicity-seeking behaviour as opposed to organizational capacity for quality policy research, with think tanks deemed to do the less rigorous former and institutes the more objective latter. Whilst such distinctions may serve an important symbolic role in the competitive market for policy analysis, the differences can often be more imagined than real. The style of 'informing' policy debates or 'educating' public opinion takes multiple forms. Moreover, such distinctions implicitly posit the purity of science and rationality against the impurities of ideology and normative understandings (see the essays in Braun and Busch, 2000). It sets up a false ontological divide between knowledge and power that denies the inherently political nature of research.

Think tanks need to have some kind of engagement with government if they are to succeed in influencing policy. However, their desire to preserve intellectual autonomy means that most try to strike a delicate balance between dependence on government and total isolation from it. The precise nature of think tank 'independence' is to be treated with flexibility. While many institutes discussed in this volume are private organizations, their degree of independence varies across a number of dimensions. Despite *legal independence*, some of the organizations may be said to have resigned their autonomy to government, a political party or a corporation. For example, in Malaysia the Institute of Strategic and International Studies (ISIS) was established at the instigation of the Malaysian Cabinet (although it has since acquired formal independence). By the same token, it cannot always be assumed that government-created think tanks enjoy an automatic bureaucratic route to decision-makers. Even inside government, policy research and analysis can be marginalized as irrelevant to the cut-and-thrust and immediacy of politics.

A number of think tanks are dependent on a single funding source, whether it be governmental or private. Accordingly, *financial independence* could be construed as developing an endowment or having numerous sponsors and a diverse funding base, so that the organization is not dependent on any *one* or few benefactors. *Scholarly independence* is a different concept, and reliant upon certain practices within an institute:

Introduction

for example, the processes of peer review and a commitment to open inquiry rather than directed research. As the following chapters show, cultural understandings of independence, the degree of think tank autonomy, and the extent of interest in policy and political issues vary dramatically not only from country to country but from one institute to another.

The world-wide spread of think tanks

Studying think tanks cross-nationally sheds light on how government institutions and political actors interpret and respond to political problems. Different institutional and cultural environments affect think tank modes of operation and their capacity or opportunity for policy input and influence. Oppressive regimes can severely limit the realm of 'safe' policy inquiry and investigation. In Egypt, for instance, international attention has been drawn to the forced closure of the Ibn Khaldoun Centre and the imprisonment of four of its scholars. In many countries, the think tank population is sparse and stunted, or quiet and uncritical, where 'independent' research is problematically dependent upon a tolerant political culture and freedom of speech.

Unsurprisingly, think tank development across nations is very uneven. By 2000, in excess of 1200 think tanks were estimated to have emerged in the USA (Hellebust, 1996), while they were and still are relatively few in number in European countries. American analysts often argue that the US system is more open, pluralistic and permeable than European political systems. They often assume (*inter alia*, Polsby, 1983; Weaver, 1989) that there are fewer opportunities for think tanks to enter the policy fray in Europe and elsewhere due to factors such as stronger party systems, corporatist modes of decision-making, strong and relatively closed bureaucracies, or weak philanthropic sectors. Such assumptions about the 'exceptionalism' of American political structures and institutions should not be taken entirely at face value. There has been a think tank boom in CEE, suggesting that other political systems provide fertile conditions for their proliferation and abundance. Indeed, think tanks are often perceived by young professionals in the region as a more viable vehicle for personal advancement than a career in decimated public sectors.

The think tank form has also spread extensively into Central and Latin America (Sherwood Truitt, 2000), East Asia (Yamamoto, 1995) and, more recently, the Middle East, North and Sub-Saharan Africa (Johnson, 1997). Quantitative data on think tanks is imprecise. McGann and Weaver (2000), employing a strict definition of 'think tank' as a private civil society body, put the total world-wide in excess of 4000. The figure is likely to be much higher.

Think tank proliferation can be explained by a variety of factors. Constitutional changes and government reform, the intensity of political debate and opposition, the attitudes of political leaders and the political culture of a society open and close opportunity for think tanks and policy entrepreneurs. Rising levels of literacy and press freedom, the development of a domestically based intellectual elite, and a history of philanthropy, independent organization and voluntarism within civil society are also relevant factors in explaining the emergence of think tanks within a particular country and internationally. The governance programmes of the EU, the World Bank, the UN and bilateral development assistance have also promoted the Western export of the think tank form. There are, however, significant differences in the organizational characteristics of think tanks between countries.

The American tax structure encourages the formation of foundations and individual giving, creating a massive source of funding for think tanks and other non-profit organizations. In Australia, Canada and Japan, the foundation sector is less developed and corporate funding of think tanks is paltry compared to the USA. Yet foundations in OECD countries have funded think tank capacity-building initiatives throughout the developing world. For instance, the Ford Foundation provided capital for the establishment of the Thailand Development Research Institute, while the Konrad Adenauer Stiftung (KAS) has funded a series of dialogues among Asian think tanks.

The federal structure of government has also aided the proliferation of US think tanks. Federal systems supposedly provide more fora into which think tanks can target their activities. However, while this may be true of the *Länder* in Germany and to a lesser extent of Malaysia, it evidently cannot explain the situation in Australia or Canada, where think tanks are less numerous than in a unitary system such as the UK. Additionally, the USA has a presidential system whereas Britain, Canada and Australia are parliamentary systems of a 'party government' type (Weaver and Rockman, 1993: 20). The checks-and-balances system of the USA provides interstices through which think tanks can emerge. By contrast, parliamentary systems involve greater centralization of legislative power and accountability, supposedly allowing for greater control over policy and exclusion of external policy actors. Furthermore, political parties in parliamentary systems (especially those with a 'first past the post' electoral system) tend to be more cohesive and disciplined. In the USA, individual legislators have considerable autonomy and face little pressure from their party to conform to policy positions. Consequently, it would seem more likely they would benefit from contacts with think tanks, experts and interest group activists. These factors appear to make the USA a more congenial home for think tanks than France, for instance, where the central bureaucracy is more powerful.

Bureaucratic structures and styles differ markedly between countries. Government appointees are more apparent in presidential systems. In the USA, administrative permeability of the executive is commonplace. By contrast, in Japan, Britain, Canada and Australia, permanent civil services dominate as a source of policy advice. The use of special advisors from universities, business, think tanks and elsewhere is not extensive in these countries. Yet since the early 1980s, there seems to be a tendency towards drawing upon external sources of advice, possibly in response to what is seen as the 'rubber stamp' role of parliaments, or a reaction against the civil service view or *pensée unique*. Thus, the 'closed' nature of these systems can be overstated. Although Japan is an exception here, it is not unknown for think tank representatives to appear before commissions of inquiry, to speak at parliamentary committees or to be incorporated into bureaucratic taskforces. Indeed, as our Argentinian contributors reveal (chapter 12), think tanks are also co-opted into policy implementation.

There is no evidence that think tanks are more likely to develop further within multi-party systems contributing to coalition government (as in Germany) or in strong two-party systems which alternate in office (as in Britain and Australia). The link with political parties is clearly central to understanding the role of think tanks in Germany. In other countries, such as Italy, the ties to political parties are less formal and substantial. In the dominant party system of Malaysia, where party competition is circumscribed, think tank numbers rocketed during the 1990s. Even in the one-party system of China, both governmental and some private think tanks have flourished since the early 1990s.

One proposition regarding think tank growth concerns government 'overload' and the increasing complexity of decision-making processes. In this view, think tank growth is indicative of a need for more information, analysis and advice as economies and societies become more complex. Big government, globalization and the flood of information from interest groups, industry and new government programmes mean that think tanks become one source of expertise able to explain the nature, causes and likely remedies of problems. Similarly, they have become useful translators of the abstract modelling and dense theoretical concepts characteristic of contemporary social science. For governments concerned about 'evidence-based policy', think tanks potentially help create a more 'rational' policy process by augmenting in-house research capacities, circumventing time and institutional constraints and alerting elites to changing global circumstances (Dror, 1984).

Rather than organizations for 'rational' knowledge utilization in policy, think tank development is also indicative of the politicization of knowledge. Denham and Garnett (chapter 14) argue that this has led to the 'hollowing out' of British think tanks. In a few countries think tanks are a means of career advancement or a stepping stone for the politically ambitious. The 'revolving door' of individuals moving between executive appointment and think tanks, law firms or universities is a well-known phenomenon in the USA but is increasingly seen in CEE countries. Similarly, Su-ming Khoo (chapter 11) reveals that a handful of Malaysian think tanks are a means of promoting the political ambitions of a few politicians whilst institutes are key support structures in the factionalism of Chinese state-party politics.

Political parties and interest groups have established formal and informal ties with think tanks, not only because the latter are a source of policy ideas and innovation, but also because they have intellectual authority that can be used to give established policy positions additional credibility. Similarly, in a number of countries, the media has developed an enormous appetite for think tank services. Mutually beneficial relationships develop, whereby think tanks represent an 'expert' source of information and commentary for journalists who, in turn, play a key role in amplifying or broadcasting think tank analyses. Another demand-side explanation for the massive growth in think tanks worldwide might arise from the 'inability of traditional bureaucracies and interest groups to put aside sectorally narrow, self-serving policies and develop innovative and integrative solutions to policy problems' (Langford and Brownsey, 1991: 2). The private provision of more diverse sources of policy advice thus represents a form of market correction. However, a political explanation might identify demand arising with the dissatisfaction of political leaders or parties with existing sources of policy advice. For instance, the establishment of ISIS was a means for the prime minister, Mahathir bin Mohamed, to circumvent the Malaysian bureaucracy and concentrate his power.

Another thesis of the recent spread of think tanks is that a long-term process of convergence has taken place. That is, the creation of (quasi-) independent policy research institutes is indicative of national intellectual and decision-making elites copying Western bodies (particularly those of the USA – see Dolowitz and Marsh, 2000; Krastev, 2000b). There is some evidence to support this explanation for think tank dispersion. One dynamic for convergence outlined in chapter 2 on institutes of international affairs is imperial ties. The Atlas Economic Research Foundation (Atlas Foundation) and the Mont Pelerin Society have been an important funding organization and intellectual society respectively that have supported libertarian and free market institutes around the world. Organizational transfer has also been fuelled by individuals trained in Western educational systems who have gained both familiarity with the think tank form and, occasionally, a desire to replicate them in their countries of origin.

While the convergence argument has some purchase, it does not explain the development of all institutes outside the Anglo-American world. Many bodies emerge as the result of initiatives and dynamics *within*, rather than outside, the host country. Furthermore, rather than mimicry, a range of organizational forms, styles and practices has emerged across nations. As the following chapters indicate, national political cultures and institutional arrangements strongly determine the type of think tank that takes root and the character of its policy involvement.

Another thesis that may partially explain the development of think tanks emphasizes the spread of democracy, often in tandem with economic development. Think tanks seem to be more prevalent in industrially advanced democratic polities. This could easily lead to the inference that think tanks are symptomatic of democratization and national prosperity. A diversity of organizations, none of which has a monopoly on policy advice, strengthens the democratic functioning of society by educating the populace and providing another forum for political debate and participation. This theme is developed in chapter 10 on Japan and to a lesser extent chapter 12 on Argentina. A comparative examination, however, suggests that there is no simple correlation. As chapter 11 on Malaysia reveals, think tanks are associated with political elites rather than the wider citizenry in a political system with the trappings if not the substance of democracy. Furthermore, think tanks can duplicate a closed and secretive environment. This is clearly the case in China. Instead of presenting opportunities for participation, their prestige can act as a barrier to policy input from more democratic sources.

Not unrelated to ideas of democratic consolidation, the majority of chapters outline 'waves of think tank development' within the countries considered here. Such waves of development will vary from country to country but each appears to bring increasing diversity. Abelson (chapter 13), Lindquist (chapter 16), Denham and Garnett (chapter 14) and Marsh and Stone (chapter 15) all note how later generations of American, Canadian, British and Australian think tanks are more advocacy oriented, partisan or ideological. Yet Lucarelli and Radaelli (chapter 6) consider that while Italian think tanks are becoming less academic in character, they are not being politicized. Asian think tanks exhibit a different evolutionary pattern from that in the West. Their proliferation has occurred later and the majority of institutes are technocratic in character. As would be expected, independent think tanks in Russia and CEE appeared only after 1989.

In many instances, the heightened activity of think tanks appears to be related to periods of economic and political instability. The rise of the so-called 'New Right' think tanks illustrates this point, as their emergence coincided with a crisis in the Keynesian paradigm in policy-making. This suggests that the 'waves of think tank development' in a particular country do not occur in a linear fashion. There are fluctuations within the industry as a whole. Indeed, think tank numbers might dip at certain times, such as during recession, war or periods of authoritarian government. Similar questions apply to individual organizations. Some think tanks experience decline or periodic crises, a number are disestablished or, alternatively, develop into different kinds of organization. Funding sources can dry up, an organization can suffer from a lack of leadership or poor management, or fail to adapt to a changing world. These factors, often internal to organizational operation, can have significant impact on a think tank's capacity for external policy influence.

Finally, beyond the nation-state, there are strong signs of think tank adaptation and evolution that may prefigure a further wave of think tank development and diversification. The activities of international organizations such as the UN agencies, the World Bank, the International Monetary Fund (IMF) and the World Trade Organization (WTO) have drawn think tanks into their ambit. As Heidi Ullrich notes (chapter 4), the European Union provides yet another institutional forum for think tank activity with the emergence of EU-wide think tanks disengaged from specific national identities. Furthermore, with the revolution in information and communication technology, policy research disconnected from specific organizational settings has become increasingly feasible and fashionable. Most think tanks have a virtual presence (see the appendix), and international research exchange and cross-national collaboration between think tanks are commonplace. The EuroMeSco network of Euro-Mediterranean foreign policy institutes is a good example. Consequently, this volume starts with the transnationalization of think tanks, detailing historical antecedents among institutes of international affairs, latterday transnational networking and the development of regional interaction in the EU. This structure may appear to be back to front, but we wish to stress the extensiveness and diversity of think tank structures and styles beyond what is often thought to be the Anglo-American norm.

Think tanks and the issue of influence

One of the most common questions associated with the study of think tanks is how to determine their influence. However, attempts to measure this are plagued with methodological problems. As a result there are wild fluctuations in assessments of think tank powers and capacities. Their impact on policy thinking is often exaggerated, while other commentators refuse to acknowledge that think tanks can have any genuine input at all.

'Influence' is a word that is itself open to a variety of interpretations. For scholars, the problem is complicated by the fact that think tanks often need to convince members, their donors and benefactors, their media contacts and decision-makers of the think tanks' influence, relevance or importance. As a result, they often claim an influence over policy that is inflated or unrealistic. Whilst some of these organizations do have links with the policy formation processes and have some kind of presence in the broader social-political system, their power or influence is limited and dependent. Thus, it may be less the case that think tanks have an impact on government than that governments or certain political leaders employ these organizations as tools to pursue their own interests and provide intellectual legitimation for policy. This is certainly the case in China.

As the politics and policy process of any country is invariably complicated, it is rare to find uncontested examples of a one-to-one correspondence between a think tank report and a policy adopted subsequently by government. In general, our contributors are sceptical of direct think tank impact on politics. Instead, they develop wider and more nuanced understandings of think tanks' policy influence and social relevance in their roles as agenda-setters that create policy narratives that capture the political and public imagination. This ability to set the terms of debate, define problems and shape policy perception has been described elsewhere as 'atmospheric' influence (James, 2000: 163). In a number of chapters, think tanks appear to be useful in periods of critical transition. Such transitions may occur with electoral change, whereby an incoming party requires transition thinking in the form of policy ideas and blueprints. 'Paradigm shift' represents another form of transition (Hall, 1990). Indeed, many of the Russian *instituteniki* were constitutive of changing policy orthodoxies that led to *glasnost* and *perestroika* in the Union of Soviet Socialist Republics (USSR) (see chapter 8).

The problem of gauging or measuring the impact of think tanks crossnationally is also fraught with difficulties. For example, the attraction of foundation funding is one potential indicator of think tank success. However, a large foundation grant to an Australian institute is more noteworthy than a similar grant to an American think tank simply because of the greater difficulty experienced by Australian think tanks in winning such funding. Similarly, the National Bureau of Economic Research (NBER) may be subject to regular attention from the media in the USA but is less so outside the USA, while ISIS in Malaysia attracts a high level of interest throughout Southeast Asia. These differences highlight the incommensurability of indicators across borders. However, these methodological dilemmas do not mean that the question of influence cannot be meaningfully explored.

Early studies of think tanks tended to adopt a macro-level focus of explanation. Many of these studies adopted power approaches to the role of think tanks in decision-making. Elite studies of institutes such as the Brookings Institution (Critchlow, 1985; Dye, 1978) have emphasized how think tanks are key components of the 'power elite', where decision-making is concentrated in the hands of a few groups and individuals. The problem with such studies is that analysis is directed towards well-known policy institutions with solid links to political parties or the corporate sector, neglecting the role of smaller, lesser-known institutes, which thrive in much larger numbers than the 'elite' think tanks.

Neo-Marxists have argued that establishment think tanks are consensus-building organizations for maintaining hegemonic control (Desai, 1994). Think tanks develop the ideology and long-range plans that convert problems of political economy into manageable objects of public policy. Furthermore, as the common economic interests and social cohesion among the power elite are insufficient to produce consensus on policies, agreement on such matters requires 'research, consultation and deliberation' to form a coherent sense of long-term class interests (Domhoff, 1983: 82). These institutes mobilize elites to redefine the terms of debate in order to translate class interests into state action (Peschek, 1987; Stefanic and Delgado, 1996). In common with elite theorists, scholars in this tradition perceive capitalists as cohesive and active in sustaining privilege. Think tanks are identified as a central component in the political mobilization of business. However, neo-pluralist and structuralist arguments that capital is divided and unco-ordinated provide better explanations for the diversity of think tanks as well as their more partisan and ideological stances (Himmelstein, 1990: 159).

In chapter 2, Inderjeet Parmar adopts a neo-Gramscian framework of analysis but extends it by focusing on the *transnational* dimensions of hegemonic projects (in chapter 7, Catherine Fieschi and John Gaffney note similar strategies of New Right groups in France). Think tanks are portrayed as one set of actors in 'knowledge networks' that incorporate professional associations, academic research groups and scientific communities organized around a special subject matter or issue (Stone, 2002). Individual or institutional inclusion in such networks is based upon professional and official recognition of expert authority as well as more subtle and informal processes of validating scholarly and scientific credibility. A neo-Gramscian understanding of such networks links private knowledge actors and institutions to the material interests and structures of globalizing capitalism (Sinclair, 2000). The emphasis is on 'organic intellectuals' whose ideas are funded, generated and disseminated by foundations, corporations, publishing houses and non-governmental organizations (NGOs).

Pluralist studies of think tanks have emphasized the competition between them for access to the political system and how the market place of ideas is open and plural. Independent or private think tanks are often portrayed as creating a more open, participatory and educated populace and representing a counter to the influence of powerful techno-bureaucratic, corporate and media interests on the policy agenda. Moreover, a more informed, knowledge-based policy process – a role that think tank experts help fulfil – could enlighten decision-making (Weiss, 1990). The problem with such studies is that not all policy groups have equal access to the political system. Policy agendas are distorted by groups exercising structural power or political patronage.

Some of the authors in this volume suggest that fluctuating think tank influence has much to do with the way in which think tanks interact in policy networks. 'Policy network' is a generic term for a variety of different conceptual models, including 'policy communities' or 'epistemic communities', 'advocacy coalitions' and 'discourse coalitions'. A policy network is a mode of governance that incorporates actors from both inside and outside government to facilitate decision-making and implementation. Through networks, think tanks can be integrated into the policy-making process. Pluralists usually stress the openness and informal participation in decision-making offered by networks. Yet policy networks can also prevent the emergence of challenges to dominant values or interests, suppressing or thwarting demands for change in the existing allocation of benefit and privilege in society. Networks potentially undermine political accountability by excluding the public. Institutional procedures entail that the system responds better to the well-organized, wealthy, skilled and knowledgeable rather than to disorganized, poorly financed, unskilled pressure groups. Thus the network literature can accommodate elite views, that networks are closed and dominated by a small number of key actors, as well as Marxist perspectives, that networks are dominated by interests representing capital.

Within policy communities, think tanks (or their scholars) are likely to acquire 'insider' status if they share the prevailing values and attitudes of the policy community. The advocacy coalition approach places greater emphasis on the view that analysis has a long-term enlightenment function in altering policy orthodoxies, and highlights the role of beliefs, values and ideas as a neglected dimension of policy-making (Sabatier, 1987). This approach is employed in chapter 6 on Italian think tanks. Discourse coalition comes from the 'argumentative turn' in policy studies and emphasizes language and political symbolism (Fischer, 1993). The focus is on how a policy problem is defined and the discourse through which the problem is understood. It is a constructivist approach that emphasizes the development of 'intersubjective knowledge' – common understandings and shared identities – as the dynamic for change (Stone, 2002: 2). Unlike those taking neo-Gramscian perspectives, proponents of this school are more likely to argue that ideas (such as policy research and analysis) can have independent impact on politics. In not dissimilar fashion, the epistemic community concept (Haas, 1992a) focuses on the specific role of experts in the policy process and the heightened influence of 'consensual knowledge' in conditions of policy uncertainty. It is a concept picked up in chapters 4 and 7 on EU and French think tanks.

The policy network literature illuminates how think tanks seek to influence political agendas and the manner in which networks involve think tanks as 'policy entrepreneurs'. Within networks, think tanks contribute policy-aware advocates, researchers and other specialists who analyse problems and propose solutions. In short, they provide intellectual resources. The scholars and executives of think tanks act as policy entrepreneurs, firstly, by promoting ideas and pushing them higher on the public agenda, and secondly, by 'softening up' actors in the political and policy system to new ideas. When an opportunity arises (for example, elections or a policy crisis), an entrepreneur's ideas might meet a receptive audience (Kingdon, 1984). Rather than concentrating on formal decision-making procedures, the policy milieu is assumed to include non-formal actors. Accordingly, the approach is also useful for understanding how think tanks extend their activities and interests beyond the nation-state into regional and global policy domains.

Think tanks bring social science research into the public domain by seeking appointment to government taskforces, international 'blue ribbon' commissions or industry delegations. The ability of think tank members to establish links with the media, trade unions, pressure groups, political parties, bureaucrats and departments is essential to their coalition building. These informal links create a route of access to decision-makers in order to promote ideas and soften up public opinion. Think tanks' agenda-setting abilities and powers to manipulate social myths, language and symbols can be assessed in terms of power over meaning (Fischer, 1993). In chapter 11 on Malaysia, for example, Khoo emphasizes the discourse of 'development' created and reinforced by elite think tanks.

Networking, policy entrepreneurship and discourse construction to capture political agendas are manifestations of the way in which knowledge has been politicized by think tanks. Additionally, the acquisition or appropriation of think tank policy research by interest groups, government and political parties for their own purposes is another manifestation. Think tanks are not only a source of policy ideas and innovation, but also symbolic of intellectual authority that can be used to support entrenched policy prejudices and political causes.

Despite its utility, the network literature has its limitations. Institutes build an infrastructure to maintain contact and keep actors in policy networks abreast of current activities and research. Networking helps promote solidarity, loyalty, trust and reciprocity. In itself, such networking does not amount to political influence, but it aids the effectiveness of think tanks in promoting policy ideas. It is tempting to equate successful networking with influence. Yet the informal access that networking might afford does not mean that decision-makers pay attention to think tanks. Networks may generate intense activity that does not necessarily translate into policy. Careful analysis is required to distinguish instances where think tanks are providing real input into policy deliberation from those (more frequent) occurrences when they do not.

In the last instance, think tanks operate alone. They are in competition with other think tanks and policy advice organizations to attract political and media attention as well as foundation, corporate and individual support. Consequently, think tanks advance themselves by successfully championing issues and placing themselves towards the centre of debate on key issues. Notwithstanding the difficulty of determining influence, it is evident that think tanks have found audiences in the circles of government, NGOs, the media and international organizations. These audiences are likely to grow rather than diminish.

Taking contemporary think tank development as a whole, they are in transition from the trends and traditions apparent in the twentieth century. The think tank industry or sector is *transcendent*, in several meanings of the word. In a simple sense, the sheer number of think tanks that have emerged world-wide since 1990 greatly exceeds the pace of think tank growth witnessed in the previous century. Furthermore, this type of organization has transcended Anglo-American exceptionalism to appear virtually everywhere and in all kinds of political systems (see the appendix). Think tanks have a 'virus-like' quality, and their dispersal has been aided by finding a niche in the multilateral discourses of democratization and development. Indeed, USAID and a number of foundations are providing seed funds and expertise for the establishment of an Afghani think tank. As editors and chapter contributors, we have gone beyond *Think tanks across nations* by incorporating a wider range of national contexts in which to evaluate think tanks. Moreover, we have sought to highlight how think tanks increasingly transcend the nation-state by developing international networks or undertaking their activities at a regional level. In particular, information technology has allowed think tanks to transcend normal publication processes and media outlets, to develop an independent 'virtual' presence open to anyone with internet access. We suggest that the degree of attention that the think tank phenomenon increasingly receives from us – and from many other scholars around the world – thus supersedes the marginal treatment that they have received in the past as a subject of social science inquiry. Finally, whilst the chapters in this volume address concrete organizations and the policy actors that enliven them, in the philosophic sense of the word, think tanks are transcendent by drawing attention to the most intangible aspect of political life – ideas.

Notes

1 This introductory chapter draws substantially upon the introduction to *Think tanks across nations*, co-written with Mark Garnett in 1998.
2 Some of the best-known studies include: Abelson, 1996, 2002; Cockett, 1994; Denham, 1996; Dickson, 1971; Ricci, 1993; Smith, 1991; Stone, 1996b; Weiss, 1992.
3 At the time of writing (2003), recently completed doctoral dissertations on think tanks include those by Stella Ladi at the University of York; Heidi Ullrich at the London School of Economics; Joseph Braml at the University of Passau; Andy Rich at Yale University; Collette Dartford at Bath University; and Kim Beng Phar at Oxford University.

Part I

The international dimension

2 Inderjeet Parmar

Institutes of international affairs: their roles in foreign policy-making, opinion mobilization and unofficial diplomacy

Institutes of international affairs (IIA) have proliferated around the world since their modest beginnings during the early 1920s, in the aftermath of the mass slaughter of the Great War (CEIP, 1953; King-Hall, 1937). Numerous European and British Commonwealth countries boast an institute of international affairs. IIA leaders have invariably been close to their nation's foreign policy establishment, frequently being 'drafted' into government service during times of war and crisis. In the public deliberation of foreign affairs, IIAs play a vital role in elaborating an elite consensus and in mobilizing public opinion behind major official foreign policy initiatives. In part, this has occurred as a result of the fundamental role played by IIAs in developing the academic discipline of international relations. Internationally, IIAs utilize their connections with their overseas counterparts 'unofficially' to discuss sensitive issues that face their own governments (Bosco and Navari, 1994; Parmar, 1999a; Wala, 1994). It is likely, given their funding from American foundation sources, that they are part of a global knowledge network promoting liberal internationalism and attitudes friendly to the United States (Parmar, 2002a). Despite playing such significant roles, however, their existence and persistence have, in the main, failed to inspire scholars to study their activities, to assess their influence, and to consider their significance in understanding 'how power works' in liberal democracies. In particular, there are few impartial studies of the Canadian, Australian, New Zealand and South African institutes.

It is clear that, since the founding of the original IIAs, the Royal Institute of International Affairs (RIIA, also known as Chatham House) and the American Institute of International Affairs (which early on changed its name to the Council on Foreign Relations, CFR), there is a fair variety of forms taken by such institutes, their culture, roles and influence. Such variety is inevitable, reflecting the diversity of their systems of government (federal, unitary), political subcultures and historical factors. Such breadth of roles and forms, however, gives rise to difficulties when trying to analyse this phenomenon, as empirical differences cannot adequately be described or explained in a short chapter. Consequently, this chapter aims to do the following:

1 to place the IIA phenomenon in an historical context;
2 to describe the original founding institutes of the 'movement', as they served as models for the ones that followed;
3 to discuss, as far as the secondary literature permits, some of the similarities between Chatham House and the CFR and those that followed, such as the Australian, Canadian and South African IIAs;
4 to place IIAs in a theoretical context, to try to suggest an adequate framework within which their functions in democratic societies might better be understood and explained.

Historical context

The IIA 'movement' was Anglo-American in origin, spreading across the world by the 1930s and after. The 'movement' arose in response to a number of major forces in world affairs, such as global warfare, imperialism, nationalism and internationalism, the growing strength of democratization movements, and particular domestic developments in the two countries. In addition, the growing importance of global communications technologies facilitated analysis of international affairs (Parmar, 2002b).

The early twentieth century witnessed the growing effects and significance of mass, urbanized and dynamically changing social and political systems, under pressure from a number of quarters – the working classes, women, progressive/liberal social reformers – to reform themselves in order better to meet the numerous challenges confronting them. In response, private and (increasingly) governmental efforts in Britain and the United States focused on scientifically analysing the effects of industrialism and urbanism on social, economic and other problems, with a view to developing 'social technology'. In the United States and Britain, the Progressive movement and 'new liberalism', respectively, challenged the existing laissez faire attitudes of government, favouring greater state intervention to deal with poverty, slums, ill health, education, and the dehumanizing side effects of the business cycle (Hall, 1988; Link and McCormick, 1983). To be sure, these were largely elite-led movements that feared social chaos and more radical socialist alternatives. Nevertheless, they challenged the status quo in domestic *and* international affairs.

Abelson (1996) and Higgott and Stone (1994) have periodized the formation of foreign affairs think tanks in the USA. They argue that the most important period was the early twentieth century and that the foundation of the CFR (1921) was among the most significant in this regard, in addition to the formation of the CEIP in 1910. A movement allied to the formation of IIAs, and to a large extent their inspiration, was the Round Table in the British Empire. The Round Table movement was inspired by Sir Alfred Milner and Cecil Rhodes, both die-hard imperialists, to construct the basis of imperial 'organic union' and closer Anglo-American relations, particularly against the rising power of Germany (Kendle, 1975; Lavin, 1995). After this period, which also saw the formation of the Rockefeller Foundation and Carnegie Corporation in the USA, and of Britain's Chatham House, the most significant was the late 1920s and 1930s, which saw such developments in Canada (1928), Australia (1932), New Zealand (1938), South Africa (1934), India (1936) and Pakistan (1948). The Chatham House 'model' also inspired a number of European institutes of international affairs, including the French Centre d'Etudes de Politique (1935), Belgian Institut des Relations Internationales (1947), the Italian Istituto per gli Studi di Politica Internazionale (ISPI, 1933), and the Dutch Nederlandsch Genootschap voor Internationale Zaken (1945). It is the description and analysis of several of the groups modelled on Chatham House that form the empirical basis of this chapter.

Chatham House and the CFR

Chatham House and the CFR, particularly the former, were the originators of what became a world-wide 'movement'. Since they provided the inspiration for so many of the IIAs that developed subsequently, especially those in Canada, Australia, New Zealand and South Africa, it is worth spending some time examining their intellectual roots, aims, leadership, activities and influence.

The formation of Chatham House and the CFR was initiated at the Paris Peace Conference of 1919–20, in the aftermath of World War I. Officials from the British and American delegations met informally to explore the establishment of an institute of international affairs with two branches, one American, the other British. The institute was to be scientific in character, an attempt to improve the levels of expertise in the making of official foreign policy and in the construction of a supportive public consensus. The aim was not to make policy but to assist policy-makers with 'sound' material from which to fashion policies and 'sound' public opinion to support them (Parmar, 1994).

Upon return to their homelands, however, the delegates found domestic opinion was unfavourable to an Anglo-American institute (anti-British isolationism in the US, anti-American feelings in Britain). Each delegation, therefore, proceeded to establish a separate national organization (the CFR and Chatham House), composed of experts, practitioners in foreign affairs, journalists, university academics, international lawyers and bankers. The two organizations were thoroughly connected to their respective foreign policy establishments (Shoup and Minter, 1977). For example, the CFR and Chatham House quickly forged good working relationships with 'their' respective secretaries of state and foreign secretaries.

The men who founded the two think tanks grew up and were educated during the 1880s to the early 1900s, a period of spectacular change at global and domestic (British and American) levels, featuring industrialization, urbanization, mass immigration, imperialism, and increasing international economic, commercial and military competition. Britain and the United States in this period were transformed, internationally and domestically, with important knock-on effects for the generation coming to maturity during the era (Kennedy, 1988; Parmar, 1999a).

Particularly important tendencies within Britain and the United States at this time were the rise of evangelical Christianity, social and racial Darwinism, the cult of manliness, scientism, and liberal social/political reform movements (Parmar, 2002b). Those who went on to form the Council and Chatham House were drawn from the elite of their society, having attended private schools and the most prestigious universities. They were also among the brightest people of their generation, deeply interested in the nature of their society and of world politics. Among the British founders of Chatham House, liberal imperial reformers, such as Lionel Curtis, played particularly significant roles (Lavin, 1995).

The CFR and Chatham House quickly became indispensable to the discussion of foreign affairs and as a source of expert personnel for policy advice. They established influential journals, *Foreign Affairs* (CFR's house organ) and *International Affairs* (RIIA), which were read by 'policy influentials' and the 'attentive public'. In addition, the institutes were vital to the growth of the new university discipline of international relations, as were the Rockefeller and Carnegie foundations (Olson and Groom, 1991). Their study groups began operating in the early 1920s and published their findings in a regular stream of reports and books that were read by the policy-making community, reported in the higher-quality newspapers, and placed on university courses in international relations.

Above all else, the original IIAs were designed to be practical, policy-oriented. Their 'finest hour' was World War II. Even before the war's outbreak, Chatham House had been requested by the Foreign Office to set up a Foreign Research and Press Service in order ultimately to assist officials in the formulation of foreign policy and postwar planning. In the Council's case, the private group offered its policy research and analysis services to the State Department in September 1939, over two years prior to American entry to the war. The War and Peace Studies programme of the CFR was one of the most interesting examples of private group–US governmental liaison in foreign affairs (Shoup and Minter, 1977; Wala, 1994). Both the Service and the War and Peace Studies project were influential in mobilizing dozens of foreign policy academics, foreign affairs correspondents and other experts for state service, and in proposing new policies (Hilderbrand, 1990; Parmar, 1994, 1999a, 1999b; Shoup and Minter, 1977).

In addition to their policy research role, both think tanks played a vital role in mobilizing public opinion to support their respective governments' policies, such as American military and other aid to Britain, Anglo-American postwar co-operation, the formation of the UN, and the Bretton Woods system (International Monetary Fund and World Bank) (Parmar, 1994; Shoup and Minter, 1977). The CFR, in 1938, had established its regional committees on foreign relations in several cities across America, with the aim of providing local internationalist fora for discussing and studying US foreign relations, for spreading the 'globalist' gospel to the 'heartlands', and as 'listening posts' for finding out what Americans were thinking (Parmar, 1999b). Although Chatham House never managed fully to establish as effective a system of local 'branches', it did make strong efforts in the case of Edinburgh, Glasgow, Manchester, Durham and Newcastle (RIIA Archives, London). In addition, both think tanks made strong mobilisation efforts with specific sections of opinion, including the armed forces (Chatham House), university students, the press, labour organizations (CFR), etc. (Chadwin, 1968; Parmar, 1994, 1999a).

Finally, the leaders of the CFR and Chatham House provided another important service to the state by acting as both official advisors and unofficial diplomats. Such roles were especially important at the numerous financial and naval conferences of the 1920s and 1930s, during controversies over British war debts to the United States, and in the negotiation of the Anglo-American Trade Agreement of 1938 (Roberts, 2001). Chatham House provides the best example of this practice through its role as the British section of the Institute of Pacific Relations (IPR), an organization dedicated to examination of the issues related to what is now called the 'Pacific Rim' (Woods, 1999). In relation to this, the Chatham House IPR committee liaised very closely with the Far Eastern department of the Foreign Office, particularly through a common link in the form of Frank Ashton-Gwatkin, a career official and Chatham House Council member. The result was that Chatham House's independence was compromised at numerous IPR conferences, as the Foreign Office financed, guided and supplied officials for the delegation and vetted private individuals. The IPR conferences brought together representatives from many nations with Pacific region interests, including the Americans, and constituted an important forum for the criticism and defence of Britain's imperial record in the area (Hooper, 1995; Thorne, 1978).

The original IIAs, therefore, were well connected with their respective foreign policy establishments, were drafted into state service during World War II, helped to mobilize sections of national opinion in support of Anglo-American co-operation and globalism, and acted as official and unofficial diplomats. They were fairly comprehensive organizations, producing original research in book form, prestigious journals, regular annual reviews of their country's foreign relations, and policy advice. They were also, in the main, independent of the state and, even when they went along with attempts by government to co-opt them, it was always because the institutes believed that, in those specific instances, it was in the national interest to do so. That is, they agreed with the state policies being pursued and co-operated on their own terms.

Subsequent IIAs

The institutes that followed the above (particularly the Chatham House) model are examined below. What were their roles? How influential were they? To what extent does the secondary literature address the issue of their connections with the official makers of foreign policy? What are the theoretical frameworks that have been utilized to make sense of the institutes of international affairs?

The main period of growth and consolidation in the IIA movement was the late 1920s and 1930s, with some further additions in the post-1945 period. The institutes formed during that period were the outgrowth of the direct influence of Chatham House and/or the IPR, as well as the Round Table movement (Hooper, 1995: 209; Millar, 1977–78). Chatham House had developed numerous branches in the Dominions, had organized several unofficial Commonwealth Relations Conferences, and participated vigorously in the IPR. Such activity, alongside internal developments within the Dominions and India, led to the formation of IIAs. Their beginnings, therefore, were very much influenced by the ideas and attitudes dominant within Chatham House (Akami, 2002; Millar, 1977–78; RIIA, 1946: 38–9).

The European IIAs modelled on Chatham House, such as France's Centre d'Etudes de Politique Etrangere, were also funded by American foundations (CEIP, 1953). From their very beginnings, however, several of them received a significant proportion of state funding, providing a challenge to their aim of remaining 'independent'. One that was originally unconnected with the state (and universities and churches) was the Italian institute, which was founded during the Fascist era. Since the 1950s, however, it has received around one-third of its funds from the state. The Netherlands institute receives 45 per cent of its income from the Dutch government (CEIP, 1953).

To make easier the comparison of the newer institutes with their Chatham House 'parent', the section below is arranged according to the same criteria as used for the British and American think tanks: aims, intellectual roots and establishment connections, foreign policy-making role, opinion mobilization and unofficial diplomacy.

The CEIP organized a meeting of 17 IIAs in 1953 and advanced the following criteria for 'membership' within a loose international club. The CEIP suggested that IIAs were: (1) 'capable of independent judgement and scholarly determination of their own programs'; (2) 'concerned with basic research in international relations'; (3) 'engaged in dissemination of information by conference and publication, but are not primarily instructional centers'; (4) 'precluded from partisan political programs' (CEIP, 1953: 30). These criteria provide a useful way of examining the available evidence in the secondary literature and permit some conclusions as to the degree to which the IIAs lived up to their own aims.

To begin, it is interesting to note that the funding of the Dominion and European IIAs was, though to a lesser extent than was the case for Chatham House, the IPR and the CFR, sourced in the same American philanthropic foundations: the Rockefeller Foundation, the Carnegie Corporation, and the CEIP (CEIP, 1930s–60s; Hooper, 1995; Legge, 1999; Millar, 1977–78). The Canadian, Australian, New Zealand and South African institutes, and several others, have benefited greatly from such funding, enabling them to establish public information services, foreign travel scholarships, publishing programmes and organizational capacity, and to meet expenses relating to international conference organization. As is clear from published research on these foundations, they targeted funds to further the forces of liberal internationalism, liberal anti-communism, and those supportive of Anglo-American (and Euro-American) cooperation (Berman, 1983; Parmar, 1999a, 2000, 2002a, 2002b).

Aims

The aims and objectives of the IIAs were identical to those of Chatham House. The Canadian Institute on International Affairs (CIIA), for example, founded as an affiliate of Chatham House, confined membership to British subjects and forbade the expression of any 'opinion' or institutional 'line' on international questions (Greathed, 1969: 106). Its aims were to encourage the research, study and discussion of Canada's foreign relations in order to promote better policy-making (Millar, 1977–78; Reford, 1976). The Australian Institute (AIIA) also pointed out that it was engaged in the 'objective, scientific study of foreign affairs' (Stone, 1996a: 117). Viewing themselves very much as an intellectual vanguard, IIA leaders believed they stood between government and public, assisting the 'government in finding the answers and to criticize it responsibly ... [while also helping to] spread knowledge and create a climate of opinion which sustains wise policy with approval' (Boulden, 1999: 644; quoting John Holmes, a CIIA leader). The stamp of Chatham House was also evidenced in the British members' domination of the Indian Institute of International Affairs (Hooper, 1995).

Chatham House was the model for the European institutes but not quite the 'parent' in its relations with them, in contrast to the Dominions' institutes. However, there is no published research on this question. A CEIP report of 1953 states only that the Italian, Belgian, French and Dutch institutes 'modelled' themselves on Chatham House, giving no indication of the actual process. Nevertheless, the institutes reflected their 'statist' character by breaking with the Chatham House tradition of remaining (relatively) free of state funding.

Intellectual roots and establishment connections

The intellectual roots of the founders of the Dominion institutes often mirrored those of their Chatham House mentors. Many of the members of the new IIAs had also been active in the Round Table movement and early twentieth-century peace societies (Reid, 1989; Stone, 1996a). Committed in general to the British Empire, the IIAs were also exercised by the desire to define more clearly their own nation's independent interests (Legge, 1999; Reid, 1989; Stone, 1996a).

According to Millar (1977–78), the early Dominion institutes were led by figures from the political and academic establishments of their country. Decades later, the AIIA had become 'a respectable and useful part of the Australian cultural establishment' (Millar, 1976: 3). The CIIA was, for instance, labelled as 'composed of MASPS – male, Anglo-Saxon Protestants' by one of its early leaders, Escott Reid. Reid commented further that, in 1938, the CIIA represented 'less than one-quarter of one percent of the Canadian people' in terms of their racial, linguistic, residential and age characteristics (Reid, 1989: 76).

The elitist character of the IIAs is further hinted at by the references in the literature to the role of prominent figures in the IIAs. For example, a former prime minister, Sir Robert Borden (1911–20), was elected president of the CIIA, while Professor A.H. Charteris of the University of Sydney presided over the AIIA. John Holmes, a leading CIIA member from the 1940s to the 1970s, noted that, at its founding, the institute was 'entirely male, attired in black ties, inhabiting the best clubs across the land, was composed of those who could, it was believed, affect decision-making [on Canadian foreign policy] by a well-placed phone call' (Reid, 1989: 76). In India, the viceroy, Lord Willingdon, was appointed president, while the chairman was always drawn from among the governor general's executive committee (Millar, 1977-78: 15). The IIAs were generally male-dominated and elitist by reputation (Reford, 1976: 27), drawing their numbers from the professions, government, the press, business and academia (Bostock, 1984: 9, 20; Forsyth, 1974; Stone, 1996a: 117). The AIIA, according to Millar, was so elitist as to have 'kept people out by a policy of elitism' (Millar, 1976: 4).

Foreign policy-making role

The attitude of official foreign policy-makers to the IIAs normally depended upon the degree of the state's own foreign policy capacity. That is, the IIAs were more successful in engaging constructively with officials when the latter needed assistance in carrying out tasks the bureaucracy could not itself perform. Before World War II, therefore, the Canadian Department of External Affairs (DEA) was small and only too willing to mobilize the CIIA (Dobell and Willmott, 1977-78: 106; Soward, 1977-78: 73). During the war, the CIIA, AIIA and the South African Institute of International Affairs (SAIIA) were mobilized to conduct background historical and other research for numerous ministries, to provide expertise in regard to particular geographical and issue areas, to provide digests of foreign press reports, and to liaise with overseas organizations such as Chatham House. John Holmes, for example, played an important role in developing Canada's policy in regard to the UN. The state needed outside assistance and found willing helpers among IIA leaders and members (Bostock, 1984; Forsyth, 1974; Stone, 1996a).

According to Millar (1977-78: 15), World War II was the period in which the IIAs proved most 'influential'. Across the Dominions and in Britain, Millar argues, IIA men 'began to move into positions of influence within government'. In particular, he claims that the CIIA 'helped build an internationalist mood within Canada'. As the war approached, Canada's External Affairs department was 'short-handed', with just 33 officers in Ottawa in 1939 (Soward, 1977-78: 72-3). The CEIP's survey of IIAs in 1953 also asserts that wartime governments drew 'extensively' on the 'research facilities and personnel of a number of the institutes' (CEIP, 1953: 23). The SAIIA offered its services for the production 'of memoranda upon the historical and political background of any international situation', but there is no evidence that the offer was accepted. The Institute did, however, supply Chatham House with reports on the domestic situation in South Africa (Bostock, 1984: 21).

Stone (1996a: 119) points out, in relation to the AIIA, that it was most useful to the (DEA) during the 1930s and 1940s, when the DEA was a new government agency and institutionally weak. Several AIIA leaders were mobilized by the state. According to W.D. Forsyth, a leading member of the Melbourne branch of the AIIA, service in the Institute had been excellent preparation for state service. He prepared secret intelligence and press reports for the departments of Information and External Affairs, and acted as a conduit for Chatham House reports to the Australian bureaucracy (Forsyth, 1974: 44). He served in External Affairs from 1942 to 1969. His Melbourne group was particularly expert in Far Eastern and Pacific affairs and was of utility to a number of government departments. Another Melbourne group member, W. Macmahon Ball, attended the San Francisco Conference on the UN in 1945, and served on several diplomatic missions to Asia (Rix, 1988: xii). In addition, as the holder of the first chair in political science at Melbourne University, Ball helped prepare a new generation of Australian diplomats (Rix, 1988: xv).

Did the IIAs influence official foreign policy during the war? According to Stone, the kind of influence the AIIA may have exerted is 'intangible' though real, as IIAs tend to blur the dividing line between state and society, and act as a channel of influence in both directions (1996a: 119–20). It is clear, for example, that the AIIA and the CIIA were very close to their respective governments during the war. In fact, they were closer to government than any other private organizations. The CIIA produced studies of Canada's consular services at the request of the DEA; it was seen as a highly respectable and worthwhile organization. Through John Holmes, it was also important in 'the formative stage of official thinking about international organizations' (Dobell and Willmott, 1977–78: 106). It is important to bear in mind that none of the institutes maintained a genuine long-term commitment to 'basic research', unlike the CFR and Chatham House. Only in the 1970s, for example, did the SAIIA begin an authentic in-house research programme, with immediate effects on its usefulness to official foreign policy-makers (Bostock, 1984: 51–9). Boulden, conversely, lamented in 1999 that Canada had failed to produce adequate foreign policy research institutions (Boulden, 1999: 647). However, the archival research still needs to be conducted in order to address adequately the question of IIA policy influence in war, and, indeed, at any, time.

Opinion mobilization

'Public opinion' and 'public education' are probably the most important factors behind the formation of the IIAs. Chatham House, the CFR, the CIIA and the rest of the IIAs shared a devotion to public enlightenment. They believed, as Fowler argued in the first issue of the CIIA's review, *International Journal*, in 1946, that good political leadership required a supportive and 'informed and thoughtful public opinion' (Fowler, 1977–78: 1).

In general, however, the IIAs' definition of public opinion was restricted to the leaders of opinion – journalists, academics, students, professionals, businessmen – rather than the broader population at large, in line with their general elitism (Page, 1977–78: 50). As Chatham House's Stephen King-Hall stated rather pointedly, the institute 'helps the man *who reads* the leading article by helping the man *who writes it*. It helps the voter by helping the MP' (Millar, 1977–78: 22). An exception was the Dutch institute, which, up to the mid-1950s at least, published much that was written for 'the general reading public' (CEIP, 1953: 98).

The CIIA began its first full public education programme in the 1930s, utilizing its extensive connections with its 'popular arm', the League of Nations Society (Reid, 1989). Although its reputation emerged somewhat tarnished by the experience of 'activism', the CIIA was able to help build an 'internationalist mood within Canada' before and during World War II (Millar, 1977–78: 24; Page, 1977–78). It began publishing regular pamphlets, *Behind the Headlines*, exploring for a broad audience the events in Europe and the Far East, reaching a circulation of up to 15,000. The CIIA, from as early as the 1930s, made extensive use of radio broadcasts. Its topical memoranda on Canadian policy on contemporary events, such as the Korean War, the Iranian oil dispute, etc. also proved effective (CEIP, 1953: 42). During the 1950s, the CIIA made further public education efforts, funded by the Ford Foundation (Millar, 1977–78: 25).

In the 1970s, the CIIA organized several national conferences, including one on Canada and the European Community, in collaboration with the DEA. Smaller meetings examined the issues of 'nuclear proliferation ... and oil and politics in the Middle East' (Boulden, 1999: 637; Reford, 1976: 27). The SAIIA was also active in the post-1945 period, successfully 'reaching a wider public' through its information library, 'sponsorship of adult education projects, lecture tours and radio broadcasts, and by the publication of study-group reports' (CEIP, 1953: 121). It is extremely difficult, however, to determine whether the IIAs influenced public opinion through their seminars, conferences and publications.

Unofficial diplomacy

The IIAs have engaged in unofficial diplomacy through international conferences, in particular (Millar, 1977–78: 22–3). The series of Commonwealth Relations Conferences from the 1930s to 1960s is a prime example of such diplomacy, as the delegations, formally private, examined the principal imperial issues facing policy-makers. The CIIA, for example, solicited assistance from the DEA to facilitate the Institute's participation in the unofficial Commonwealth Relations Conferences organized by Chatham House (Reid, 1989: 72).

Over several decades, the CIIA has arranged conferences involving IIAs in the Commonwealth, and between them and the CFR and the CEIP (Reford, 1976: 28). The issues examined at such conferences have included the policy of détente between the United States and the USSR, relations with the European Community, Anglo-American relations, and the politics of oil (Reford, 1976: 27). In regard to superpower relations in the 1970s, the Canadian institute actually brought its Eastern European counterparts – from Poland, Hungary, Romania and Russia – into East–West dialogue (Reford, 1976: 28). According to Boulden, the CIIA 'played a significant role in supporting the Department of External Affairs in various international functions before and after the Second World War' (Boulden, 1999: 636). Frequently, leading institute members engaged in official and unofficial diplomacy as the situation required (Soward, 1977–78: 78–85), leading to the development of a 'revolving door'. As Alex Inglis notes, the institute's first three secretaries – Escott Reid, John Baldwin and John Holmes – 'all went into government service and rose to the top of the mandarinate' (Inglis, 1977–78: 92). Much the same may be noted of the AIIA: several men from the Melbourne branch served in official and unofficial diplomatic capacities in Southeast Asia, Japan, Canada and the United States (Forsyth, 1974: 47). In recalling his role at the San Francisco conference that founded the UN, W.D. Forsyth noted that much of the thinking behind the Australian official paper on colonial problems and trusteeship had been developed in 'Melbourne in 1938 and 1940 in the AIIA circle' (Forsyth, 1974: 48). Once again, of course, the shortage of personnel to staff overseas diplomatic missions encouraged the DEA to turn to the AIIA for assistance. In addition, the AIIA has provided a forum for foreign diplomats to be heard across their branches and at local universities (Stone, 1996a: 120, 133).

The relative weakness of the foreign services of Australia and Canada, especially before and immediately after World War II, provided an ideal opportunity for institutes to try to influence outcomes. Whether the institutes even attempted to do so, however, remains an important question for further research.

What may be concluded in regard to the IIAs in relation to their 'parent' bodies and in relation to the CEIP's view of them as independent, non-partisan disseminators and researchers in international relations? First, none of the IIAs reviewed above, except for the SAIIA (and that only since the 1970s), had developed a genuine programme of independent research, unlike the CFR and Chatham House. Their credibility and usefulness to government and the scholarly community (and thus to other attentive publics) suffered thereby (Boulden, 1999). It is far more difficult to be so unqualified in regard to the IIAs' commitment to the maintenance of their independence of thought and judgement. Many of them receive regular financial support from their government, raising the *possibility* of compromised independence. They appear, however, to have preserved their non-partisan character, which probably accounts for their longevity. Most interesting in this regard are the Italian and South African institutes, both of which have survived extreme right-wing regimes. In disseminating information and thought on international questions and their nation's interests and foreign relations, the IIAs have probably been most successful. Even in this field, however, the lack of research makes it impossible to draw any firm conclusions. It may well be that IIAs have added to the wisdom of the attentive publics, diplomats and policy-makers, that they have been lighting '"quiet lamps and candles" in studies, in government and media offices, and in countless homes as well' (Fowler, 1977–78: 4).

Theoretical framework for analysis

Although there are several frameworks that may be applicable to the study of IIAs (as detailed in other chapters of this volume), the aim here is to suggest the relevance of the Gramscian perspective (Gramsci, 1971). This view, it is argued, contains all the key elements that permit a sound explanation of the role of the institutes. It permits a fundamentally important role for ideas and intellectuals, social classes and elites, organized (responsible) private societies and groups, and most fundamentally the state. This is a rare combination not shared by rival theories of power such as pluralism, statism and corporatism. The latter theories' conceptualization of power as a zero-sum game, as power of one force 'over' another, the private group over the state or vice versa, is severely limited. The Gramscian notions of 'state spirit' among 'private organizations' of the 'ruling class', particularly among intellectuals, and of the reliance of the state on non-state forces to elaborate a societal consensus behind a hegemonic project (of globalism, internationalism, Anglo-American cooperation, etc.), are broadly validated by the evidence (incomplete though it is) reviewed above.

The Gramscian view contends that the British and American states were engaged in the planning and construction of a 'new world order' during and after World War II and that this project relied also on the mobilization – for policy-related research, public opinion mobilization and unofficial diplomacy purposes – of formally private forces across the world, especially in the US, Britain and its empire (Augelli and Murphy, 1988; Parmar, 1999a). It is contended here that the American foundations and the IIAs were key unofficial elements in this programme, connecting the dominant states – the US and Britain – to a pool of experts and practitioners linked with each other, their respective nations' elites and official foreign policy-makers (Berman, 1983). Thus, a hegemonic project was being constructed to institutionalize Anglo-American power in the postwar world (Shoup and Minter, 1977).

The role of IIAs, particularly in the 'Anglo-Saxon' countries, was essential to the project. They participated only too willingly as they shared the general goals and ideals of liberal internationalism, interdependence, and international security, undergirded by Anglo-American power (Augelli and Murphy, 1988; Parmar, 2002b). In this regard, the institutes cannot be seen as self-interested pluralistic pressure groups attempting to force their respective states to take a particular line. Their states were already moving in the same direction but, owing to the inadequacies of their foreign policy-making capacities, needed outside assistance. Once mobilized, the IIA men in government accepted their place in the division of labour, carrying out tasks assigned to them as the situation demanded.

The attitudes of the leaders and the conclusions drawn by scholars who have studied IIAs seem to bear out such an interpretation. Certainly, this is the case with regard to Chatham House and the CFR (Parmar, 1994, 1999a; Wala, 1994). Of the Canadian institute's relationship with the DEA, Alex Inglis concludes that the CIIA 'has acted neither as a foreign policy association nor as a council of foreign affairs. In other words it has avoided being a group of insiders defending established policy and it has stopped short of being a group of outsiders seeking to define and urge policy alternatives'. He further notes that the relationship can 'best be described as free but co-operative, respectful but compromising (in the good sense of the word)' (Inglis, 1977–78: 88). John Holmes of the CIIA and of the DEA notes that while intellectuals must assist the state 'in finding the answers' and 'criticize it responsibly', they must also 'spread knowledge and create a climate of opinion which sustains wise policy with approval and, when required, sacrifice' (Boulden, 1999: 644). The available published evidence on the AIIA also bears out this interpretation of its role (Forsyth, 1974; Legge, 1999; Stone, 1996a). The CEIP's survey of the institutes as a whole argued that although they are 'non-governmental in character, they nevertheless maintain close contact with responsible public officials ... [They] are active in informing and educating both leaders and the public at large' (CEIP, 1953: v).

The institutes that followed the formation of Chatham House and the CFR were unlikely to be exactly the same as their role models. Except for the European institutes, about which almost nothing (in English, at least) has been written, the Dominions' institutes were 'grafted' onto societies that were developing in conditions rather different from those prevailing in London. Also, they were not at the centre of an empire; neither were they 'great powers'. Having little experience of independent foreign policy-making, their state machinery for such purposes was inadequate, as was the pool of unofficial expertise and research capacity. Consequently, the goals of their state and society differed qualitatively from those of the USA and Britain. Nevertheless, within those boundaries and limitations, the institutes managed to help build the pool of private foreign affairs experts and the machinery of policy-making and diplomacy, particularly as their states began to assert their own interests.

That they have, in general, suffered relative decline since their 'finest hour' is widely acknowledged. They have been accused of being old-fashioned, 'stuffy' and out of touch. They face competition from numerous sources that did not exist when they were formed: a greater number of university-based research groups, a wider range of reviews and international affairs journals, and the newer, more aggressive 'advocacy' think tanks, among others. The consensus in regard to the Australian, Canadian, British, American and other IIAs is that they need to modernize, to reach out to a broader constituency, to make themselves more relevant to the demands of a 'globalized' world (Boulden, 1999; Clough, 1994; Grose, 1996; Stone, 1996a). Two principles, however – of nonpartisanship and 'objectivity' – have served the institutes well over the years and ought to be maintained. Nevertheless, their significance probably lies in the fact that they represent the founding generation of a 'transnational elite' that transcends national boundaries, constituting the building blocks of the contemporary world order (Dobell and Willmott, 1977–78: 109–10).

3 Diane Stone[1]

Think tanks beyond nation-states

Many think tanks have become transnational actors in regional affairs and global politics. The transnational boom in think tank development has been prompted by foundations, corporations and other non-state actors demanding high-quality research, policy analysis and ideological argumentation. It has been fuelled by grants and other funding from governments and international organizations seeking to extend policy analytic capacities, aid civil society development or promote human capital development. Accordingly, the main focus in this chapter is to address the supply and demand forces that propel these institutes into the global agora. However, it is first necessary to specify who or what they target beyond the nation-state and to track trends in transnational development. This is covered in the first section. The second section investigates the supply and demand forces behind think tank transnationalization and the manner in which think tanks occupy territory as (global) civil society organizations. The third section looks at think tank incorporation into transnational networks, with a particular focus on the Global Development Network (GDN). While this chapter is concerned primarily with why these organizations become transnational, questions are also raised about the policy impact and accountability of think tanks in the global agora. The 'agora' is both a market place for economic transaction and a public space where democratic principles and practices might be instituted.

Transnational trends

The primary targets of think tanks are legislatures and executives, bureaucrats and politicians at national and subnational levels of governance. Think tanks seek access to policy communities to inject new ideas into policy debates. A policy community is taken to mean all actors or potential actors who share a common 'policy focus' and who, over time, succeed in shaping policy (Richardson, 2000). Members of a policy community (individual politicians and bureaucrats, interest groups and their staff, and experts within government, universities or policy institutes) interact regularly, developing a shared understanding concerning problems that are deemed important and devising possible solutions. Think tanks from outside a country also target official actors, although such institutes have less legitimacy and greater difficulty in gaining access to and inclusion within these policy communities. At the same time, policy communities are also becoming transnational in orientation and composition.

Think tanks were a new organizational phenomenon of the last century. As noted in chapter 1, there have been three broad waves of think tank development. The first policy research institutes were established as state-based entities catering to elite national audiences in response to growing levels of literacy and pressures for public debate. International connections were virtually unknown. The second wave from 1945 was characterized by more extensive think tank development, but institutes remained state-centric, given the sources of financing and the domestic character of their audiences. Aside from a handful of foreign policy centres, strategic studies institutes or development institutes, relatively few think tanks either pursued research agendas that developed transnational policy themes, or interacted cross-nationally on a regular basis.

The third wave of development is the phase in which think tanks are most clearly acting transnationally – that is, extending their activities to function within the domestic political system of more than one state – and in global and regional fora. In many ways, they are political barometers of broader trends and respond to wider environmental factors. The Organization of Petroleum Exporting Countries (OPEC) oil crisis of 1974, the increasing salience of environmental issues and, latterly, the breakdown of authoritarian regimes, the deepening and widening of the EU, the collapse of the USSR and subsequent nation-building has created new political spaces in which think tanks can operate. More frequently they are responding to transborder policy problems of pollution, and to international movements of finance and human capital, by adopting broader research agendas in recognition of compromised state sovereignty and various processes of economic and political globalization. The expansion of international agendas, challenges to state sovereignty and the growing power of transnational policy communities are perhaps the most significant reasons behind think tank transnationalization.

The massive proliferation of think tanks world-wide has also been propelled by the increasing availability of foundation support and development aid for such organizations. For example, the Secretariat for Institutional Support for Economic Research in Africa (SISERA) was created in 1997 by USAID, the Canadian International Development

Agency and the International Development Research Centre to provide technical support and financial assistance for policy institutes (Seck and Philips, 2002). As noted in chapter 12 on Argentina, the world-wide phenomenon of 'third sector' associational growth and the nascence of global civil society have prompted think tank growth and extension of activity. Along with cheap flows of information, the number and depth of transnational avenues of contact have expanded, providing greater opportunity to organize and propagate think tank views. Similarly, the transnationalization of think tanks parallels that of academia, with its 'invisible colleges' and cross-national research partnerships (KFPE, 2001). Research staff who are employed in institutes such as the Stockholm International Peace Research Institute (SIPRI), RAND or the Institute of South East Asian Studies (ISEAS) are often drawn from an increasingly internationally mobile community of academics, consultants and other experts. Indeed, many have a transnational presence as a consequence of the media – CNN or the BBC – requiring pundits or 'talking heads' to speak authoritatively on matters such as the 'war on terrorism' or the decay of the ozone layer.

Since the late 1980s, a growing number of think tanks have extended their activities beyond their home states. A few American institutes have opened offices abroad; for example, the Heritage Foundation in Hong Kong and the Urban Institute in Russia. The International Institute for Strategic Studies (IISS) in London has an international fellowship scheme that draws in talent from around the world and that allows IISS to maintain contact with other institutes (and universities and ministries) for years subsequently. Similarly, the Overseas Development Institute (ODI), also based in London, has a fellowship scheme that places researchers in developing countries. Convened by the Japan Center for International Exchange (JCIE), Global ThinkNet is a dialogue forum for the heads of some of the world's leading think tanks.

Think tanks that are genuinely international are less apparent. The Trilateral Commission is a think tank-like organization that is transnational in its form of organization (Gill, 1990). The Club of Rome and the World Economic Forum (WEF) (in Davos, Switzerland) may also qualify. Transnationalisation also results in think tank hybrids – international policy salons like the elite Evian Group, the more plebian Third World Network (TWN) or research units inside NGOs like Transparency International. Such developments further undermine efforts to fashion watertight definition's of 'think tank'.

Regionalization appears to be a stronger dynamic than globalization. In regional fora, think tanks target regional groupings such as Asia Pacific Economic Cooperation (APEC) or Mercosur. As discussed by Heidi Ullrich in chapter 4, the EU acts as a policy magnet for think tanks. ISEAS, based in Singapore, is a good example of an institute with a regional identity. More generally, the Association of South East Asian Nations – Institutes of Strategic and International Studies (ASEAN-ISIS) are key players in regional policy debates on security and economic affairs (Kraft, 2000). The policy challenges of transition have prompted a proliferation of institutes in CEE (Krastev, 2000; Struyk, 2002). Both the Latin American and Caribbean Economic Association (LACEA) and the Economic Research Forum (ERF) in the Middle East and North Africa are networks of economic policy institutes. Although other regional groupings are not characterized by the extensive institutional development and pooling of sovereignty of the EU, the common traditions, shared histories of colonialism or communism and cross-border policy problems create a dynamic for regional dialogues in which many think tanks can find a role.

Globalization is also a phenomenon that has prompted changes in think tank activity and research agendas (Stone, 2001). This is evident in three areas. Firstly, as the number of think tank publications on globalization testifies, think tanks are observers and interpreters of globalization. Secondly, the changing focus of think tank activity is symptomatic of globalization. That is, these organizations are both transnational and (to a lesser extent) globalized in response to the compromised autonomy of the state, the formation of regional blocs, and the more general phenomenon of non-state actors interacting on the global stage alongside international organizations and nation-states. Third, in a small way, think tanks are also constitutive of globalization. They propel political, social and economic forms of globalization respectively by promoting their staff into transnational policy communities, by forming transnational networks and alliances with other non-state actors, and through policy studies that advocate and criticize economic forms of global integration. Many seek to address a 'global audience', and can be seen as contributing to the emergence of global civil society.

One of the most effective mechanisms through which think tanks have become transnational is via networks. An important distinction needs to be made between policy networks and knowledge networks. The knowledge networks of think tanks are composed of organizations with shared perspectives, joint interests and common scholarly agendas, 'homogenous rather than heterogenous in their fundamental views' (Struyk, 2002: 83). By contrast, policy networks are more heterogeneous and designed to mediate between members with differing interests.

Knowledge networks exhibit different styles. An 'open assembly' arrangement is a network 'established primarily for knowledge sharing, membership is unrestricted ... network coherence is weak' (Struyk, 2002: 83). Examples include the African Knowledge Networks Forum (AKNF). The Open Society Institute (OSI) funds a network of 17 policy institutes addressing problems of transition, but is an example of a network under 'donor leadership or official patronage'. ASEAN-ISIS, LACEA and ERF also have official patronage and selective membership. In these cases, network coherence and leadership are stronger. Selective membership procedures also operate in some networks headed by a single private think tank, such as JCIE's Global ThinkNet (Struyk, 2002). Another example, is the California-based International Center for Economic Growth (ICEG) network of over 300 institutes in approximately 100 countries.

Think tanks are drawn into 'global public policy networks' (or what could also be called 'transnational policy communities'). In many issue areas, governments and international organizations do not have the ability to design and/or implement effective public policies alone. 'Global public policy networks', composed of NGOs, government agencies, business groups and international organizations, are helpful in some issue areas to come to terms with these challenges. The transnational character of policy problems establishes rationales for research collaboration, sharing information and co-operation on other activities that creates a dynamic for the international diffusion of ideas and policy transfer. An example is the Consultative Group on International Agricultural Research (CGIAR). It has 16 international agricultural and natural resources research institutes, several committees and a consultative council collectively working towards food security and poverty reduction through scientific research and policy-related activity.

Few of these transnational networks existed prior to the 1990s. But what is their political significance? At one level, such interactions are symptomatic of globalization; advances in communications and lower travel costs have enabled actors with common research interests to communicate transnationally on a regular basis. However, these networks are also symptomatic of the role of knowledge and expertise in global governance. Furthermore, transnational networks present many advantages for knowledge organizations; they create the overlapping personal and communications infrastructure for fast and effective transfer of new ideas and policy approaches between global and local levels. Potentially, networks help increase the effectiveness and efficiency of implemented projects by incorporating a wider range of knowledge and expertise. Similarly, there are potential benefits of improved co-ordination and policy transfer.

The policy network literature – with its variety of different conceptual models, including 'policy communities' or 'epistemic communities', 'advocacy coalitions' and 'discourse coalitions', outlined in chapter 4 – helps to explain the character of think tank influence, incorporating actors from both inside and outside government into decision-making and policy implementation (see Stone, 2001). Pluralists usually stress the openness and informal participation in decision-making offered by networks. Yet it has also been recognized that policy networks can prevent the emergence of challenges to the dominant values or interests in society, suppressing or thwarting demands for change in the existing allocation of social benefits and privileges. Depending on the political context of a country, think tanks can reinforce either of these tendencies. Transnational networks are also exclusive or inclusive depending on the policy field, the degree of technical expertise required in the issue area, and the extent of official involvement. Access to and participation in think tank and other networks are not necessarily open. Furthermore, the more informal character, loose structure and non-institutional features of networks make transparency and democratic norms of accountability all the more difficult.

Think tank prominence at a global or regional level is often reflective of the extent of think tank consolidation in the home country. Transnational institutes still require a strong domestic constituency and local sources of sustenance. Transnational activity requires finance, leadership skills and vision as well as expert personnel to carry the organization forward into regional and global fora. Not all institutes command sufficient material and ideational resources. Furthermore, there are often 'drag' factors that keep many institutes primarily focused on national policy issues and domestic audiences. Institutes that operate in global arenas tend also to be elite, well-established and high-profile bodies in their national context. The vast majority of think tanks are not known beyond their national borders and lack the size, stature, recognized experts and resources of institutes based in OECD countries to sustain a presence beyond national borders. In short, Northern think tanks are more prominent than institutes from the South. Nevertheless, despite disparities in organizational capacities, the general trend among think tanks world-wide is an increasing diversity and depth to transnational activity. The question that arises is why think tanks have become more prevalent in global and regional domains.

Transnational supply and demand for analysis, advice and advocacy

Adopting a global or regional scope reflects competition at the national level in countries such as the USA, Canada, Germany and the UK, and a need to expand organizational horizons to maintain status or to be consulted by national governments. Transnational activity is an adaptation to secure relevance and organizational expansion. By contrast, in political systems that are more closed, moving onto a global or regional plane of interaction may be a way for think tanks to circumvent authoritarian controls and exclusion from domestic policy communities. A think tank can find alternative sources of support from NGOs, donor agencies or groups in other states. In other words, there are often internal organizational imperatives for transnational activity. Yet think tanks also respond to the more general conditions of domestic and international undersupply of research and analysis.

Firstly, in many countries, knowledge activities that were once funded by the public purse have suffered from fiscal restraint and state retrenchment. This is particularly evident in CEE and Africa. Secondly, knowledge development has the character of a public good that dampens investment in its production. Indeed, knowledge has been cast as a 'global public good'. These problems have been noted by multilateral and bilateral development agencies that initiated numerous capacity-building programmes within national polities (e.g. KFPE, 2001), but increasingly in a regional and global context – specifically the GDN, as discussed below. These development agencies have also dovetailed policy agendas to promote good governance and incorporate civil society stakeholders in their support of think tanks. This has entailed the 'export' of the US think tank 'model' to developing and transitional countries.

Many think tanks in developing and transition countries adopt the rhetoric of being civil society organizations, claiming they contribute to the enhancement of a tolerant, plural, educated and democratic citizenry. Think tanks provide services and perspectives needed by the public that are not always produced by either the state or the market. Not only do policy research institutes supposedly provide a distinctive service in raising the standard of debate or broadening the agenda, but they advocate the views of minority groups, taking on a representational role. It is not unusual to see some think tanks adopt the mantle of protectors of the principles and philosophies underpinning democratic societies. Furthermore, it is often in their interests to do so, given that the discourse resonates so well with development agencies and foundations. Finally, these organizations indirectly aid good governance and dynamic economies, as they represent a constituency desirous of information, data and transparency, and are geared towards co-operative activity that creates a set of institutionalized expectations that other social actors will reciprocate. As noted by one Eastern European observer:

> The conviction that open public debate contributes to the quality of policy decisions constitutes think tanks as powerful instruments for the democratisation and rationalisation of the policy process. It is this democracy-building function that has encouraged the export of American think tanks over the past 10–15 years. (Krastev, 2000: 144)

However, domestic policy entrepreneurs have also found their own reasons for establishing think tanks.

In many cases, policy entrepreneurs are educated overseas, are familiar with think tanks in other countries and seek to import and adapt the form to their own country. Additionally, think tank entrepreneurs are often willing to invest time and energy in developing regional or international links. Indeed, they often have a vested interest in organizational expansion, for principled reasons as well as for the more self-interested motives – seeking political visibility abroad, informal entrée to decision-making fora, policy experience and personal contacts through networking – that frequently position individuals to make beneficial career moves. Possession of knowledge resources often represents a passport into the global agora; a means of occupational advancement, with the growing pre-eminence of the professional and technical classes; and the emergence of global public policy networks.

Think tank founders have responded to changes in their public sector environment. On one dimension they have taken advantage of new funding opportunities and a culture of public activity in many countries that favours privatization, deregulation and contracting out. However, such contracting out does not occur only at the national level. Increasingly, international organizations, transnational corporations and foundations are providing funding for analysis as well as funds to assist think tanks to function beyond the domestic domain; for example, to develop policy capabilities for accession to the EU. By making their organizations more transnational, by developing global research agendas and by plugging themselves into networks, the executives and scholars of these organizations meet changing demand from private and public actors at the global level.

Think tank entrepreneurs also look to other established think tanks in making a stronger claim for legitimacy in a process of institutional (mimetic) isomorphism. The existing institutional environment exerts considerable pressure for new organizations to conform to the 'conventional' or taken-for-granted rules promulgated by the organizations that emerged beforehand. For example, the ASEAN-ISIS prompted new think tank growth in Cambodia and Laos. Within an international context the American think tank form is often taken as a template for development elsewhere. Mimicry occurs when founders in other countries say they want to establish a Brookings-style institution in their own country. A cross-national pattern of new think tank development in response to existing think tanks is evident. Lindquist suggests that Canadian think tank development was initiated partly because of a perception of being outshone by American think tanks: 'The felt need for an independent institute had more to do with the self-image of a nation, or the image held by its policy elite' (Lindquist, 1989: 298). Maroc 2020 – a Moroccan institute now defunct – drew some inspiration from Malaysian think tanks.

On the demand side, there are groups of people in diplomatic and military circles, amongst other private actors in the media, law firms, NGOs, consultancy companies and international organizations, who require high-quality research and analysis. For example, philanthropic foundations are an important source of demand, and hence of funding and support, for independent policy research. Foundation executives and other sponsors have the ability to define what are emerging policy agendas (such as development studies in the 1960s) and to legitimate particular kinds of professional expertise (Parmar, 2002a). Other actors in society interact with or support think tanks because the latter provide useful resources. For instance, the media can find expert commentary from so-called 'independent' and 'scholarly' think tanks. Interest groups, trade unions, churches, NGOs and social movements can find ideological succour or normative arguments to bolster their advocacy.

One way to make sense of the different types and varying quality of research and analysis provided by policy institutes is to think of them as being shaped by demand for something that is more, better or different (James, 1987). Demand explanations help explain the market for independent research as well as the nature of its diversification as think tanks meet differentiated tastes. As demand for more information, research and analysis has grown, so has demand for *different kinds* of information and research. To summarize the manner in which think tanks meet the diversity of demand for more, better or different research, information and analysis, their services are categorized below into three types: (1) knowledge, analysis and expertise; (2) advocacy and argumentation; and (3) organizational and technical services.

Knowledge, analysis and expertise

In developing countries, or in countries facing reconstruction after war and civil unrest, think tank research supplements government research. For example, the Malaysian Institute of Economic Research (MIER) provides some forecasting services and analysis regarding the economy that is suited to business needs and is not provided by the Malaysian government. Additionally, foreign think tanks may be contracted by governments to provide information, analysis and research in areas where government or universities have a weak analytic capacity. However, it is less pertinent to argue that think tanks are meeting excess demand for research in advanced economies, given the size and strength of bureaucracies, semi-autonomous government research bureaux and universities. In such circumstances, elite think tanks seek to provide superior forms of policy advice by mustering the best thinkers and practitioners.

Governments, when they contract research from a foreign institute, are often looking for superior quality or a different kind of analysis from that which could be produced in-house or by local institutes. Commissioned research can be used to reinforce government policy preferences, or it can act as a standard to which local research work can be compared. Think tanks can only meet this demand if they produce knowledge that appears relatively unbiased and results from a process in accordance with professional norms, and characterized by transparency and procedural fairness. This is very often achieved by mimicking academic norms of inquiry.

However, some establishment think tanks meet a different form of demand: elitism and exclusivity. Selective membership or high entry costs (for example, membership fees) represent a form of gatekeeping and a practice that promotes homogeneity of members, and hence a greater likelihood of similar needs and interests. Such procedures can operate as a form of quality control by limiting participants to those who are 'suitably qualified'. It is also a means of managing the public standing of a think tank and indicating that certain organizations are, in some way, superior. As entry is exclusive, competitive and elite, an organization can lay claim to superior standards or to being an exceptional distillation of wisdom and expertise.

The substance of what international organizations demand from non-state knowledge actors varies considerably. International conferences draw upon think tanks to provide expert analysis on specific issues. Some leading think tank directors may find themselves co-opted onto the advisory councils or consultative committees of international organizations. For example, a number of Association of Southeast Asian Nations (ASEAN) institutes have been semi-incorporated into international organizations or multilateral negotiations, through, for example, processes of 'informal diplomacy' (Kraft, 2000). Think tanks have been encouraged to conduct studies to bring additional knowledge and perspectives into an international organization. For instance, the World Resources Institute (WRI), in partnership with the World Bank, the UN Development Program and the UN Food and Agriculture Organization, helped launch the Tropical Forestry Action Plan (Mathews, 1996). In other words, think tanks can often provide local or specialized knowledge that is better than that produced by the contracting organization. Similarly, the UN convened a think tank policy dialogue in 1999 in order, firstly, to identify how its research requirements converged with or could be met by the ongoing research agendas and work of the independent research community, and, secondly, to investigate possibilities for partnerships (ODC, 1999).

Advocacy and argumentation

Think tanks often provide intellectual legitimation of norms even though they engage in processes of mystification to establish institutes as independent, scholarly and relatively dispassionate sources of expertise. Groups want ideas fashioned into a format to bolster their arguments and interests; that is, in a simplified, palatable form that can be used to inform and mobilize their constituencies. 'Without access to expertise (or counter expertise)' NGOs 'cannot effectively participate in the policy process' (Fischer, 1993: 36). By necessity, NGOs will align themselves with certain think tanks or support the establishment of new think tanks while corporations will fund institutes that concord with preferred policy perspectives. Activist organizations like Greenpeace can draw upon the analysis of respected institutes such as the World Watch Institute to reinforce its own research or advocacy on sustainable development. Those who desire policy analysis that supports the case for a free trading system are likely to find policy options and analyses of high but accessible standard produced by organizations such as the Institute for International Economics (IIE). Alternatively, analysis that is broadly supportive of the interests of labour can be found among a loose network of like-minded progressive institutes that include the TransNational Institute (TNI) in Amsterdam and the Institute for Policy Studies (IPS) in Washington, DC.

Many Western think tanks are sometimes viewed as disseminating ideas that bolster the prevailing liberal hegemonic order of free market economies and liberal democratic polities. They use their superior resources, whether it be funding, professional personnel or entrée to transnational policy networks, to promote normative policy positions. Such elite think tanks represent one organizational component of a transnational grouping of global norm-setting elites (Gill, 1990). Some think tanks have become more political, ideological or partisan in response to the competitive environment for funding, political and media attention, and to demand from business, political parties and NGOs that recognize not only the importance of ideas in policy but the need for intellectual legitimation.

Organizational and technical services

The kinds of relationship between think tanks and official agencies are multi-fold, but a frequent mode of interaction is a low-key service role. For example, institutes provide services such as ethics training to government employees or are commissioned to organize conferences and seminars. Think tanks create channels of communication between formal and informal policy actors by starting newsletters, compiling databases and building networks. They gather information and prepare submissions, develop policy blueprints or draft legislative proposals. When operating at a domestic level, think tanks facilitate the downward flow of information from national decision-makers to local levels of decision-making, as well as to the 'educated public'. When operating at global or regional levels, think tanks facilitate the horizontal flow of information between transnational policy elites as well as to other non-state actors. In terms of international agreements or new policy regimes, think tanks are often well placed to alert domestic constituencies to changes in the external environment, and to report on negotiations, treaties and agreements. Numerous EU think tanks can be found diffusing ideas and information to national audiences about tax harmonization, the implications of European Monetary Union (EMU) or the technical requirements for meeting various EU directives. Think tanks are also important organizations for communicating and educating domestic constituencies into 'soft law' in the form of guidelines, recommended practices, non-binding resolutions and such like. Think tanks also monitor policy implementation and provide evaluation in global public policy networks.

There is demand for the production of knowledge but also for information to be managed. International organizations and governments require organizations to sift and edit knowledge. Think tanks represent a legitimate and neutral vehicle to filter, to make sense of the conflicting evidence, sets of argument and information overload. The 'politics of credibility' – of status, trust and reputation – is an important dimension of demand for think tank services in the 'information age' (Keohane and Nye, 1998). Think tanks are just one group of organizations amongst many others pressing upon governments and international organizations with ideas, information and analysis. Yet think tanks can set themselves apart as 'filters and interpreters' of information:

> to understand the effect of free information on power, one must first understand *the paradox of plenty*. A plenitude of information leads to *a poverty of attention*. Attention becomes a scarce resource, and those who can distinguish valuable signals from white noise gain power. Editors, filters, interpreters and cue-givers become more in demand, and this is a source of power. There will be an imperfect market for evaluators. Brand names and the ability to bestow an international seal of approval will become more important. (Keohane and Nye, 1998: 89, my emphasis)

'Think tank' is an informal 'brand name' for organizations able to 'edit and credibly validate information' reliably. Indeed, the 1999 UN think tank meeting identified a role for them to act as a 'quality check system', vetting NGOs and their worthiness for interaction with the UN, including:

- communicating and translating global values and agreements to regional and local audiences;
- reviewing international agreements and recommending the formulation of national and regional policy options;
- convening and building alliances among NGOs and civil society;
- training and teaching fledgling NGOs on organizational management, planning and advocacy (ODC, 1999: 7).

Indeed, it may well be the case that 'think tank' is a preferred label to 'NGO', given the massive proliferation of NGOs since the early 1980s.

Transnational networks, development and think tanks

Much transnational activity of think tanks has been propelled by the development agendas of aid agencies. The World Bank Institute (WBI, previously known as the Economic Development Institute) is a good example. The World Bank identified think tanks as key organizations for democracy promotion, civil society enhancement and capacity building. During the 1990s, WBI partnered the Washington-based Center for International Private Enterprise (CIPE, an affiliate of the US Chamber of Commerce) to conduct 'capacity building' and training events for think tanks. This activity culminated with the World Bank launching in 1999 the Global Development Network (GDN), an association of research institutes and think tanks. One objective was to mobilize World Bank knowledge and that of its member countries to address pressing development issues whilst also recognizing growing public pressures for participation in policy choices. 'In this context, think tanks constitute crucial civil society institutions that transcend government changes and offer a consistent source of knowledge for quality improvement of locally generated economic policies' (EDI, 1998: 2). Additionally, as part of the World Bank's efforts to restructure and deepen its knowledge base, think tanks represent a source of local knowledge that can be woven into the knowledge management system of the World Bank. Furthermore, communication channels between Bank staff and the outside world are expanded.

Many think tanks emerge out of civil society from the entrepreneurial efforts of local intellectuals and politicians, concerned business people and educators, and other community leaders. However, think tanks can reflect, reinforce and amplify divisions in society and exaggerate societal tensions. It is equally possible for think tanks to act as a force to limit and contain civil society pressures. They do not inevitably establish dynamics for democratization, participation and public, inclusive debate. Issues of power and conflict come to the fore. Sometimes, think tanks are so close to government that their civil status is compromised. State-sanctioned bodies may simply articulate and expound the interests of the state, or the ambitions of certain political leaders, or the concerns of the military. Whilst many think tanks adopt the mantle of civil society, in some instances this is a facade. It is easy to adopt the rhetoric of civil society but more difficult to engage in substantial relations with other civil society actors – churches, mosques and temples, women's groups, associations promoting literacy, birth control or clean water initiatives. Many think tanks are less successful in developing long-term relationships with organizations that are deemed to be of lower social status, groups that are perceived to be radical or disruptive in their demands, or bodies that are in competition with think tanks for media, political and foundation attention. In many respects, think tanks can be viewed as sanitized civil society organizations that sometimes act as a buffer between other civil society organizations and the state. Consequently, it is necessary to take into account the manner in which the GDN may accentuate tensions in (global) civil society and create divisions among groups.

Think tanks are composed of intellectual, political and economic elites, and the organizational structure itself is often of a secular, Westernized format. This is a feature that makes them attractive to other elite actors such as foundation representatives, political parties and World Bank officials. There are similar intellectual and organizational connections, often common educational backgrounds, and sometimes previous contact through transnational networks. Think tanks are the kind of elite civil society organizations with which many international civil servants are very comfortable. In other words, development agencies like the World Bank are one elite engaging with a civil society elite.

A second set of issues revolves around the operationalization of 'knowledge' in capacity building for think tanks, the development of 'knowledge management system' and World Bank training programmes. Think tanks are being engaged in 'partnerships' in which a local think tank, or a regional network, acts as amplifier of World Bank values, perspectives and priorities. Furthermore, in an era of information overload, think tanks become essential to the World Bank as 'editors, filters, interpreters and cue-givers' (Keohane and Nye, 1998: 89). This is a source of power for think tanks that sets them apart from other civil society actors in a privileged position. The regional and global networks that the World Bank and other international organizations are helping to build with think tanks potentially create a 'club-like' tendency.

A related issue revolves around the type of knowledge that is being deployed. The regional networks sponsored by the World Bank (for example, LACEA and ERF) do not incorporate the full range of think tanks that have emerged on the world scene. Instead, capacity building concentrates on a particular grouping of think tanks. This is exemplified by the membership of CIPE's 'Economic Freedom Network', which was created to 'advance the cause of economic freedom, democratic consolidation and business development' (www.cipe.org/efn/). The Network includes organizations such as the Centre for the Study of Democracy in Bulgaria, the Free Enterprise Institute in Peru, and the Lebanese Center for Policy Studies. At one level, this focus on capacity building for economic development think tanks – especially those of a market-liberal disposition – is not surprising. Just like any organization, the World Bank is more likely to engage with others that exhibit common values and norms. Furthermore, for practical reasons it is less interested in the large numbers of foreign policy and security studies institutes that run their own networks, since these policy domains are of more limited relevance to World Bank programmes. However, the inclusion of 'social democratic' or 'progressive' think tanks is less apparent. Similarly, environmental think tanks – institutes that often have strong views on questions of economic development – are few. These research institutes represent alternative forms of knowledge that are yet to find a voice through the GDN.

The structural power of World Bank patronage should not be underestimated. The GDN represents a means of structuring the supply and demand for development knowledge at regional and global levels. Political themes and policy approaches are reinforced by the multiplication of organizations at a domestic level and through building regional networks to share information, spread policy lessons and develop a consensus. The GDN significantly strengthens the advocacy and agenda-setting capacities of certain think tanks by amplifying economic development knowledge in preference to alternative voices and visions. Think tanks in other 'global public policy networks' may play similar roles.

Conclusion: think tanks and the global agora

The transnationalisation of think tanks is a trend that will continue to unfold. However, it is apparent that those think tanks operating at a regional or global level tend to come from strong, domestically based think tank communities. Accordingly, international organizations, foundations and aid agencies represent a powerful exogenous source for prompting think tank development in countries where there may be legal, human capital, financial and other constraints in the way of their development. However, think tank transnationalization presents some broader reflections on three issues: that is, the changing nature of global society; the character of global governance; and the scope for representative democracy.

The implication of this study for our understanding of global society is two-fold. First, think tank transnationalization is illustrative of the evolution, diversification and consolidation of civil society organizations in global and regional fora. However, the massively increasing numbers of NGOs and other non-state actors, their networks and dense patterns of exchange, along with their advocacy and policy demands, are creating congestion – the so-called 'paradox of plenty'. In short, civil society developments can be dysfunctional. In these unfolding conditions of 'plenty' and 'gridlock', think tanks are carving out a role, on the one hand, as editors and interpreters and, on the other, as expert sources of knowledge. Yet unequal outcomes are inevitable, not only between think tanks but also between think tanks and other civil society organizations. Think tanks' dominance as 'interpreters' in seeking preferential relationships with governments and international organizations runs the risk – from a civil society perspective – of think tanks becoming divorced, distant or detached from other groups that are less well resourced, less well connected and less politically competent and entrepreneurial. As such, think tanks represent a vehicle from which to observe the competition, emerging hierarchies and tensions in global society as a whole.

The second issue concerns policy-making at global and regional levels. In the absence of a sovereign authority – a world government or global federation – political opportunities are provided to non-state actors. They acquire some agenda-setting powers, input to decision-making and informal authority through transnational policy communities. The policy process at global and regional levels may well be more porous to non-state actors. This is not to suggest, however, that all non-state actors have equal entry. In these processes, think tanks emphasize their scholarly credentials as knowledgeable, expert, reputable and intellectually reliable organizations in order to gain a comparative advantage in access to decision-makers, information and finance. Think tanks that share the normative position of powerful patrons are better positioned for inclusion in transnational policy communities. Public policy, whilst still dependent on the state, is informed by a wider range of actors and structures at this level. Governance can be *informal* and emerge from strategic interactions and partnerships of national and international bureaucracies with non-state actors in the market place and civil society.

Thirdly, think tank transnationalization raises questions about representative democracy in the global agora. These organizations often claim that they perform a representational role, articulating diverse viewpoints and challenging orthodoxies. Indeed, in the absence of political parties generating policy ideas and visions at this level of governance, it is arguable that think tanks, NGOs and other civil society organizations are adopting this function. They press for greater transparency and accountability from national governments and international organizations. Without the ballot box to confer authority, the independent status of most think tanks and other civil society organizations is advantageous. Where asymmetries of information exist, consumers are more prone to 'trust' the non-profit supplier of policy advice claiming to act in the public interest. Yet such claims must be treated with caution. Given the current dominance of Western institutes, the representation of policy perspectives may occlude the articulation of policy perspectives from groups in developing countries. Equally important, think tanks and many NGOs are administered and staffed by professional elites who are often unrepresentative of the communities for which they seek to speak – whether it be specific groups or the general public – and to which they are largely unconnected.

These issues are outlined only in a cursory fashion here. The objective of this chapter has been the more limited one of outlining the dimensions of think tank transnationalisation. The supply and demand dynamics of think tank expertise are complex, and the role of knowledge and advocacy in politics cannot be understood without reference to the relationships between those who produce it and those who consume it. However, the key question and future research agenda will be to address think tank influence and transnational policy impact in conditions where knowledge is power.

Notes

1 This chapter is a substantially amended and updated version of 'Think Tank Transnationalisation', *Global Society*, 14(2), 2000 published by Taylor and Francis.

4 Heidi Ullrich

European Union think tanks: generating ideas, analysis and debate[1]

In contrast to the growing number of studies of think tank activity in other political systems and regions, there has been a conspicuous lack of work on EU think tanks. This chapter is an attempt to add to the existing literature on EU think tanks and to stimulate further work in this area. Its primary concerns are to identify the various types of EU and EU-oriented research institutes and think tanks and to begin to appraise their role in the EU policy environment. In order to accomplish these objectives, it is necessary to address several issues. First, the rapid growth in scale of EU think tank activity over the past decade or so is analysed and explained. Secondly, a typology is offered to distinguish between the various types of EU think tank. Thirdly, the conceptualisation of EU think tank activities and actors is considered through the application of various components of the policy network approach. Finally, the issue of influence is investigated to determine the degree of impact think tanks exhibit in the EU policy process.

Explaining the growth of EU think tanks

There has been a significant increase in the number of EU think tanks since the early 1990s. Additionally, many of those active earlier have significantly enlarged and/or refocused their programmes to adapt to the evolving European policy environment. EU think tanks, working individually and increasingly in collaboration with other institutes, now cover a wide spectrum of European policy issues, ranging from broad questions of institutional reform and enlargement to much more specific topics, such as financial regulation and the creation of a single market for European advertisers.

The growth in EU think tank activity may be seen as a response to both the deepening and widening of the EU itself and the corresponding increase in the quantity and complexity of policy-making activities at the EU and member-state level. As the policy environment expands in scope and demands on government policy-makers in terms of time and expertise become greater, there is an increasing need for specialist knowledge, new ideas and policy alternatives.

Additionally, the rise in the number of EU think tanks may be seen as part of the more widespread phenomenon of increased policy-relevant activity by non-state actors, witnessed since the start of the 1990s. In the EU, the trend of increased non-state actor activity was partly a result of the difficulties surrounding the ratification of the Maastricht Treaty between 1992 and 1993 and the acknowledged need for greater transparency in policy-making. Recognizing a need to incorporate the views of citizens to reduce the perceived democratic deficit within the EU political system, European politicians and bureaucrats have encouraged the increased involvement of non-state actors.

The EU's relatively transparent and open policy-making process provides think tanks with potentially numerous targets for their research and ideas. Sherrington (2000: 175) notes that: 'Given the multi-level nature of EU policy-making, there are also a variety of access points, or target audiences for think tanks ... Consequently, there is a much wider constituency for think tanks at the EU level.' This broad constituency is a primary reason for the burgeoning scale and diversity of EU think tank activity in recent years.

Defining EU think tanks

Much of the literature on think tanks has been preoccupied with the difficult issue of definition. Given the complex, multi-level policy-making environment of the EU, it is argued here that rather than seeking to develop an all-encompassing definition, perhaps more critical to gaining an understanding of EU think tanks is defining their role in the policy process. According to EU think tank researchers themselves,[2] this can be characterized as follows:

> Firstly, to develop ideas for the policy agenda for about two years down the line [since] there is a need to take up the issues of today and then link them with the future. Secondly, to promote intelligent ideas. Thirdly, to pull policy-makers away from the here and now and get them to see the implications and deeper meanings of issues. (Interview with member state official, Brussels, March 2001)

> To provide independent analysis and policy options. (Interview with think tank director, Brussels, January 2001)

> Think tanks act as facilitators or catalysts [within the EU policy process]. They also bring together those who would not have any other occasion to come together. These include academics, civil servants, associations and

lobbyists, civil society organizations and non-governmental organizations ... A broad field of people who are working in the same field, but have different perspectives. (Interview with an official in the European institutions, Brussels, January 2001)

Taken together, these comments produce constructive defining characteristics that provide a useful basis for analysing the large variety of think tanks operating within the EU policy environment.

Towards an EU think tank typology: making sense of complexity

EU think tanks share many defining characteristics but also vary in their methods of operation, size, sources of funding, target audiences and the political environments in which they operate. Given this diversity of characteristics and contexts, it is useful to place them within a typology to provide a framework for analysis. The typology developed here identifies four categories:

1 *The EU's internal think tank:* The Group of Policy Advisors (GPA), widely known by its French name, Cellule de Prospective, operates within the European Commission to provide both expert policy advice to the president of the Commission and his Cabinet, and a link with external research institutes and associations.
2 *Brussels-based EU think tanks:* The handful of Brussels-based EU think tanks differ in at least two important respects from their member-state counterparts. First, their location in the heartland of EU activity gives the former more frequent access to both EU and visiting member-state officials. Second, their independence from any member-state government means that they are relatively immune from the influence of national political and policy agendas, which may in turn enhance their credibility at the EU level.
3 *Member-state EU-oriented think tanks:* This category includes numerous member-state EU and EU-oriented think tanks with varying objectives and distinctive methods of operation, due to the nature of their particular domestic political system.
4 *University-based European research institutes:* The major university-based European research institutes, while cherishing and claiming their independence in terms of research, often collaborate with each other or with other think tanks on specific research projects. Thus, a mutually beneficial relationship is formed.

While typologies serve as an analytical tool, some caution is warranted in their interpretation. This is particularly so in the case of the EU, given the multi-dimensional nature of the policy-making environment. Even within the categories of this typology, significant differences in objectives are evident. These differences, most apparent among the Brussels-based and member-state EU think tanks, may be divided into three main groups reflecting their primary functions: (1) generating ideas; (2) policy-oriented analysis and outreach; and (3) furthering debate. Table 4.1 positions selected EU think tanks within these three categories of activity.

Table 4.1 Selected EU think tanks: a typology

Type of think tank	Generating ideas	Policy-oriented analysis	Furthering debate
Internal		Group of Policy Advisors (GPA)	
Brussels-based	Centre for European Policy Studies (CEPS)	European Policy Centre (EPC)	Friends of Europe
Member-state: UK	Royal Institute of International Affairs (RIIA)	European Policy Forum (EPF)	Centre for European Reform (CER) Foreign Policy Centre (FPC) Federal Trust for Education and Research
Continental	Centre of European Studies and Research (ELIAMEP) Clingendael Institute German Council on Foreign Relations (DGAP) Germany Institute for International and Security Affairs (SWP) Institut Français des Relations Internationales (IFRI) Institut für Europäische Politik Instituto Juan March de Estudios e Investigaciones Max Planck Institut für Gesellschaftsforschung	European Institute of Public Administration (EIPA) EU Institute for Security Studies (EUISS)	Bertelsmann Stiftung Friedreich Ebert Stiftung (FES) Konrad Adenauer Stiftung (KAS) Notre Europe
University-based research institute (RSC)	Robert Schuman Centre (RSC) (European University Institute (EUI), Florence) European Institute (EI) (London School of Economics (LSE))		

The EU's internal think tank

Established in 1989 by the then European Commission president, Jacques Delors, the history of the GPA, formerly the Forward Studies Unit (FSU), reflects the evolution of the Commission within the expanding EU policy environment, the policy needs of successive Commission presidents and the relationship between the latter and the directors of the Unit/Group. The degree of impact shown by the GPA on EU policy has ebbed and flowed according to the approach to policy-making within the Commission, the amount of direct access the FSU/GPA has had to the president, his Cabinet and the other commissioners, and the strength of the Commission. Under the direction of Delors's advisor and friend, Jérôme Vignon, the FSU initially benefited from having close relations with the president and his Cabinet. The objectives of the Unit under Vignon included 'identifying the issues of tomorrow', developing new ideas, and acting as a catalyst for debate within the Commission (interview with EU official, Brussels, January 2001).

Following the resignation of the Delors Commission in 1995, Delors's successor, Jacques Santer, shifted the FSU's primary mandate to a longer-term perspective and distanced himself from its activities. Despite a reduction in visible impact on EU policy, however, elements of the Unit's research could still be detected in areas such as the Local Employment and Development Initiative and the European Council's decisions on employment and social issues. Medium- to long-term research continued under the direction of Jean-Claude Thébault, Vignon's successor, including the publication of a collaborative work entitled Scenarios 2010 that presented five possible scenarios of 'Europe' by that date. According to observers both within the Commission and in the wider EU policy environment, this work served as a point of reference for the activities of several member-state ministries. None the less, the overall influence of the FSU on EU policy remained relatively weak.

However, with the appointment of Ricardo Levi, a personal advisor and friend of Commission president Romano Prodi in the spring of 2000, the Commission's internal think tank returned to its original mandate of providing policy advice directly to the president. As described by Levi, the role of the renamed Group of Policy Advisors is that of a 'back-up [to] the President's cabinet' (interview, Brussels, March 2001). Recognizing the need both for specialist advice and analysis within the relatively under-staffed Commission, and for the expansion of its network across Europe, the GPA recently established the Group of Economic Analysis (consisting of senior experts from academia, finance and research institutes), which reports directly to the president. This group is similar to the successful 'High-Level Groups', such as the 1992 High-Level Group on the Operation of the Internal Market, that offer expert (and supportive) advice to the Commission.

Brussels-based think tanks

Brussels-based EU think tanks generally fit neatly into categories defined by their activities. Evidence gathered through extensive interviews suggests that there is little collaboration between them. While they are interested in each other's activities, staff members seldom interact. However, except when they are bidding for the same project, there is little competition either. This may be due to each fulfilling a slightly different need of EU policy-makers. The downside, though, according to a director of an EU think tank, is that this lack of competition may be the cause of weakness among the Brussels-based think tanks: 'There is not significant competition. As a result, they are not as good as they might be. They don't generate enough buzz' (interview, Brussels, March 2001). The following section briefly examines the three major institutes in terms of size and significance.

Centre for European Policy Studies: CEPS is highly regarded among policy-makers and other researchers both in Brussels and in the member-states for its high-quality research and capacity to generate new ideas and analysis. Although active since 1980, CEPS was officially founded in 1983. Thus, it was the first EU think tank in Brussels, and is still considered by some outside CEPS to be 'the only true EU think tank' (interview, Brussels, March 2001). This reputation stems from its emphasis on rigorous research and balanced analysis. Daniel Gros, the current director, and Karel Lannoo, its chief executive, seek to ensure that CEPS 'invests in its intellectual capital' through encouraging its staff to expand their research capabilities continuously (interview with Karel Lannoo, Brussels, January 2001). The relatively large number of researchers (23 at the time of writing) is reflected in the broad range of CEPS' activities and large number of publications (over 75 published in 2000). The main focus of publications is on economic policy and politics, institutions and security issues. In addition to targeting corporate decision-makers, CEPS aims to reach mid-level civil servants both in the Commission and in national ministries. In general, this strategy seems to be successful. A report on EMU written by Gros in the late 1980s reportedly worked its way up to senior German and EC officials, with some aspects reflected in the 1989 Delors Report (interviews with various think tank researchers, Brussels, January 2001).

European Policy Centre: since its launch in 1997, the European Policy Centre (EPC) has clearly distinguished itself from CEPS by focusing on outreach activities and policy-oriented analysis rather than research. Its leadership (including Belmont Centre founders Stanley Crossick, John Palmer, Hywel Ceri Jones and Max Kohnstamm) is well known in EU policy circles. Palmer attributes the EPC's authoritative reputation to the fact that the personnel involved in its activities know who the 'key players' are (interview, Brussels, January 2001). Part-time senior-level advisors who supply policy-relevant essays supplement the small number of full-time research staff. The EPC is membership-driven with projects broadly determined by its sponsors, which currently include over 200 corporations, professional associations, diplomats, regional governments and civil society organizations. Members, the majority of which are corporations, professional associations and diplomatic missions, are considered crucial voices within the EU policy process. The EPC sees itself as providing a forum for its members to engage in dialogue with EU and member state officials.

Friends of Europe: established in 1998, Friends of Europe sees itself as a reflection group rather than a true think tank. Media reports have branded it 'an eminent group', which is well deserved given an advisory board that reads like an EU who's who. Its secretary general, Giles Merritt, states that the group is calling for a 'deeper and wider debate' on the future of Europe (interview, Brussels, March 2001). Friends of Europe aims to influence EU policy and to 'muscle in on the political debate'. Members of the advisory group, headed by the highly regarded Vicomte Etienne Davignon, hold various responsibilities including fund-raising, establishing networks with national institutes in order to 'denationalize' them, and most importantly acting as a catalyst for debate. The group's strategy is to be more 'heterogeneous and democratic' than the other Brussels-based think tanks. In practice, this approach is evident in their membership and activities. In addition to their official membership, numbering approximately 400 at the time of writing, events are also open to all interested members of the public.

Member-state think tanks

There are several variable elements amongst EU think tanks based in member states. First, although this category of think tank often reflects the political and policy-making environments in which they operate, some are clearly affiliated to national political parties. Secondly, EU member-state think tanks vary in the amount of time they devote to EU, as opposed to purely domestic, issues. Thirdly, EU think tanks vary in accordance with their geographical location. A researcher familiar with both UK and continental think tanks observed that in general, 'continental think tanks are typically more academic in nature, while UK think tanks are frequently based on youth, dynamism and innovation' (interview, January 2001). As Day (2000: 104) notes, while think tanks in the UK tend to resemble their US counterparts in terms of structure, there is 'definitional blurring' when one considers think tanks across Western Europe as a whole. However, despite their differences, the activities of member-state EU think tanks generally fall within the three broad areas of generating ideas, policy-oriented analysis and furthering debate. In the following section, selected EU think tanks from the UK and the continent are briefly discussed.

United Kingdom: RIIA (also known as Chatham House) has a well-established reputation for developing ideas, producing high-quality research and serving as a forum for debate, which are arguably its three primary contributions to the EU policy process. The aim of its European Programme is to encourage and contribute to the EU policy debate through a variety of activities including research, books, briefing papers and other publications, seminars and conferences. The researchers, drawn from academia, have recognized expertise in European issues. Current work includes enlargement, the economic and political issues surrounding UK membership of the euro, co-operation in justice and home affairs, and the related issues of migration and bilateral relations within the EU. Like many EU think tanks, Chatham House actively participates in regular meetings with a wide network of continental and US think tanks. According to Julie Smith, head of its European Programme, such networking not only encourages collaborative research, but 'can also contribute to more effective EU policy debate on a multi-lateral level' (interview, London, January 2001).

Having a mandate of providing its members with policy-oriented analysis is the European Policy Forum (EPF), established in 1992. Separate fora, including telecommunications and media and financial issues, began operations in 1997. With its funding coming almost exclusively from corporate members, it is little surprise that EPF supports European policies with a preference for market solutions. Activities include seminars and conferences based on the participation of members, academics, media representatives and member-state diplomatic officials. EPF does not publish to the same extent as other EU think tanks in the UK. Graham Mather, its president and a former Member of the European Parliament, describes its ideology as being 'positive on Europe', but at the same time favouring a decentralization of EU institutions (interview, London, February 2001). Comparisons may be made between the EPF and the EPC in Brussels in terms of activities and type of membership.

EU think tanks active in the UK may be identified as those advocating a 'progressive' or a more 'traditional' approach. Among the more 'progressive' are the Centre for European Reform (CER) and the Foreign Policy Centre (FPC). These think tanks have more similarities than differences. There is also significant overlap with the style pioneered by the 'postmodern think tank' Demos. While claiming to be independent, financially and intellectually, both were officially established in 1998 with the encouragement of the prime minster, Tony Blair, and the then foreign minister, Robin Cook, although CER was active earlier. Access to senior national policy-making circles has benefited the CER and the FPC and contributed to their well-respected reputations. Additionally, the directors and staff members are young and dynamic with visible enthusiasm for developing a 'new way' of looking at the European policy debate and proactively seeking out media coverage for their activities. Both target the full spectrum of policy actors, although the CER often emphasizes the needs of its corporate members. However, the two also differ in several respects. While the CER focuses exclusively on European issues, the FPC incorporates Europe into broader foreign policy issues, reflecting its view that topics should be studied in ways that are 'joined up', rather than in isolation. Moreover, while staff members at the FPC are predominantly British, CER employs a significant number of non-British Europeans. According to Steven Everts of CER, this gives the latter 'a more European perspective' (interview, London, February 2001).

Stimulating debate through a more 'traditional' approach is the Federal Trust for Education and Research. Established in 1945, its underlying aim is to stimulate and inform public debate on federal issues of relevance to the national, continental and global levels. Martyn Bond, its current director, emphasizes that this debate should be at a 'rational' level. Establishing trust between academics and policy-makers and educating civil society are seen as two critical means of ensuring this type of debate. Although a primary principle of the Trust is not to advocate a specific EU policy, it does not prevent the authors of its publications from doing so. Bond views its particular strengths as its promotion of a 'simple' idea (namely, encouraging 'democracy' at all levels), its 'lateral' thinking and its 'intelligent' approach to issues (interview, London, March 2001).

Continental: like their counterparts in the UK, continental EU think tanks may also be divided into categories according to their primary activities. Those focused on research and generating ideas include the Institut Français des Relations Internationales (IFRI) in France; the German Council on Foreign Relations (DGAP) and the German Institute for International and Security Affairs (SWP) in Germany; the Clingendael Institute in the Netherlands; the Hellenic Foundation for European and Foreign Policy (ELIAMEP) in Greece and the Instituto Juan March de Estudios e Investigaciones in Spain. Organizations primarily involved in policy-oriented analysis for a specific constituency include the European Institute of Public Administration (EIPA) in Maastricht and the EU Institute for Security Studies (EUISS) in Paris. Aiming to further debate on European issues are Jacques Delors's Notre Europe, DGAP's Forum on European Foreign Policy, the outreach programmes of the Bertelsmann Stiftung, including its extensive conference network, international forum and European summer school, and Germany's party-affiliated institutes such as the Friedreich Ebert Stiftung (FES) and the KAS. There are a large number of EU and EU-oriented think tanks active throughout the 15 member-states. However, despite increasing collaboration between think tanks across national borders, within individual countries the relationship is characterized by competition.

University-based EU research institutes

Amongst the various types of think tanks described in the literature is that of the 'university without students'. Although this description is true of most think tanks, using this as a defining factor may prevent the inclusion of the growing number of university-based EU research institutes that are actively contributing to the EU policy debate. This investigation argues that several such institutes within the EU should be included within a broad definition of EU think tanks. This is due to the strong policy-relevant research, publications and conference activities that several university-based research institutes in the EU member-states are engaged in. 'Think tanks have one thing in common: the individuals in them attempt to make academic theories and scientific paradigms policy-relevant' (Stone, 2000b: 154). Therefore, university-based EU research institutes share an important element with other EU think tanks. Although this discussion limits itself to the Robert Schuman Centre (RSC) at the European University Institute (EUI) and the European Institute (EI) at the London School of Economics (LSE), other highly regarded university-based institutes that fall into this category include the Centre for Applied Policy Research (CAP) in Munich and the Mannheim Centre for European Social Research (MZES).

Established in the autumn of 1993, the RSC, based at the EUI, has described itself as 'an academic centre [aiming to] contribute relevant policy research on the main issues which contemporary European society must address and, in particular issues bearing on the construction of Europe' (*The Economist*, 2000). Under the leadership of its first director, Yves Mény, several plans were implemented, including firstly the expansion of its formal relations with other European research institutes as well as EU and national government institutions. Secondly, Mény focused on developing the core RSC's academic team, who in addition to possessing academic excellence were required to 'link academic research with the outside world' (EUI, 1999: 20–1).[3]

Under the new directorship of Paul Taylor, the primary objective of the EI at the LSE is to become an instrument for projecting the collectivity of LSE's substantial European research to the outside world. There are several autonomous research centres and programmes within the EI, including the Hellenic Observatory, the Economic and Social Cohesion Fund and the European Political-Economy Infrastructure Consortium. Taylor notes that although each group has a defined intellectual space, he is working to make them more cohesive (interview, London, March

2002). Through its research, public lectures and weekly series of meetings, the EI aims to contribute to the broader European debate as well as provide expertise to EU policy-makers.

Think tank networks

A further variable adding to the complexity of analysing EU think tanks is the increasing use of formal and informal networks, often transnational, among the various organizations. In the case of the EU, these networks are forming within and across the categories of the typology as well as with states outside the EU. Due to the unique features of the EU policy environment, including that it is multinational, multi-lingual and multi-level, policy networks operating across national borders and contributing to debates in both Brussels and member-states are particularly important. These networks of intellectuals take shape through interaction at conferences, collaboration between EU and EU-oriented think tanks, international institutions and associations that draw upon national contributions. Such transnational networks allow EU think tanks to gain broader perspectives on European issues and incorporate different approaches to EU policy issues. Within these networks, a European 'policy elite' has emerged that facilitates linkages between Brussels-based EU institutions and the national debates within the individual member-states.[4] Notably, a researcher within an EU think tank argued that while historically debates over Europe had been primarily national in their outlook, due to the increase in think tank networks and collaboration on research projects, as well as the growing frequency with which European policy actors are meeting in think tank sponsored forums, a truly European debate could be said to be developing (interview, London, February 2001).

The Trans European Policy Studies Association (TEPSA) is an example of an initially informal network becoming formalized. TEPSA was established in 1974 among the Belgian Groupe d'Etudes Politiques Européennes, the Istituto Affari Internazionali (IAI) in Italy and the Federal Trust in the UK, who were all working on European issues from an educative standpoint. By the mid-1990s members recognized that due to the growth in participants, a more formal structure was needed. TEPSA currently consists of 15 member-state EU think tanks and research institutes as well as six associated members, four of which are located in the applicant countries. TEPSA's aims include the establishment of dialogue between the different nationalities of the EC and developing a common TEPSA view. Advantages of belonging to this formal network include the availability of first-hand knowledge on organizing a conference in any particular member's country and, of particular relevance for national associations from newer member-states or candidate countries, the assistance of other TEPSA members in learning the intricacies of the EU policy process and gaining easier access to EU policy-makers.

However, among members of EU think tanks, differences in opinion exist on the benefits of forming networks. The head of one Brussels-based EU think tank stated that think tanks 'gain strength out of unity' (interview, Brussels, March 2001), while formal alliances were seen by some as being managerially cumbersome: 'What would be the value-added of having more structured relations with other think tanks? More committee meetings?' (interview, London, February 2001).

Conceptualizing the role of EU think tanks: simplifying complexity

Although the typology offered above provides a useful framework to distinguish the various types of EU think tanks, it does not offer significant insight into the role EU think tanks play in influencing EU policy, specifically within transnational networks. This requires a conceptual framework. A potentially useful conceptual model is that of policy networks, particularly when broadly defined as a mode of governance that incorporates actors from both inside and outside government to facilitate decision-making and implementation.

However, rather than applying only the general notion of policy networks, this study suggests applying its various components, including the concepts of policy communities, epistemic communities, advocacy coalitions and policy entrepreneurs, to conceptualize the role played by EU think tanks in influencing EU policy. These groups are seen to be frequently complementary, with significant potential for conceptual synthesis. Additionally, it may be useful to investigate the relevance of each component during various stages of the EU policy process. These various groups, or perhaps individuals in the case of policy entrepreneurs, may be identified as explanatory factors in analysing both the manner in which and the reasons why a specific EU policy emerges.

Conceptualizing EU think tanks in this manner offers a more comprehensive approach to explaining the role of EU think tanks in the multi-level EU policy environment. This section provides a brief introduction to the various conceptual components as applicable in the case of EU think tanks. However, it is not within the scope of this chapter to test the applicability of these approaches in the case of EU think tanks and policy development. To do so requires rigorous analysis of examples of specific instances of policy change within the EU (see Ullrich, 2001).

European Union think tanks 63

Policy communities

Members of a policy community include a wide range of policy actors, among them politicians, civil servants, interest group and non-governmental organization representatives as well as recognized experts. Actors within policy communities 'interact strategically, while engaging in exchanges involving the sharing of information, expertise, and political support' (Coleman and Perl, 1999: 696). Research indicates that numerous policy communities consisting of EU think tank researchers, national and EU bureaucrats, politicians, academics and corporate representatives are active within the EU policy environment. Although these various communities often differ in terms of nationality and specific policy issues, think tanks provide a primary domain in which these various policy communities overlap. Thus, EU think tanks could be one factor in the development of a Europe-wide policy community. Notably, EU think tank-sponsored fora exclusively for fee-paying corporate members (referred to by some as 'new' policy communities, as compared to the more traditional 'old' policy communities that involve a mix of government, corporate and citizen representatives) have been described as 'private diplomacy' (interview, London, February 2001). The increase in new-style policy networks is due to the large number of mergers across EU member-state boundaries, encouraging corporate representatives to become part of a policy community that is not separated along national lines.

Epistemic communities

Epistemic communities have been defined as 'a network of professionals with recognized expertise and competence in a particular domain and an authoritative claim to policy-relevant knowledge within that domain or issue-area' (Haas, 1992a: 3). Although epistemic community members are generally found in think tanks and university-based research institutes, they may also be active within government ministries and national and international profit and non-profit organizations. Epistemic communities are of specific interest in tracing the development of new ideas and policy alternatives. In order for specific epistemic communities to be legitimized within the policy process, their ideas and policy tools generally need to be accepted as well as used by other policy actors.

The existence of epistemic community members is thought to be more likely within think tanks that emphasize the generation of ideas and university-based EU research institutes. For example, with a dual mission of carrying out scientific research and evaluation while at the same time promoting environmentally sound policies, evidence points to the group of natural and social scientists working in the Institute for European

Environmental Policy (IEEP) as being part of an environmental epistemic community (Sherrington, 2000: 185). Additionally, the European Network of Economic Policy Research Institutes (ENEPRI), sponsored by CEPS, and the London-based Centre for Economic Policy Research (CEPR), with its wide European network of economists, exhibit elements of epistemic communities. That these epistemic communities operate within EU think tank and policy institute networks indicates that within the European policy environment, epistemic communities may tend to be transnational in nature.

Advocacy coalition

Like epistemic communities, advocacy coalitions place a premium on knowledge. Consisting of a diverse range of policy actors, such as politicians, civil servants, researchers and interest group representatives, advocacy coalition members 'seek to better understand the world within a particular policy area in order to identify means to achieve their fundamental objectives' (Sabatier, 1993: 33). However, a key distinguishing variable of advocacy coalitions is the emphasis on the belief system rather than knowledge in itself. The beliefs of members guide their actions and shape their ideology and interests. Thus, unlike epistemic communities, advocacy coalitions offer a 'more overtly political and value-based' approach to the policy process (Dudley and Richardson, 1996: 69). In fact, Radaelli argues that the advocacy coalition approach 'offers a link between policy and politics' (1995: 171).

The advocacy coalition framework is particularly applicable to explaining policy change. Confronted with new knowledge and expertise, members of advocacy coalitions may alter some of their beliefs through a process of policy-oriented learning, thus allowing for changes to current policies. Given that members of advocacy coalitions contribute alternative policies to the policy process as well as serve as advocates of specific policies, they are more likely to be active in think tanks that focus on policy analysis and outreach.

Policy entrepreneurs

Kingdon identifies policy entrepreneurs as 'advocates for proposals or for the prominence of an idea' who are particularly noted for 'their willingness to invest their resources – time, energy, reputation, and sometimes money – in the hope of a future return ... that might come to them in the form of policies of which they approve, satisfaction from participation, or even personal aggrandizement' (1995: 122–3). Since many of the potential policy entrepreneurs within EU think tanks, often members of advisory boards, have retired, this description might be limiting. However, Kingdon continues by explaining the motivation of some identified policy entrepreneurs: 'They enjoy advocacy, they enjoy being at or near the seat of power, they enjoy being part of the action. They make calls, have lunch, write memos, and draft proposals' not only to promote their own visions or values, but because they 'simply like the game' (Kingdon, 1995, 1st edn, 1984: 130). The link between policy entrepreneurs and think tanks has been described by Stone (2000a: 211): 'These organizations [think tanks] are independent policy research institutes but are not simply learned societies. Instead, many act as policy entrepreneurs within both domestic and international policy domains proffering policy advice on cross-national problems of pollution, pandemics, trade and so forth.'

In the case of the EU policy process, the source of policy entrepreneurs' influence derives not only from their expertise in a particular policy field but also from their intimate knowledge of the EU policy process and access to elite policy communities and government policy-makers. Additionally, the existence of a well-placed and highly regarded policy entrepreneur within an advocacy coalition may increase its chances of gaining dominance in the policy environment. Acting as a policy entrepreneur is generally a choice made by individual policy actors based on various motivations. Thus, within the EU, they may be active in the full range of think tanks. However, given that policy entrepreneurs tend to be involved in the policy debate, there may be a greater likelihood of such actors within think tanks focusing on policy analysis or furthering debate.

The idea that various subgroups within the broader concept of policy networks may operate within think tanks is not new (see Stone, 1996b). However, this research concludes that a combination of these groups, active at various times and to various degrees at each stage in the policy process, may be useful for conceptualizing the role played by EU think tanks and their staff within the multi-level EU policy-making environment.

The impact of EU think tanks on the EU policy process

EU thinks tanks, regardless of whether they engage primarily in generating ideas, policy analysis and advocacy or stimulating debate, seek to have a degree of impact on the EU policy process. However, the difficult issue of measuring the degree of influence that think tanks have on the policy process has been debated by many (see *inter alia* Campbell, 1998; Yee, 1996). Rather than entering the debate over measurement, this study addresses four issues related to the impact of EU think tanks on the European policy process: (1) whether influence is direct or indirect; (2) the sources of influence; (3) areas where EU think tanks exhibit impact; and (4) the limitations of such influence.

Influence: direct or indirect?

There is virtually unanimous agreement among EU think tank communities and constituents that to the extent to which influence may be said to exist, it must be considered indirect. The director of one Brussels-based think tank admitted that: 'Regarding influence, one can't say that "x" caused "y". There could be 50 reasons why something happened. All one can do [to determine influence] is look back at previous papers and see if any valuable ideas came from them' (interview, London, February 2001).

In addition to widespread recognition of influence being indirect rather than direct, many of those interviewed were of the view that judgement of the degree of think tank influence required a period of at least two to three years between the development of a specific idea and the time when it could be said to have been taken up by policy-makers. To compensate, one researcher pointed out that 'Think tanks try to influence the climate of opinion, rather than have a direct link [to policies]' (interview, London, February 2001).

Sources of influence

The influence that EU think tanks have on the EU policy process derives from three interrelated sources:

1 *Authority based on expertise:* As pointed out by a senior EU think tank staff member, in order to have influence, think tanks 'must have good information, good statistics and good research' (interview, Brussels, January 2001). Expertise may be in a specific issue area, such as that possessed by researchers in EU think tanks focusing on research and analysis and in university-based research institutes. However, in the case of the EU, expertise may also be intimate knowledge of the EU policy process and/or having access to the key policy actors.
2 *Promotion of an independent, balanced view:* Preliminary research of the views of EU policy-makers indicates that the outputs of EU think tanks, particularly those operating in Brussels, are seen as credible sources of information and policy advice due to their independence. An official in a European institution stated that some EU think tanks had 'moral authority' because of their independent status (interview, Brussels, March 2001).
3 *Legitimacy:* The issue of legitimacy largely stems from having recognized authority. Several EU think tank researchers mentioned that their legitimacy was strengthened by their need to defend their reputation. The expertise of researchers was also a factor in the existence of think tank legitimacy. Policy-makers focused on the unique features of some EU think tanks, noting their ability to bring a wide group of important policy actors together, as well as their strong track-record of addressing EU policy issues.

The impact of EU think tanks on the EU policy process

The results of research show that the activities of EU think tanks have three types of impact on the EU policy-making process:

1 *Serving as a forum for debate:* Bringing EU policy-makers together through their fora was mentioned on numerous occasions by those interviewed as one of the key impacts EU think tanks have on the EU policy process. Through offering various policy actors, including civil servants, politicians, academics, lobbyists and members of the interested public, a forum for debate, think tanks allow for the sharing of ideas, broadening of perspectives and exchange of information. An official in a European institution exuberantly remarked: 'Think tanks are an excellent forum for discussion. Here they have influence!' (interview, Brussels, March 2001).

2 *Serving as a catalyst for debate:* In addition to serving as a forum for debate, EU think tanks can also have an impact due to their ability to be a catalyst for debate. This stems from their analysis of policies, development of alternative ideas and providing relevant information. Through proposing policy ideas and concepts, EU think tanks generate debate, primarily in the agenda-setting stage of the EU policy process.

3 *Developing medium-to-long-term ideas:* Unlike policy-makers, particularly those within government institutions, EU think tanks have the ability to address long-term issues and overarching themes as well as those that others may at first dismiss as unrealistic. An observer within a European institution noted that 'Think tanks think ahead with their proposals. These proposals may not be feasible, but [someone] must keep the fantasy' (interview, Brussels, January 2001). However, given its long-term nature, the results of this impact may not be traceable to an individual think tank.

The limits of influence

Despite evidence of EU think tanks having some impact in the EU policy-making environment, the overall conclusion is that this impact has been relatively limited. An official in a European institution argued that while their studies and analyses are comforting, EU think tanks do not substantially add to the policy-making process. However, there is some indication that at least some people working in think tanks recognize the limits of their impact: 'We want to contribute to European affairs and integration. However, we won't change the destiny of the continent' (interview, Brussels, January 2001).

Conclusion

This chapter has discussed the role of EU think tanks in the EU policy environment. Within the framework of a four-level typology, the primary EU think tank activities are generating ideas, analysis and debate. The need to conceptualize the activity of EU think tanks is critical to a better understanding of the organizations and their researchers. Expanding on the findings of earlier think tank studies using a broad policy network approach, this chapter suggests that using the individual conceptual models of policy communities, epistemic communities, advocacy coalitions and policy entrepreneurs potentially offers a more complete picture of think tanks' activities and motives.

Regarding influence on the EU policy process, evidence suggests that the impact of EU think tanks is limited. However, these organizations play important roles in serving as a forum for debate, generating debate and developing medium-to-long-term ideas rather than focusing merely on short-term policy issues. Until further empirical research is carried out, the extent to which EU think tanks influence EU policy remains uncertain. What is more certain is that as the policy process becomes ever more complex there will be a continued increase in the number and activity of EU think tanks. Thus, there is an increased need for academic researchers and interested policy-makers to investigate the topic of EU think tanks through generating their own ideas, analysis and debate.

Notes

1 I would like to thank Andrew Denham, Philippa Sherrington, Julie Smith, Diane Stone and William Wallace for providing useful comments on earlier versions of this chapter, as well as Anne Corbett for her sound advice. Earlier versions also benefited from comments received at the 2001 Political Studies Association Conference at the University of Manchester and the 2002 International Studies Association Annual Convention, New Orleans.
2 Much of the information in this chapter derives from in-depth interviews carried out with the directors, researchers and policy analysts of EU think tanks, primarily in Brussels and London, but also including Berlin and Florence. Additionally, to gain a more balanced view, EU policy-makers, the primary consumers of think tank output, were interviewed, including officials within the European institutions as well as member state civil servants based both in Brussels and in their respective capitals.
3 Helen Wallace replaced Mény in the summer of 2001.
4 This information draws on personal comments made by William Wallace.

Part II

European think tank traditions

5 Martin Thunert

Think tanks in Germany

In Germany, as elsewhere, 'think tank' is an imprecise and elusive term covering many different types of research and consulting organization scattered across the country. Germany has a long-standing tradition of state-sponsored 'applied basic research', especially in economics, but hardly a vigorous legacy of independent policy analysis and research. It is therefore necessary to use 'think tank' in its broadest sense, that is, to describe non-profit private and public organizations devoted to examining and analysing policy-relevant issues and producing research outputs in terms of publications, reports, lectures and workshops, in most cases targeted to identifiable audiences with the hope of influencing decision-making and public opinion.

Recent estimates of the number of think tanks (or their functional equivalents) operating in Germany vary, ranging between seventy and ninety institutions (see Day, 2000). If one broadens the definition to include various church-sponsored academies (which sometimes serve as part-time think tanks), operating foundations or university research centres, the number easily exceeds 100.

More than half of the German policy research institutes were founded in the last quarter of the twentieth century, although a large proportion of the biggest and best-funded think tanks date from pre-1975. Compared to other countries – especially to the United States and Britain – the percentage of publicly financed think tanks is very high – at least 75 per cent. There are about a dozen large non-university institutes that have annual budgets of between 5 million to 14 million euros and employ between thirty and eighty research staff. With the exception of the private Bertelsmann Stiftung, these larger institutes receive funding from the federal government or the *Länder*, joint funding from both levels of government as well as from research bodies such as the Max Planck Society or the Fraunhofer Society. Contract research is an important funding source for many German think tanks. The important role of state governments as sponsors and financiers of think tanks reflects Germany's federal structure.

By and large, the German think tank landscape fits into the mould of international think tank typologies (McGann and Weaver, 2000), although the sector of private and advocacy-oriented policy research institutes is less developed than in Anglo-American countries. It is also sometimes hard to distinguish between research-oriented academic think tanks on the one hand and institutions of basic research touching on policy-relevant questions on the other. It has proven quite difficult, if not impossible, for members of this diverse group of think tanks to recognize that they may belong to a clearly identifiable community. Table 5.1 provides a breakdown of think tank types in Germany.

Table 5.1 Types of think tanks in Germany (as percentage of all think tanks)

Type[a]	Percentage
Academic think tanks	⩾ 50
Contract research	10–15
Advocacy institutes	30–40
Party think tanks	10–15

Source: Author's survey
[a]Organizations may fall under more than one category.

Generally speaking, German think tanks are post-World War II creations. However, the origins of some policy research institutes date back to the Weimar Republic and even to Imperial Germany. Four of the six large economic research institutes, the Hamburg Institute of International Economics (HWWA) (1908), the Kiel Institute of World Economics (IfW) (1914), the German Institute for Economic Research (DIW) (1925) and its western branch, the Essen-based Rhine-Westphalia Institute for Economic Research (RWI) (1926), were postwar relaunches of previously existing institutes. A few other bodies, the Economic and Social Science Institute (WSI) of the German Federation of Trade Unions (DGB) and the FES, close to the Social Democratic Party and named after the first president of the Weimar Republic, had forerunner institutes prior to the Nazi period. However, rather than taking a chronological approach, this chapter discusses the German think tank landscape according to the categories outlined in Table 5.1.

Academic think tanks

Academic think tanks are by far the largest group of think tanks in Germany. An even larger number of institutes profess to adhere to the ideal of an independent academic research institute engaged in applied basic research. Academic think tanks can be divided into the following subgroups:

1 created by government, but working independently within public sector guidelines;
2 non-university institutes (mostly 'Blue List'/ Leibniz-Society institutes);
3 university-affiliated centres of applied policy-relevant research;
4 academic think tanks with considerable private funding.

Government-created institutes

The federal government created two large research bodies in the area of international affairs in the 1960s: the SWP, inspired by the RAND Corporation of Santa Monica, California, and the Federal Institute for Russian, East European and International Studies (BIOSt). Until the year 2000 the SWP was based in Ebenhausen, a small village near Munich and 600 km from the seat of government, while BIOSt was located in Cologne. Significant overlap in the work of both institutes and cost-cutting efforts by the federal government led to a merger of both institutes in the late 1990s and the relocation of the newly merged think tank to Berlin in late 2000. With a staff of 145 – half of them researchers – the merged institute, SWP–German Institute for International Affairs and Security, is the largest international affairs think tank in Europe today.

Between the 1970s and the 1990s, state governments became important sponsors of academic think tanks, sometimes with a strong emphasis on advocating certain policy areas or policy directions. In the early 1970s, Scandinavian think tanks such as SIPRI and the Peace Research Institute Oslo (PRIO) served as the operative models for peace research institutes founded by Social Democratic *Länder* governments in Frankfurt (the Peace Research Institute Frankfurt – HSFK/PRIF) and Hamburg (the Institute for Peace Research and Security Policy at the University of Hamburg – IFSH). Some of Germany's larger states, like Northrhine-Westphalia or Baden-Wuerttemberg, became particularly active as sponsors of think tanks in the 1990s: Northrhine-Westphalia launched the Science Center Northrhine-Westphalia, an umbrella organization of four state-based research institutes, which attempts to combine the concept of an academic advanced studies centre with that of a pragmatic think tank. The Wuppertal Institute for Climate, Environment and Energy, the Bureau for Future Studies (SFZ), and the Bonn International Center for Conversion (BICC) have gained a reputation beyond Germany's borders. Other *Länder*-based think tanks are the Baden-Württemberg Academy for Technology Assessment in Stuttgart, or the Centre for European Economic Research (ZEW) in Mannheim and the Franco-German Institute in Ludwigsburg.

'Blue List'/Leibniz-Society institutes

The largest group of academic think tanks consists of the so-called 'Blue-List' institutes.[1] Among this diverse group of eighty-three non-university research institutes, most of which receive financial assistance from the federal government and the states on a fifty-fifty basis, about a dozen institutes undertake applied research that is policy-relevant. The most visible institutes among this group are six large economic research institutes with a combined staff of more than 400 economic researchers. The joint funding of these economic think tanks through the national and state governments not only reflects Germany's federal structure, but expresses the desire to encourage competing views on economic policy and on Germany's economic development. Twice annually, experts from these six economic research institutes issue a Common Report predicting the short- and medium-term performance of the German economy. The six expert institutes are meant to arrive at joint conclusions, but the opportunity to express dissenting views in the form of minority opinions is given. In recent years, four of the six institutes concurred in the majority opinion based on the assumptions of neo-classical economics, while one or two institutes (usually the DIW and the RWI) have been noted for their adherence to neo-Keynesian paradigms. The Common Report receives the attention of the media as well as of the government, the Bundesbank, interest groups, and other actors in the economic policy community. It influences public debate about the legitimacy of government economic policy more than it influences policy decisions.

Other Blue-List institutes that conduct work of some policy relevance, but which have a less deliberate policy orientation, include the Social Science Center Berlin 'for Social Research' (WZB), which was founded in 1969 at the suprapartisan initiative of federal members of parliament and was inspired by the Brookings Institution in Washington, DC, and the German Overseas Institute (DÜI), an umbrella organization that incorporates a group of Hamburg-based area-studies institutes with an expertise on Asia, the Middle East, Africa and Latin America. Most member-institutes of other scientific associations, such as the Max Planck Society for the Advancement of Science, are too devoted to long-term, basic research to be regarded as policy-oriented think tanks. Among the notable exceptions are individual researchers and research units at the Max Planck Institute for the Study of Societies in Cologne, at the ZEW Mannheim, and the Fraunhofer Institute for Systems and Innovation Research (ISI) in Karlsruhe.

University-affiliated centres

Many German think tanks are affiliated with universities or operate in a semi-academic environment. With a staff of 50 researchers, CAP at the University of Munich is one of the largest institutes of its kind. CAP is somewhat unusual for a university-based research institute as it draws a substantial amount of its core funding from governmental (European Union) and private sources (such as the German Marshall Fund and the Bertelsmann Foundation). CAP founding director Werner Weidenfeld was a long-time advisor of former chancellor Helmut Kohl and serves on the board of the Center for Strategic and International Studies (CSIS) in Washington, DC. A thorough analysis of the management styles and strategies of major American think tanks such as CSIS, the American Enterprise Institute for Public Policy Research (AEI) and the Brookings Institution preceded CAP's creation in 1995. Weidenfeld concluded that independent policy research and consultancy has a bright future in Germany and that carving out a niche for a new institute would be worth while.

In addition to CAP, the 1990s brought a new dimension to this already close relationship between universities and think tanks. Some academics turned into policy entrepreneurs and created university-based policy research units – usually much smaller in scale than CAP. Examples include the Oswald von Nell-Breuning Institute for Business Ethics (NBI) at the Jesuit College in Frankfurt and the Institute for Development and Peace (INEF) at the University of Duisburg, inspired by the Worldwatch Institute. Another Munich-based academic research centre, the Center for Economic Studies (CES), operates as the academic arm of the Institute for Economic Research (IFO), which belongs to the Blue List/Leibniz Society. In most cases, it is not easy to draw a line between academic research and policy-oriented work. Two notable recent additions to the field of university-affiliated academic think tanks are the Centre for European Integration Research (ZEI) and the Centre for Development Research (ZEF) in Bonn. Founded in the mid-1990s, both academic think tanks received substantial government grants to compensate Bonn for the loss of its status as Germany's capital.

Privately financed academic institutes

There are at least two major exceptions to the rule of government-created and publicly financed academic think tanks. One is DGAP. DGAP was founded in 1955 in Bonn as an independent, non-partisan, non-profit organization. The models for this, the oldest German think tank dealing with international affairs, were the CFR in New York and the RIIA in London. DGAP's goals, its organizational structure as an elite network-cum research institute and its mode of financing are indeed strikingly similar to that of the older Anglo-American flagship institutes.

The second major exception is the Bertelsmann Stiftung, which was founded in 1977 at the seat of its parent corporation Bertelsmann AG in Gütersloh. In the 1990s the Bertelsmann Stiftung emerged as a heavyweight player in privately funded policy research with resources matching or exceeding those of the largest government-funded institutes. Boasting a constantly expanding staff of more than 200, this operating foundation organizes and carries out projects in close co-operation with partners in public and private scientific institutions. Members of the foundation have increasingly sponsored and organized expert meetings for the federal president and the Chancellery. Some of the foundation's units, such as the Centre for Higher Education Development, operate like think tanks, whereas others specialize in running specific programmes.

Finally, while having a more limited research capacity than the Bertelsmann Foundation, a growing number of other corporate foundations are becoming catalysts for policy-relevant ideas by organizing and sponsoring dialogue activities that bring together experts and practitioners. They include bodies such as the Thyssen Foundation, the Koerber Foundation and the Herbert Quandt Foundation, and academies like the Burda Academy for the Third Millennium as well as Protestant and Catholic academies. More recently, international think tanks and branches of American think tanks have expanded their activities or set up shop in Berlin: among them are the Aspen Institute, the American Academy and the Berlin office of RAND-Europe.

Contract research

Almost all publicly funded research institutes look for additional 'third funding' to finance project research (Weilemann, 2000:171). Hence, the number of think tanks creating a considerable portion of their revenue from some kind of contract research is quite high. However, contract research rarely defines their institutional purpose entirely. Contract research is a territory that non-profit think tanks must share with for-profit ones such as the Swiss-based Prognos Group, with corporate think tanks, and increasingly with large commercial management consulting firms.

Advocacy institutes

Increasingly in Germany, there exists a whole range of institutions that do not restrict their activities to seemingly objective scientific research, but see themselves primarily as advocates for specific solutions to public policy problems or for their own political worldview.[2] Interest-based policy research organizations affiliated with either the DGB, the Confederation of German Employers' Associations, the Protestant and Catholic Churches, or certain single-issue interest groups (such as the Taxpayer's Union) are among the oldest think tanks in Germany, dating back to the 1950s and 1960s. The WSI, think tank to the DGB, became an important training pool for future academics and political activists. The Federation of German Industry expanded its own research unit, the Institute of German Industry–Cologne, Germany's largest privately funded economic research institute.

The 1970s and 1980s saw the emergence of a small number of more independent advocacy-oriented think tanks, often founded by entrepreneurial academics or politicians. In 1977, for example, with the help of corporate sponsorship, Kurt Biedenkopf, a prominent maverick politician from the Christian Democratic Union and later the state-premier of Saxony (until 2002), and the economist Meinhard Miegel founded the Institute for Economics and Society (IWG), a miniature version of the AEI. In the same year, Germany's first environmental think tank, the Öko Institute, opened its doors in Freiburg. Hans Filbinger, a former conservative state-premier from Baden-Wuerttemberg with a questionable record in the World War II Wehrmacht, created an institute to continue his life's work after his death, the right-wing Weikersheim Study Centre (SZW), in the early 1980s. In 1982, a group of market-oriented academics set up the Frankfurter Institute/Foundation for Market Economy and Politics and its research council, the Kronberg Circle. A small number of market-oriented institutes, such as the Small Business Institute (ASU-UNI) and the Ludwig Erhard Foundation, have followed suit.

The decision to convert the Frankfurter Institute from a loose dialogue forum into a fully fledged advocacy think tank in the 1990s was influenced by the success of the Heritage Foundation and the CATO Institute in the United States, as well as by the free market think tanks in Britain. The products of the Frankfurter Institute, which despite its name moved to Berlin in the summer of 2001 to enhance its visibility among policymaking circles and subsequently renamed itself the Foundation for Market Economics, closely resemble those of American advocacy tanks. While policy briefs and one-pagers are not yet the dominant product of German advocacy institutes in general, their activities are clearly more devoted to marketing, communication and convocation than are most of their more academic counterparts. Advocacy tanks align themselves with sympathetic actors – from governmental bodies, national newspapers, business firms or the non-profit sector – within advocacy coalitions (Sabatier and Jenkins-Smith, 1983). They market value-driven policy recommendations through op-ed opinions, host one-day conferences with prominent keynoters, undertake educational activities targeted to tomorrow's elites, and are eager for appearances on television news programmes.

The prominence, proliferation and alleged influence of think tanks world-wide has not gone unnoticed by a growing number of young German policy entrepreneurs in their late twenties or early thirties, who only a decade or two ago would have sought a political career in a political party or in a non-research-oriented NGO, rather than create advocacy think tanks running on a shoestring budget and essentially a lot of unpaid or low-paid volunteer work. For this new and internationally oriented generation of think tank founders and 'activists', think tanks are as natural an inventory of the political space in a late-modern democracy as are parties, interest groups and NGOs. These new 'mini-tanks' such as the Foundation for the Rights of Future Generations (SRZG) based in Oberursel and Frankfurt), Deutschland Denken (Cologne), BerlinPolis, the Global Contract Foundation (GCF) and others, are minuscule in comparison to the state-funded and scholarly oriented think tanks and university institutes. Some of these mini-think tanks exist more as network institutes on the internet than as organizations with office space and staff. It is noteworthy of this newest wave of German think tanks is that their funding structure, the idealism of their young activist founders, their emphasis on marketing and advocacy and their concentration on a few carefully selected issues closely resemble those of some of the American and British advocacy institutes in their early years. Beyond their shaky financial situation, these new creations have in common a belief that societal, economic and political reforms in Germany are moving too slowly and that the interests of a younger, post-baby-boom generation are not well represented in political discourse. There is no agreement, however, about the priorities and the desired direction of reforms. Most of these new mini-tanks are refreshingly unideological and pragmatic, but by no means apolitical.

Party think tanks

The fourth distinct group of think tanks are the political party-affiliated think tanks, or 'political foundations', as they prefer to be called. These organizations are more prominent and better funded in Germany than nearly anywhere else. The semi-official status of political parties in the Basic Law (Article 21) and the desire not to channel various educational, research-oriented and international activities directly through the party system, but also not to keep them outside the influence of political parties, have resulted in a huge – albeit shrinking – amount of public funds (approximately 400 million euros in 2000) flowing into political foundations. Today there are six such foundations (Table 5.2). Each of them is related to one of the parties represented in the Bundestag. When their associated party is in government, the foundations are often perceived erroneously as semi-official bodies by many outside observers.

Table 5.2 German political foundations

Political foundation	Date established	Party
Friedrich Ebert Stiftung (FES)	1925	Social Democratic Party (SPD)
Konrad Adenauer Stiftung (KAS)	1964	Christian Democratic Party (CDU)
Hanns Seidel Foundation (HSS)	1967	Christian Social Union in Bavaria (CSU)
Friedrich Naumann Foundation (FNS)	1958	Free Democratic Party – Liberals (FDP)
Heinrich Böll Foundation	1996	Bündis90/Greens
Rosa Luxemburg Foundation	1998	Party of Democratic Socialism (PDS)

It is difficult to distinguish potential think tank functions from the other activities of party foundations. Think tank activities may account for up to 15–20 per cent of a party foundation's budget. The remainder is given in tied grants for development aid, student scholarships, civic education and archival work. Most foundations host in-house academies, research and consulting units, or study groups that focus on foreign policy, on economic and domestic policy, or on empirical social research, thereby fulfilling the typical think tank functions. Neither the policy expertise nor the think tank functions of party foundations are uniform. International networking with like-minded civil society organizations is one of their most important functions and their most common denominator. Apart from that activity, political foundations may differ in their institutional and policy priorities. For example, during the 1990s, the KAS merged several smaller institutes into a large Department of Political Research, equipped with powerful empirical research tools and a particular expertise in local government and security policy (Weilemann, 2000: 179–86). During the early and mid-1990s, when the Free Democratic Party was in government, that party's liberal Friedrich-Naumann-Foundation (FNS) was good at 'flying kites', testing the ground for new and generally more radical (that is, libertarian) ideas than the party establishment initially was ready to accept in the party platform. Today, the party platform is very much in line with some of those libertarian ideas.

The health of the political foundations' in-house think tanks depends on the willingness of the foundation leadership to sponsor think tank activities and on the availability of suitable policy entrepreneurs as well as experts for the job. All too often, important posts (especially abroad) are given to deserving but retired, or even failed, politicians. (The KAS would make an excellent case study in this respect.) Power relationships within the party and the foundation, and between the foundation and those in the parliamentary and the government party, as well as the overall funding and staffing situation are other important variables for the success of these party think tanks. Yet, public funding laws governing the party foundations, in combination with public distrust of politicians and partisan politics, may prompt the foundations to hide possible behind-the-scenes partisan consulting activities from the wider public and to make party foundations appear as if they are civil society organizations acting in the public interest. Despite the close personal and ideological links to their 'mother party', the foundations are not always willing external affairs instruments of the party leadership or extended arms of the party's in-house research departments. Conversely, pragmatic party politicians often ignore the findings and recommendations of the party think tanks in favour of the views of more politically powerful interests and of the preferences expressed through opinion polls and focus groups.

Main features of German think tanks

Type of research

The majority of the larger academic institutes, the party think tanks and a significant number of established advocacy think tanks produce their research in-house. Most think tanks in Germany are neither single-issue institutes nor full-service institutions – although the Bertelsmann Stiftung and the larger party foundations, such as the KAS, the Hanns Seidel Foundation (HSS) and the FES, are possible exceptions. The majority of think tanks can be classified somewhere in between. During the 1980s and most of the 1990s, economic and financial issues were paramount, followed by the environment, technology policy, social and labour market issues. Recently, European integration research (including 'European Central Bank-watching') has been booming, while foreign policy (including research on defence, peace and human rights) has been boosted, with a new focus on international affairs, in the wake of the war in Kosovo in 1999 and the terrorist attacks on the United States on 11 September 2001.

Finances

The most important source of income for German think tanks is still the state, primarily at the national and regional levels, but increasingly at the European Union level as well. Governments on all levels continue to be willing to finance external policy research organizations such as think tanks, as witnessed by the founding and state-sponsorship of research institutes on European integration and development policy studies in Bonn, and research on peace and human rights as well as finance. Increasingly, however, the proportion of state funds devoted to the core funding of institutes' activities – which research institutes prefer because it gives them maximum discretion – has been reduced in relation to project funding. Many of the generously core-funded academic think tanks as well as the party foundations suffered budget and staff cuts in the second half of the 1990s.

In the past, the availability of generous state funding made up for the relative absence of a strong philanthropic tradition of think tank funding in Germany. As Germany has changed its foundations laws and thereby created stronger tax incentives to establish philanthropic foundations, Tthis might be changing in the futureis going to change, albeit slowly. In the 1990s, some operating as well as grant-giving foundations such as the German Marshall Fund and a number of smaller foundations began shifting their funding priorities from basic academic research to applied and policy-related work. A very small number of family foundations have been following the American example of funding specific advocacy institutes or party think tanks which they believe share the funders' values and their ideological persuasion. The main beneficiary of this trend has been the HSS, which received a 35-million-euro grant from the conservative Ingeborg and Maria Tausend-Foundation in 1999.

Location

In terms of geography, Germany's policy research infrastructure is highly decentralized. Think tanks, with the exception of foreign and security policy institutes, are by no means assembled in the capital, Berlin, but rather are spread across the country with regional concentrations in Munich, Frankfurt, Cologne-Bonn, the Ruhr area, Berlin, Stuttgart and Hamburg-Kiel. This wide scattering of locations is a result of Germany's unique federal structure, of the important role played by the *Länder* in the financing and foundation of think tanks, of their close attachment to the (equally scattered) academic world, and of the structure of the German media landscape. Very few of the think tanks' most important channels for disseminating their research and policy ideas – the national newspapers and magazines – have headquarters in the German capital.

Staff

Until recently, recruitment at think tanks has almost exclusively followed academic patterns. Many senior staff at academic think tanks hold doctoral degrees, most in economics, followed by political science/international relations and the natural and applied sciences. Senior positions at established think tanks often require qualifications similar to a medium-level or even senior professorship (chair) at a university. In the past, many of the older and larger academic institutes offered a high degree of job security through semi-tenured research positions. In the 1990s, however, job security for new appointments was cut back drastically. This was partly a result of overall budget constraints and the rise of project funding, but also a reflection of the directors' desire for more flexibility in creating new research groups and as a way to avoid the bureaucratization of think tanks.

The revolving-door phenomenon that allows people to move freely in and out of government, however, is still extremely rare in Germany. One of the reasons for a certain career path rigidity is structural: unlike the United States, most parliamentary democracies are administered by civil servants even in the upper echelons of the ministerial bureaucracy. There are few administrative positions available for political appointments from the policy research industry. One strategy to bypass this structural problem is the creation of special advisors and of policy units staffed with external experts in the offices of the head of government as well as of cabinet ministers. Another is the creation of informal and ad hoc consulting arrangements, such as temporary commissions or kitchen cabinets (also known in German as 'chimney rounds'), outside the formal governmental structures of decision-making. Whereas reform-minded governments in the 1970s and early 1980s tried the former approach – to strengthen their policy capacity by bringing in external policy experts to work in planning units and internal think tanks – other governments more recently have relied on flexible and less permanent advisory structures such as task forces and temporary commissions. Think tanks are by no means in a privileged position in these advisory structures. They have to compete and co-operate with experts and representatives from stakeholding groups and other action-oriented leaders from established interest groups (Thunert, 2001).

In the past, the career paths of think tank staff were largely separate from those of civil servants or political practitioners and resembled academic career patterns. In general, this is still the case today, but the exceptions are becoming more frequent. Not only have some prominent policy wonks from economic and environmental think tanks embarked on political or administrative careers, but a small but increasing number of younger think tank staff no longer aspire to later career in universities and in academic research. On the other hand, and due to the decentralization of the policy research industry, the social capital of young people working for a spell in a think tank (for a modest salary), as part of a career progression in related fields such as journalism, the media, academia, management and political consulting, and politics, is still underdeveloped in Germany. Finally, there are constant calls for more interchange of personnel and thus of ideas between business, education, politics and the media, but such calls seldom result in practical change. More working groups, planning teams and policy units in the top echelons of politics would very much accelerate such an exchange of personnel and ideas.

Potential impact of German think tanks[3]

How think tanks affect political decision-making is more complex than is the case with straightforward political counselling. First of all, think tanks participate in the political decision-making process via the media. Secondly, policy experts active in think tanks also participate in thematic and issue networks as well as in epistemic communities. The weight carried by individual think tank experts in a particular issue network depends on the situation and the issue in question and often needs to be examined qualitatively on a case-by-case basis. In a political system with corporatist structures of interest-mediation like the German case, individual experts or think tanks are at a political disadvantage in making policy-relevant recommendations when compared with the representatives of interest-based associations. The former do not have the battalions behind them to back up their arguments and thereby make them more politically appealing to decision-makers. It has been a common feature of German politics in recent years that decision-makers have actively sought advice from think tanks and policy experts, but eventually yielded to interest group and political pressure in the final stages of policy-making. It is thus almost impossible to make any generalizations about the influence exercised by think tanks. What has been studied, however, is the strategies of think tanks in their pursuit of influence. These surveys have yielded data that can help illustrate how think tanks decide on their strategies and target groups. However, these data represent mean averages from which individual institutes may vary substantially.

Strategies of German think tanks

The most important target groups for German think tanks are other research institutes and universities on both the national and international level, followed by the members, caucuses and committees of the Bundestag, then the bureaucracies of the government ministries. These are followed in turn by individual political parties and certain segments of the quality press, and at some distance by boards of management and company directors, trade unions and non-governmental organizations.

Although many German institutes judge their communicative proximity to decision-makers on a national and local level to be satisfactory, contact with political leadership on both the European and the global levels generally leaves much to be desired – individual exceptions such as CAP nothwithstanding. However, as far as networking with educational and other civil society institutions is concerned, at an international level German think tanks hold their own.[4]

The German institutes are clearly very press-oriented: their most favoured target groups include the political and economic editors of German quality dailies and weeklies. Strategic alliances of think tanks with sympathetic print media became an important dissemination tool. In contrast, the majority of think tanks have in the past entertained rather distant relations with television. But in recent years relations between economic policy experts in the big institutes and the business editors of the TV and radio stations have improved. An important exception to the press orientation of most institutes has always been those institutes that specialize in international affairs and foreign policy. As far as the latter are concerned, crises are good for business. During the Kosovo war in 1999 and after September 11, 2001, for instance, representatives of such think tanks were seen on TV almost daily. Most think tanks recognize that in an age in which people are loosening their ties with specific political parties and with mass organizations in general, communication with the so-called public at large as a target group must receive a higher priority than has hitherto been the case. In addition, the internet has opened up opportunities for offering interested citizens direct access to expert opinion and information, thus bypassing the traditional media. In general, aggressive self-promotion of the institute and its products is a strategy that has been more cautiously adadapted in Germany than elsewhere, but some recently appointed think tank directors have been pushing their institutes into this direction.

Assessing think tank influence

Influence in the policy-making process depends a great deal on such variables as the policy field (closeness or openness of policy communities in a given policy field), the institutional source and the location of the think tank (closeness to government or closeness to civil society) and the stage of the policy-making process. The advisory needs of decision-makers are not uniform across branches of government, agencies or time. The contents and forms of advice giving differ with respect to the inherent dynamism of each policy area. In dynamic and potentially innovative areas such as biogenetics or European integration, advisory structures tend to be more flexible, focused and timely, since the pressure for decision-making in hitherto uncharted policy territories is high. In such areas, think tanks and their researchers compete with other external advisors on

Think tanks in Germany 85

a level playing field. In long-established and more predictable policy areas, governments and advisors can rely on past experiences and the timetables of long-standing – and in most cases institutionalized – consulting relationships. This offers opportunities for established think tanks which, like the six economic research institutes, are members of institutionalized consulting relationships.

External influence is likely to occur at three stages of the policy-making process: first, agenda setting and problem definition; second, policy selection and policy enactment; and third, policy implementation and evaluation. Policy-relevant knowledge fulfils different roles at different stages of the process. Expertise appears as warning and guidance during the first stage, as support, legitimation and ammunition in the second, and as assessment at the third. Few if any German think tanks are active simultaneously at every stage of the process, nor does their expertise fulfil every one of these roles. Table 5.3 illustrates the intensity of activity, visibility and thus possible influence of different think tank types at each stage.

Table 5.3 (Estimated) policy impact of think tanks

Type of think tank	Impact on agenda setting and problem definition	Impact on policy selection and enactment	Impact on policy implementation
Academic think tanks (and members thereof)	**	**	**
Contract research	*	**	***
Advocacy institutes	***	*	*
Party think tanks	***	**	**

* low visibility/activity; ** medium visibility/activity; *** strong visibility/activity.

Academic think tanks have a moderate but consistent influence on each stage of the policy-making process. Yet their role in providing warnings about impending problems and guidance on how to approach these problems, as well as some degree of legitimacy for policy solutions, is perhaps their strongest asset. In German culture, which values 'Wissenschaftlichkeit' (a scientific front), their academic status gives their warnings and their forecasts more credibility than those of quasi-interest and advocacy groups, and, in turn, academic credibility enhances their usefulness as sources of information and analyses.

Advocacy institutes and party think tanks are stronger in the early stages of the policy process – particularly medium and long-term agenda-setting – than academic think tanks, but their overall influence is more intermittent. Some independent advocacy think tanks and certain units or researchers of some academic institutes have cautiously started to adapt the strategies of their American counterparts to provide ammunition and intellectual support to advocacy coalitions during policy selection and enactment. Party think tanks can become powerful intra-party agenda-setting resources, especially when their party is in opposition and their access to governmental policy capacity is rather restricted. Legal regulations prevent party think tanks from becoming too closely involved in political strategy or in the drafting of party manifestos. As agenda-setters and discussion forums, they rather guide and reshape the understanding of broader policy questions – particularly in the area of foreign policy – for their party and even beyond.

Finally, it should be noted that while the sole influence of contract research institutes should be primarily on policy evaluation or problem assessment, some of these organizations have stepped beyond a purely passive approach. A number of them have begun producing unsolicited policy evaluations and recommendations.

The future of German think tanks: opportunities and constraints

German think tanks possess great potential for playing a more significant role on the political and public stage in the future. The forecasts and analyses of the experts are becoming increasingly important in public debate. 'Policy gurus' and 'spin doctors' motivate and orient members of both the public and political elites. Competition between established institutes, some of the more flexible and practically oriented newcomers to the German scene, international institutes and commercial advisors, for a hearing, for ideas and for money, will become harder. Ideas used in public policy-making are also being developed commercially in Germany – especially at the interfaces between technology, the environment and society, and in the worlds of finance and fiscal policy, as well as in public management. In an age of global information and consultancy markets, both large commercial consulting agencies and non-profit organizations and think tanks at home and abroad stand ready to take up commissions in Germany.

Co-operation between those who offer and those who need policy advice can be optimized. The think tanks must show initiative, practise more applied research, and rely more on an agenda of their own and less on commissioned and contract work. The reality in Germany is, however, that think tanks, especially the larger academic institutes, are getting conflicting messages from their target audiences and their funding environment.

The first part of the message urges them to become more policy-relevant and more strategic. Politicians in elected office increasingly depend on, and thus ask for, a mixture of policy advice and political consulting. A survey conducted among policy-making civil servants in the premiers' offices on the state level (echoed by similar studies on other levels of government) showed that marketing and communication expertise (public relations, polling, 'spin' skills, etc.) are deemed as important as, and sometimes more important than, detailed policy expertise (Mielke, 1999). A similar message was communicated to foreign affairs think tanks in Germany. In 1995–6, the president of the Federal Court of Audit conducted a report on the co-ordination and rationalization of federally funded research on international affairs (Federal Court of Audit, 1996) The report was based on a survey among senior civil servants in key federal ministries, who were asked to report on their utilization of research provided by federally funded international affairs research institutes. Among the responses were criticisms regarding the usefulness and the policy-relevance of such research. These criticisms were echoed by the then head of the planning staff of the German Foreign Office (Klaiber, 1996). According to this key think tank audience in government, high-caliber staff of academic think tanks are too inclined to indulge in theoretical abstraction and to write and speak in a vocabulary that does not travel well into the worlds of political decision-making or business. Research is not timely and is sometimes out of synch with the foreign policy agenda of both governments and non-state actors. Some policy institutes are seen as too academic, detached and uninvolved, providing avalanches of information, not strategic recommendations. The report led to a consolidation of federally funded foreign policy research institutes and to their relocation to closer geographical proximity with their target audiences in Berlin.

While these responses show that policy advice cannot be strictly separated from political advice, many researchers in academic think tanks continue to shy away from providing a mix of both, resorting instead to purely scientific advice. Legacies from the past, especially the manipulation of knowledge first by the Nazis and later by the ruling Communist Party in East Germany, have accentuated the tendency of many think tanks – even those that advocate a particular policy paradigm – to present a scientific front and to sacrifice general comprehensibility to academic standards. There are other reasons as well. Since the 1990s, most publicly funded academic think tanks have been evaluated by the Science Council (Wissenschaftsrat), a joint federal-state advisory body with an explicit mandate to make recommendations and statements on developments in higher education and other research establishments like the publicly funded think tanks. The criteria by which academic think tanks are being evaluated are the standard academic criteria used in the evaluation of university departments and of institutions of basic research. The idea-brokerage functions of think tanks are not taken into consideration, and some academic think tanks have received a negative evaluation by the Science Council precisely because they were considered too policy-oriented and too disconnected from the cutting edges of academic research. The almost exclusive reliance on state funding has thus become a mixed blessing for those academic think tanks which would like to become more policy- and marketing-oriented.

A new generation of recently appointed think tank directors in established institutes, policy-oriented academics at university-based research centres and in consulting bodies, as well as younger researchers in new think tanks, is slowly changing the political culture of policy research in Germany. This new generation does not treat applied policy-oriented research with the same suspicion as it was viewed with twenty or thirty years ago. One may even state that the validity of the once widely held equation that excellence in basic research implies policy irrelevance and vice versa is now being called into question. Some of the new think tank directors and council members – especially in economic and foreign policy research institutes – challenge their staff to produce more internationally competitive, cutting-edge research, to venture into thinking the unthinkable and to become more policy-relevant and audience-oriented at the same time. Whether this is too ambitious a challenge for the German think tank community and those who fund it remains to be seen.

Notes

1 In 1975, the Federal Government and the *Länder* enlarged the Framework Agreement on the Promotion of Research to include independent research institutions of supraregional importance and national scientific interest, and institutions performing service functions. Those qualifying for this financial assistance were listed in an implementing agreement in 1977 that was printed on blue paper. Hence the name 'Blue List', which has recently been renamed the Wissenschaftsgemeinschaft Gottfried Wilhelm Leibniz (Leibniz Society).
2 In the large academic think tanks too, the value-oriented political preferences of individual experts tend, in some cases, to result in unambiguously biased recommendations.
3 The following paragraphs, including Table 5.4, reflect (1) surveys and interviews conducted by the author and others that have yielded data that can help illustrate especially how think tanks decide on their strategies and target groups, and (2) an internal survey conducted by the Federal Court of Audit among the ministerial recipients of external policy advice in the field of foreign policy (Federal Court of Audit, 1996).
4 For a more detailed analysis of international activities of German think tanks see Thunert, 2000.

6 Sonia Lucarelli and Claudio M. Radaelli

Italy: think tanks and the political system

This chapter sets out to examine the role of think tanks in the context of the changes to the Italian political system in the 1990s. We draw on three sources of information: a set of in-depth interviews with officials of *major* think tanks, a mail survey of Italian policy research institutes conducted in 1996, and recent data on the international research of major institutes (for a full report see Lucarelli and Menotti, 2002a).[1] In the first section, we describe Italian think tanks, with particular emphasis on their relationships with the academic world and their lack of ideological propensity. In the following section, we analyse the major sources of challenges and transformation of Italian think tanks in recent years, looking at the domestic impact of the end of the Cold War, both at the level of policy issue areas and at the deeper level of procedural and institutional changes in the Italian political system. In the third section, we suggest a possible interpretation of how think tanks have affected public policy in Italy. In doing so, we build on the advocacy coalition approach developed by Sabatier and Jenkins-Smith (1993; Sabatier, 1999).

A profile of Italian think tanks

We define as 'think tanks' all private, independent organizations that carry out at least one kind of policy-oriented activity. Some might argue that this definition is too loose, because it fails to take account of whether these organizations have all the features that are normally associated with think tanks – at least those operating in English-speaking countries – such as control over their own research agenda, some degree of independence from government funding, and an inclination to disseminate their research findings to a larger audience, particularly through the media, in order to affect the policy process. Our argument for applying such a broad definition is that, although in Italy there might be very few US/UK-type think tanks, most of the private independent organizations we have identified share some features of the traditional think tank model, at least to some degree. Most of them have some control over their research agenda; many of them have access to non-government funding, or at least to untied public funding, which constrains their ability to conduct independent analysis less; and most of them attempt to disseminate their research and devote resources to the promotion of debate.

Broadly speaking, and bearing in mind that there is more than one grey area, there are four types of think tanks in Italy:

1 Policy institutes generated by political parties, organized sections of political parties and the trade unions. These think tanks are intimately linked to the political system, and their independence is low.
2 Think tanks that contribute to the political and intellectual debate with a substantial degree of independence. Their aim is to influence the political culture of the country in the long term and the political debate in the medium term. Rarely do they engage in professional policy analysis.
3 Think tanks specializing in professional tasks, such as policy evaluation and impact assessment. Typically, they interact more with public administration than with party leaders and ministers.
4 Policy clubs – to be described below – which are more fora of discussion among like-minded politicians and intellectuals than organizations producing research on a regular basis.

Italian think tanks vary widely in size, as measured by their total annual budget. For example, our 1996 survey of 69 think tanks showed that in 1995 the median size of their budget was about 375,000 euros, and the average about 1.25 million. About 40 organizations (58 per cent of the total) had an annual budget below 500,000 euros, while only 12 surpassed 2 million euros and only 3 the 5-million mark. Even the largest Italian think tanks would be considered of medium size in the US.

The majority of research institutes devote resources to all three broad functions of a think tank: policy research, promotion of debate, and education for public service. Thus, there is a rather low degree of specialization among Italian think tanks. However, while most organizations engage in all three activities, they devote very different amounts of resources to them, at least on average. Not surprisingly, policy research takes the lion's share. Apart from the traditional areas of public policy (macro-economic policy, foreign policy, health policy, local economic development, industrial policy, public administration reform, etc.), in the 1990s many research institutes started to devote growing attention to the EU.

This is due partly to the decision of the Italian government to qualify for the single currency. The run-up to the euro was a catalyst of major transformations with implications far beyond the domain of public finance (see Radaelli, 2002). But it is also due to the deepening of the integration process in the EU. Issues such as cohesion policy, the foreign policy of the EU, EU competence in the areas of justice and home affairs, and more recently enlargement have spawned debate and policy research in all EU countries. In Italy, according to a survey article published some time ago (Giuliani and Radaelli, 1999), EU studies were somewhat neglected for a long period. But the situation is changing swiftly, and the proliferation of degrees in European studies contributes to the intensification of research on the EU.

The integration process as such, and the economic, legal and political aspects of decision-making in the European Union system (Community level and sublevels of governance), are now common topics for research in nearly all research institutes. In 2001, a survey of research institutes dealing with international issues (Lucarelli and Menotti, 2002a) showed that among the 41 institutes dealing with international *economic* issues, 21 had a research branch on European integration (51.2 per cent), the highest percentage for a single issue, followed by 'processes of globalization and internationalization', on which 17 institutes work (41.5 per cent). In the *political science* section of the survey, 20 institutes – out of 46 – worked on European integration issues (43.5 per cent) and 14 on international conflicts (30.4 per cent). Finally, among the 45 more *legally* oriented institutes we find that 25 deal with the EU as a research area (55.5 per cent), followed by 14 working on human rights (31.1 per cent).

The analysis of funding sources reveals that these organizations are dependent on research contracts – but to a lesser extent than one might anticipate. To be sure, contracts for specific projects on behalf of government clients were also reported in the 1996 survey by 61 per cent of the organizations, the most widely quoted source of funding. However, 'untied contributions' are also reported from a variety of sources: central and regional governments, individual and corporate supporters, and proceeds from own endowment. The last is reported in only 16 per cent of cases.

Funding influences the scope and type of research undertaken. As most of the leading policy institutes do research when a client or group of clients asks for a particular product, self-determination of the research agenda – a typical feature of independent Anglo-American policy institutes – is comparatively limited in Italy. Stone (1996b: 15) has observed that, in order to preserve autonomy in their research agendas, 'think tank managers often require that funding be untied so that they may be free in determining the questions they address and in arriving at their findings'. By contrast, Italian think tanks are more similar to 'contract research organizations' than to 'universities without students' (Weaver, 1989). However, qualification of this statement is needed when referring to major research institutes. In the first place, untied funding is more diffuse than it appears: a small but significant proportion of the products of Italian think tanks is not tied to particular funding. Examples include the activities of Fondazione Agnelli and some activities of the Centro Studi Investimenti Sociali (Censis). Moreover, the relationship between client and institute is dialectic. Typically, the client comes forward with a vague idea, and ample scope is given to the think tank manager for reformulating the initial request. One of the key slogans within policy institutes is that 'the supply educates the demand for research'. In the remainder of this section we analyse two further relevant features of major Italian think tanks: their relationship with the academic world and their ideological orientation.

The relationship between academia and the world of research institutes is quite intense, so much so that in *Think tanks across nations* we spoke of the ubiquity of professors in think tanks (Radaelli and Martini, 1998). Leading academics have a foot in the academic world, and another in politics. Indeed, one can see the same academic bringing the results of his or her research to the attention of ministers and opposition leaders either via a think tank report or directly, as consultant to a department. Some academics (pre-eminently from law, but recently also from economics and political science) went so far as to cross the bridge and become directly involved in politics, as MPs or (in a few cases) ministers or under-secretaries of state.

Indeed, it seems that not only are academics ubiquitous in think tanks, but they also know the world of politics very well. So much so that leading academics can also become high-profile figures in the press, as tragically shown by the terrorist assassination of Professor Marco Biagi – a top consultant of the Department of Labour and Welfare – in 2002. But this chain 'university–think tanks–political life' is the case only in some disciplines, namely law, economics, political economy and political science.

Foreign policy seems different, however. Whereas the Treasury has made great use of economic models and of a rigorous social science approach to key issues such as pension reforms (Radaelli, 2002), the Department of Foreign Affairs has always shown less interest in theory-based suggestions for policy, methodological rigour, and even some classical areas of investigation for think tanks and academics. It is more difficult for a professor of international relations to become an 'advisor of the Prince' (either directly or through a think tank) than it is for a professor of economics to get involved with the policy activity of the Treasury, the Department of Public Administration or the Department of Labour. The problem is not the 'ivory tower' syndrome. Indeed, international relations professors are involved with the activities of foreign policy think tanks such as the Istituto di Politica Internazionale (ISPI), the Centro Militare di Studi Strategici (CeMiSS), the IAI and the tiny but lively

Archivio Disarmo. Thus, there is potential in terms of getting academic experts involved in real-world debates. The problem is that the cognitive framework of foreign policy does not go further than poor, stripped-down versions of realism or pseudo neo-liberal institutionalism, as documented by Lucarelli and Menotti (2002a, 2002b). We found an extremely low propensity (indeed, reluctance) towards theoretically informed research on the part of policy-makers and civil servants. The problem is compounded by the low institutionalization of international relations in Italy. In May 2002 we found only five full professors of international relations, twelve associate professors and three lecturers (out of the 158 members of the wider 'Political Science' disciplinary group).

Turning to ideological orientation, the type of think tanks characterized by ideological commitment to free-market ideas or, in foreign policy, hard geopolitics, aggressive language and fierce competition for political impact (what Stone calls the 'new partisans': Stone, 1996b; see also Fischer, 1993) has not as yet fully materialized in Italy. Across the English-speaking world, 'new partisans' seized visibility and influence in the 1980s. By contrast, the ideological propensity of Italian think tanks has remained low. True, political change during the 1990s has now produced a starker demarcation between the centre-left and the centre-right. In the past, the pivotal party in all governments was the Christian Democratic party. By contrast, Italians can now choose between the centre-right and the centre-left when they go to the polls (Bufacchi and Burgess, 2001). This provides a structural incentive to engage in political debate by transforming policy institutes into advocacy tanks. However, this has not yet been the case, with some qualifications.

Firstly, Italy has always had some think tanks with a clear ideological orientation (such as the Fondazione Einaudi), but they have never been as aggressive and committed as their Anglo-American counterparts. Secondly, the advent of bipolarism has triggered a debate in classic think tanks – such as Il Mulino – as to whether it is still possible to remain independent in a bipolar political system, and if so, how (Della Loggia and Panebianco, 2002). Thirdly, classic think tanks face competition from new hybrids with a clear propensity to advocacy. We would call this new hybrid the 'policy club'[2]. The latter does not employ permanent researchers. It is more a club of like-minded politicians and intellectuals that contributes to the political-cultural debate by publishing an occasional report, or by organizing a high-profile conference. Most of the new policy clubs are known to the public because of their flagship periodicals[3]. Policy clubs have raised the ideological temperature in political debate, but – as mentioned above – most traditional independent policy research institutes have not embraced advocacy.

The new hybrids have been much more aggressive and ideologically oriented than the classic Italian think tank. Their high visibility in the media is objectively a challenge for traditional think tanks. Although it must be remembered that policy clubs represent more cases of editorial success (or at best loose networks of like-minded intellectuals) than real organizations, the possibility is that bipolarism (a centre-right pole and a centre-left one competing for office) will question the meaning and feasibility of independence.

As far as domestic politics is concerned, advocacy clubs include Ideazione (right-wing), MicroMega (left-wing) and Liberal (open to both mild right-wingers and mild centre-left intellectuals, but clearly oriented towards dialogue with the Catholic tradition). In 2002 a new hybrid came to the fore: Officina (the name means 'workshop') produced a report on institutional change for the prime minister, Silvio Berlusconi. It was covered by all newspapers and television channels.

In EU affairs, the most successful club is the Foundation Italiani-Europei, led by two former prime ministers of the centre-left, Massimo D'Alema and Giuliano Amato. Their monthly publication has been instrumental in launching the debate on the European dimension of Italian politics and Italian economic policy.

In foreign policy, the success of the *Limes Review of Geopolitics* has been striking. Limes managed to fill the gap of information on international politics for a non-specialized public, using colourful language, a vague geopolitical appeal and an elusive atheoretical approach (at best a narrow realist perspective). The *Review* is widely read in diplomatic circles. This might have reinforced a certain unsophisticated approach to foreign policy that was already shared by many, however. Interestingly, Limes has not developed into a proper think tank, nor does it have a clearly defined ideological position.

On balance, apart from hybrids such as Ideazione and MicroMega, we do not see signs of marked ideological orientation. As we mentioned above, this seems surprising given the development of two distinct electoral poles (the centre-right and the centre-left). The lack of think tank partisanship is less surprising, however, if one observes that a clear pro-market drive was almost completely absent from Italian politics in the 1980s (Regonini and Giuliani, 1994). And even the electoral alliance based on Berlusconi's Forza Italia is far from representing a pro-market cartel (Bellucci and Bull, 2002).

Strategies of overt ideological commitment are, in any case, far from optimal for think tanks operating in the Italian context. To see this, one only has to consider the difference between the electoral market and the policy-making process. Indeed, the electoral debate has always been quite ideological (Sartori, 1976). In the past the conflict was between the Catholics and the communists; more recently Berlusconi has been successful in keeping the ideological temperature high in electoral campaigns. The new 'policy clubs' aim to influence this public debate more than the actual policy-making process. The latter, in fact, is made in less confrontational arenas by policy networks (Dente and Regonini, 1987). Laws are approved in Parliament by large majorities (Capano and Giuliani, 2001: 20). Given that one of the aims of traditional policy institutes is to (1) get research funding from whoever is the incumbent, and (2) impact on policy rather than on the electoral market, Italian think tanks have always avoided the bitter confrontation of ideological politics. Within many larger think tanks there are good contacts with a large part of the political spectrum.

In foreign and defence policy, the trend exposed above was even reinforced during the Cold War by a 'locked-in' foreign policy. There was little public expectation of a specific Italian role in international politics. Most of the limited political debate was mainly of an ideological nature and reflected the socio-political pro-American–anti-American (left-wing) divide in the country. In general, international relations research has steered clear of ideology. The situation, however, changed with the end of the Cold War when more space was left for a higher level of attention to international politics and more open ideological inclination.

Challenges and transformation for the major think tanks

In this section we analyse the main challenges that think tanks in Italy have faced since the end of the Cold War and evaluate the impact of such challenges on their current and future activities and impact. Italian politics in the 1990s was characterized by three major crises (Rhodes and Bull, 1997). The end of the Cold War destabilized the identity of major political parties. New political parties had to learn how to play a new electoral game: the changes in electoral laws (both at the national level and for regional and local assemblies) may have not been optimal. In any case political actors had to learn swiftly how to make electoral profits from these changes. This is the first crisis – one could call it the party crisis.

At the same time, investigations of political corruption reduced the legitimacy of conventional politics: many MPs and local politicians were taken to court, and top politicians arrested. The legitimacy crisis was compounded by the advent of an anti-welfare party, the Northern League, which argued for radical devolution and at times even secession of the north (Della Porta, 1996; Gilbert, 1994). This second crisis was a legitimacy crisis. Finally, the imperatives of European integration began to bite seriously: the convergence criteria for the accession to the euro-zone produced major policy change in public finance and redefined Italian identity in Europe (Radaelli, 2002). These effects, then, had repercussions on think tanks in various ways.

Foreign and international politics: the missed opportunity?

In the first place, the end of the Cold War has transformed international politics, opening the way for a more active Italian foreign policy, and raising public interest in international issues. The explosion of ethnic and nationalist confrontation in the neighbouring Balkans, as well as the developments in the European integration process (the euro, but also the definition of a common foreign and security policy, slowly integrated by a defence capacity) raised public concern for international relations. Books like Samuel Huntington's *Clash of Civilizations* (1996) were promptly translated into Italian and became best sellers. Public interest in foreign policy is further evidenced by the striking success of the review *Limes* (founded in 1993).

The net effect of this transformation was, however, partially disappointing. If it is true that most research institutes became more international in orientation, it is equally true that research on international politics has not profited enough. Academic research institutes and individuals were unable to use this opportunity to bring international relations (IR) literature, with its theoretical complexity, to the attention of the wider public and of policy-makers. Private research institutes, at the same time, were only partially able to grasp the new opportunities. Temporarily, some IR scholars became 'advisors to the Prince' (Carlo Maria Santoro and Stefano Silvestri, for example, became under-secretaries of defence). The main tangible results concern European studies, as mentioned above. In fact, the developments of integration have transformed the EU from an international issue into a domestic one, as indicated by recent research projects under way in Italy on the topic of 'Europeanization'.

Changes in the domestic environment

The transformations of the 1990s have also changed the external environment for most think tanks. On the one hand, the major political party, the Christian Democrats, split into a number of small parties, thus making the landscape of recipients of policy research more uncertain. On the other, new political formations, such as the Northern League and Forza Italia, have either shown limited interest in policy analysis (Northern League) or used marketing research rather than the conventional think tank products (Forza Italia). In addition, the anti-corruption investigations of the magistrates have taken a large number of local politicians and (to some extent, at least) prominent civil servants out of business. Classic think tanks have to reposition themselves in a new bipolar political system (Della Loggia and Panebianco, 2002). They also face competition from the new policy clubs. Turning to institutes close to political parties, those that were close to the Socialist Party or the Christian Democrats lost their political master: they either no longer exist or have undergone radical change.

Changes in the market for research

As shown in *Think tanks across nations*, the market for research has become more international and more professional. However, the capability of Italian think tanks to stimulate collaboration with foreign institutes, create European networks and consortia, and ultimately 'push' the international market remains low. A further effect of the change in the market of research has to do with the role of academics in the world of think tanks. We have already argued that the presence of academics in many, mainly domestically oriented, Italian think tanks has been overwhelming. However, in future, the role of academics even within 'domestic' policy research institutes could be less crucial than it has been in the past. Most of the products which are now demanded in this market are not typical academic studies. To a large extent, evaluation research, regulatory impact analysis and feasibility studies (three areas where the Italian government has made use of these techniques by the public administration compulsory) are professional (not academic) activities. In turn, this may create the preconditions for an increased role for professionals (as opposed to academics) within think tanks.

In sum, Italian think tanks have held course in a period of dramatic political transition. The situation has been compounded by the necessity to internationalize, by new tendencies in the professionalization of social science research, and by the challenge of hybrids (policy clubs) with high visibility in terms of public opinion. Following the ratification of the Maastricht treaty, Italian macro-economic policy has been characterized by fiscal austerity, which has made the market for public funding more competitive. Perhaps, after years of relatively easy growth, the time for consolidation and adjustment has come.

Think tanks and advocacy coalitions

Were think tanks able to make an impact on a political system characterized by a party crisis, a legitimacy crisis, and the 'national emergency' of meeting the Maastricht criteria for the euro-zone in time? Did they manage to overcome the challenges of a post-Cold War environment and of a new market for research? In this section we suggest an interpretation of the impact of think tanks in the 1990s. We look at two main episodes of change in the 1990s, that is, the change of electoral laws and the run-up to the euro.

By any standard, they were *the* topics of that decade. The theme of engineering political change by changing electoral laws became the centre of political discussions and initiatives. It was grounded in the belief that political inertia (that is, lack of alternation in office) was due to the mechanisms of the electoral law. Political corruption was also said to thrive on electoral mechanisms such as preferential voting. Finally, poor policy delivery was linked to the electoral mechanisms as well.[4]

A network of intellectuals, academics and politicians not belonging to the core of party political power started to challenge the existing electoral national law by using the referendum. The latter gives Italians the possibility to strike down laws. It was an obvious move to target electoral law via the referendum once it became clear that the Parliament would not have been able to produce changes in the mechanisms for the selections of MPs (Bufacchi and Burgess, 2001).

The expectation at the beginning of the 1990s was that new electoral laws would limit the opportunities for political corruption and would generate more alternation in government. The network mentioned above mobilized Italian public opinion on electoral reforms first, and later on the utopia of fully fledged constitutional change (Regonini and Giuliani, 1994).

The structural adjustment of public finance was the most important exogenous shock to the Italian political system. It triggered changes in macro-economic policy, but also institutional change. By tying their hands in agreeing to the European commitments enshrined in the Treaty on European Union signed at Maastricht, Italian policy-makers set the conditions for dramatic policy change in economic policy and for institutional change (Radaelli, 2002). More importantly still, this transformation of the agenda disempowered the old political parties. The power basis of the *partitocrazia* was curbed by the 'sound finance' imperatives of the EMU, whilst at the same time a technocratic policy elite was empowered by the 'external constraint' on domestic policy (Dyson and Featherstone, 1999).

Let us now turn to the issue of influence. The latter (that is, the impact on public policy) has been debated at length by the comparative literature on think tanks and political advice (Gaffney, 1991; Stone, 1996b). In the short term, 'Rarely is there a one-to-one correspondence between a book or a study and a particular policy change. There are numerous intervening forces that mediate and alter the impact of research that shroud any cause and effect relationship that may exist between policy institutes and government decision-making' (Stone, 1996b: 219). However, there is a long-term impact of policy analysis which is represented by the 'enlightenment' of political actors (Weiss, 1979). It is therefore useful to situate the study of influence within an appropriate time-frame. A decade seems an appropriate span of time (Sabatier and Jenkins-Smith, 1993) because it enables one to uncover the deep impact of policy studies, such as the impact on the policy paradigms used by politicians in office. This type of impact goes well beyond any single policy decision. As mentioned above, electoral change and fiscal adjustment are two good candidates for the analysis of the 1990s.

The 'advocacy coalition approach' elaborated by Sabatier and Jenkins-Smith (1993; Sabatier, 1999) acknowledges that a broad view of 'political influence of knowledge' is needed, and therefore sets out to explain how knowledge is transmitted into the policy process over a decade or so. Advocacy coalitions are 'People from a variety of positions (elected and agency officials, interest group leaders, researchers, etc.) who share a particular belief system – that is, a set of basic values, causal assumptions, and problem perceptions – and who show a nontrivial degree of co-ordinated activity over time' (Sabatier, 1993: 25).

Adversarial coalitions compete for the control of policy arenas. The result of the competition between coalitions, however, is not decided by power alone. Learning within (and, more rarely, across) coalitions, policy fora and persuasion are at least as important as power. Sabatier and Jenkins-Smith formulate the hypothesis that policy-oriented learning across coalitions is facilitated by the existence of a forum (1) dominated by professional norms and (2) prestigious enough to attract professionals from different coalitions. More generally, the cognitive element of politics is so crucial in this model that knowledge and beliefs represent a *constitutive* aspect of coalitions (that is, one of the components that define coalitions). One testable hypothesis offered by this approach is that non-incremental policy change requires (1) significant perturbations external to the subsystem (that is, an exogenous shock) and (2) a skilful exploitation of the opportunities generated by the exogenous shock by the (previously) minority coalition (Sabatier and Jenkins-Smith, 1993).

Turning to the Italian case, what is the role played by think tanks in the two processes of change described above? Let us start with the change of electoral laws. The initial steps were triggered by a network of academics engaged in politics (Regonini and Giuliani, 1994). As mentioned above, their core belief was a causal chain linking institutional reforms (the independent variable) to governmental efficiency in reaching decisions, and finally to increased policy performance (the dependent variable). This causal chain was a constitutive aspect of the coalition for electoral reform.

The advocacy coalition framework argues that a coalition comes into existence only when a multitude of actors join together, embrace a set of shared beliefs, and set out to control a policy arena. This is precisely what happened in Italy. Between the second half of the 1980s and the early 1990s, the network of 'academics in politics' described by Regonini and Giuliani expanded into a wider advocacy coalition. It included the leaders of the mass movement supporting the electoral referenda of the 1990s, interest groups (such as the Confederation of Italian Industry,

Confindustria), and magistrates fighting corruption. In other terms, an advocacy coalition was formed.

Yet think tanks as organizations did not get involved in electoral reform and debates on constitutional change because they specialize in social and economic policy and in intergovernmental delivery systems, not in macro-questions of constitutional design. One possible exception is Il Mulino and its related research institute Carlo Cattaneo[5], with their emphasis on electoral and institutional reforms in the first half of the 1990s. But most Italian policy institutes have always advocated bottom-up solutions (often based on societal mechanisms), the reform of public administration, and a micro-debate on policy instruments rather than on macro-constitutional engineering. The Fondazione Agnelli made reform of the state one of its main areas of activity in the 1990s (Fondazione Agnelli, 1996). But this area of activity consisted of research on the organization of the state, the key issues being lesson-drawing in administrative reform (Dente, 1995) and federalism.

Our argument is that think tanks as organizations were at the periphery of (and in most cases excluded from) the *advocacy coalition of electoral-institutional reforms*. However, by drawing attention to networks rather than to specific organizations, Regonini and Giuliani's study detects another element of influence. Although think tanks as organizations did not participate in the coalition for institutional reform, some of their charismatic leaders were *personally* involved in it. Individuals such as Romano Prodi, the founder of Nomisma, Luigi Spaventa of the Centre for European Research (CER), and especially Arturo Parisi (Fondazione di Ricerca di Istituto Carlo Cattaneo and Fondazione Segni) were deeply attracted (at least for a few years in the early 1990s) by the idea of changing the Italian political system through electoral reform and institutional design. They made public statements in favour of institutional reforms and – in the case of Parisi – took part in the movement for electoral change. Their engagement was not accompanied by major studies on electoral and constitutional reforms undertaken by think tanks. Neither can one argue that think tanks contributed to the community of discourse emerging in those years around these topics. The choice of some think tank leaders was a personal political preference. In terms of the dichotomy between insiders and outsiders, think tanks as organizations were outsiders.

Could it be argued that think tanks have been insiders in the other area of policy change, fiscal adjustment? To begin with, the technocratic policy elite promoting fiscal adjustment has included, in addition to the senior civil servants mentioned by Dyson and Featherstone (1999), individuals from CER, Nomisma, Prometeia and the Istituto per la Ricerca Sociale (IRS). But what about think tanks as organizations? Since the early 1990s or so, think tanks have spawned a debate on the macro-economic policy implications of Italian membership of the European Union, thus emphasizing the 'external constraint'. They have disseminated ideas, policy slogans and data on European economic integration and the deterioration of Italian public finance. They have also echoed the preoccupation of the European Commission and EU partners with Italian economic policy reliability. Following the Maastricht treaty, the message of think tanks on the need 'to join Europe' became even more persistent. The CER reports and newsletters on public finance, the analysis of current economic trends provided by IRS, and the project funded by the Fondazione Rosselli on 'the costs of non-Europe' (Amato and Salvadori, 1990) stressed the need for a radical change in the conduct of fiscal policy. Simply put, policy institutes have provided arguments, data and a climate of opinion. They sought to change the paradigm of macro-economic policy. Of course, they did not act in isolation, but within a *coalition for fiscal adjustment*.

What members comprised this coalition? As shown by Dyson and Featherstone (1999), the most powerful actors in the pro-fiscal adjustment coalition were technocrats based in the Treasury and politicians with an academic background, like Giuliano Amato, with additional support from the Bank of Italy and employers' organizations (with the qualifications indicated by Radaelli, 2002). Knowledge and interests have been in a symbiotic relationship within this coalition encompassing segments of the political system, such as the Republican Party, a small but very influential number of top socialists (for example, Giuliano Amato and Giorgio Ruffolo, who in turn participated in initiatives launched by Fondazione Rosselli and CER in the 1980s and early 1990s) and even the technocratic rump of the Christian Democrats. Beniamino Andreatta, a minister, a senior figure within the Christian Democrats and at the same time leader of the Agenzia di Ricerca & Legislazione (AREL) institute, is a good example of a man bridging the worlds of knowledge and political action.

The battle over economic reform, however, was fought by two coalitions, one advocating radical reform of public finance, and the other advocating the status quo, formed around what journalists labelled the *partito unico della spesa pubblica* (roughly, the grand party for public spending). The latter can be described as a cross-party coalition of politicians and constituencies with the aim of distorting public resources for micro-corporatist interests and electoral consensus. Hence it could be labelled the (cross-partisan) *public expenditure coalition*.

Having broadly outlined the two coalitions, the question remains whether think tanks played a role in economic policy change. We have already argued that they contributed to the emergence of a climate of opinion in which a radical turn in economic policy paradigms was perceived as indispensable for membership of the single currency club. At the same time, the key actors within the fiscal reform coalition were the core government (the Treasury and prime minister) and a large part of the business community, not think tanks. However, as mentioned earlier, economists from different political orientations were 'socialized' into the discourse on fiscal reform through their participation in think tank initiatives.

This draws attention to our hypothesis that think tanks operated as policy fora. Indeed, although think tanks were certainly closer to the fiscal reform coalition than to the public expenditure coalition, their role as independent and competent observers of economic policy made them ideal policy fora. The latter – as explained by the advocacy coalition framework – are instrumental in generating cross-coalition learning. In the case of economic reform, think tanks brought economists from different advocacy coalitions closer. A discourse on economic policy 'framed' in terms of 'objective' economic analysis has disenfranchised economists from political parties. Even economists relatively close to the parties then in government came to agree on the necessity of radical change in economic policy. It is no mystery that, at the beginning of the 1990s, in addition to the personalities mentioned above, senior economic advisors to the Socialist Party, the Christian Democrats and, as far as the then opposition is concerned, the Communist Party converged in their assessment of the Treaty of Maastricht. One of the authors of this chapter conducted for a think tank a study based on a panel of experts (mainly economists) involved in politics in the aftermath of the Treaty of Maastricht (Prospecta, 1992) and found no evidence of disagreement on 'what should be done' among the experts interviewed, although they had very different party affiliations.

However, across-coalition learning *per se* did not produce any policy change. Indeed, the turning point was represented by the robust ammunition provided by the Treaty of Maastricht. Clearly, the public expenditure coalition tried to ignore as far as possible the message coming from hundreds of alarming reports on public finance produced by policy institutes in the 1980s, but eventually had to surrender to the imperatives of Maastricht and their political implications in the 1990s. As argued by the advocacy coalition approach, an external shock (in this case, the Treaty on European Union) altered the balance of resources available to the two coalitions. The fiscal adjustment coalition was empowered by the provisions on economic policy enshrined in the Maastricht treaty and was able to capitalize on this empowerment, thus showing political creativity.

To sum up, the advocacy coalition approach provides a conceptual framework for the analysis of knowledge utilization over the long term. The institutional reform coalition attracted individuals from think tanks. However, as Italian think tanks have specialized in social and economic policy rather than constitutional policy, their involvement as organizations was minimal. In the arena of economic policy, think tanks provided a policy forum and, in the long term, facilitated the emergence of an economic policy discourse based upon the paradigm of 'sound finance' and convergence. Their distinctive role has been not as a key actor within a coalition but, rather, as a policy forum.

Conclusion

Our first conclusion is that Italian think tanks are undergoing a process of rationalization and consolidation. Their external environment became more turbulent in the 1990s, due to the political crisis, the imperatives of internationalization and new market challenges. Italian think tanks have not been able to profit fully from the opportunities opened by the end of the Cold War, as shown by the example of knowledge 'misutilization' and 'non-utilization' in foreign policy.

The second conclusion is that think tanks at times have influence in the context of the competition between advocacy coalitions. This has been the case with economic policy change, but not with electoral-institutional change (with the exception of Il Mulino and of specific think tank leaders). Think tanks should be characterized as policy fora rather than members of one of the two coalitions in the debate on fiscal adjustment. Thus think tanks were agents of learning in the 1990s: by acting as policy fora, they generated cross-coalition learning. The analysis of two policy areas has shed light on broader advocacy coalitions. Therefore, our third conclusion is that further research should investigate not policy institutes *per se*, but rather the wider political activity of advocacy coalitions in which think tanks operate.

This leads to our fourth conclusion, which emphasizes the need for an appropriate conceptual framework. Here we have argued that an adequate framework should include the long-term impact of policy analysis, and the symbiotic relationship between interests and knowledge. We have made the choice of employing the advocacy coalition approach, but additional studies should test alternative approaches. In doing so, the study of think tanks could avoid the risk of becoming a 'cottage industry' and thus contribute to crucial issues in theoretical policy analysis, such as policy change and knowledge utilization.

Notes

1 This chapter draws on 'Think Tanks, Advocacy Coalitions, and Policy Change: the Italian Case' by Claudio Radaelli and Alberto Martini, which appeared in *Think tanks across nations*. Here, greater attention has been devoted to think tanks working in the field of international and foreign policy.

We are grateful to the research team that assisted with previous research and to the institutes that have responded to our updated questionnaire. The authors are indebted to Diane Stone, Giliberto Capano, Furio Cerutti, Rosa Balfour and Roberto Menotti for useful comments and suggestions. The usual disclaimer applies.
2 It should be observed that policy clubs of this type (that is, oriented to partisanship) are not entirely new, as shown by the examples of the left-oriented circles revolving around periodicals such as *Quaderni Piacentini* and *Quaderni Rossi* in the 1960s and 1970s.
3 Il Mulino is a classic think tank that also publishes a well-known periodical. Although the monthly *Il Mulino* has not espoused partisanship, it has faced a more competitive editorial market since the advent of the new policy clubs in the second half of the 1990s.
4 With hindsight, one can see many reasons to cast doubts on this belief.
5 Il Mulino arose out of the Association Carlo Cattaneo, established in 1956. The Association developed into an institute 'for research and study' in 1965.

7 Catherine Fieschi and John Gaffney

French think tanks in comparative perspective

There is no sound definitional French equivalent to the English term 'think tank' and we struggled to reconcile French reality with the rigorous demands of social science. A few years ago when we began the research for this volume, the various librarians and information specialists we approached could point us to no headings in card catalogues or databases. Thankfully, the past few years have seen an increased used of the web by think tanks. Outfits such as the Centre National de la Recherche Scientifique (CNRS) or the IFRI, who were barely present on the web four or five years ago, have now developed extremely sophisticated and informative sites; associations with few financial resources have made the most of the web to make their publications available and develop links and hyperlinks to other associations. This seemingly strictly technological development had two important consequences. First, the sites, by presenting links to other think tanks, political parties, associations and clubs, contribute to the identity of the relevant think tank itself. This makes it much easier for the outsider to grasp the ideological nebula of which the think tank sees itself as a part. Secondly, access to French search engines and research on the basis of key words relieve the definitional burden somewhat and reveal that in the past few years – perhaps in part due to an Anglo-American spill-over effect on the web – the term 'think tank' figures more prominently in French society, at least in its virtual form.

Several questions arise when defining a think tank. Which grouping or type(s) of grouping shall we take as constituting a think tank in the French context? What is its relationship to established political parties? What is the capacity (and desire) of those involved to influence politics, and more particularly policy processes and outcomes? What are their backgrounds and expertise? Do they make any claims to neutral expertise or are they more ideologically oriented? More practically, how are they funded? Does their source of funding curtail their autonomy? To these questions one needs to add that French think tanks have often had a greater impact on the wider *political* process than is apparent if one confines oneself to their direct impact on the *policy* process (see below). French think tanks are, in fact, often not at all closely linked to the policy process. This means that they are more difficult to assess in terms of both their aims and their effectiveness: policy impact is difficult to measure when it is obvious, even more so when it is incremental, a 'by-product' of think tank activity.

After definition and an analysis of some of the specific formative characteristics of the French context, we shall examine the ministerial *cabinets*. The next section deals with the political clubs, the reasons for their emergence, their subsequent personalization and their pivotal role in the French political system. Our final section analyses groups that more closely resemble Anglo-Saxon think tanks: the national research institutes, the independent policy research groups and the intellectual think tanks of the French New Right.

Definition and context

Our definition of think tanks involves a compromise between a classificatory and generalizable definition, and the recognition that France presents particularities that modify generalization. In the French case, the main difficulty in defining think tanks lies in the relationship between think tanks and the state/policy sphere, given that the line between intellectual, or at least a particular type of intellectual, and politician is blurred. This blurring is sustained by the higher education system as well as by a long historical tradition (Gaffney, 1991).

A useful concept in a basic classification of think tanks applied to the French context is that of the 'epistemic community' (Haas, 1992a). Epistemic communities are 'politically motivated intellectuals seeking to inform limited areas of policy on the basis of their expertise' (Stone, 1996b: 36). This allows for a very broad range of think tanks to be taken into account, all the while placing the necessary emphasis on the ideological and/or scientific coherence and policy interest of the institution. Much of this discussion applies to think tanks everywhere, but in the French case ideological positioning is structured in a forceful and influential way by the political culture. We will return to this theme; however, it is important to state that if think tanks are the means by which policy and intellectual convictions inform one another, then the French case is particularly interesting given the specific nature of these ties. First, though, there are three contextual factors which structure the definition itself.

A first factor is that a non-profit attitude to research and a degree of financial independence from vested government and corporate interests further the think tanks' claim to produce scientifically sound, rational research (see McGann and Weaver, 2000). Alongside the question of independence from the state and its structures, think tanks are also normally considered as needing to be independent from the pressures exerted by the private sector. In the USA, think tanks benefit from extensive corporate support. The scientific quality of the research produced is not necessarily diminished by the use industry or private vested interests make of it, even if they have actively contributed to its undertaking. This view, however valid, is an Anglo-American one and reflects different understandings of the relationship between state and civil society. In UK and American political thought, civil society rests upon a liberal ethos, placing at its core the role of the market. Civil society is in fact conceived of as a market place of ideas. The French conception of civil society virtually excludes the private sector, hinging on a direct relationship between the state and the individual, a relationship constructed on the basis of the notion of the Republic (mediated only grudgingly by political parties). Intrusion by the corporate sector, in the form of funding for research institutes or think tanks, is invariably perceived as a fundamental affront to the values of the Republic.

French think tanks are smaller than their American, Canadian or German counterparts. For example, the largest American think tanks, such as the Brookings Institution, the Environmental Law Institute or the Heritage Foundation, have a minimum permanent staff of 200 and a budget ranging from US$ 5 million to 20 million (5.1 million to 20.5 million euros). In Britain, the largest think tanks (the Centre for Economic Policy Research (CEPR) or the IISS) have permanent staff of around 15 to 20, and their budgets range from £1 million to 2 million (1.5 to 3.1 million euros). Even the smallest of British think tanks, such as Demos or the Adam Smith Institute (ASI), have a minimum of 5 to 7 permanent staff and budgets ranging from £200,000 to £360,000 (310,000 to 560,000 euros). France offers a sharp contrast (excluding the state-funded and affiliated national research institutes examined below), with think tanks generally working with a maximum of 5 full time staff and a budget often well under $0.5 million. The data in Table 7.1 (2001) is indicative only but gives an illustration of the varying sizes and budgets (when revealed) of French think tanks.

Secondly, the geographical concentration of the myriad of political think tanks in Paris is also not without significance and demonstrates how organizational forms designed almost by definition to call into question the centralization of the state imitate the state's very structures. In terms of personnel, moreover, graduates from the prestigious École Normale d'Administration and the Institut des Études Politiques dominate. The corollary is that members of Parisian political think tanks will be not only geographically close but socially as well. The French think tanks are *very French* (in the sense of being fragile, Parisian, elitist and historically aware) and bear out in this domain at least, the continuing phenomenon of the 'French exception'.

Table 7.1 Sample of French think tanks

Think tank	Number of staff	Budget (euros)	Location
Association pour la Démocratie et l'Education Locale et Sociale (ADELS)	22	Undisclosed	Paris
Autogestion Initiative Locale et Économie Sociale (AILES)	18	112,000	Paris
Centre National de la Recherche Scientifique (CNRS)	25 000	8.7 million	Paris
Club de l'Horloge	5	328,000	Paris
Convergence Ecologie Solidarité	6	547,000	Paris
Groupement de Recherche et d'Étude sur la Civilisation Européenne (GRECE)	2	Undisclosed	Paris
Institut Français pour les Relations Internationales (IFRI)	50 (20 permanent)	Undisclosed	Paris

A helpful way of looking at French think tanks is to view them from two perspectives. The first is that of their relationship to France's political institutions and formal political structures. There is a spectrum of interaction with formal structures depending upon the type of think tank involved and its ideological affinity with a political party, or with a government or government ministry. It is not only the nature of the relationships between think tanks and formal politics which is of theoretical and empirical interest to our study, but that of formal structures to one another – the state apparatus to the political party, the education system to the bureaucracy, the political elites to the wider electorate, and so on – which arguably call into existence and sustain the French think tank. The second perspective concerns their enacted relationship to the wider political culture. The think tanks' scope and influence are ascertainable, in part, in terms of how they are perceived, what assumptions are made about them and what their role purports and is perceived to be.

A defining characteristic of political think tanks, therefore, is their relationship to the state and the state's apparatuses within the framework of the wider culture, that is to say, the *interrelationship* of the two perspectives mentioned. In theory, as we have mentioned, the French state has no interlocutors – parties, associations, think tanks, interest groups – no intermediaries between it and the people. The French notion of popular sovereignty upon which republicanism is built posits no mediation. In practice, and in part because of such a primitive view, the state, the nation, teems with mediating institutions, and exercises a systematic – and indeed systemic – relationship with interest groups and pressure groups of various kinds in its policy elaboration and legislation. This has been the case throughout the last two centuries, and the Fifth Republic is no exception.

The seedbed of these pressure groups is not only professional and other interest groups, but also the estimated half a million (and rising) active 'associations' in France (mainly sporting and cultural groups, sometimes no less politically significant for that). A think tank is neither a pressure group nor an association, but sometimes the dividing lines between the three types of organization are unclear. It is in this environment of a somewhat atomized nation-state that we need to view the think tanks and their role: that is, within the framework provided by a strong, centralized unitary state which needs to enter into a whole series of informal and semi-formal relations with other sites of political activity, opinion and expertise, because of its very centralization and the relative neatness of its political institutions – small political parties, very low union membership and little activity in local politics.

It is important to emphasize here that what determines the roles and aims of think tanks in this context is not vested interests or their source of funding, but their coherence of ideological belief and their expertise. It is, moreover, through these two fundamental characteristics that they acquire their third defining trait: political impact; although, as we shall see, this is not transmitted through the political system via formal channels and institutions alone.

Therefore, we define a think tank in the French context as a group of experts who share an ideological orientation (and often a similar educational and social background) and a wish for their research and reflection to influence the political process. This community's primary function is to engage in research projects, informed by an ideological base, and to ensure that the results of the research or reflection have a political impact. Political impact can range from concrete policy proposals, through electoral support for a particular candidate, to the fostering of public debate on particular topics. The defining features are therefore ideological coherence, expertise and impact. In our classification of think tanks in France some clearly share the characteristics of think tanks in other countries, while others are more exclusively French phenomena.

Definitional caveat

Even within our relatively indulgent view of think tanks as coherent groups which organize in order to influence the political agenda, identifying and classifying them remains dauntingly difficult. Associations, *cercles*, *cercles d'étude*, *de réflexion*, centres, clubs, alliances, conventions, fora – or simply groups with names or acronyms which resemble exhortations rather than an organization – Agir, Convergences solidarités and so on – are everywhere. Yet a phone number (so often unanswered) and a name (so often difficult to get hold of) do not in themselves constitute a think tank (or should not). The list, moreover, is endless and ever-changing; as impossible to identify in its totality as many of its constituent clubs or think tanks are to contact by telephone, get documentation from, or interview. Such profusion and confusion are themselves, however, significant and revealing of the overall situation: such activity and organization *assume themselves* to be politically consequential and part of a vast and respected French tradition. They also bear witness to the French belief in ideas and their role in a politically healthy culture.

Ministerial *cabinets*

The ministerial *cabinets* place great strain on our definition of think tanks in France. Yet to by-pass them would be to exclude from analysis a political institution – unique to France – that mimics what all think tanks yearn to be: that is, groupings of experts, ideologically committed, practically orientated, who offer advice to government ministers, often short-circuiting that of the ministry's civil servants, and who have great influence upon agenda-setting and policy elaboration. The *cabinets*, which are ad hoc groupings around newly appointed government ministers, have taken on a formal role within the governmental system (even though they have no basis within the Constitution).

Cabinets have existed in one form or another since before the Revolution, as political entourages surrounding individuals. It was the Third Republic (1870/75–1940), suspicious of the Second Empire's civil servants, which saw the phenomenon embed itself in formal politics. The Third, Fourth and Fifth Republics have codified and regulated the *cabinets* (they now comprise a dozen or so advisors). Today they complement and rival the ministerial bureaucracy, providing all kinds of support, from legislative proposals to ordering taxis. In many ways, the *cabinet ministériel is* the functional equivalent of the think tank in other countries. The member of the *cabinet* is, although normally civil-service trained, invariably a member of a political party and has usually been associated with a particular principal personality, offering expertise, advice and support and therefore constituting part of his or her entourage. For more than a century, the movement of individuals from the civil service, into politics, perhaps into business or the universities, and back again has not been unusual, or normatively questionable, as it is for example in the UK, on condition that certain procedural forms are observed.

Since the mid-1980s, a new phenomenon has developed, what we might call the *cabinet*-in-waiting. With much greater alternation between the right and left in government, the ideological and personal groupings around a person or area of expertise need to be maintained while a government is out of office, hence the profusion since that time of small political clubs which mirror the *cabinets* themselves (Gaffney, 1988). Consequently, the relationship of the *cabinets* to government and even more importantly to the political parties is of crucial importance, as it is for another quintessentially French phenomenon: the political clubs.

The political clubs

With respect to the role of political parties in France it is important to bear in mind the mistrust, if not disregard, in which parties have been held since their emergence. Parties were for a long time associated with factionalism and weakness. They were in the first instance held as a negative legacy of 1789, suspected of carrying forth into future eras the factionalism and backstabbing politics of the darkest hours of the Revolution. In many ways, the parties were depicted as the enemies of the Republic. Where the Republic was united and embodied public concern and government for the people and by the people, the parties were disruptive, petty and the incarnation of individual or factional interests. The Third and Fourth Republics' weaknesses were seen as stemming directly from the power which the parties wielded within the National Assembly, to the detriment of strong, efficient government.

Hostility still exists, but from 1958 onwards it has been in greatly reduced form. Ironically, de Gaulle, who so disdained the parties, was in large part responsible for their rehabilitation. His new Republic, although curtailing their influence – and effecting something of a showdown with them in 1962 when revising the Constitution to allow for the election of the president by universal adult suffrage – never posited an alternative to them. By heightening presidentialism within the Republic, however, he did institutionalize a kind of permanent antagonism between presidential and party principles. De Gaulle's mistrust of what he referred to as 'la politique politicienne' (party political machinations) and 'les féodalités' (parties as feudal lords) was accompanied by the curtailment of the National Assembly's powers and the relegation of the parties to their legislative and budgetary functions. Presidential politics went hand in hand with strong political parties in order to sustain not only potential candidates but also the democratic regime itself. In a regime built on the dual basis of republicanism's historical legacy and strong presidential politics, political parties have had periodically to renegotiate their legitimacy.

Creating a club has been one of the ways in which parties have sought to be perceived as more than the apparatus of 'la politique politicienne'. This is even more true in the case of those clubs whose function is to promote the image and the opinions of a particular presidential candidate. Examples in the 1980s and 1990s include Solidarité Moderne for Laurent Fabius; Convaincre for Michel Rocard (later, in 1996, Rocard founded Action pour le Renouveau Socialiste (ARES)); République Moderne for Jean-Pierre Chevènement; Club 89 for Jacques Chirac; Allons z'Idées for Jack Lang; and Démocratie 2000, founded in 1985, and then Clysthène for Jacques Delors.

Clubs in France reflect the need to elevate politics above partisan lines, and the political club often depicts itself as being called into being when the political party is seen to have failed in some of its essential functions, such as offering the prospect of political power, providing policies, articulating an ideology, or, most importantly, defining or redefining political morality and 'vision'. The reasons for clubs serving a corrective function to political parties are complex, and raise questions about the primacy of the role of the political party itself in the French polity. In the German case, for example, the well-financed foundations are in a harmonious and permanent relationship with the political parties. In the UK, there are problems regarding their legitimacy vis-à-vis the party (the Fabians, for example, have always 'known their place' in terms of the British Labour movement and would face fierce criticism if they questioned it). In France, the legitimacy of the club is not contested. On the contrary, it is considered a vital part of the overall political process, but its *systematic* role vis-à-vis the political party is contested. It therefore resembles the UK think tank in one respect and the German in another, but its relation to the political party is, though organic, in many ways dynamically oppositional. The clubs are therefore always in an unstable, transitory, cyclical relationship with the political parties they 'serve'. As well as fulfilling their daily 'ordinary' tasks, the political parties, when 'healthy', are perceived as rallying points for opinion – *rassemblements* – which rise and fall on the scale of political opportunity depending upon their 'fitness'. It is also worth pointing out that the nature of French political party rhetoric is very different from its Anglo-American and Northern European counterparts. When this rhetoric seems no longer to correspond to political reality – that is, when the rhetoric remains 'moral' but action is perceived as not being so – there is a perceived fracture for which the club must offer a remedy. Good recent examples of this were the dislocations within the left as a result of repressive (often socialist-led) government policy in Algeria during the 1950s, and the search for political purpose in the 1960s. The clubs in France thrive, therefore, in crises or perceived crises, and are always in a mutually legitimating relationship with political parties. This notion of crisis is underpinned by the fact that club activity invariably accompanies the loss of power by political parties, and the beginning of a period of regrouping and redefinition of aims, strategy and policy.

The parties are also subject to surges of indifference or hostility, often followed by vulnerability to what the French call 'adventures', which may posit regime change and are normally accompanied by personal leadership appeals that contest party legitimacy. This personal element within the overall political equation raises issues of fundamental importance. Just as personal leaders – especially during the Fourth Republic – could make anti-regime appeals for support and allegiance, in the Fifth Republic, because of the presidential system and its effects upon the polity, the personalization of power and of political allegiance have become the hallmarks of political activity. 'Persons' therefore work within the overall system as well as against it. This means two related things for clubs and political parties. The first is that the definition or redefinition of political activity and allegiance (and morality, etc.) traditionally undertaken by the club must address the question of the acute personalization of power in the Fifth Republic. The second and related point is that individuals themselves will take on a more nodal function, making claims to be 'representative' of a tradition or part of it, and acting as brokers within parties, or between them, heightening their own position, and acting as rallying sites for opinion. 'Unstable' parties, or parties in complex alliance relations with others, witness this kind of activity constantly. So too do the clubs. Clubs set up by individual figures in the highly fractioned ecologist movement offer a very good example. Individuals such as Brice Lalonde, Antoine Waechter and Noel Mamère moved throughout the 1980s, 1990s and even more recently in perpetual relation to one another, setting up *cercles de réflexion* and claiming to represent various strands of ecologism in order to reinvigorate (and influence) the organized political movement. The same is true for individuals positioned *between* strong political parties; the sphere between the socialist and communist movements has long been one of proliferating *cercles* or *entourages* around figures such as ex-socialist Jean-Pierre Chevènement or ex-communist Pierre Juquin. The irony in the case of ecologism, socialism ... and communism lies in the claim of each to be fundamentally uninterested in following leaders; once again we can see how the club imitates the structures it contests.

As with the ministerial *cabinets*, the political clubs are a hybrid phenomenon which, while not corresponding to a strict definition of think tanks, do nevertheless exhibit think tank characteristics (ideological coherence, political/policy impact and some – if little – research). They shed important light on the nature of relationships, formal and informal, political, ideological and social, and how these inform and structure politics in France. Often members of these political clubs are or have been themselves members of ministerial *cabinets*, and are involved in other groups and other clubs.

Tracing the evolution of the political clubs in France from bona fide clubs to personalized political outfits sheds some light on the process through which many of these groupings designed to contest aspects of the political regime ultimately end up mirroring its defining features. The clubs of the 1960s, which sprang up right across the political spectrum in response to the Algerian war and the advent of the Fifth Republic, were based upon a venerated French tradition of political clubs which thrived during the French revolutionary period of the late eighteenth century (themselves in part a version of the pre-revolutionary and female-influenced *salons* of the Enlightenment). This pedigree reflects a recurring (Parisian) insistence upon the role of the discussion of political ideas.

The most famous of the 1960s clubs was the Club Jean Moulin (founded in 1958 in reaction to the alarming coup d'état of 13 May in Algiers). It published a regular bulletin with a circulation of 2,000 and produced in the course of the decade a dozen or so highly influential books (for example, on constitutional reform and the rebuilding of the left). In transit through the Club were most of the figures who were to play a role in left and centre-left politics in the subsequent decade. (However, in terms of what we said above about the subsequent personalization of club activity, few of the founding figures of the 1960s clubs went on to major political careers.) We can make three points here. Firstly, the Club Jean Moulin, like its contemporaries, was born in reaction to a perceived crisis (both of the regime and of the left more generally). Secondly, it flourished in the absence of a strong left party, nurturing, redeveloping, 'keeping safe', as it were, the torch of the non-communist left. Thirdly, it was eclipsed at the moment the left united, and the clubs merged, in wave upon wave, into the new Socialist Party between 1969 and 1974.

Between 1958 and the late 1960s there were scores of clubs set up. In fact, many of them united with one another to form 'Unions', 'Conventions' or 'Federations' of clubs in order to give themselves more political influence at the national level (for example, François Mitterrand's Convention des Institutions Républicaines). In terms of their language and identity it should be mentioned that the 'voice' of the clubs was heavily influenced by, and in turn influenced, the emergence of neo-Marxism as the main discourse of the left in the period 1960–80. The rigour of Marxism gave many of the clubs an intellectual integrity they might otherwise not have had, although such a discourse also added to the pretentiousness, the inappropriateness and ultimately the sterility of much club inquiry. Moreover, the teleology within Marxian thought reinforced the idea that the clubs were tributaries flowing back to the main mighty river (a reunited left). It also eclipsed the other strong though younger tradition within the French left, that of Christian democracy (Jacques Delors, a representative of this tradition, was himself a member of the second most important 1960s club, Citoyens 60, which claimed to provide a meeting-place for the centre-left).

The long-lasting effect of and upon the political clubs was their reconciliation of the left with the normative values of the Fifth Republic, the most dominant being that a person could represent a tradition or political family. Indeed, the clubs of the 1960s were superseded (1969–74) at the very point at which the left had reconciled itself to a *Gaullien* allegiance to an exemplary individual – in the case of the left, the 'convert' to socialism, François Mitterrand. The clubs, therefore, served a systemic function (which they would doubtless have denied). Rather than redefine the left in terms of rediscovering it beneath the rubble of the Algerian war and collapse of the Fourth Republic, their true 'function' was to align French socialism with the ideological parameters of the Fifth Republic, and take part in a mythical 'homecoming' of the left – the clubs, the trade unions and the political parties – around the mythologized status of a heroic individual. This was to bring the left to power, but also present it and the club tradition with unexpected challenges.

Throughout the 1970s, with the reunification of the Socialist Party, the leadership of François Mitterrand, and the Alliance between the socialists and communists, there was little club activity outside the rallying of opinion to the left. After the left gained power in 1981, winning both the presidency and a socialist majority in the National Assembly, what had been apparent to some now became real for many and was to last throughout the 1980s and into the 1990s. Socialism had lost its voice. There was an adage in British left politics after World War II that socialism was whatever a Labour government happened to be doing at the time. In France, socialism in the 1980s seemed to have become whatever François Mitterrand happened to be thinking.

Such as it was, the 'rethinking' that was being done by groups of experts around the Socialist Party, members of the ministerial *cabinets*, themselves involved in study projects, and so on. Nevertheless, for most of them and for the left generally there was little ideological terrain to occupy, simply a painful and dramatic conversion to the reality of government and the market economy. Modernization not socialism, rationalization not major social reform, were the new watchwords.

The conditions, however, were being created for a renewal of the political clubs, even though the left was to remain in government until 1993, with Mitterrand serving as president until 1995. By the mid-1980s, the earlier 'wishful thinking' about socialism had given way to several years of practical government and the experience of office. This was a very curious phenomenon. The articulated voice of socialism had been handed over to the president because of the nature of the institutional system, and the 'lyrical illusions' had been destroyed by the reality of office. Yet what we might call an unexplored discursive space had been created in which a new rhetoric, marrying republicanism and social democracy, for example, was now possible. The ministerial *cabinets* of the left had increased dialogue and exchange with other progressive thinkers such as trade unionists and members of associations. It was clear that the left would need to prepare for the post-Mitterrand period just as the Gaullists had had to prepare for *l'après de Gaulle*. Social democracy, feminism, managerialism, localism, regionalism, republicanism: the revival of a leftist ideology or the creation of a new blend of political thought now had to address some of the successes of the left in the Fifth Republican government where once it had had to address only its failures.

These 'clubs' are now an active part of the political scene, and virtually every figure of any political significance is associated with a political club dedicated to the renewal of ideas within the Republic. All have shifted their focus from 'political' to 'social' questions reflecting the concerns of both the political class and the public, and the intractable and growing problems of unemployment, job and other insecurity, and the phenomenon of 'exclusion' (homelessness, poverty, ghettoization, social marginalization and globalization).

Think tanks and the longer-term perspective

The national research institutes

The national, state-funded research institutes, such as the CNRS (founded in 1939, the mother organization to which many of these institutes are affiliated), Institut National de Statistiques et d'Études Economiques (INSEE) and a range of others, fulfil many of the functions carried out by independent research institutes in other countries. For example, the CNRS runs approximately 1,500 laboratories and research centres responsible for the majority of French scientific research in all fields. INSEE (founded in 1946) provides detailed social, economic and political statistics, and the Institut National d'Études Demographique (INED) provides detailed demographic information. The Conseil Scientifique de l'Audio-visuel (CSA) acts as both a media monitoring device and a research centre on the French media. The entire network of national institutes can usefully be conceived of as a research chain through which information is collected, analysed, diffused, and used for further research in other national research centres down the line. Regardless of the activity undertaken by institutes, the nature of their staff provides continuity in that researchers and managers at every level are mostly recruited from the Grandes Écoles (elite national colleges). It ensures that the system as a whole produces researchers with the skills and outlook concomitant with its aims.

The role of the national research institutes is of importance because it spans several sectors. The research chain has numerous links to other chains, that is, to other sectors: education, industrial, political and cultural. The scientific institutes provide expertise and research to the industries located both in the private and in the public domains. They also provide the staff for the Grandes Écoles, some of which, such as the École Normale Supérieure, tend to set – for better or for worse – France's cultural parameters. As such, their role is multiple and central. They resemble, in part, large North American think tanks such as the Hoover Institution or the Brookings. The links between the research institutes we have just examined and the French state are so close as to make them an integral part of the state apparatus. Nevertheless, the personnel overlap between these institutes and the education sectors (as well as the ministerial *cabinets*), and their claims to research and political/policy impact, warrants their inclusion in a survey of French think tank activity.

The policy research groups

There are a number of think tanks in France whose roles and aims within the French political/policy process are as ill-defined as they are interesting. These groups have several characteristics in common: they are indeed epistemic communities and bring together a number of experts who carry out research in well-defined fields and who share values and principles. Often these experts are drawn from universities, but the groups in question seek to bring them together – and this very explicitly – with party political actors, trade union representatives and social workers: that is, professionals who might be able to report on the state of a particular sector, on the basis of their professional expertise, while also being well placed to implement the results of any research emanating from the scholars active in the think tank. The desire to bring an element of pragmatism to politics is present in all of the groups that we have chosen to include in this chapter. However, the policy research groups stand out in their belief that politics is overwhelmingly defined at the local or grass-roots level. Their practical stance is, therefore, necessarily highlighted by the nature of their ties to the local community, indeed by their very conception of the local community as the appropriate site of enabling political power. That is not to say that these groups are neighbourhood-based or strictly local organizations: they share a national outlook and significant ties with universities and other groups across France.

Nevertheless, part of their mission is to foster 'nationally applicable' research at the local level. One such group is Autogestion Initiative Locale et Economie Sociale (AILES). Founded in 1986, AILES – an acronym meaning 'Wings' – brings together former members of one of France's largest trade unions (the Confédération Française Democratique du Travail (CFDT)) and former members of the Communist Party and the PSU (Unified Socialist Party). Most members are linked either to a national research institute or to a university, and combine various political activities and commitments with research activities (Dominique Taddei of the association was both professor of economics and deputy mayor of the city of Avignon).

One of the characteristics of this group is its links with other similar groups. AILES has close ties to the Association pour la Démocratie et l'Education Locale et Sociale (ADELS), whose main activity is the dissemination of information about local democracy and political participation. Initiatives de Citoyenné Active en Réseaux (ICARE) is another group involved on the one hand in formalizing ties between associations, research groups and local groups and on the other in promoting research on grass-roots participation. It serves as a hub for a hundred or so organizations and associations that share in its aim of 'revitalizing' local citizenship initiatives.

The phenomenon of French think tanks is such that this chapter seems neatly divided into think tanks that have an explicit connection with the French state and that are partisan, and large, monolithic French research institutes such as the CNRS funded by the French state. The groups we have referred to above may define themselves as think tanks but are, in practice, small partisan associations, producing little research and having little political impact despite their growing network. One think tank stands out as an exception to all this, IFRI. Founded in 1979, it is perhaps the only French think tank that bears a similarity to its Anglo-American counterparts. IFRI publishes a well-established journal of research on international relations (*Politique Étrangere*), and brings together academics and members of the corporate sector (whose intellectual credentials are deemed worthy enough) in debates and discussions whose aims are to further the presence of French political interests throughout the world. It is not affiliated to any political party and prides itself on a thriving academic culture and significant scholarly input.

The New Right: GRECE and the Club de l'Horloge

The French New Right was responsible for the creation of two controversial think tanks, both of which claimed to give new impetus to ideologies discredited by World War II. The Groupement de Recherche et d'Étude sur la Civilisation Européenne (GRECE), founded in 1968, and the Club de l'Horloge, founded in 1974, were the cornerstones of the French New Right. It is beyond the scope of this chapter to give an exhaustive description of the ideological tenets of either of these. What is of relevance to our study here is that the ideological inclinations of each of these think tanks and the means they chose to encourage debate and disseminate their research offer striking examples of what we have called the 'intellectual' think tanks. GRECE and the Club de l'Horloge sought to have an impact on politics not just through research and debate, but also through the adoption of an intellectual stance often seen as the preserve of left-wing intellectuals.

The emphasis placed on cultural and intellectual debate, and the importance of the creation of a *space* in which GRECE could give voice to its concerns and theories, make GRECE one of France's foremost think tanks. It was a reaction to events even prior to 1968: in other words, the New Right precedes GRECE by several years. The New Right in France should be understood as originating around 1962–63 as a result of the Algerian crisis and, even more directly, as a result of the combined failures of the ultra-anti-Gaullist movements for 'l'Algérie Française' (1956–62) and of the extreme right-wing parliamentary movements such as the Mouvement Nationaliste du Progrès and the Rassemblement Européen de la Liberté (Taguieff, 1994). GRECE was the intellectual expression of a frustration with the weakening of France's hegemonic strength, and the failure of the traditional nationalist right to deal with this decline (Duranton-Crabol, 1988). What was new in postwar France was the way in which this right wing expressed itself, both through GRECE and through the Club de l'Horloge.

The Club de l'Horloge is probably the most well-known and most respected think tank of the New Right. In a sense it is the bridge between the old and the new right, bringing together political personalities and scholars in workshops and fora centred on political themes. Individual membership of the Club de l'Horloge often overlaps with membership of more centre-right parties and in many cases with membership of GRECE. (Yvan Blot, president of the Club de l'Horloge, was a leading personality of the centre-right Rassemblement pour la France (RPR), while Bruno Megret of the breakaway Front National–Mouvement Republican was also a member of the Club and of the RPR before joining Le Pen's party.) But where GRECE was highly active, technocratic and robust if not abrasive in its intellectuality, the Club de l'Horloge presented a more classic scholarly face. The members it flaunted were older, more established political personalities, the scholars more quiet and less media-prone.

Central to their project was a 'cultural struggle' to unsettle, or rather displace, the ideology that constructed the postwar liberal and social-democratic consensus. In order to do so, GRECE and the Club de l'Horloge adopted a left-wing strategy: a Gramscian project of molecular cultural change. To some extent, by bringing right-wing ideas centre stage, they succeeded.

Conclusion

French think tanks operate in a conflictual relationship to the political party, offering themselves as alternatives, particularly as regards sources for policy and doctrine. Think tanks are best understood when seen within the overall political system; that is, one needs to see not simply their role vis-à-vis government agencies or political parties, but their place in the overall institutional and cultural configuration, both diachronically (in a rich tradition) and synchronically (within the Fifth Republic). Given the now relatively common alternation between right and left in government and, even more pertinently, the 'cohabitation' phenomenon in French politics (whereby the dual executive is split and a president and prime minister from different political parties are brought together, as in 1986–88, 1993–95 and 1997–2002), this extra or alternative 'site' for policy elaboration or ideological renewal is amplified as parties are forced into or out of power. 'Cohabitation', in particular, has heightened the importance of the political clubs. While they did not become more transparent or more stable, they nevertheless seemed to serve as a locus of debate while political parties (in particular the socialist party and the RPR) were busy playing the game of 'cohabitation'.

There is also an element of 'wish-fulfilment' on the part of contemporary think tanks which raises the question of cause and effect in political relations. In a country with such a strong tradition of intellectually driven political renewal and the heroic role of the politically committed philosopher, it is difficult to disentangle teleological thought from inquiry, teleology from political action, and self-importance from political contribution.

Perhaps most significant in terms of the essential character of contemporary think tanks and the Fifth's Republic influence upon them is the tendency towards personalization as an organizing principle within them. Today, many of them are just fan clubs with no proper reflection upon political questions. Sometimes they pretend to be less tied to their leader than they are, claiming that the personalization that exists is simply part of a deeper movement, or a reflection of the demands of the modern media. What is significant in terms of our analysis is to note that it is the Fifth Republic itself that has done this to the organization of political groups and political ideas.

8 Mark Sandle

Think tanks, post communism and democracy in Russia and Central and Eastern Europe

Few parts of the globe have undergone such a momentous period of change as Russia and Eastern Europe since 1989. The events which swept the ruling communist parties from power have transformed the political, economic, social and cultural landscape. The struggle to create viable postcommunist states has encompassed a wide variety of challenges faced by the peoples of Russia and Central and Eastern Europe, including democratization, economic reforms, environmental problems, ethnic issues, minority rights and social policies. What role have think tanks played in this period? This chapter will provide an overview of the evolution of policy research institutes across this region and assess their contribution to the policy process. A broader issue – the impact of think tanks on the development of democracy and civil society – will also be addressed. Is it accurate to argue, as many commentators do, that think tanks in Russia and Central and Eastern Europe have strengthened democracy? Or can their activities be seen more as a result of the failure of liberal politics and the crisis of the intellectual in postcommunist societies?

Communist roots

The Soviet model

An awareness of the communist origins of the think tanks is vital. While there were variations between the different states of Eastern Europe and the Soviet Union, a similar structure existed which configured the relationship between ideas, policy-making and power in particular ways. The basic model that underpinned communist intellectual life was generated in the Soviet Union. Intellectual life was monopolized by a vast politico-ideological complex and expressed through a monist belief system: Soviet Marxism-Leninism. A broad conglomerate of departments, agencies and organizations undertook the production, dissemination and control of ideas, overseen by the Communist Party secretariat and its apparatus, all totally funded by the state. Broadly speaking, there were three different levels of research institute. Those under the tutelage of the Academy of Sciences offered the greatest degree of intellectual freedom, followed by the universities. Secondly there were the institutes attached to and supplying information for particular ministries, but having little influence over the policy-making process. Finally there were those institutes within the Soviet Communist Party (CPSU) itself, usually staffed by political consultants and engaged in work relating to broader ideological and political questions (Hough and Fainsod, 1979; Krastev, 2000a: 280).

Although the size, structure and functions of these institutes varied, they did possess a core of common features. All researchers were employees of the state, and their lifestyles were relatively privileged. Secondly, the institutions were comparatively large bodies, employing up to 700 staff. Thirdly, they were highly specialized entities, designed to cover all aspects of the study of a particular topic or region. Fourthly, there was little or no competition between them; consequently they enjoyed a monopoly of research expertise and information (Antonenko, 1996: 1). Finally, all policy-making was tightly controlled by the leading bodies of the CPSU, notably the Central Committee and the Politburo. Knowledge, power and policy-making were fused within one massive hierarchy. The research institutes were very active and productive, but opportunities for influence and (relative) autonomy were highly restricted. Although it is tempting to date the moves towards greater democracy and openness from the Gorbachev period (1985 onwards), this temptation should be resisted. The history of intellectual life and policy-making in the USSR/Eastern Europe prior to 1985 is not a static, uniform one. There were chronological, functional and geographical variations from the picture outlined above. In general, research institutes came to play an increasing role in the intellectual life of the socialist bloc states after 1956, and were more influential in those states that took the greatest steps towards liberalizing their political systems.

After the death of Stalin in 1953, there was a gradual loosening of intellectual constraints in the USSR as the CPSU increasingly sought to draw 'expert' knowledge into the policy-making process. The increasing complexity of governing a maturing industrial society, maintaining Soviet hegemony in a new international socialist bloc, and responding to the twists and turns of Cold War diplomacy meant an increased reliance upon expertise to make informed policy. It was at this level – policy-making – that institutes were able to develop a degree of autonomy from the state and, in doing so, to attempt to exert a modicum of influence. In the course of discussing policy alternatives in areas such as economic policy, foreign affairs, welfare, housing and legal reform, it became possible for institutes within the Academy of Sciences to open avenues of influence over policy research and formation. This was aided by a growing awareness amongst the political leadership of the dwindling analytic capacity of the party-state bureaucracy. Dominated by careerists who made a living out of avoiding responsibility and evading decision-making, the bureaucracy was mediocre, resistant to change and hostile to creativity (Arbatov, 1992: 142–8). In this context, the party elite began to solicit 'expert' contributions, but without shifting any control of policy outside the apparatus itself.

In the USSR the institutes enjoyed a greater degree of influence from 1956 until 1968 (the invasion of Czechoslovakia), when a period of domestic retrenchment and conservatism set in. Input into the policy process took a number of different forms. In direct terms, the institutes outside of the party-state hierarchy responded to initiatives from the latter, usually in the form of research reports, proposals or analytical studies. The institutes and their employees (or *instituteniki*) also contributed to the wider political and intellectual climate by publishing ideas and proposals via a number of different outlets. Many institutes generated in-house journals. Yet these institutes operated under severe constraints that restricted their influence and activities markedly. Ideological constraints restricted the spectrum of alternatives. Prior censorship limited what could be discussed. There was only one 'client' for research: the monopolistic, dominant state. There was no 'public sphere' and hence no arena of autonomy in which to operate.

In general terms, the most intellectual autonomy could be found in those fields that were of the least ideological or political significance, such as ancient history, ethics and logic. In policy terms, the most important factor affecting the influence of think tanks was arguably the extent to which their proposals corresponded to the goals of the party leadership at the time, or reinforced the latest ideological diktat. Also important in this regard was the field in which researchers worked. Those areas that were of most importance to the leadership, such as economics, or were the least ideologically sensitive, such as foreign relations, allowed the most leeway for activity and influence. Significant in this regard were institutes such as the Institute of the World Economy and International Relations (IMEMO), the Institute for the Study of the USA and Canada (ISKAN), the Central Economic and Mathematical Institute and the Institute of Economics and Industrial Organization (Arbatov, 1992: 158). Secondly, the role of key political figures or prominent intellectuals was also important. The surest way for an institute to guarantee its autonomous status, or for individuals to gain access to the policy-making process, was through the patronage of a leading political figure. At the same time, the opposition of conservative figures could see the closure or emasculation of entire institutes, or the isolation and ostracism of individuals.

Eastern European variations on a theme

In the pre-Gorbachev period, the organization of research, ideological controls and policy-making was remarkably consistent across the countries of the socialist bloc. One of the key components of Soviet control across the region was the imposition of the Stalinist 'model', based on one-party rule, industrialization via heavy industry, the collectivization of agriculture and so on. This was replicated in the sphere of intellectual life. The model of a gigantic Academy of Sciences network, alongside a highly controlled university sector reinforced by particular research groups clustered around specific ministries, was imposed on the countries of Eastern Europe, with similar results to that of the Soviet model.

However, each country did forge a particular type of Soviet model, not just intellectually, but also in areas such as agriculture, industry, ethnic relations and the roles of, for instance, the church or trade unions. The relationship between degrees of liberalization and the activity and influence of research institutes appears to have been a strong one. In particular, Polish and Hungarian institutes were able to develop a significant degree of autonomy. Hungary, above all, stands out in this regard. The economic reforms (embodied in the New Economic Mechanism) from 1968 onwards allowed institutes working in fields such as economics and labour studies a greater degree of latitude to produce reports and proposals for the state and to discuss possible alternatives. At the other end of the spectrum, the German Democratic Republic (GDR), Czechoslovakia (after 1968) and Bulgaria were the least willing to grant influence or autonomy in the policy-making process. These variations were important in shaping the postcommunist world of think tanks and research institutes.

The Gorbachev phenomenon

The accession of Yuri Andropov saw the start of the shift in the configuration of power within the politico-ideological complex. Between 1982 and 1991, there was a gradual loosening of the ideological and political constraints on intellectual activity, combined with an overhaul of the personnel and the institutions engaged in the production of both ideology and policy. The hegemony of reformist thinking in the party leadership not only created a genuine sphere of autonomy for intellectuals and academics, but also fundamentally changed the relationship between the CPSU, the bureaucracy and research institutes. The status of the last changed, especially under Mikhail Gorbachev, from 'outsiders' to 'insiders', as a clear policy coalition of party reformers and Academy of Sciences *instituteniki* emerged.

It was not until Gorbachev came to power in 1985 that the trends Andropov initiated were codified and institutionalized. The Gorbachev leadership shifted the configuration of forces in three ways. First, there was a new intellectual climate characterized by *glasnost* (openness) and *novoe politicheskoe mishlenie* (new political thinking). Secondly, a renewal of personnel occurred within both the party and the institutes, and new institutes were created. Thirdly, a policy coalition comprising the party leadership, selected institutes and sections of the media and the bureaucracy was established.

In short, *glasnost* began to change the rules of the game. Although limits to discussion and publication still existed, the period after 1986 saw them gradually eroded, as Soviet society began to create a public sphere marked by pluralism, dialogue, diversity and conflicts of opinion. It was now possible to use the media to disseminate a range of different views. Although the internal structure of institutes – their size, functional specialization and state funding – remained unchanged, their activities were profoundly affected by this change in their external environment.

Arising out of these changes to the external environment and in personnel came a shift in the relationship between the party, the bureaucracy and think tanks. Research institutes were drawn directly into the policy-making process. Their policy input ranged from drawing up practical recommendations in selected fields, to dynamic shifts in the world-view of the CPSU. Examples of policy coalitions in practice were the collaborative efforts of the State Agricultural Committee (*Gosagroprom*) and the Agricultural Academy, and the creation of SOVNA-PECC (the National Committee for Economic Cooperation on Asia-Pacific Affairs) which comprised members of IMEMO, ISKAN, the Ministry of Foreign Affairs, trading organizations and Far Eastern local authorities for Asia-Pacific and Siberian development (Shimotomai, 1990: 94).

Reformist think tanks under *perestroika* (restructuring) enjoyed something of a golden era. Relative intellectual freedom, access to the policy process and the political leadership, access to information from abroad and unrestricted funding brought them to the centre of the political process. Their experiences under Gorbachev demonstrate the importance of ideas and expertise in shaping policy, but also in fostering a set of values and norms amongst a key section of the policy-making elite.

The impact and legacy of think tanks in the Soviet model

Clearly, the institutional architecture of the Soviet state created serious constraints on the emergence and growth of autonomous policy research institutes. The absence of a 'public sphere', the state control of intellectual life and the control exercised over the policy-making process by the party-state bureaucracy made it exceptionally difficult for them to think and act autonomously, and hence exert influence in the policy process. In addition, the threats of unemployment, exile and incarceration tended to promote conservatism amongst many institutes and their personnel.

Yet this very architectural configuration also facilitated the growth of these institutes once the leadership had decided to create them, as the bureaucracy required increased levels of expertise in policy-formation. Access to resources was not a problem. The functional and geographical divisions of the bureaucracy (including its nominally federal structure) afforded the research centres numerous access points. The analytical weakness of the Soviet bureaucracy – a function of the recruitment policy which rewarded political loyalty and obedience, conservatism and conformity – forced the leadership to turn to experts when the tasks of governing and reforming a modern industrial society became apparent after the death of Stalin.

The development and consolidation of think tanks under communism was also closely linked to the wider correlation of political forces within the system. The close linkages between reformist political figures and institute heads, and the use of institutes by reformers to 'push' innovative policy proposals, ties the development of think tanks to wider political developments. The victory of the reformers under Gorbachev tilted the balance firmly in favour of the Academy of Sciences over the party-state bureaucracy.

Given the constraints within which Soviet think tanks were operating, questions about the influence or impact of think tanks are highly pertinent. Two issues stand out. First, did the research institutes bring a greater degree of 'rationality' (Dror, 1984) to bear upon the decision-making process? Undoubtedly, Soviet think tanks did widen the scope of policy alternatives, due to the analytic weakness of the bureaucracy, and also because the CPSU deliberately sought out this advice. However, the important qualification to this is that the range of policy alternatives was extremely narrow. Think tanks did provide alternative advice and analysis, but this was a very limited selection of alternatives. The second issue concerns the character of the influence that think tanks attempted to exert over the policy process. Did they have an educative function, shaping the climate of public opinion? Or were they 'enlighteners' (Weiss, 1990), setting the terms of discourse within which policies were formulated? In other words, did they produce a 'paradigm shift' within the official ideology that eventually fed into the policy process?

The educative function – informing the public of policy issues and so widening the scope of the debate – was not feasible given the controls on the dissemination of information exercised by the CPSU. It can be argued, however, that think tanks did perform a quasi-enlightenment function. Institutes often developed new ideas and concepts which overturned the existing orthodoxy (the example of the radically different world-view espoused by IMEMO is particularly apt). However, this shift only fed into the policy process because of the correlation of political forces and due to the links between the institutes and the key political figures. The think tanks provided a reformist discourse, but this only became embedded in the policy process due to the wider political and institutional configuration of forces under *perestroika*.

Think tanks after communism

The communist legacy continues to loom over the activities of policy research institutes and think tanks in Russia, the former Soviet republics and the states of Eastern Europe. The particular configuration of knowledge/power as it evolved in the communist period has shaped the think tank sector in each country. This has been accentuated by the dynamics of postcommunist political and economic development. A comparative survey of think tanks across this region throws up some very interesting patterns. Before turning to a comparison of think tanks, a few preliminary remarks are in order.

The literature on think tanks in the region has grown almost as quickly as the think tank phenomenon itself. (McGann and Weaver, 2000; Kimball, 2000; Struyk, 1999; Johnson, 1996a, 1996b; Quigley, 1995). The attention of Western analysts has been drawn in two directions. At a micro-level, and usually taking the US example as the starting point, analysts have attempted to examine how and why think tanks emerge, to detail their internal organizational structures, funding and personnel, and to assess their specific influence over the policy process. At the macro-level, Western analysts have tended to locate the growth of think tanks as a function of the march of democracy and the market across the globe amidst the wreckage of the collapse of communism and the disillusionment with socialism. Both directions have been underpinned by an explanatory paradigm which is driven by an external cultural frame of reference, be it the US model of think tank growth and organization or the deterministic, teleological approach of 'transition' politics: onwards to democracy, markets, liberalism, privatization and consumerism. This differs somewhat from the writings of some 'local' analysts, such as Ivan Krastev, director of the Centre for Liberal Strategies based in Sofia. Their contextualization is primarily local, be it national or regional, but also tends to be less deterministic in its approach. The emphasis is upon the contingency of the postcommunist situation, and the significance of the communist legacy in shaping the organizational structures, values and outlooks of postcommunist think tanks even if only in the negative sense of a conscious rejection of what came before. The different starting points end, unsurprisingly, in rather different destinations.

Turning to the think tanks themselves, broadly speaking, issues of personnel, funding and political uncertainty have dominated their activities (Kimball, 2000; Manaev, 2000; Struyk, 1999). In some countries, think tanks have struggled to recruit able and talented policy experts (Johnson, 1996a, 1996b). They have also struggled with funding. A reliance on Western funding has created problems of dependence, and of a perceived pressure to adopt Western agendas or values (Kimball, 2000). Domestic sources of funding have also often carried 'strings', somewhat compromising the attempt to develop an autonomous sphere of activity. These practical issues are overlain by a wider problem relating to the relationship between think tanks and the society out of which they arise. Analyses have tended to highlight the emergence of think tanks (albeit in various guises) as an expression or outgrowth of a healthy, mature civil society as well as part of the process by which a civil society is being 'constructed' (McGann and Weaver, 2000). The attempts to create viable political and economic structures amidst the wreckage of communism have placed the think tanks in a paradoxical situation: trying to effect change whilst establishing themselves as viable entities within a constantly evolving and rapidly fluctuating situation. The simultaneous imperatives of educating the new governments as to how think tanks can assist them, whilst actually carrying out research and advocacy to demonstrate their usefulness, have been problematic. This has been exacerbated by the high turnover of governments in some states, which means that the process of education has to begin all over again with new personnel (Johnson, 1996a).

Perhaps the most significant observation to be made about the think tank phenomenon in Central and Eastern Europe is the proliferation of new research institutes. The Freedom House Directory of Think Tanks in Central and Eastern Europe (1999) included approximately 136 institutes. This is remarkably rapid growth since only 1989. While some have evolved out of the old Academy of Sciences research institutes, most are new organizations. Why has there been such a proliferation? The wider literature on think tanks has explained their proliferation in a number of ways: the complexity of government, information overload, the huge growth of the media and the inability of traditional policy agencies to solve political problems. Are any of these factors pertinent to Central and Eastern Europe?

The collapse of communism produced a massive institutional shake-up, which fractured many of the links and practices of the old policy process. The new system contains three distinctive elements that led to this prolific growth of research centres. The first is funding. The drastic reduction in funding for the Academy of Sciences led talented researchers to create their own analytical centres, or join new ones, which now co-exist alongside the old research institutes. The deteriorating economic conditions compelled many analysts in the public sector to seek an alternative career path within independent policy research institutes. But this proliferation has also had an external impetus. Many Western foundations and agencies have been instrumental in providing funding, as part of a wider agenda to 'hothouse' policy research institutes on the Western model, which are seen as a central part of a 'healthy', 'mature' civil society. Krastev (2000b: 144) comments that: 'What the United States is eager to export in the post-Cold War world is not only particular economic policies (deregulation and competition) and values (multiculturalism and respect for human rights) but also a specific process of policy making.'

This external funding context, driven by the assumptions of Western groups, has been central in the proliferation of think tanks, and of particular types of think tank. The internal context has also been important, particularly that of increased competition and fragmentation. The previous situation of virtual 'monopolies' of expertise has given way to a more competitive environment. The new political and economic environment (multi-partyism and new political institutions) created fragmentation and new axes of differentiation. Alongside functional specialisation, the new conditions created differentiation along political/ideological lines (Bruckner, 1996: 1–3; Antonenko, 1996: 1). Budgetary constraints have clearly hindered many governments in the region from developing sophisticated, informed policy analysis. New think tanks have stepped into this void. A final factor is the increased complexity of governing. The difficulty of understanding the problems facing each state in the region, and of devising policies to create viable economic and political systems in the wake of communism, has generated a need for expertise that many governments were unable to meet.

Have any general trends in the development of think tanks across the region become apparent? One of the conceptual problems facing analysts is to decide what is, and what is not, a think tank. As noted in the introduction to this book, 'think tank' is notoriously difficult to define. While different scholars have used different criteria to identify think tanks, any attempt to compile a comprehensive list has been hampered by the economic and political uncertainty in the region. Many organizations have had a short shelf-life. The nature of the postcommunist state, and its relationship with independent organizations vary widely within the region. This has made it difficult to establish what 'independent' means in a postcommunist context.

Various ways of categorizing the new think tanks have been used. The Freedom House surveys (1997 and 1999) used three broad guidelines in order to establish what would count as a think tank:

1 A substantial amount of their activities were targeted at research and advocacy.

2 Their primary interests fell in what Freedom House considered to be the major research fields: the economy, environmental issues, legal changes, security and democratization.
3 Legal status: institutes were expected to be fully independent, and for the most part registered as NGOs.

This way of categorizing think tanks across the region has been criticized by Raymond Struyk, who highlights instead two key features of any acceptable definition: independence and typically (though not exclusively) non-profit-making entities. He omits government and university-affiliated institutes (Struyk, 1999: 21–2). Struyk's (1999: 62–3) analysis of thirty-seven public policy institutes in four countries (Russia, Armenia, Bulgaria and Hungary) outlined six ways in which think tanks emerged:

1 privatization of a former state research institute;
2 former colleagues in state research institutes combining to create a new institute;
3 high-profile public figure creating a new institute;
4 institute attached to a political party;
5 institute created to make a profit;
6 'spin-off' institute.

Jonathan Kimball (2000) uses a much simpler means of categorization. Think tanks, he argues, can be divided into 'universities without students' on the one hand, and advocacy organizations on the other. Overall, although there are substantial difficulties in establishing clear criteria for defining think tanks in Eastern Europe, these can best be surmounted by examining the policy research institutes within the specific national context in which operate. This allows for the peculiarities of each country's communist legacy and experience of postcommunism to be taken into account.

Think tanks in operation: comparisons across Central and Eastern Europe

Although comparative analysis can be fraught with problems, it is extremely useful in coping with the complexity of analysing think tanks in Central and Eastern Europe. Comparisons enable patterns, similarities and unique instances to be highlighted, contributing to our overall understanding of a complex phenomenon. The following analysis will take a broad view of a spectrum of countries and their think tanks, from those with dynamic and extremely highly developed institutes (Poland and Hungary) to those with a far less developed think tank sector (Albania) and also interesting cases (Russia, Bulgaria and Slovakia). Before turning to this examination, can any general patterns be detected across the region, aside from the quantitative growth in think tanks?

A few general patterns have emerged. First, although think tanks have increasingly diversified in terms of their sources of support since 1989, a reliance on Western funding is still apparent. This includes financial programmes of the EU, Western governments and independent foundations (Soros, for example). Secondly, think tanks have consolidated their internal structures and operating procedures: budgets and levels of staffing have grown gradually, and formal management structures have been put in place in most institutes. Similarly, although think tanks have diversified their activities, there is still a marked concentration on economic and business issues, and to a lesser extent social policy and aspects of the development of democracy/civil society. Outside of these general trends, there are significant variations between countries. Let us start with Russia.

The Russian case

The period since 1991 has seen a proliferation of new research centres. Alongside the old institutes from the Academy of Sciences – many of which have struggled to survive in the new political and financial climate – a bewildering variety of analytical research centres has blossomed. The funding situation has provided a substantial obstacle to the think tanks developing autonomy from particular interests, be they political or business. Political parties, banks and Russian companies have all sought out research from the new centres, which are driven by economic necessity to seek out work wherever they can. The embryonic state of the Russian political system, and the severe economic constraints within which they are working, have made it almost impossible for any centre – new or old – to function satisfactorily and autonomously.

All these factors affected the internal structures of the new research centres. In the first few years after 1991 the old communist institutes became much smaller, with a great deal more specific, short-term contract work. Even the established old institutes shrank substantially – IMEMO had its staff reduced from approximately 700 to around 300 by 1995 (Kislov, 1996) – and new centres averaged about 15–20 full-time staffers in 1996/97. This figure has grown somewhat since this time, and Russian think tanks are on average the largest in the region. The centres now cover a broad range of policy issues, as opposed to the prior functional specialization. This is in the main due to the overriding need to generate income, leading to a diversification of activities. This, in turn, has led the new centres to employ researchers on short-term contract to undertake specific projects. The new centres shifted their focus towards the use of the media to disseminate their ideas (Antonenko, 1996). However, their activities have also been shaped by the nature of postcommunist Russia. The sheer size of Russia and its federal structure have given think tanks openings for influence amongst many layers of government: national, regional and municipal. The context of their activities and their internal structures have shown radical changes from the think tanks under communism.

One of the critical features of the post-1993 period has been the relative strength of the Russian presidential administration vis-à-vis the parliament and the government. This has made access to the presidency critical to the development of channels of influence for the think tanks (Antonenko, 1996). Interestingly, the old Soviet culture and practice of personal links between political figures and researchers appear to have been reproduced quite swiftly:

> At the Presidential level all 'in-house' analytical information is prepared in the Presidential Analytical Centre and by presidential advisors. In most cases, members of the respective Presidential advisory groups were originally connected with one of the Academy of Sciences institutes (advisors were usually the directors of institutes). In their work for the Presidential Administration, official analysts therefore usually still refer to their old institutes, which have often been transformed into new centres, to provide intellectual support. (Antonenko, 1996: 4)

The arena in which they have been able to exert most influence is in the State Duma, which has the most undeveloped in-house analytical capabilities. Political parties have also used new centres extensively in their activities. In this regard, think tanks such as the Centre for Political Technologies and EpiCentre: Centre for Political and Economic Research have been very active. The domination of decision-making by the presidency, and the analytic strength of the presidential analytical centre, have tended to restrict the opportunities for think tanks to become involved in the policy-making process, especially those without the necessary personal contacts (Antonenko, 1996).

However, for those with access to the presidency, then the scope for influence is very wide. Under President Yeltsin, the Institute of State and Law (in the Russian Academy of Sciences) played a central role in advocating a decree privatizing the ownership of agricultural holdings, burying one of the key features of the Soviet communist system. This was an institute that had adapted and survived, having been a key research institute in the Soviet era. In terms of new institutes, those worthy of note are the Centre for Ethnopolitical and Regional Research (which advises the president and his administration on ethnic issues), the Fund for Efficient Politics (information and media issues) and the Institute for Strategic Analysis and Development of Entrepreneurship (business issues).

The issue of access/influence via personal contacts is the main continuity with the past. The impact of contemporary think tanks is mediated far more through the media and the corporate sector than in the past. The destruction of the party-state politico-ideological complex has removed the huge bureaucratic apparatus as the main access point into the policy-making process. Consequently, Russian think tanks began to seek influence through a wider variety of means than before, whilst working to establish themselves within the policy-making process (Bruckner, 1996: 2–3). Russia has generally seen a gradual increase in think tank activity, and this activity is generally viewed positively within the policy-making community. Russian think tanks have grown in size and diversified their activities. Many new institutes have grown up and become established since 1991, although the old institutes and the Academy of Sciences continue to play an important role. Although the dominance of the executive branch of government has in some senses restricted the avenues of influence for think tanks, the continuing importance of personal contacts and the size and complexity of federal government in Russia ensure that there are still many access points to the policy process.

Poland, Hungary and Bulgaria

Think tanks in Poland, Hungary and Bulgaria are widely viewed as the most dynamic and effective within the region. However, the reasons for this differ markedly from country to country. Poland is seen as having the most developed think tank sector in the region, mainly due to the growth of its civil society and economy since 1989. The Freedom House survey identified twelve institutes, many of which have been in operation for over ten years. The origins and operating procedures of Polish think tanks reflect some of the general trends across the region, although the existence of think tanks outside of the capital is unusual. Polish think tanks, because of their experience, have also been active in supplying training and advice to policy-makers, politicians and others in countries across the region. This, particularly in the case of the Gdansk Institute for Market Economics (GIME), is a direct result of the communist legacy. Gdansk, as the spiritual home of the Solidarity movement, has continued to exert influence in postcommunist Poland.

Polish think tanks have been created by the flight from academia, but also by the high turnover in government. The former finance minister Leszek Balcerowicz was a key player in the setting up of two institutes: the Centre for Economic and Social Research and the Foundation for Economic Education (Johnson, 1996a). The Foundation Lech Walesa Institute employs many of Walesa's former advisors from his time as president (Kimball, 2000). The existence of these personal contacts has enabled Polish think tanks to maximize their influence over the policy process. The main area of interest for Polish think tanks has been the economic/business sphere, as the Polish government has grappled with the problems of making the transition to a market economy.

A good example is GIME. This institute grew out of a group at the heart of the Solidarity movement. Created in December 1989, it had already been debating and discussing the issues of postcommunist economic transition. It has gained a reputation as the leading authority on privatization and maintained excellent access to government through personal contacts; its former president, Janusz Lewandowski, was appointed minister of privatization in 1991. GIME has gone on to exercise significant influence over government policy towards the semi-legal or 'grey' sector of the Polish economy. By 1999, it had a large budget and employed forty full-time staff (*Economic Reform Today*, 1996).

The Hungarian experience is similar to that of Poland. Freedom House identified eleven institutes in 1999. Again the focus was primarily upon economic and business matters, although security also played a prominent role. Questions of Hungary's integration into NATO and the EU have pushed think tanks into these areas. Of all countries in the region, Hungary probably exhibits the most significant degree of continuity between communist and postcommunist research institutes. In particular, many of the current institutes emerged out of the Hungarian Academy of Sciences, or former ministries within the Hungarian government (Kimball, 2000; Struyk, 1999). The close links between these institutes and the state have continued, particularly in terms of funding and contracts for their services. This has made it difficult for Hungarian think tanks to acquire Western funding, as potential donors have been uneasy about their apparent lack of independence from the state. Despite this, think tanks have been able to develop financial viability because of the maturity of the Hungarian economy. A particularly influential institute has been Agroconsult, which has provided extensive advice on land privatization and property rights for the Ministry of Agriculture and the State Privatization Agency (Struyk, 1999: 72).

The Bulgarian case provides an interesting counterpoint to the Hungarian and Polish examples. Here, the dynamism and success of the think tank community are seen as a consequence of political and economic instability, rather than of the more developed and stable economic and political systems in Poland and Hungary. Freedom House identifies sixteen functioning policy research institutes. Kimball argues that the weakness of the economy – only Albania has a less successful economy in the region – means that expertise is not lured into the business sector, and instead has remained within the think tank sector. Additionally, political instability – constant turnover of governments and personnel – has made the political system less attractive for policy specialists. The think tanks have benefited as a result, and have been able to attract significant support from Western agencies (Kimball, 2000). The most influential Bulgarian think tanks – the Centre for the Study of Democracy, the Centre for Liberal Strategies, the Institute for Market Economics and the Open Society Foundation Sofia – have developed substantial numbers of highly qualified staff, been involved in a range of different areas, and exerted significant influence on the policy process (Struyk, 1999). For example, the Centre for the Study of Democracy was asked by the Bulgarian government to draft their law on foundations, and has played a central role in developing policy on privatization in local government (*Economic Reform Today*, 1996).

Slovakia and Albania

Although there are policy research institutes in Slovakia and Albania (Freedom House identified twelve and six respectively) their effectiveness has been quite limited, although for very different reasons. This is primarily a result of economic instability and political hostility/intolerance. It is interesting to compare this with the Bulgarian case. In Albania, the ethnic conflicts, economic problems and investment scandals have seriously hampered attempts to create a viable political and economic system and posed huge barriers to those groups seeking access to the policy process. In addition, the government has passed restrictive legislation, attempting to regulate the scope of activities of NGOs within its borders. The most effective think tank in Albania has been the Albanian Centre for Economic Research, which has undertaken research on economic reform, as well as engaging in collaborative work with other institutions in Bulgaria and Hungary (Kimball, 2000).

In Slovakia, the government also passed restrictive legislation that has caused a clear divide in the think tank community: for or against the government. This has resulted in a high degree of politicization of the community. Although the legal and political framework has been less than helpful, Slovakian think tanks have been able to benefit financially. Western agencies, especially the Phare programme and the OSI, have been keen to fund Slovak think tanks in order to help the pro-reform institutes to survive and operate (Kimball, 2000).

Overall, think tank communities have grown up in every country very rapidly in the period since 1989. The levels of effectiveness, independence, influence and financial viability vary greatly from country to country depending upon a particular correlation of historical legacies and economic and political circumstances, ranging from the dynamic examples (Russia, Poland) to struggling ones (Albania). Although there are substantial obstacles to further development – most notably funding – think tanks are likely to play an increasingly significant role in the policy process in the region.

Think tanks, democratization and the crisis of the liberal elite

One of the underlying themes in much of the analysis of think tank development in Central and Eastern Europe is the overt link between democratization, marketization and think tanks. Think tanks are examined within the paradigm of the march of democracy and the market economy across the globe in the wake of the demise of communism. Thus they are held up as symbols of the growth of civil society. On another level, though, think tanks are actively promoted as generators and defenders of democracy, civic freedoms and a market economy. This view is shared by practitioners, advocates and analysts alike. For example, Grigorij Mesežnikov of the Institute for Public Affairs in Slovakia argued that, 'Between 1994–98 think tanks played an important role in preventing Slovakia from completely slipping from the path of democratic and market-oriented reforms' (Mesežnikov, 2001). It is argued that think tanks enhance pluralism in society by providing a range of alternative perspectives (Parsons, 1996), and that they contribute to the process of building and consolidating democracy.

In terms of pluralism, the Russian case is an interesting one. The growth and activities of think tanks in the Soviet period contributed to the gradual erosion of political and ideological monism, through the extension of participation outside of the party-state bureaucracy. The think tanks between 1956 and 1991 promoted the demonopolization of party-state control over the policy process. But how 'pluralist' was this? Not only were there a highly restricted number of institutions, but they operated within a fairly narrow ideological paradigm: 'reform communism'. The institutes and their staff which were drawn into a coalition with the party elite and the bureaucracy under Gorbachev represented a narrow section of opinion. They were a group of 'liberal' intellectuals, who shared a number of common attitudes: a positive view of the West, concern with humanistic and civic values, greater openness and individual autonomy, and greater emphasis upon the consumer and private initiative in the economy. In effect they were 'liberalizers' and 'Westernizers', rather than 'democratizers', preferring to graft Western civic and economic practices onto a more tolerant and participatory Soviet political system.

Demonopolization does not automatically equate to democratization. Think tanks in the Soviet system rendered it more pluralistic whilst simultaneously restricting the extent of this pluralism. There is some evidence to suggest that the hegemony enjoyed by a number of institutes after 1985 excluded voices and ideas from the policy process. What emerged was an elite of experts and intellectuals within the party and the institutes who shared a common set of norms and values, but who could not stem the tide of popular pressure for change unleashed during 1989. The think tanks in Soviet Russia did contribute to the process of democratization, but only in an indirect sense by promoting the end of the political and ideological monopolies of the CPSU and Marxism-Leninism. In the sphere of policy-making, they became forces for elitism and exclusion, marginalizing the citizenry and restricting the scope of debate. In the post-Soviet period, the old institutes and new research centres also seem to be institutionalizing these same tendencies of exclusion, elitism and expertism, as a coalition of business elites, analytical centres and key political figures emerges. The limitations on the political discourse of the transition process provided by this new coalition threatens to sustain one of the enduring divides in Russian history, between the rulers and the ruled, the elite and the masses.

Interestingly, practitioners themselves are beginning to question the democratic efficacy and reformist credentials of the think tanks in the region. Ivan Krastev (2000a: 276) argues that 'the rise of think tanks can be interpreted as a new strategy for the institutionalisation of the liberal political agenda following the electoral failures of liberal parties in the region'. His argument is that in the early 1990s the liberal political and economic agenda was steadily undermined by the problems and tensions of building viable economic and political systems. In this context think tanks have emerged as attempts by liberal intellectuals and politicians to 'preserv[e] the liberal agenda' (Krastev, 2000a: 283). This agenda – privatizing, anti-Keynesian, supply-side economics – came under pressure from popular unrest after 1992, and the rise of the think tanks was, according to Krastev, directly linked to the criticism of and opposition to the liberal programme. They became advocates of the liberal agenda, rather than independent research institutes. Additionally, the rise of the think tanks needs to be seen as part of the wider crisis of the intelligentsia in Central and Eastern Europe. The collapse of communism has created widespread antipathy and cynicism towards overarching narratives and 'grand ideologies'. Nationalism and consumerism have rushed in to fill this void. But where does this leave the intellectual as interpreter, critic and thinker? For those antithetical to the emotional appeal of nationalism, the refuge of practical policy advocacy provides an interim haven for liberal intellectuals.

Krastev's argument points to the need to locate any analysis of think tanks in the region within the political, economic and cultural context of postcommunism. Think tanks need to be interpreted within this local paradigm, before positing them as part of a global process of democratization, rational decision-making, cultural convergence or government overload. The development of think tanks in Central and Eastern Europe provides us with an intriguing window through which to view the politics and economics of a region undergoing widespread change.

Part III

Think tanks in democratic development and economic transition

9 Ming-Chen Shai with Diane Stone

The Chinese tradition of policy research institutes

The role of 'establishment intellectuals' in contemporary China's policy-making process has attracted increasing scholarly interest since the early 1980s, when the Chinese leadership initiated its programme of economic reform. In part, this interest has been stimulated by the contribution of intellectuals in Eastern Europe and the former Soviet Union to the collapse of their communist regimes in the late 1980s (see Sandle, chapter 8 in this volume). Inevitably questions have been raised as to whether a similar development is possible in China. This question has assumed more significance in China as establishment intellectuals have increasingly come to play a major role in providing political leaders with expertise and policy advice in a range of reform areas, including the 'four modernizations' that took place from the beginning of the 1980s. In other words, as a result of the changing political and economic needs of the Chinese Communist Party (CCP) and the impact of Deng Xiaoping's pragmatic leadership, Chinese establishment intellectuals have been given 'a more open intellectual environment than at any time since 1949' (Goldman, 1999: 283).

In this new political climate, many official and semi-official research institutes have been established by the Chinese government. Within these institutes, establishment intellectuals have come to occupy influential positions in the policy process, thereby highlighting the increasing regularization of that process in China (Barnett, 1985: 143). Nevertheless, these establishment intellectuals have continued to suffer from political oppression, as illustrated by the Bai Hua incident in 1981,[1] the anti-spiritual pollution campaign of 1983, the critiques of bourgeois liberalization in 1985 and 1987, and finally the tragedy of Tiananmen Square in 1989. The intellectuals' treatment at the hands of the state has tended to go through alternating cycles of 'loosening' and 'tightening', and this reflects their ambivalent role as servants and critics of the political regime.

Accordingly, this chapter addresses the roles of China's official and semi-official think tanks in Beijing's policy-making process and seeks to fill in some of the gaps in our understanding of the behaviour of Chinese think tanks, with specific reference to the political culture within which establishment intellectuals operate. It draws upon a number of interviews conducted with scholars based in Chinese and Taiwanese think tanks over the period 1998–2000.[2] The chapter is organized as follows. The next section explores the historical role of China's establishment intellectuals since 1949. The third section outlines the relationship between individual advisers and the state, and some of the main policy research institutions that they occupy. The following section argues that the activities of 'establishment intellectuals' are heavily constrained in Beijing's policy process and are likely to remain so in the foreseeable future despite increasing opportunities for intellectual exchange, public debate and policy input.

Political culture and the role of think tanks

There is a fundamental difference between the communist and non-communist worlds. In the Anglo-American context, think tanks play a recognized role as civil society actors in educating the community and contributing to public debate (Dror, 1984; McGann and Weaver, 2000; Stone, 1996b: 16). By contrast, this chapter argues that the majority of Chinese think tanks maintain close patron–client relations with certain political leaders and operate within a closed policy context that is distant from civil society. Consequently, these institutes tend to filter and exclude voices and ideas from the policy process and to contain public debate.

Early studies of think tanks focused mainly on Western societies and paid little attention to the role of think tanks in Communist regimes in general and China in particular. Viewed through the lens of Western analysis, think tank development in China can lead to erroneous assumptions. With the changing needs of state and society, some Western scholars took it for granted that newly emerging think tanks in China after 1980 represented the (belated) emergence of China's civil society. Moreover, they argued that because think tanks provide alternative advice and analysis, this would assist political pluralization (Brook, 1997; Goldman, 1999). The problem here is that Western scholars have tended to overlook the harsh political realities in mainland China and are too sanguine about the emergence and power of civil society.

The place of China's think tanks in policy-making represents more an organizational means for the party-state either to maintain ideological hegemony or to consolidate the vested interests and strengthen the political positions of political leaders during internal power struggles. In other words, the growth of think tanks is the product of deliberate decisions by the party-state machine – that is, by the party cadres, who are also state bureaucrats. In short, Chinese think tanks (official or semi-official) cannot be regarded as 'independent' research institutes to the same degree as their Western counterparts. Instead, the political connections of establishment scholars to their political patrons shape the role of think tanks in the policy process. The emergence of a few Western-style think tanks does not undermine the centrality of the official institutes. In the main, think tank scholars have no intention of challenging and replacing the regime, but want to maintain the existing structures of political authority by persuading the state to change itself and thus help the political leadership to overcome its difficulties. The characteristic attitudes of think tanks towards the state result in a very strong 'statization of society' which suppresses civil society. Before exploring further the role of China's think tanks in policy-making, it is necessary to explain briefly the different roles and characteristics of think tanks in Western and Asian societies.

Most members of think tanks in Asian societies see their organizations as (necessarily) politically dependent. To a large extent, their perceptions of state and society are influenced by the broader cultural and historical context, whereby think tanks play an active role in providing the government with policy suggestions but do not (or should not) challenge the prevailing ideological values. In contrast to think tanks in Western societies, those in, say, Malaysia and Japan are less able to resist the intervention of the state's administrative power (see Ueno and Khoo, chapters 10 and 11 in this volume). Similarly, in Singapore there has been critical debate about the lack of independence of key research institutes as mouthpieces of the government and the 'revolving door' between think tanks and senior government figures (Jayasuriya, 1994; Wong, 1995).

In the case of Taiwan, whose political tradition and culture are similar to those of China, think tanks are not independent from the supervision of the former ruling party (the KMT), with the notable exception of the Academia Sinica. Other think tanks, such as the Institute of International Relations (IIR), which is affiliated to National Zhengzhi (Chengchi) University, the Taiwan Institute of Economic Research (TIER) and the Institute for National Policy Research (INPR), have strong political connections with individual government leaders. In this political climate, policy research institutes serve as ideological articulators, defending the policy conducted by government under the guise of academic freedom. For example, the INPR is categorized as a non-governmental research institution (INPR, 1998: 1). However, as became evident during interviews, the solidity of the relationship between political leaders, such as Lee Teng-hui (former president of the Republic of China), and the president of INPR, Hung-Mao Tien, cannot be underestimated when analysing the role of INPR in the policy-making process. As interviews confirmed, the influence of Taiwanese think tanks depends on the personal connections of their presidents or directors with political leaders, and the willingness of most researchers to be recruited by the ruling party (the KMT) to high-ranking official positions.

Thus, it is difficult for think tanks in East Asian societies to maintain their academic independence and intellectual autonomy. Not only do political leaders have different expectations of researchers, but researchers generally hold different goals and beliefs to their Western counterparts. Certainly, the domination of society by the state in East Asia has placed major obstacles in the way of encouraging research institutes to provide independent policy suggestions. Accordingly, compared with think tanks in Western societies, research institutes in China can be called 'think tanks' only in a much looser sense. China's think tanks are both instruments for political leaders, to help them legitimate their political position, and analytical bodies whose role is to formulate better solutions when dealing with increasingly complex political problems.

Chinese think tanks can be classified as follows: official, semi-official and privately owned. In reality, the boundary between official and semi-official think tanks is blurred. First, all the institutes affiliated with government, military and the propaganda system are classified as 'official research institutes'. These institutes are in a vertical bureaucratic relationship with their official sponsoring agency; a phenomenon better known as 'stove-piping' by American scholars (or 'silos' in British parlance), where horizontal co-ordination of policy research is weak and research products are transferred upwards, not downwards (Glaser and Saunders, 2002: 600).

Secondly, this chapter has classified university institutes as 'semi-official think tanks' because to a large extent they are close to and mainly supported by governmental organizations. Finally, since the end of the 1980s, a handful of private think tanks have emerged (examples include the Asia Institute (AI) and the China Development Institute (CDI). Nevertheless, in some respects these privately owned research institutes should be viewed as semi-official think tanks, because the directors or some members have official backgrounds and use their personal connections within the bureaucratic systems. Wang Daohan, the chairman of the Association for Relations Across the Taiwan Straits (ARATS), is also the honorary head of the AI and the Center of International Studies Shanghai Municipality (CISM). To view the AI as functioning as a privately owned think tank can be misleading. The interlocking memberships and directorates blur the private and public distinction and reiterate the dominance of the state.

Although the chapter appendix is not comprehensive, it conveys the scale of the Chinese think tank sector and accurately reflects the fact that most of the organizations are located in Beijing, near to the centre of power. Not listed here are the increasing number of locally based Chinese think tanks. For instance, Shanghai has a thriving think tank community but, once again, the majority are state sponsored and Shanghai's mayors have used them to assist in planning for this rapidly industrializing city (Wu, 1994). However, neither distance from the centre nor market-driven reform processes have provided fertile conditions for institutes to put down roots in civil society. The reintegration of Hong Kong has not brought many private think tanks into China. Furthermore, despite Hong Kong's being one of the most 'Westernized' regions of China, 'think tank practice and the concept of a non-government policy community has yet to take root' there (Chin, 2000: 51). Consequently, while Chinese think tanks undertake some functions similar to those of Western ones, the Chinese institutes lack the legal trappings of independence, and the financial autonomy to develop their own research agendas and operate in a political culture that limits dissent and freedom of expression. In other words, rather than being societally generated, Chinese think tanks are a product of the state.

Establishment intellectuals and the Chinese state

Traditionally, intellectuals in China have been seen as official scholars who are members of the government bureaucracy. Peter Ferdinand (1991: 10) argues that the literati of the old empire shaped the formation of the imperial bureaucracy. Accordingly, this chapter argues that due to a long cultural tradition based on the unity of ruling and teaching (*zheng jiao he yi*), relatively few Chinese intellectuals can be viewed as intellectuals who are willing to criticize the existing political regime.

Peter Moody (1977) argues that there is a clear distinction between establishment and non-establishment intellectuals. Similarly, Merle Goldman (1981) claims that a 'sense of responsibility' is the hallmark of those scholars belonging to the category of 'establishment intellectuals'. Drawing on Goldman's concept, Bonnic and Chevrier (1991) argue that 'establishment intellectuals' are those scholars singled out by political leaders in order to shape the legitimacy of political authority. For the purpose of this chapter, we define Chinese 'establishment intellectuals' as follows:

1 They are intellectuals serving and operating within governing institutions such as official and semi-official think tanks or universities.
2 They are experts, generally well educated, specializing in political and economic issues serving the ruling party's interests.
3 They play a crucial role in policy-making by providing leaders with policy suggestions through informal channels.
4 They seek to join official associations or to be recruited into the bureaucracy, which leads them to play an ambivalent role as both servants of the regime and critics of society.

Under the 'party-state' structure, establishment intellectuals depend on the political regime to protect their interests and therefore cannot be seen as civil society actors reinforcing and protecting public and private interests or mediating the intervention of the state in social affairs.

It is only since the late 1970s that intellectuals and policy research institutes have developed as institutional entities within the bureaucracy. Earlier, under Mao Zedong's regime, the impact of first-generation think tanks on either domestic or foreign policy was very limited. The style of policy-making was highly personalized because political power was concentrated in the hands of a few top CCP leaders under the command of Mao. This was especially true during the Cultural Revolution, when the policy-making process was dominated by the leader's ideological considerations, which led to an ill-institutionalized policy process. This is exhibited in the case of the China Institute of International Studies (CIIS), which was dormant from 1967 and only reactivated in 1979 (Cheung, 1987: 96).

One consequence of the Cultural Revolution was the 'absence of a generation of scholars' arising from 'a ten year alienation from educational training and isolation from the international intellectual community' (Muta and Noda, 1995: 350). This trend was not reversed until Deng Xiaoping reached the pinnacle of the power structure in 1978. Chinese leaders began to re-evaluate the abilities of professionals and specialists and placed particular emphasis on the establishment of think tanks in order to facilitate the progress of the 'four modernizations' (of agriculture, industry, science and technology, and the military) proposed by Deng Xiaoping. In this regard, Deng differed from his predecessors by trying to enhance inner-party discussion by allowing experts or scholars to express their opinions freely on controversial issues. Deng attempted to establish a systematic and professional policy formulation process in order to help legitimate his personal authority (Nelson, 1984: 6). Today, this personal high-level patronage of expertise appears to have been continued under the premiership of Zhu Rongji (Tanner, 2002).

Both Hu Yaobang and Zhao Ziyang (former general secretary of the CCP and a protégé of Deng Xiaoping) supported Deng's policy towards intellectuals and helped legitimize the perspective that experts could help solve the economic and social problems resulting from the reform programme. Establishing numerous research centres or 'think tanks' under the State Council, Zhao Ziyang understood that building a system of technocracy would play an important role in tackling both economic and political problems, and that the Chinese political system would be pushed forward in a more institutionalized manner. Reflecting on these departures in policy, one think tank scholar identifies three developments that enhanced the position of intellectuals and second-generation think tanks:

First, to meet the needs of the reform and open door policy, and the increasing demands of information, China must both understand the external world and strengthen the study of its domestic situation ... Second, the proposition advanced by Deng Xiaoping that 'intellectuals are one part of the working class', has won nation wide support, ... third, 'democratization and scientification of decision-making' has been advocated by the central government and has further pushed forward the development of academic research work. (Luo, 1991: 75)

To implement the 'four modernizations', Chinese leaders saw the necessity of reducing the emphasis on ideology and class struggle in order to improve professionalism within government. This was exemplified by Zhao Ziyang's proposal of separating the party from the government at the Thirteenth Party Congress in 1987. Zhao attempted to build the professional and technocratic bureaucracy to deal with the domestic and foreign issues confronted by leaders after the economic reform. Although Zhao was defeated by the conservative factions who rejected his proposal, arguing the necessity for party control over the government, the trend of recruiting experts into research institutes to improve the quality of policies was retained as a fundamental element of the 'four modernizations'. Many research institutes abolished by leaders during the Mao era were allowed to reopen, while new institutes have been established.

Acknowledging the shortage of trained personnel, the CCP began to recruit intellectuals into the party organization and the state bureaucracy at both local and central government levels. Several research centres were established during Zhao Ziyang's tenure as premier. These included the Economic Research Center (ERC), the Technical Economic Research Center (TERC) (later the Economic, Technical and Social Development Research Center (ETSDRC), the Development Research Center (DRC) and the China Center for International Studies (CCIS).

The CCIS was established in 1982 to provide policy suggestions on international affairs and domestic political and economic development. Its director, Huan Xiang (now deceased), had strong personal ties with key political leaders, including Deng Xiaoping and Zhao Ziyang. The DRC was established in 1980 as the main research unit under Zhao Ziyang and headed by Ma Hong, an economic specialist and personal advisor of Zhao. However, both the CCIS and DRC have lost influence as a result of both leadership changes and the broader political climate since the Tiananmen Square tragedy of 1989. In this regard, both political culture and personal connections determine whether research centers are influential or not. The implications are that 'the centers' authority has not and probably will not soon become highly institutionalized' (Halpern, 1992: 131). Indeed, 'gaining influence with Zhu Rongji is still the most important way to affect policy' (Naughton, 2002: 626).

An institute's influence largely depends upon the role and personal authority of its president or director. Most directors are retired military officers and diplomats. Some think tanks are units within several important government agencies (*xi tong*), such as the Ministry of Foreign Affairs, the General Staff Headquarters and General Political Department under the People's Liberation Army (PLA), and the Taiwan Affairs Office and State Council (Swaine, 1996). They influence decision-makers significantly because the directors or presidents have personal ties of *guanxi* (social connection) that have aided their career development.

Establishment intellectuals are appointed by top leaders to important positions in the bureaucratic process and enjoy regular communication with the leadership through both formal and informal channels. For example, establishment intellectuals can provide policy advice through personal meetings with leaders. As one interviewee noted, they may also be called upon by party leaders to attend special and secret groups to offer new ideas and analysis. 'Chinese leaders usually form informal research groups or 'private advisory groups' through their affiliations with educational institutions ... The recommendations of these groups are usually more influential than the ones brought up by formal bodies such as government think tanks' (Muta and Noda, 1995: 351; see also Naughton, 2002: 631).

In general, think tanks benefited from the reforms to education policy (such as overseas study) in mainland China after 1979, which helped propel the technocratic era of policy planning. The contemporary party elite emphasized the importance of education as the path towards the goal of fostering economic modernization. This had positive implications for research institutes, their staff recruitment, and more consistent and sophisticated input into Beijing's policy process. Chinese students have been encouraged and sponsored by the government to go abroad to study. Some of these intellectuals began to introduce Western economic and political theory into China. Many of these Chinese students are from China's research institutes (such as the Chinese Academy of Social Science (CASS)) and often return to their original post.

Think tanks and the policy process in China

Although China's political system has shown tendencies towards increasing professionalization and institutionalization of policy-making, it remains a relatively closed society dominated by a few political leaders. The force of patronage and social connections remains strong. Indeed, the policy functions of think tanks are shaped by the implicit reciprocal relationship of mutual interest between intellectuals and political leaders. This chapter argues that there are four specific roles played by think tanks in Beijing's policy processes: (1) information filters; (2) policy defenders;

The Chinese tradition

(3) introducers of new ideas; and (4) interlocutors with foreign interests. These roles provide little scope for the engagement of Chinese civil society with the state.

Information filters

Think tanks are information filters in the sense that their members provide leaders with analysis based on the filtering of abundant raw data from either the news organizations, such as the *People's Daily* and *Xinhua* agency, or world-wide intelligence systems. In so doing, they provide political leaders with an invaluable pool of processed information. To a large extent, political actors are unable to gain access to comprehensive information from society at large and are unable to grapple with social and economic problems without the advice, recommendations and expertise of specialists. Therefore, the function of think tanks as information filters is to conduct the preliminary task of removing repetitive or substandard information in order to shortlist essential reference materials on aspects of either international or domestic affairs for political leaders. In practice, political leaders often limit themselves to the options filtered by think tanks.

The main challenge facing research fellows in China's official and semi-official think tanks is to decide how to process information and research materials. Because many intellectuals regard themselves as channels through which the leaders are exposed to complaints from society, in deciding how to process information, scholars do have some power in shaping agendas and how problems are perceived. In other words, the information-filter function of think tanks is extremely important in problem definition. However, this does not mean that intellectuals challenge the leaders' own political status and power. Moreover, think tanks play a crucial role in providing suggestions or research results *after* top leaders or the directors of research centres have set the agenda. In this way, think tanks help decision-makers to clarify the various societal interests involved in complex problems.

Policy defenders

The vast majority of Western think tanks are independent of their governments even if they have strong connections with key political actors such as political parties. In China, however, think tank analysis serves to justify the policies of political leaders and legitimate their official positions. Thus, think tanks tend to become policy defenders for the regime and legitimate prevailing values and ideologies (see also Muta and Noda, 1995: 354). For example, Liu Zhifeng (1996), a member of CASS, argues that China should develop its own democracy according to Chinese characteristics, and believes that Western ideas concerning popular elections and competitive party systems are not appropriate in China. In a similar vein, Xu (1996: 112) noted that 'when there is a big problem about people's starvation, anyone who has a sense of social responsibility and righteousness should co-operate with the ruling party in order to solve this problem'. Or as Zhao (1996: 107) puts it, 'a scholar who is allowed to discuss foreign policy issues in public is expected to explain and justify the official line'. Accordingly, think tanks function in an essentially task-oriented manner rather than as critical agents.

Being policy defenders also means that experts and scholars are regarded as the instrument of their political patrons, acting to legitimate the incumbent's political position and oppose his political rivals. For example, during the political conflict between Hua Guofeng's relatively orthodox 'whatever faction' and the more pragmatic 'practice faction' of Deng Xiaoping in 1978,[3] Hu Yaobang realized that in order to defeat the remaining Maoists of the 'whatever' faction, he had to seek the assistance of intellectuals to help justify the new pragmatic line and legitimate Deng's leadership. Hu invited many intellectual leaders to participate in this political struggle to defend Deng and his pragmatic policies. It appears that the CCP still controls the activities of these experts in terms of their ideology and loyalty. While the autonomy of Chinese experts has expanded since the establishment of China's open door policy, 'it is still intermittent and conditional' (Goldman and Cheek, 1987: 19). As a result, acting as a policy defender is a politically expedient strategy for think tanks or influential scholars to preserve their own social interests and political privileges. As indicated in some interviews, advocacy of policy ideas out of line with the personal interests and values of leaders can lead to a loss of social status and position for intellectuals. The members of think tanks are thus forced to recognize the limits in terms of the official line set by leaders if they wish to participate in the policy-making process. The relations between leaders and think tanks are based on a kind of instrumental orientation in which both leaders and intellectuals acknowledge the reciprocal benefits between them.

Introducers of new ideas

Although political leaders set the political framework within which members of think tanks and scholars offer advice, experts and specialists do raise some important Western ideas; for example, ideas concerning checks and balances and the separation of the party and the state (see Luo, 1991), or foreign practices in public security and professionalized crime fighting (see Tanner, 2002). However, it can be difficult for scholars and think tanks to strike a balance between their policy-analysis interests in innovation and their policy-defender responsibilities.

The Chinese tradition

Chinese think tanks can be relatively autonomous within the state bureaucracy when the government wants them to be. For example, during the period of political reform under Zhao Ziyang, there were some scholars who were responsible for providing theoretical recommendations and for co-ordinating various opinions made by panels affiliated with the office of the Central Discussion Group for Reform of the Political Structure (Wu, 1997). These intellectuals persuaded Zhao to draw up a draft scheme or blueprint for political reform. Internal party dialogue was viewed by reformists as a strategy to open up the political system in which bureaucrats at all levels could become more responsive to popular opinion and tip the balance towards political reform. Zhao Ziyang and his personal advisors believed that only through dialogue could China become an open society under the rule of a reformed Communist Party. Reputedly, this was opposed by anti-reform elements in the CCP leadership. Nevertheless, at the 1987 Party Congress, Zhao adopted this principle as CCP's official policy.

While intellectuals rarely challenge the principles of government policy in public, they can use their expertise to affect the content of policy slightly and even to influence the perceptions of political actors indirectly. For example, some Chinese experts specializing in the Taiwan issue have discussed – *unofficially* – the possibility and applicability of a 'confederation of great China'. These analysts have argued that the idea of 'confederalism' (*bang lian zhi*) offers a better way to solve the Taiwan issue than the formula of 'one country, two systems'.

To some degree, this role qualifies the earlier argument that due to the influence of situation-oriented and cultural norms, establishment intellectuals have little courage or desire to challenge the policy ideas of top leaders. Yet they can express their own ideas provided they have the political patronage of a leader with similar policy beliefs or a willingness to engage with new thinking. For example, Peng Ming, the chairman of the United Association for China's Development, claims that many high-ranking military officials and even Wang Daohan, the chairman of ARATS, do not reject the idea of 'con-federalism'(*China Times*, 16 September 1998: 2). In this case of CCP policy towards Taiwan, some researchers can introduce new ideas which deviate slightly from the official line and alter the policy agenda because they have close links with specific political leaders (*hou tai*). While this chapter contends that think tanks are the means used by political actors to transmit the ruling ideology to the people or to contest the policy positions of their political enemies, on occasion think tanks should also be regarded as careful and circumspect introducers of new ideas.

Interlocutors

A more recent development has been the involvement of think tanks in convening meetings with foreign counterparts and hosting delegations. Such meetings have been instrumental in providing Chinese policy elites with some insight into the perceptions and intentions of foreign powers. At the same time, these dialogues are also regarded as a means to influence foreign perspectives on Beijing's policies and as private fora to express objections to other countries' policies, such as US arms sales to Taiwan. In other words, in addition to gathering information from foreigners through participation in international conferences or more long-standing dialogues with foreign researchers, some institutes have become involved in Track II diplomacy (Glaser and Saunders, 2002: 606; Gill and Mulvenon, 2002: 622). With the presence of Chinese government officials, institute meetings are a mechanism to transmit particular policy messages, while for foreigners these meetings are invaluable for insight into the nuances of Chinese policy.

Conclusion

With rapid and dramatic changes in world politics, Chinese researchers are presented with a wider range of opportunities to provide their expertise to leaders. Although they are still unable to challenge the political tune set by leaders, their perception of Western political and economic paradigms will to some extent affect new Chinese leaders' views about the development of political and economic reforms in mainland China. Although some Chinese scholars have questioned the introduction of Western theory and policy perspectives since the Tiananmen incident in 1989, these researchers understand that China has to be aware of the issues happening around the world. In so doing, they argue that it is necessary to understand the market economy in the capitalist system before criticizing it.

Especially by comparison with the era of 'better to be on the left than to be on the right' from the early 1960s to the end of 1970s, Chinese establishment intellectuals working for research institutes have more opportunities than ever before to make contact with the outside world. Many Chinese students have gone abroad to study, especially to the United States. Since the 1980s, China's think tanks have increased their academic contacts with their Western counterparts by exchanging perspectives and ideas with experts abroad. Because many mainland scholars are eager to communicate with the outside world or are in some cases educated in the West, they tend to acknowledge the values of Western theory in terms of democratic politics and the market economy.

The Chinese tradition

This raises a number of issues for the future. Are they likely to reconsider their own roles in the Chinese decision-making system on the grounds that they are disappointed with the constraints they face? If so, will researchers working for either official or semi-official think tanks seek more intellectual autonomy, thus threatening to weaken the control exercised by the political regime? It remains the case that the political control of the party-state remains pervasive and sets clear parameters for the autonomy of Chinese establishment intellectuals in think tanks. However, there are some indications of a changing political culture and strengthening public sphere in which some intellectuals are willing to challenge political authority or provide redefinitions of collective interests.

New trends are evident among a nascent third generation of think tanks (Glaser and Saunders, 2002: 600–4). More independent bodies are emerging and a significant number of scholars are more inclined to seek a public profile for themselves or their institute via the media. Chinese broadcasters are more open, while an increasingly commercialized publishing industry has provided both new outlets for policy analysis beyond the research institute system and a source of income. More horizontal interaction between institutes is occurring as 'associations' emerge to bring together experts with overlapping interests, or when a foreign institute co-ordinates joint research among Chinese institutes. In general, increased interaction with foreign scholars since the 1980s has helped widen research agendas and analytical perspectives. Younger scholars educated in the West can be more open-minded, less concerned with preserving bureaucratic norms, and more interested in making internationally recognized contributions to their academic discipline. Sociopolitical connections of *guanxi* still shape possibilities for influence, but some Chinese analysts are also building reputations on merit and, on occasion, their books attract the attention of top leaders. While decision-making processes are highly personalized, at the same time there are strong pressures towards institutionalization and professionalization, not only in the research institute sector but more generally throughout the society and economy, as China becomes more integrated into the world economy. These factors in combination promote greater openness in Chinese policy processes, but do not necessarily translate into better scholarship or improved decision-making.

Notes

1 Bai Hua wrote a film script, *Bitter Love*, to criticize Maoist policies during the Cultural Revolution implicitly. This film was viewed by the party leaders, including Deng Xiaoping, as an attack on themselves because they implemented Mao's policies. In order to denounce the trend of 'bourgeois

liberalism' in theoretical and artistic circles, encouraged by Hu Yaobang, Deng launched a campaign against Bai Hua and other writers in 1981.
2 Twenty-six people were interviewed by Ming-Chen Shai. They were in either China or Taiwan and specialized in the affairs of the Taiwan Straits. Those interviewed did not want their identities revealed.
3 The 'two whatevers" refers to the statement that 'we will resolutely uphold whatever policy decisions Chairman Mao made, and unswervingly follow whatever instructions Chairman Mao gave'. See *Renmin Ribao* (*People's Daily*), 7 February 1977, 'Study the Documents Well and Grasp the Key Link'. Deng Xiaoping upheld two slogans, 'seeking the truth from facts' and 'practice is the sole criterion of truth', to legitimate his 'practice faction'.

Appendix: major research institutes in China

Think tank	Leading scholars	Research interests	Type of institute and periodicals	Date established and location
Asia Institute (AI)	Wang Daohan, Chen Qiwei, Tian Zhongqing, Lu Guoliang, Guan Li	Collecting and analysing, information on politics, economics and social development in Asia-Pacific countries China's economic development	Privately owned institute	1988 Shanghai
Asian Economic Research Institute (AERI)	Pan Hongxuan, Yao Weng-gang, Qiu Yijuan, Cao Guoqi, Zhao Xiaolei, Cui Xiejun, Xiong Shiping, Hu Yonggang, Huang Wenzhuo, Zuo Dongping	Development of countries in Asia China	Academic Shanghai University of Finance and Economics *Financial and Economic News Daily*	1993 Shanghai
Center for American Studies (CAS)	Ni Shixiong	Sino-US relations and Taiwan issues	Academic Fudan University	1985 Shanghai
Center for Cross-Straits Cultural and Economic Exchanges (CCSCEE)	Unknown	Unknown	Should be regarded as a branch of the Ministry of State Security	unknown Beijing

Think tank	Leading scholars	Research interests	Type of institute and periodicals	Date established and location
Center for Economic Research (CER)	Lin Yifu	China's economic reform Modern economic theory	Academic Beijing University	1994 Beijing
Center for Peace and Development Studies (CPDS)	Xin Qi, Bao Lixian, Zhao Llanqi	Strategy analysis and intelligence regarding Taiwan, Hong Kong, and Macao (especially in Taiwan affairs)	General Political Department	Unknown
Center of International Studies Shanghai Municipality (CISM)	Wang Daohan, Pan Guang, Huang Renwei, Li Yihai, Cai Zhiyun	Asia-Pacific	Government (under the SASS since 1988)	1985 Shanghai
Center of Taiwan Studies (CTS)	Yan Jin, Zhao Jianming, Wang Jinzhao, Zhang Nianchi	Taiwan's economic development, political situation, and relations across Taiwan Straits	Branch of Institute of Asian-Pacific Studies	1990 Shanghai
China Center for International Studies (CCIS)	Huan Xiang, Li Luye, Zhan Shiliang, Shi Chunlai, Cheng Ruisheng	International affairs (Asia-Pacific, US, Japan and Russia) Politics, economy and security	Government (State Council) CCIS *International Review*	1982 Beijing

Institute	People	Topics	Type	Founded / Location
China Development Institute (CDI)	Li Luoli, Tang Jie, Guo Wanda, Liu Luye, Feng Subao, Sun Hao, Long Long, Guo Jianbo	International/domestic economic development Investment/economic ties across Taiwan Straits	Privately owned institute (in effect, very close relations with government (State Council))	1989 ShenZhen (Guangdong Province)
China Institute for Economic Reform (CIER)	Chen Yizi	Economic development in China (society, politics)	Government *China Development and Reform*	1984 Beijing
China Institute of Contemporary International Relations (CICIR)	Shen Qurong, Xu Dan, Lu Zhongwei, Song Baoxian	International economic and current strategic issues, domestic economic development Japan, US, Asia-Pacific	Government (State Council) *Contemporary International Relations*	1960 (regained its full strength in 1980) Beijing
China Institute of International Studies (CIIS)	Yang Chengxu, Qu Bode, Xhou Xingbao, Xing Hua	World economic situation Interrelations among major world powers	Government	1956 (rebuilt its staff and re-established itself as a leading policy research institution in 1979) Beijing

Think tank	Leading scholars	Research interests	Type of institute and periodicals	Date established and location
Chinese Academy of Social Science (CASS)	Hu Shen, Wang Renzhi, Liu Ji	Thirty-two research institutes Economics, social and political development, international relations and legal issues	Government	1977 Beijing
Chinese People's Institute for Foreign Affairs (CPIFA)	Liu Shuqing, Ma Xusheng, Zhang Wenpu, Xia Daosheng	Carrying out people-to-people diplomacy	Government (Foreign Ministry) *Foreign Affairs Journal*	1949 (suggested by Zhou Enlai) Beijing
College of International Relations (CIR)	Wang Zaixi	Most students graduating from CIR will be assigned to CICIR	Under the control of CCP *International Affairs Study Journal*	1978 (reopened) Beijing
Development Research Centre (DRC)	Wang Huijiong, Ma Hong	Policy consultation for government	Government (State Council)	1980 Beijing

Institution	Leader(s)	Research Focus	Affiliation / Journal	Year	Location
Economic, Technical and Social Development Research Center (ETSDRC)	Ma Hong	Technical economics, monetary and fiscal policy, economic development, current economic situation and pricing problems	Government (State Council)	1985	Beijing
Energy Research Institute (ERI)	Zhou Fengqi, Zhou Dadi, Han Wenke, Hu Xiumin	Comprehensive research on China's energy situation	Government (State Planning Commission) *Energy Information News*	1980	Beijing
Environment Strategy Center (ESC)	Qu Geping	Environmental strategy Population growth	Government (National Environmental Planning Agency)	1987	Beijing
Institute of American Studies (IAS)	Wang Jisi, Tao Wenzhao, Li Mingde	American studies Sino–US relations	Affiliated to CASS *Quarterly Journal of American Studies*	1981	Beijing
Institute of Asia-Pacific Studies (IAPS)	Zhang Yunling	Politics, economy, foreign relations, societies and culture in Asia-Pacific South Asia, American studies and US–Asia-Pacific relations	Affiliated to CASS *Contemporary Asia-Pacific Studies*	1988	Beijing
Institute of Asian-Pacific Studies (IAPS)	Zhou Jianming, Wang Shaopu	Asian-Pacific Japan, Korea Southeast Asia	Under SASS *Asian-Pacific Forum*	1990	Shanghai

Think tank	Leading scholars	Research interests	Type of institute and periodicals	Date established and location
Institute of Industrial Economics (IIE)	Zhou Shulian	Research on all aspects of the industrial economy	Affiliated to CASS *Economic Management*	1978 Beijing
Institute of International Relations (IIR)	Yuan Ming, Liu Jinshi, Chen Lemin, Zi Zhongyun	China, former Soviet Union, US China's relations with its East Asian neighbours	Academic Beijing University	1985 Beijing
Institute of Russian and East European Studies (IREES)	Xu Kui	Analysing developments in former Soviet-bloc states of Europe	Government *Journal of Russian and East European Problems*	1964 Beijing
Institute of Taiwan Studies (ITS)	Xu Shiquan	Taiwan affairs in terms of economic, political and social issues Programme of 'Peaceful Unification'	Affiliated to CASS *Taiwan Studies*	1984 Beijing
Institute of Taiwan Studies (ITS)	Mao Jiaqi, Cai Zhiqing	Taiwan's politics and economy, and relations between both sides	Academic Nanjing University	1991 Nanjing

Institute	Key People	Focus	Affiliation	Year/Location
Institute of Tech-Economics (ITE)	He Shigeng	Offers comprehensive studies of tech-economic options to government	Government (State Planning Commission) *Techno-Economic Research*	1981 Beijing
Institute of World Economics and Politics (IWEP)	Zhu Li, Ye Guang	World politics and economics	Affiliated to CASS *World Economy*	1979 (two institutes merged to form the joint institute) Beijing
Institute of World Economy (IWE)	Wu Yikang, Wang Yueyang, Zhang Youwen	World economics and politics	Under SASS *Research of World Economics*	1978 Shanghai
International Studies Research Centre (ISRC)	Huan Xiang, Guo Zhengyuan	International studies Economic issues	Government (State Council)	1984 Beijing
Research Center of Taiwan, Hong Kong and Macao	Huang Jiashu	Analysis of negotiation across Taiwan Straits	Academic People's University	1993 Beijing
Shanghai Academy of Social Science (SASS)	Yan Jin	Social science Sixteen research centers appointed by government as national bases for studying Deng Xiaoping Theory	Government Close to Shanghai government Close to CCIS in Beijing	1958 (fully re-established after 1978) Shanghai

Think tank	Leading scholars	Research interests	Type of institute and periodicals	Date established and location
Shanghai Institute for International Studies (SIIS)	Yu Xintian, Yang Jiemian, Wu Jinan, Zhang Zuqian, Zhao Huasheng	Current international affairs Particular interests in Asia-Pacific, Europe, US, Japan	Government (Foreign Ministry) *SIIS Journal*	1960 (suggested by Zhou Enlai) Shanghai
Taiwan Research	Xu Bodong	Taiwan's economic development, political issues, and relations across Taiwan Straits	Academic Beijing Lianhe University	2000 (and earlier informally) Beijing
Taiwan Research Institute (TRI)	Fan Xizhou, Li Jing, Han Qinghai, Liu Guosheng, Li qiang, Li Fe	Taiwan's economics, politics, history and literature Relations across Taiwan Straits	Academic Xiamen University *Taiwan Research Quarterly*	1980 Xiamen

Sources: Shambaugh, 1987; JCIE, 2000; Muta and Noda, 1995; Guo Ruihua, 1996; www.asian-affairs.com/Frame/framethinktanks.html; www.iceg.org/iceg_mi_nosub_detail; www.pku.edu.cn
[a] According to David Shambaugh, CIISS has no real office to support research staff. Indeed, 'the institute is often referred to by Chinese as *xuehui* (association)', denoting a more informal organization'. See Shambaugh, 1987: 298.

10 Makiko Ueno

Think tanks in Japan: a new alternative

Since September 11 2001, the governments of the world have faced tremendous challenges in dealing with the consequences of terrorism and the US war against it. The attacks on the World Trade Center and the Pentagon have sparked passionate debate around the world about redefining the concepts of national security and individual freedom, the values of democracy, state–society relations and global economic growth. At this critical time, Japan faces its own intractable problems: dramatic demographic change, huge public debt, and an economy that has been in stagnation for almost a decade. With an ever-falling fertility rate, the total population is projected to decrease after a peak of 127 million in 2006, and the population of those 65 and older will reach almost 29 per cent by 2025 and 36 per cent by 2050. In early 2002, Japan's public debt amounted to 130 per cent of GDP – one of the highest rates recently experienced in the industrialized world (Oshio, 2002). As the world's second largest economy, Japan's GDP is 532 trillion yen, about half that of the United States. Since the early 1990s, the average growth rate of the GDP has been 1.5 per cent. Japan's economy has been shrinking and is now showing a hint of deflation.

These are deep-seated problems that require broad intellectual efforts to solve. Strong policy-making capacity is a must for a country wrestling with this high level of policy challenge. Currently, however, Japan seems incapable of resolving these problems effectively. One of the nation's handicaps in this regard is its lack of the kind of think tanks that might provide policy solutions. Moreover, the think tank-like institutions that do exist in Japan are now receding, due to financial constraints, at a time when Japan needs genuine think tanks more than ever.

When Asia's financial crisis hit in the late 1990s, some Western economists considered that it was a temporary blip, because Asian countries have enormous market potential due to large pools of skilled labour and strong consumer power. Others saw the crisis as a longer-term problem that was brought on by failures in financial policies, reflecting a deeper malaise in societies that lack political transparency and Western-style democracy. Among Americans, the general understanding is that a market economy and political democratization together propel a healthy nation, like two wheels of a vehicle. Though far from perfect, it is claimed that a market democracy is the only system to offer the kind of dynamism and flexibility that societies need to flourish in the twenty-first century.

Below I revisit the subject of Japanese think tanks and democracy. Based on my chapter in *Think tanks across nations* and supplemented by work done by myself and other scholars (Ueno, 1993, 2000; Suzuki and Ueno, 1993; Struyk, 1999), this chapter discusses the shortcomings of Japan's think tanks and the country's version of democracy. The idea of creating an independent think tank in Japan is further from being realized today than it was just a few years ago, even though Japan needs such an institution now more than ever. Nevertheless, I still hold out hope for improvements in Japan's policy-making capabilities. Specifically, I argue that democratizing the national budgetary process – which could be helped along by a think tank devoted to this endeavour – could be a critical breakthrough for Japanese democracy.

A brief history of think tanks in Japan

If we define a think tank as a non-profit institution outside of government that generates policy analysis and alternatives on domestic and international issues based on serious policy research in order to serve citizens and policy-makers, there are almost no think tanks in Japan. Yet the latest edition of the Japanese publication *World Directory of Think Tanks* lists 24 think tanks in Japan, out of 320 think tanks in 77 countries (NIRA, 2002). According to the directory, Japan is second only to the United States in the number of think tanks, for which it lists 76 such entities. It is interesting to note changes between the 1996 and 2002 versions of the directory, which reflect general trends. The newer edition dropped 10 Japanese think tanks and added 12, including 5 for-profit entities. The listings include institutes that are affiliated with government or industry, indicating a broadening of the definition of non-profit and independent think tanks in Japan. In contrast, for the United States the latest version of the directory lists increasing numbers of non-profit, public policy institutions.

Japan has many so-called think tanks other than those referenced in the NIRA directory. The nation experienced three boom eras for think tanks: the early 1970s, the late 1980s, and from the late 1990s to the present. The first peak began in 1970, Japan's 'year of the think tank', when, at the instigation of political, economic, labour and academic circles, the public and business sectors created think tank-like institutions that focused on industrial policies and economic development. On average, 15 think tanks were formed every year between 1970 and 1975, including some of Japan's leading institutions. Almost all are research arms of government ministries or private industry: the Mitsubishi Research Institute (founded in 1970 by the Mitsubishi Group), the Japan Research Institute (approved in 1970 and overseen by the Economic Planning Agency and the Ministry of International Trade and Industry), the Nikko Research Center (founded in 1970 and supported by the Nikko Security Insurance Group), the International Development Center of Japan (overseen by the Ministry of Finance and several other ministries and founded in 1971), the Hitachi Research Institute (tied to the Hitachi Group and founded in 1973), and the National Institute for Research Advancement (NIRA, founded in 1974). These institutes were based in Tokyo, but in the 1970s the think tank 'craze' even spread beyond the capital. The Kansai Institute of Information Systems (KIIS) was founded in 1970 with the support of the Kansai region's business group.

Japan's second peak era for think tank formation occurred between 1985 and 1988. The for-profit institutions founded during this period were mainly funded by large banks, insurance companies, and other financial institutions that were profiting from the economic growth of the 1980s. Their research focus was on corporate and financial strategies. Among this second wave of think tanks are the (Long Term Credit Bank) Research Institute (LTCB, founded in 1983), the Sanwa Research Institute and Consulting Corporation (1985), the Asahi Bank Research Institute (1986), the Sakura Institute of Research, Inc. (1986), the Fujitsu Research Institute for Advanced Information Systems and Economics (1986), the Sumitomo-Life Research Institute, Inc. (1987), the Daiwa Institute of Research (1987), the Dentsu Institute for Human Studies (1987), the (Nippon Life Insurance) Research Institute (NLI, 1988), the Fuji Research Institute Corporation (1988), and the Sumitomo Trust Bank Research Institute (STB, 1988). The Institute for International Policy Studies (1988), established by the former prime minister Yasuhiro Nakasone, was and still is a unique think tank in Japan; its aim is to maintain Nakasone's influence on current politics.

Since the late 1980s, the Urban Institute has been working to introduce to Japan the concepts of a non-profit sector and an independent think tank (Struyk, Ueno and Suzuki, 1993; Ueno, 1993). Due in small part to those efforts (Telgarsky and Ueno, 1996; Shimokobe, 1996) and in large part to the nation's economic and social problems, Japan reshaped its think tank community in the late 1990s. The 21st Century Public Policy Institute of Japan was formed in 1996 by several academics and former journalists aiming to formulate policies from citizens' perspectives. Other initiatives point to a similar goal. The 21st Century Public Policy Institute, funded by Keidanren (the Japan Federation of Economic Organizations), was created in 1997 to strengthen Keidanren's policymaking capability. The Tokyo Foundation, funded by the Nippon Foundation, was founded to promote policy research in 1997. The Japan Initiative was set up in 1997 by a young ex-bureaucrat. These new think tanks intended to break new ground by raising a voice independent from government by forwarding policy alternatives.

Using a very broad definition of think tanks (that is, not limited to non-profit institutions or those whose research findings are accessible to the public), there are now about 332 such institutions in Japan (NIRA, 2001). Half of these are non-profit public corporations that were created with the approval of government ministries and local government and enjoy limited tax exemptions; most are small-scale entities with fewer than twenty members of staff. The other half are for-profit institutions set up by banks, security firms and large corporations; these have more staff, some over fifty people. The main areas of research of Japan's best-established institutes are, in this order, economic forecasting and development, national and local land use and land development planning, information and communications, science and technology, environment, international affairs, resources and energy, household and consumer economics, and culture and the arts.

Non-profit think tanks in Japan often work on research contracts from national and local governments or semi-governmental agencies awarded through personal connections rather than open, competitive bidding. For-profit think tanks, which are generally corporate arms, conduct economic and business forecasts and provide consulting services to clients including local- and national-level governments. It is almost unheard of for non-profit or for-profit think tanks in Japan to evaluate public policies and programmes and provide policy alternatives either to the government or to the public. Historically, think tanks have been used by the government to promote economic growth and to devise blueprints and development plans for national investment in public works. In fact, Japan has no think tanks independent from government or industry that carry out critical policy analysis and programme evaluation in areas of national development, national security, defence and the military, peace, human rights, the constitution or democracy.

The current situation

In early 2001, as part of government reform, Japan's ministries began to create what are called *Dokuritsu-Gyosei-Hojin* (Independent Administrative Institutions, or IAIs). Following an international trend of government privatization, these are agency spin-offs that are fully subsidized by a ministry's appropriation to carry out some of the latter's

Think tanks in Japan   167

functions. The earliest such spin-off is the Research Institute of Economy, Trade and Industry, which was created in 2001 by the Ministry of Economy, Trade and Industry (or METI, the former Ministry of International Trade and Industry). The institution's president is a prominent economist, and it claims to be a quintessential Kasumigaseki think tank (Kasumigaseki is the Tokyo location where central government offices are located). IAIs could point to a new trend in government policy-making and Japanese think tanks. It is not clear, however, that these institutions will engage in serious policy analysis and research. Although it is too early to tell, they may be an important step on the long road to opening up the ministries' policy-making process.

NIRA has been the only institution in Japan to promote think tanks and policy research, even though Japan's definition of policy research does not imply or include analysis and evaluation of public policy. Authorized by the National Institute for Research Advancement Act of 1974, NIRA calls itself a joint public–private organization. It was established at the initiative of 145 eminent figures from the industrial, labour and academic communities. NIRA was funded by a US$250 million endowment, half of which came from the public sector and half from the private sector. It finances its research activities through the interest earned on this endowment. NIRA has played a significant role in bolstering Japan's think tanks by distributing research grants and supporting the formation of a think tank community. But NIRA has been facing huge challenges to its institutional survival. Under Japan's prolonged economic downturn and record low interest rates, NIRA has been forced to reduce its activities and grants. In addition, due to ongoing government reforms and the fact that the government has the right to withdraw NIRA's endowment, the institute may change its status. Its future remains uncertain.

Japan's economic recession as a whole has hit the industry and business sector hard, especially the financial and construction industries, which sponsored so many of the think tanks started in the 1970s and the 1980s. At the time of writing in mid-2002, funds for think tanks in Japan are shrinking. Many think tanks have closed their doors or reduced their staff and activities, retreating further from policy research. On the other hand, since the early 1990s, both national and private universities have been busy setting up new public policy schools and departments. In the current economic situation, many graduates of these programmes realize that it will be difficult to find appropriate jobs through which to apply their knowledge.

Japan's democracy: obstacles and opportunities

Japan has a fundamental problem in realizing democracy: its people lack a firm understanding of the principles of governance and of the relationship between government and the people in a democracy. Democracy is a process rather than a perfect end-state. Moving forward in this process requires three conditions: relevant policies informed by modern scientific and technological knowledge; political leaders who embrace democratic principles and who value debate on policy priorities; and well-informed citizens who are educated and motivated to participate in their own governance. To arrive at these conditions, a society needs built-in systems and institutions along with democratic elections and an equitable distribution of power.

Japan's post-World War II agenda targeted two priorities: peace and economic growth. Seeking to democratize Japan, the American occupation of 1945–52 started to implement political, financial, educational and land reforms. But before democratic ideas could firmly take root in Japanese society, the United States was forced to turn its attention to the Korean War and the threat of communism. In the light of Japan's devotion to economic growth, the US dropped efforts to introduce democratic reforms and self-sustaining democratic systems and institutions. Left intact, however, were Japan's US-designed postwar constitution, whose Article 9 prohibits Japan from maintaining a military force other than for self-defence, and the Japan–US Security Treaty, which defines mutual responsibilities regarding security and economic co-operation.

The Liberal Democratic Party (LDP), Japan's ruling party, was founded in 1955 through the merger of two conservative parties whose predecessors had dominated politics in pre-war Japan. Its constituency included farmers who were protected by huge government subsidies, and the businesses and industries that were guided by government industrial policies – especially the construction industry, which was funded by huge public work projects that drove Japan's high growth. The LDP, with American support, grew without any serious political challenge.

In the 1950s, Japan's Socialist and Communist parties were formed in opposition to the LDP. These two parties were pro-peace and thus supported Article 9 of the constitution, but they were anti-United States, thus advocating an end to the Japan–US Security Treaty. They also held the potential for implementing democratic reforms in Japan and contained within their ranks a number of pro-democratic Japanese liberals who, because of their Marxist and socialist sentiments, were considered 'anti-government'. As the result of their anti-Vietnam war and other activities in the 1960s and early 1970s, these opposition parties isolated themselves ideologically. With Japan's growing economy and higher living standards, these parties became increasingly irrelevant (and fragmented). After the Cold War, these Japanese liberals lost even more ground. This left the LDP in power, virtually unobstructed, from 1955 until the mid-1990s. In 1993, the LDP was forced to form coalitions with Japan's opposition parties, but its policies have remained largely intact and in the late 1990s made a comeback.

For forty years the core of the LDP's policy agenda has been economic growth and national development. Economist Yukio Noguchi (1995) argues that Japan's economic success is due less to the political reforms imposed on it by the postwar US occupation forces than to the continuity of a unique wartime structure that was put in place from the late 1930s until the end of World War II and that was adopted by the LDP. Underlying this structure were the strong 'national fundamentals', comprising the divine imperial regime and a strong military, and the idea that a strong nation is one in which the government and people are one unified entity. The concept of the national fundamentals is the source of Japanese people's reluctance to act against their government.

Postwar reconstruction required the development of a strong economy. Japan's economic philosophy was based on three priorities: placing production first, co-operating for the sake of the national interest, and denying free market competition (Noguchi 1995). Politicians and the public have focused almost exclusively on economic growth (characterized by industrial policy and government investment in public works). They leave the government bureaucracy to monopolize policy-making within a ministry, absent from debate and scrutiny from within, let alone outside of, government. Japan has spent five decades pouring money into its national infrastructure such as dams, bridges, bullet trains, ports and roads. Yet the quality of life for urban families – measured, for instance, by small living space per person, meagre park space, long and arduous commuting between home and jobs – remains low relative to that in other industrialized nations. On top of national leaders' myopic focus on the economy has grown an 'iron triangle' of co-operation (some would say collusion and 'cronyism') between government bureaucracy, private business and LDP politicians. Driving this closed inner circle has been national development's emphasis on public works. Public works investment was 8 per cent of Japan's GDP in 2001 – a higher rate than that of any of the leading Western economies. This emphasis has greatly enriched the construction industry and contributed to the 'back-rubbing' that so commonly takes place among the triangle's three players.

The government scandals from the late 1990s to the present reveal how this system works. In one such scandal, Ministry of Finance (MOF) officials in charge of overseeing private banks were found to be receiving bribes, including bargain home prices, in return for special treatment, including permission to sell special bonds and notification of when the MOF would be investigating bank offices. The Minister of Finance and two vice-ministers resigned from their positions in early 1998 as a result of their exposure, and several officials committed suicide. But corruption of this kind has been going on for years and is endemic within many different government sectors.

Why Japan has not democratized

A number of factors help to explain not only why Japan has not democratized to the same extent as the industrialized Western countries, but also the relatively passive and limited role of Japanese think tanks.

Links to the past

Japan's democratic foundation, imposed on it by the United States after the war, did not and could not entirely displace the previous imperial institutional structure. Many Japanese still value implicitly certain elements of that structure, which was based on the paternalistic authority of the emperor and which helps define Japan's national identity. Japan remains linked to its past through symbols such as its national flag; its official calendar system, which counts years based on imperial reigns; and the reintroduction of its national anthem (phased out after 1945), which blesses the emperor's eternal sovereignty. The Japanese Ministry of Education (newly named the Ministry of Education, Culture, Sports, Science and Technology) has full control over education and cultural issues, and typically censors textbooks. Since the early 1970s, Saburo Ienaga, an octogenarian professor emeritus of the Tokyo University of Education, has challenged the government over the constitutionality of textbook screening. This policy favours limited, 'official' views of history (such as of Japan's World War II Rape of Nanking and the role of 'comfort women' during the war). Involving the fundamental question of whether the state has the right to control school administration, curricula and educational content, this protracted court battle finally ended in 1997, when the high court accepted some of Ienaga's claims but upheld the Education Ministry's right to continue screening textbooks. Receiving many death threats for his battle, Professor Ienaga was supported only by a voluntary citizens' movement rather than by any institution. Other local leaders, educators and media journalists who have questioned affirmative links to the war and the emperor have also received death threats from ultra-nationalists. Such a highly charged atmosphere makes it difficult for any politician or party to state openly opinions that upset the status quo. The prime minister, Junichiro Koizumi, makes repeated visits to the Yasukuni Shrine, which honours Japan's war dead, including several executed war criminals from World War II, despite the strong condemnation these visits elicit from Japan's Asian neighbours. His insistence on continuing these visits reflects the basic nature of the Japanese leadership and political environment.

Dread of conflict

The imperial system rested on people's faith in a beneficent father figure: the emperor. Society operated under an unspoken social contract whereby persons in positions of authority from the emperor downwards ruled mercifully. This characterizes the Japanese ideal of leadership. The ruled, in turn, obediently complied with the leadership. To this day, many Asian societies value the stability and security of this Confucian-based system, which has been implemented by authoritarian government bureaucracies. As a result, these societies tend to avoid dissent and conflict with those around and above them. But this desire for harmony is not suited to today's competitive world, where democratic nations need to rely on the constructive conflict born of pluralism and free debate, to better themselves and the well-being of their people.

Hesitance to pursue democracy

On the surface, Japan is a democratic country whose leaders are freely elected. Yet national policy is typically made by government bureaucrats behind closed doors. Further, the very concept of democracy is not only misunderstood but feared. Japan's ancient rulers were informed by the belief that to maintain a stable reign they needed to keep their people ignorant. The confused steps towards democracy that Japan took in the strange vacuum of the Cold War era still linger in the minds of the political and academic communities. Politicians who use the term 'democracy' often risk being labelled unpatriotic, left-leaning or pro-socialist liberals. University students, let alone ordinary citizens, rarely approach the topic. The name of the Liberal Democratic Party is, therefore, deceptive. Japanese opinion leaders and the media commonly espouse the notion that 'excess democracy' is the root of America's problems and therefore should not be brought into Japan. Indeed, neither the current prime minister nor any of his nine predecessors (except one from the socialist party) since 1990 has ever raised democracy as part of the national agenda.

Being outside of the English-speaking world is a strong barrier to understanding Western logic and wealth-creating concepts, knowledge and practices, including democracy. Further, it is not surprising that many words are not successfully translated or appropriately interpreted, since different cultures sometimes do not share common concepts and lack equivalent words. For example, the word 'democracy' translates into Japanese as *minshu-shugi*, literally 'people-master-ism', which suggests an ideology rather than a system of government, and one that is closely related to socialism or communism.

Moreover, few Japanese people question the nation's lack of private, independent space in either the literal or the figurative sense. A clear distinction between the public and the private does not exist in Japan as it does in Western societies. The fundamental problem is that the Japanese people do not have a firm understanding of the democratic principles governing relations between the government and the people as stated in the country's constitution, which was basically suggested by the US Occupation Army. The English version of the Japanese Constitution proclaims 'We, the people', as in the US Constitution; but in Japanese, *Nihon-kokumin* indicates the Japanese nation. The Japanese writers of the constitution at the time were unable or unwilling to come up with a more equivalent word in Japanese for the Western concept of 'the people'.

The US-designed constitution marks a complete U-turn from the Meiji Constitution that preceded it. Japan's constitution stipulates three distinctive branches of government power, but rather than operating separately they are intricately linked and mutually dependent, which runs counter to a more recognizable democratic system. People living in the West, especially Americans, view democracy as so basic that it is taken for granted. However, for most of the world, democracy is not a natural political state.

Lack of accountability and self-evaluation

A society that honours authoritarian government and continuity, shuns conflict and checks and balances, and fears the instability that can arise from pluralism is also apt to lack the concepts of accountability and self-evaluation that characterize well-developed democracies. Accountability is a clear necessity for a democratic government. It is needed not only to keep public officials from abusing their power and to ensure that they use money prudently and treat citizens fairly, but to accomplish public purposes. Democratic accountability means accountability for the state of finance, fairness and performance (Behn, 2001).

Japan's government lacks the desire or motivation to maintain accountability or the mechanisms for self-evaluation; the very concept of policy analysis and evaluation is alien to most Japanese. In contrast with the United States, policy analysis is not an established discipline within Japanese academia; it is not regarded as a pure science, and until very recently Japanese universities offered no structured public policy analysis, evaluation or public management programmes. Also, policy-making has been monopolized by career bureaucrats, most of whom have graduated from the law departments of a few top national universities. No training ground has existed to nurture strong policy analysts either inside or outside of government to carry out objective and practical policy analysis and evaluation. In the United States, not only does the government, through departments such as the Congressional Budget Office (CBO), the Congressional Research Service and the US General Accounting Office, evaluate its programmes from within. Furthermore, an entire research industry outside government revolves around studying the efficacy of public policies.

Lack of budget debate

A state's capacity to govern depends on its capacity to budget. The budget is the most important policy vehicle for affecting countries' economic and social priorities. Having a broad range of stakeholders who provide input into the budgeting process is indispensable to a strong democracy. Because of the shortcomings of Japan's parliamentary and political systems, over the years MOF has controlled and monopolized the budget. The Ministry's huge power rests on the information and knowledge it accumulates through its close ties to major LDP politicians. Until recently, budget proposals prepared by MOF passed within only a few days, because legislators could not provide counter-arguments or alternative options based on robust facts.

The US public's strong participation in the budget process (via citizens' groups, think tanks and congressional representatives) is the most resilient part of American democracy. The important step to democratizing the budgeting process in the United States was the creation of a non-partisan, government institution: the CBO. This resulted from the enactment of the Congressional Budget and Impoundment Control Act of 1974. The legislature can influence the budget by asking specific and well-informed questions and by debating priorities based on information provided by CBO. These critical arguments are imperative in the budgeting process.

Current and enduring problems

In early 2002, the world economy shows some signs of recovery, led by the US. However, Japan's revival as a star of the Asian economic miracle seems to be more distant than ever. A 1993 World Bank report on Asia's economic success argued that a key element is a strong, bureaucrat-dominated civil service. This report reinforced Japan's satisfaction with the status quo and with traditional Asian values, and thus helped to delay the kind of broad-based reforms needed to get Japan back on a dynamic economic track.

On top of these fundamental obstacles to a more democratic system in Japan is a relatively new cynicism towards and distrust of government among Japanese society. These attitudes have been building up since the early 1990s. Apathy and lack of interest exist among many strata of the population. Japanese citizens think their voices do not count because they have been ignored for so long. Recent exposés of government corruption have fuelled public cynicism towards bureaucracy and politics as well. This is particularly the case among the generation of people in their late fifties and early sixties who experienced strong political and social turmoil. Many of the best and brightest of this generation, who constituted the main force of student movements of the 1960s and early 1970s, excelled in the science, technology and engineering fields. Either they were forced out or they turned their backs on mainstream politics and the government bureaucracy. They were subsequently co-opted by corporate Japan and became loyal soldiers devoted to Japan's economic growth. They now constitute a conservative force, thereby shrinking the pool of potential talent that might have contributed to reforming Japan's political system. Japan's affluence of the last quarter century has failed to produce a nation's most important resource: strong, diverse and creative human capital. Notwithstanding these comments, there are some developments that could help to break the rigid mould within which Japan's government has traditionally operated.

Emerging non-profit sector

Japan's economic downturn, which adversely affected think tanks in the late 1990s, as previously mentioned, was accompanied by political disaffection. This same downturn has drawn public attention to the nation's need for a non-profit sector. The large number of Japanese newspaper articles on non-profits reflects this growing interest. One Japanese scholar suggests that change is coming to Japan because of the emergence (if on a small scale and in a limited manner) of three conditions that are needed to develop a civil society: the presence of a pluralistic society, recognition of the intrinsic value of the 'private', and popular awareness of the public interest (Iokibe, 1999). Although Japan's private business sector is less aware of its broader role in a market democracy, a concept of 'corporate philanthropy' is slowly surfacing within that sector.

One example of positive movement is new legislation, enacted by parliament in March 1998, called the Law to Promote Specified Non-profit Activities. This law was spurred, in part, by the slow response of government in providing rescue services during and after the Kobe–Awaji earthquake of 1994. Spontaneously created voluntary citizen efforts helped to fill the void of government assistance during the disaster, showing the public the crucial role that non-governmental groups can play. Enactment of this law was driven by citizens and politicians, not by government bureaucrats – a first in Japan's legislative history. Although limited in scope and lacking tax-incentive measures, this law for the first time gives legitimacy to certain entities that promote one of twelve citizen-initiated non-profit activities. In fact, this law is not sufficient to create a strong non-profit sector, but it does give credence to the concept of a non-profit sector to promote a wide range of citizens' activities. Since this legislation was implemented, citizens' groups have gained strong momentum. To date, 6,500 entities have been approved under the law (Cabinet Office www.cao.go.jp). Their activities fall mainly in social service delivery, though, using the recently enacted Law Concerning Access to Information Held by Administrative Organs to access the government information, in the future, they could engage in policy research and would be stakeholders in either the local or the national level of the policy-making process.

In addition, two new efforts aimed at boosting the policy market are taking place. One project, initiated by Heizo Takenaka, the current minister of economy and fiscal policy, is forming a network to promote policy analysis as a professional discipline rather than as an ivory-tower academic endeavour. The project is using the US-based Association for Public Policy Analysis and Management as a model. The association has connected policy researchers in existing think tanks, government research institutions and public policy schools to advance policy analysis and the policy market in Japan. The second effort is to reform local governments from the bottom up. Modelled after efforts to reinvent government and measure government performance in the United States and elsewhere, a forum consisting of local government officials, businesspeople and think tank researchers has been set up to examine and measure local government performance.

Government reform and policy evaluation law

In January 2001, the Japanese government implemented a large-scale reform of the government organizations founded on the Basic Law on the Administrative Reform of the Central Government, enacted in 1998. This reform provided a new structure consisting of a Cabinet Office and twelve ministries (the old structure had one Office and twenty-two ministries) and introduced a new system of IAIs, as mentioned earlier. The new system was put in place to enhance the political leadership of the prime minister. The reorganization, coupled with a new inter-ministry co-ordination system, is aimed at bringing more efficient and effective decision-making to government. One of the goals is to reduce the number of government employees by 25 per cent over a ten-year period.

Other essential elements of the government reform this time were to strengthen the functions of the Cabinet and affirm the leadership of the prime minister (Headquarters for the Administrative Reform of the Central Government, 2001). Japan's national budget in fiscal year 2001 was 83 trillion yen (US$615 billion). Under the Japanese Constitution, the Cabinet is responsible for preparing and submitting the budget to the Diet, though, as mentioned before, over the years MOF has controlled the public finances and the budget. The new Cabinet Office is intended to have a strong hand on the budget; however, the prime minister's effort to democratize the budget has shown the limits of the current system.

In the parliamentary system, it is difficult for the Diet to acquire the budgeting power the US Congress has. The legislature needs an institution that provides budget information and research and that is staffed with experts in various areas of policy research: budget analysis, tax analysis, macro- and micro-economic analysis, and policy analysis and evaluation. Only this kind of non-partisan, independent budget institution with collective efforts can provide policy options that open up an approach and perspective, other than the MOF's, to a nation's budget and future.

In addition, the government enacted the Law on Policy Evaluation Performed by the Administration, and set the *Standard Guidelines for Policy Evaluation*. Under this initiative, all ministries are mandated to implement 'policy evaluation' suggested by the *Guidelines*.

For example, the Ministry of Land, Infrastructure and Transport (MLIT) was created in the reorganization by combining four entities: the Ministry of Construction, the Land Agency, the Ministry of Transport, and the Hokkaido Development Agency. These ministries and agencies used to set policies for the powerful construction and civil engineering industries, and implemented huge public works, thereby creating national economic growth. These public works are part of the Comprehensive National Developments Plans that Japan has formulated since 1962.

MLIT's proposed budget for fiscal year 2002 was 8 trillion yen (US$60 billion), which made up 10 per cent of the government's general accounting budget. Eighty per cent of Japan's public works investment is provided through this ministry's budget. The industries that the public works support together employ a labour force of 6 million people, accounting for 8 per cent of GDP. Despite the huge public outlays for public works projects, until now there has been almost no substantial research effort to analyse and evaluate the Comprehensive National Development Plans.

The MLIT has a staff of some 64,000. For the first time the ministry has set up an evaluation office and assigned a staff of ten to work under a director general for policy planning. This group, with no clear financial allocation and scarce experience, is tasked with evaluating the ministry's performance and its programmes. The MLIT has also set up an advisory committee and invited to sit on it third-party specialists. Finding outside individuals qualified as evaluators, let alone policy analysts, is difficult but necessary in order to bring some objective views to the ministry's evaluation work.

Since the *Standard Guidelines for Policy Evaluation* are limited to measuring a ministry's management performance, it is too early to expect ministries to come up with any concrete policy analysis and alternatives that will solve the nation's problems. However, if the ministries implement the evaluations with strong financial backing and rely on outside expertise to conduct them, this government initiative could give real momentum to strengthening the nation's policy capacity.

Conclusion

The absence of systematic policy research in the Japanese government contrasts heavily with the case of the United States, which is supported by strong human and financial resources. A large number of scholars, academics and former government executives carry out broad policy assessments, applying empirical methods to analyse public policies and programmes (Struyk, 1999). For instance, when William Gorham became assistant secretary of planning and evaluation for the Department of Health and Human Services (formerly the Department of Health, Education and Welfare) in 1966, this body became the first department-level domestic policy analysis unit in the US government. He headed a staff of thirty, which grew to several hundred within a decade (Weiss, 1992). He brought in many policy analysts from inside and outside of government. Gorham created the concept of including funds for evaluation in each of the agency's programme appropriation requests – a clause stipulated that up to 1 per cent had to be allocated for that task. This provision was extended to other domestic programmes within a few years and helped create a flourishing policy evaluation industry in the United States (Gorham, 1998).

Despite the administrative and other reforms in the last decade, societal values and Japanese political structures and culture do not accommodate a strong policy research industry. Consequently, a market for policy research within government or outside it, where research and analysis can be produced and 'traded' in order to deal with ever-pressing social, economic and political problems, is underdeveloped. Failure to face the realities of change brings heavy penalties for a nation; as the result of Japan's resistance to political change it is experiencing such penalties already, in the form of economic stagnation and of cynicism and apathy among the public towards politics and politicians.

Pluralism is a social strategy that encourages the existence of many kinds of institutions, conflicting perspectives and beliefs, and competing economic units. In authoritarian political systems there is one dominant source of power and initiative, one ideology, one 'correct' answer. Such systems do not give rise to progress. Japan's economic problems are crying out for new approaches. Nurturing a market for policy research, enlarging the policy capacity of government, and engaging interest among the public for policy debate could go a long way in helping the Japanese out of their current situation.

A decade ago, no one in Japan knew much about independent think tanks. Indeed, in the mid-1990s the Urban Institute faced strong antagonism to introducing Western-style think tanks. Several prominent persons in Japan said it was too soon to do so and too disturbing to the status quo. Now people say that think tanks are of no use in fixing Japan's failed economy, and that they are out of fashion.

Since 11 September, Americans have begun to realize the great gap of understanding between the United States and the rest of the world. Asia, especially Japan, has strong barriers to learning Western logic and knowledge and to developing the capacity for policy-making. Exacerbating these barriers are language and xenophobic attitudes including anti-American sentiments that have recently spread throughout Asia. Nevertheless, Asia can learn from the US experience about how to create national resilience, which comes in part from robust democratic institutions. Abhist Vejajiva, a minister in the Thai Cabinet, predicted in 1998 that without assistance from the outside, Asian governments would move 'away from first-best policies, toward second-best policies, implemented by third-best officials, serving fourth-best politicians' (*The Economist*, 17 October 1998).

What Americans can do to help Japan meet the challenges of a changing world is to introduce the democratic mechanisms with which Japan can build its own policy research capability. A key ingredient in producing that capacity is to found an independent institution that is able to engage in policy research and analysis that is backed up by rigorous social science research through the team efforts of foreign and domestic policy analysts. Such an institution will link Japan and Asian countries to the global intellectual community by means of a common currency used by democratic societies – policy analysis. The longer-term goal of this kind of think tank would be to foster self-sustaining policy analysis expertise in Japan. Although no one institution can change a society, a democratic nation should at least furnish the environment to nurture the capacity for change.

11 Su-ming Khoo

Think tanks and Malaysian development

This chapter takes a critical approach to Malaysian think tanks and examines their roles as technocrats, partisans and visionaries. It interprets their emergence within the context of Malaysian development. Three main forces drive the agenda of 'development' in Malaysia: strategic economic concerns, competition between political elites, and civil society struggles for inclusion in the political arena. Malaysian think tanks have evolved vis-à-vis these agendas and the changing political landscape has offered them varying opportunities and constraints over time.

Think tanks became a noticeable part of the Malaysian intellectual landscape in the 1980s. Malaysia's strategy of accelerated growth and economic liberalization, dubbed 'Malaysia Inc.', provided the context for their emergence. There was growing need for a strong (though not necessarily democratic) governance model that would enhance links between government and industry and adopt more strategic approaches to development and globalization. This context provided opportunities for policy entrepreneurs who could bridge the government and corporate sectors.

The 1990s saw the development of the 'Vision 2020' policy, which broadened the idea of development and created new possibilities for policy actors interested in social and cultural policy. Sustained economic growth provided the backdrop to a burgeoning intellectual landscape in Malaysia and the wider Asia-Pacific region. New discourses of national and regional identity began to emerge, with a sense of positive anticipation that the twenty-first century would be the 'Asian Century'.

The 1997 Asian financial crisis triggered changes as the Malaysian government struggled with economic downturn, financial problems and political crises. Although economic recovery had begun by 1999, political stability and the intellectual climate were severely affected. The political optimism, cultural liberalization and intellectual pluralism that characterized the early and mid-1990s dissipated as economic crisis led to political turmoil. The arrest and trials in 1998 of the deputy prime minister, Anwar

Ibrahim, had a major impact, leading to large-scale public protests and demands for political reform.

Malaysian think tanks

Malaysia resembles other East Asian 'developmental' states (South Korea, Taiwan, Singapore) with a relatively authoritarian state playing a dominant role compared to the market or civil society. The government is the major intellectual arbiter and this means that think tanks find it difficult to be completely autonomous or independent. In the words of a senior analyst at ISIS, they inhabit a 'grey area' between the private and public sectors (interview, March 1995).

Malaysian think tanks may employ culturally different terms of reference to their Western counterparts. Some have strong Islamic orientations and may combine Islamic ideas with secular ones (Noda, 1995). Malaysian think tanks have actively engaged with 'Asian Values' and 'reverse Orientalist' ideas (Christie and Roy, 2001: 5). The 'Asian Values' discourse stresses Malaysia's cultural affinity with East Asia, looking to Asia instead of 'the West' for intellectual and economic guidance. Exact formulations of 'Asian Values' differ, but most include deference to authority, a consensual or 'polite' discursive culture that avoids open conflict, the importance of collective interests over individual freedoms, conservative 'family values', respect for learning and a strong work ethic. However, these 'Asian Values' are not uniformly present across all nations and sections of Asian society (Christie and Roy, 2001: 6–7). Its main advocates are authoritarian leaders in Malaysia, Singapore and China, who have tended to use the idea to defend their regimes in the face of domestic and international criticism.

Malaysian politics is characterized by two main features: ethnic politics and policies and 'money politics'. Ethnicity is a major organizing principle, although ethnic positions may not always be explicitly stated. An uneasy tension exists between a pluralist 'ethnic bargaining' model that is inclusive towards Chinese, Indian and non-Malay indigenous minorities (who together form 45 per cent of the population) and the de facto recognition of Malay-Muslim majority rule. Ethnic bargaining is reflected in the structure of the ruling Barisan Nasional (BN, National Front) coalition, with three original ethnic components: the United Malays Nationalist Organization (UMNO), the Malaysian Chinese Association (MCA) and the Malayan Indian Congress (MIC). This coalition has expanded to include fourteen parties currently, most of which are ethnically based. Component parties of the Barisan coalition have established think tanks to support their particular ethnic and political agendas, while opposition parties such as the Democratic Action Party (DAP), the Islamic

Party (PAS) and the National Justice Party (Keadilan) have tended to work with NGOs and social movements.

Malaysian think tanks emerged in roughly two phases of development, the 1980s and the 1990s, though the academic Centre for Policy Research (CPR) was established a decade earlier. ISIS, MIER and the Institute of Development Studies, Sabah (IDS) form the established 'core' think tanks, which employ a substantial number of research staff and have institutional links with government. The 'revolving door' operates to some extent, linking the larger and more established think tanks with government agencies and academia, with staff being seconded between these different spheres. Think tank staff often participate in government-initiated ad hoc committees and panels, which are important sites for policy innovation.

ISIS is the dominant think tank in Malaysia for several reasons. It is considered to be the most prestigious think tank, being well funded and with the highest political connections. It is the 'grandfather of Malaysian think tanks', having served as an organizational model and training ground for newer think tanks. Policy entrepreneurs have drawn on ISIS experience, recruiting ex-ISIS staff and learning from the ISIS model through a system of placements and fellowships. Following the ISIS model, Malaysian think tanks are set up as independent, non-profit companies regulated by the Companies Act. This confers greater independence than NGOs have, as they are generally registered as societies and come under the more restrictive bounds of the Societies Act.

ISIS, MIER, the IDS and the Malaysia Institute of Islamic Understanding (IKIM) are partly government funded, through grants to their endowment funds varying from RM$20 million for ISIS to RM$2 million for MIER (RM$1 = 0.29 euros in 2002). MIER obtained half its endowment from the private sector and also derives revenue from sales of information and membership fees. Most think tanks rely on commissioned and project-based research for much of their funding. Smaller and newer institutions may partly depend on politically connected private sector benefactors, as well as international foundations and aid programmes for commissioned research. Key international funders include the Canadian International Development Agency and the German KAS and FNS. Smaller think tanks established since the 1990s tend to have noticeable associations with political figures, reflecting the pattern of political competition. Some of the newer think tanks also have strong connections to NGOs and social movements.

The IDS and the Sarawak Development Institute (SDI) are state think tanks that reflect state politics and development agendas. There are thirteen states in the Malaysian Federation and the state–federal dynamic is a key factor that can change through time. State governments have a significant role in relation to natural resources and economic development, and chief ministers of states play an important role as gatekeepers and brokers of economic and policy opportunities.

Changes in leadership and policy direction have meant differing opportunities and constraints for think tanks in their varying roles as technocrats, partisans and visionaries. The following sections locate think tanks within the context of national development thinking, reflecting changes in political leadership and the shifting balance of power at a variety of levels – state, national and regional. To understand these complex dynamics, it is helpful to divide the historical background into four phases, beginning with the New Economic Policy (NEP) of the 1970s, followed by the Mahathirist era of the 1980s. Political culture shifted in the early 1990s, enabling think tanks to expand their roles and modes of operation. The current post-Asian Crisis period presents a more uncertain picture, with democratization emerging as an urgent question.

The NEP and the preconditions for think tanks

The NEP set some preconditions for the emergence of think tanks. Following ethnic riots in 1969, the government introduced measures to meet the demands of Malay economic nationalists. Malaysia's founding prime minister, Tunku Abdul Rahman, was ousted and multiethnic political bargaining was replaced with a more radical Malay nationalist government led by Tun Abdul Razak. The government maintained order at the expense of legitimacy and 'government processes became cloaked with obsessive secrecy' (Means, 1991: 112). A state of emergency was declared and the constitution was amended to prevent open debate on 'sensitive issues'. Civil liberties were curtailed, using legal measures to allow detention without trial and to limit freedom of information, the freedom of the press, freedom of speech, and freedom of association and assembly (Means, 1991).

Consultation was limited to the National Consultative Council appointed by Razak, though he also began to seek informal advice from sources outside the government (*Sun*, 30 March, 1995). Universities had played a key role in public mobilization and debate during the late1960s and early 1970s, but the new Universities and University Colleges Act restricted political activity for students and academics. Key aspects of public policy, such as the system of preferences for ethnic Malays, were removed from public discussion, and censorship and self-censorship became established norms in Malaysian political culture.

The NEP's two main aims were (1) eradicating poverty and (2) restructuring education, employment and capital. The latter took precedence, focusing on the restructuring of business and industry to increase Malay ownership and control of the economy. There was a major education and training drive and the introduction of Malay quotas and incentives to create a Malay middle class of professionals and entrepreneurs. One of the NEP's major consequences was the state-driven convergence of business and politics (Gomez and Jomo, 1997). The Razak government combined political and economic objectives, setting up trust agencies to enable the transfer of corporate equity to *bumiputera* (Malay and other indigenous) ownership, and to provide training and employment for the new *bumiputera* technocrats. Political parties became directly involved in corporate business, ostensibly on behalf of their ethnic groups. 'Money politics' became predominant and corporate power was concentrated in the hands of politically connected elites (Mehmet, 1988; Gomez, 1990). As business and politics converged, intra-party conflict and leadership competition came to reflect these indivisible interests, especially within the ruling Malay party, UMNO.

The analytical distinction between government and an autonomous private sector is thus problematic in the Malaysian case. The corporate sector is dominated by politically connected oligopolies. Power is best understood in terms of politically linked 'distributional coalitions', 'small, powerful and influential groups, organized as cartels, seeking rewards through collusion, transaction costs and other forms of non-competitive bargains' (Mehmet, 1988: 135).

The CPR

It is not surprising that few independent organizations were established in the 1970s, given the increased restrictions on intellectual and associational freedom. The CPR was established in 1974 as a research centre within the University of Science Malaysia in Penang. It aimed to produce policy-oriented research for local and national government agencies, which were undergoing expansion to meet the needs of the NEP. The CPR's research programme was oriented towards the first NEP policy aim of 'eradicating poverty', targeting poor, marginalized groups and producing seminal research on poverty, income inequality and agrarian issues. According to the former Director of the CPR, K.J. Ratnam, a major motivation behind its establishment was the concern to develop local expertise, since development policy had tended to rely on foreign experts (interview, June 1995). There was only a limited amount of primary research on social and economic issues, and policy planning was still relatively underdeveloped. As the 1970s progressed, policy and planning divisions proliferated within the government, and competition and replication began to characterize government policy-making.

The CPR's research priorities fitted well with the 1970s development agenda under Razak's leadership, as he was personally supportive of rural development issues. By the 1980s, its research strengths had become overshadowed by Mahathir bin Mohamed's new concerns of strategic industrialization and growth.

Mahathirist transformations

The Mahathir administration took over in 1982, consolidating the political-economic complex of the NEP, but also making significant changes. The trend towards authoritarianism continued, but the independent administrative role of the bureaucracy was increasingly replaced by the corporate agendas of a highly politicized private sector. Khoo (1995) notes that Mahathir, more than any previous leader, drove policy-making with a personal vision of industrial transformation. He ordered the country to 'Look East', and used the slogan 'Malaysia Inc.' to mark greater co-operation between government and the private sector. Almeida and Wong observe:

> Think tanks were shaped by the new thinking in the country in the first half of the 1980s. The Mahathir Administration came into office in 1982 and not long after introduced a programme of 'radical' reforms. Among them are three, which, we argue, directly influenced the thinking about think tanks. These are a wider role for the private sector; the need for a smaller, more efficient civil service; and the additional need for a close working relationship between the private and public sectors [the concept of 'Malaysia Inc.']. (1991: 7)

The think tanks of the 1980s embodied and contributed towards the 'Malaysia Inc.' discourse, which promoted the open alliance of political power and corporate capital. The emphasis shifted from the public to the private sector and politics-in-business entered a new phase as Mahathir advocated privatization, benefiting specific corporate capitalists (both Malay and non-Malay) with access to political patronage. The reformist and deregulating role of think tanks must thus be understood within a national context of 'money politics' where government, corporate and individual interests converge. It is true to say that Malaysian think tanks, especially the 'Mahathirist' ones, have played a significant role in propagating the ideological hegemony of capitalism (for comparison see Alpert and Markusen, 1980: 174), but it is capitalism in a highly politicized and culturally inflected local form.

However, Malaysian think tanks do not simply represent the concerted, self-interested actions of a political-business elite. Malaysian think tanks frequently produce public-spirited policies, ideologies and plans (cf. Stone, 1996b: 15). Individual think tank directors and staff may be motivated to reform the country 'from within', especially given the difficulty of influencing 'from without' in Malaysia.

Despite considerable constraints, NGOs developed during the 1970s as independent and often critical 'outsiders' advocating public-spirited policy. Malaysian NGOs mobilized and evolved during the 1980s, partly in reaction to growing authoritarianism and the widespread corruption and environmental scandals that broke out (see Means, 1991). The Consumer Association of Penang became a significant advocate for alternative development and in the 1980s established an environmental NGO, Friends of the Earth, Malaysia (Sahabat Alam Malaysia), and TWN, an 'NGO think tank' that networked like-minded NGOs and activists in Asia, Africa and Latin America. TWN plays a critical advocacy and lobbying role, presenting an alternative and critical 'Southern' perspective on international economic, trade and development issues.

Islam entered the political mainstream during the 1980s as Mahathir, recognizing that Islam was becoming a powerful, potentially oppositional force, sought to appropriate its ideological legitimacy. In 1982, he co-opted Anwar Ibrahim, the charismatic leader of the Muslim Youth Movement, into the ruling government. A massive government Islamization drive followed, expanding and centralizing Islamic affairs within the bureaucracy, mobilizing financial instruments such as the Islamic Bank and Pilgrim Savings Fund (LUTH) and building prestigious institutions like the International Islamic University (UIA). Mahathir 'mainstreamed' Islam, providing government support for a moderate, reformist and pro-capitalist form of it. As a result, mainstream modernization became officially and profoundly Islamized.

ISIS: bypassing the bureaucracy

Mahathir's desire to bypass and downsize the bureaucracy was a major reason underlying the founding of ISIS (interview with the director-general of ISIS, 10 April 1995). He was critical of bureaucratic inefficiency and actively sought to cut across the established chains of command and find alternatives (Khoo, 1995: 129–30). Public sector inefficiency had become a considerable burden by the 1980s, exacerbated by the problems of plummeting commodity prices and growing foreign debt. A major influence behind Mahathir's economic reforms was Daim Zainuddin, Mahathir's finance minister 1984–91 and 1999–2001, and special economic advisor 1992–98. Daim led the 1980s privatization drive, building up a powerful corporate clique with UMNO connections (Gomez, 1990, 1994). Daim initiated ISIS' first commission to find ways to slim down the civil service and bypass bureaucratic vested interests. An independent policy institute provided the new government with more flexibility and opportunities for policy inputs to come from 'outside', while enabling Mahathir and his close associates to retain autonomy over decision-making (Almeida and Wong, 1991: 17).

ISIS' structure reflects a government-oriented but somewhat independent position. Mahathir instigated ISIS and appointed its first chairman and half of its Board of Directors. The seniority of the appointees demonstrates its influence. These include the head of the military and key cabinet positions: the minister of finance, the heads of the Prime Minister's Research Department and the Implementation and Co-ordination Unit, and the Ministers of Home and Foreign Affairs. Despite these strong governmental links, ISIS derives some independence from its institutional structure and the standing of its founding director-general (now CEO), Dr Noordin Sopiee, who established a tradition of relative intellectual independence. ISIS staff perceive themselves to be freer than civil servants or academics. Noordin argued that ISIS was 'revolutionary ... beyond the clutches of the civil service' and 'independent of civil service intrigue', 'having tremendous independence to come up with ideas' (interview, 10 April 1995). 'We believe that our duty demands that we be objective and independent. We serve no function and we do not serve the country if we merely declaim the accepted conventional wisdoms and parrot the current orthodoxy' (Askiah Adam, 1995). Noordin acted as a personal advisor to Mahathir and helped to develop key policy position and platforms such as the 'Vision 2020' speech, which drove government policy in the 1990s (Malaysian Business Council, 1991).

ISIS research staff work in a number of specialized bureaus, carrying out commissioned research that is less directly political and more technocratic. It has contributed to industrial, technology and education policy in collaboration with the government's Central Economic Planning Unit, the World Bank, Asian Development Bank and UN Development Programme. It functions as a kind of secretariat for the World Bank, co-ordinating and hosting World Bank policy meetings.

The regional integration of ASEAN has traditionally relied on a combination of business leaders, academics and public servants. ISIS has established itself as the key national body engaged in this 'second-track diplomacy' (Kraft, 2000). It co-ordinates the regional think tank network (ASEAN-ISIS), and is responsible for the major regional policy dialogue event, the Asia-Pacific Roundtable. ISIS acted as the secretariat of the Council for Security and Co-operation in the Asia-Pacific and was a key force behind the articulation of the East Asian Economic Grouping/East Asian Economic Caucus concept. ISIS played a key role in persuading Mahathir not to withdraw from the Commonwealth in 1987 and in Malaysia's subsequent repositioning as a voice for developing countries. The think tank was active in the drive to promote Asia-consciousness amongst policy elites, convening the Commission for a New Asia, an elite group of sixteen visionaries charged with creating a manifesto for an

'Asian Renaissance' in the 1990s, 'a kind of Vision 2020 for Asia' (Commission for a New Asia, 1994).

MIER: an expression of 'Malaysia Inc.'

MIER was formed in 1986 as a partnership between the government and the private sector. It was initiated by the Prime Minister's Economic Panel and promoted by the Council on Malaysian Invisible Trade. MIER is best described as a technocratic institution that embodies the 'Malaysia Inc.' approach. It reflects the 1980s devolution of policy to the corporate sector as the 'engine of growth'. MIER's route to influence is technocratic in a financial-business sense. Its links are to the Treasury and the Central Bank (Bank Negara) and it is housed in the Bank Negara building. It produces independent economic and financial information and analysis, and plays a 'bridging role', connecting business, academic and government sectors.

MIER has an economically strategic, rather than a politically visionary role. It resembles the Taiwanese government research institute, TIER, which was, in turn, inspired by the Japanese model that brings together business, government and academia to solve economic problems (Anon., 1991: 30–5). MIER openly acknowledges the duality of its private and public sector stakeholders, but sees them as being integrated within 'Malaysia Inc.', in which state, corporate and public interests are harmoniously interdependent.

MIER runs a Malaysian Economic Database, produces economic forecasts, surveys business conditions and consumer sentiment, and publishes a monthly economic bulletin. These serve the large companies that are able to use macro-economic information and forecasting to their strategic advantage. This may corroborate the idea of greater interdependence between government and the private sector in East Asia (cf. Weiss, 1995), but it also shows that larger corporations can retain independence. MIER's output is both complementary and alternative to the official governmental analysis, since it provides information at shorter intervals than the official sources (quarterly and annually, whereas the government's Economic Planning Unit issues figures at two-and-a-half- and five-year intervals). MIER's analyses and forecasts have demonstrated its independence and ability to differ from the central government's 'party line', notably in its preference for lower growth rates and concern over inflation.

The IDS: state struggles with federal hegemony

The IDS is the Sabah state think tank. Its history illustrates how the link between think tanks and power can become problematic when the relationship between state and federal authorities becomes contentious. The

IDS was established in 1985 as the Institute for Public Policy and Analysis by Jeffrey Kitingan, brother of Pairin Kitingan, then chief minister of Sabah and head of the opposition party, the PBS (Parti Bersatu Sabah, Sabah United Party). Renamed the IDS in 1986, it functioned between 1987 and 1994 as part of a wider initiative to restructure the state bureaucracy, following PBS' electoral success.

The inclusion of Sabah in the 1963 Malaysian Federation incurred considerable opposition, especially from non-Malay elites who preferred self-rule. Federation was secured through an informal agreement according the state some economic and political autonomy. This notional autonomy was systematically eroded between the 1960s and the mid-1980s by the federal government's increasing attempts to 'integrate' Sabah into the Federation, politically, economically and culturally (see Loh, 1992: 225). Kadazans are non-Malay, mainly non-Muslims who form Sabah's largest indigenous group. The PBS successfully mobilized Kadazan cultural nationalism in opposition to Federalist, Malay-Muslim dominance, resulting in a surprise victory over the Federal government in 1985.

The PBS restructured the Sabah Foundation, a quasi-governmental organization conceived as a non-political, non-profit instrument to channel timber profits to indigenous Sabahans, but which had become a powerful state-level broker of money politics (Ansari, 1977). Jeffrey Kitingan restructured the Foundation and by 1988 had transformed it into an institution promoting 'People Development' (Kitingan, 1987). This was a populist social programme that emphasized culturally sustainable, self-reliant, humanistic and participatory models of rural development, modelled on a pilot programme developed in Tambunan, the Kitingan brothers' home district.

Although the PBS joined the ruling BN coalition in 1986, relations between state and federal authorities remained tense and the government continued to see the party as a threat. Its leaders were accused of 'fanning parochial sentiments' and being 'anti-federal' (Loh, 1992: 225) and Mahathir was furious when the PBS left the ruling coalition to rejoin the opposition in the 1990 elections. Jeffrey Kitingan was imprisoned on charges of inciting secession and his successor at IDS, Dr Maximus Ongkili, another PBS stalwart, was also detained. Jeffrey Kitingan's orientation shifted during his detention and he began to diverge from the PBS agenda championed by his brother, Pairin. Jeffrey Kitingan developed a pro-federal 'New Sabah' policy and subsequently established a party, AKAR (Angkatan Keadilan Rakyat, People's Justice Force), which joined the ruling BN coalition. The federal government began to bypass state government, effectively starving the opposition PBS administration of funds (Loh, 1996). Through a combination of carrot and stick measures, the federal authorities were able to undermine the PBS and build up a pro-federalist power base, capitalizing, in part, on the political split between the Kitingan brothers.

The federal government regained power over Sabah in 1994 and the integrationist 'New Sabah' doctrine prevailed. Since then, the IDS as the state think tank has switched from supporting a PBS agenda to supporting a more federalist stance under the BN. Its remit was to introduce a 'paradigm shift' for Sabah, promoting 'integration' through new development programmes, involving some RM$500 million in 'special development funds'. The 'Outline Perspective Plan, Sabah 1995–2010' was produced jointly by the IDS and the State Department for Development as the main strategic instrument for state development, with the overt aim of 'bringing Sabah into line' with the federal vision of development.

The IDS still, however, retains significant points of difference from the Mahathirist mainstream. It continues to engage in advocacy for the poor and rural sector, working for marginalized groups in ways similar to the 'People Development' model developed during the 1980s. The institute has established expertise in the areas of ecologically and culturally sustainable, 'bottom-up' development. The old may be harmonized with the new through projects exploiting traditional rural knowledge in innovative ways, such as the strategic development of traditional herbal remedies for new-age agro-industry.

The IDS's expertise in development communication and rural development means that it continues to work effectively with NGOs involved in participatory development. It is involved with the Commonwealth Association for Local Action and Economic Development, an international NGO supporting people-centred development organizations. The IDS is an active member of the Association for Development Research and Training Institutes for the Asia-Pacific and has strong links with the Asia-Pacific Development Centre, an intergovernmental institute that brings together regional and international NGOs working in the areas of gender and development, environment and natural resources. The IDS reflects both 'development from above' and 'development from below', since it continues to develop alternative models of development that include civil society, local indigenous culture and sustainability in the development equation.

The MCA Task Force and the Institute of Strategic Planning and Analysis

The Institute of Strategic Analysis and Policy Research (INSAP) was established by the MCA, the leading Chinese component of the ruling BN coalition. The think tank developed out of the MCA Special Task Force, formed in the mid-1980s and mobilized in 1988 when the government commissioned a National Economic Consultative Committee (NECC) to discuss policy post-1990, when the NEP was scheduled to expire. The NECC included 150 political, academic and non-governmental representatives from all ethnic groups, and its deliberations culminated in the submission of a substantial report to the government.

The MCA Special Task Force played a leading role in the NECC. Led by Yong Poh Kon, a successful Chinese entrepreneur, it reflected the MCA's broad objective, which was to push post-NEP policy towards greater liberalization for Malaysia's ethnic minorities, especially in policy areas affecting Chinese businesses and education. The task force tactfully avoided any outright questioning of NEP's ethnic policy, recommending that more emphasis should be placed on growth instead of redistribution. Some liberalization had already occurred through Mahathir's reforms of the mid-1980s, so these suggestions were uncontroversial. Although the NECC report should have been the major consultative document paving the way for post-1990 policy, it was basically ignored. Mahathir set up the NECC as a sop to the MCA, but he may never have meant to take its findings seriously (Jomo, 1994: 29). However, the NECC report may have indirectly influenced the 'Vision 2020' agenda, which provided the keynote for Mahathirist policy in the 1990s (Jomo, 1994: 29).

Like the MCA Special Task Force that preceded it, INSAP was unable to gain much influence outside the MCA's own circle. INSAP has no permanent staff, relying on honorary members who are corporate figures, politicians and academics. One INSAP member criticized it for relying on 'feel' rather than empirical research (personal communication, 14 June 1995) and it is constrained in a similar way to the MCA itself. Being a junior member of the ruling coalition means that it is necessary to avoid the displeasure of the senior partner, UMNO. As a party think tank, INSAP's ability to influence ultimately depends on the degree to which UMNO is willing to compromise its own interests.

The 1990s

The involvement between think tanks and individual politicians became more apparent in the 1990s as leadership contests demanded more sophisticated campaigning methods. The 1980s saw the predominance of intra-party factional struggles, especially over leadership positions within the ruling party, UMNO (Means, 1991). Power had moved upwards, concentrating in the position of the prime minister and intensifying competition over key UMNO posts and ministerial portfolios. The proliferation of think tanks in the 1990s partly reflects the emerging leadership contests, with the ultimate question of who might succeed Mahathir. For example, the Institut Kajian Dasar (IKD) is linked to the former deputy prime minister, Anwar Ibrahim. Najib Razak, currently defence minister, is the patron of the Malaysian Strategic Research Centre (MSRC), and the current deputy prime minister, Abdullah Badawi, became the patron of the Centre for Intellectual Promotion and Technological Advancement (CIPTA) as he emerged as a likely contender for the top post.

While the 1980s combined economic liberalization with heavy-handed authoritarianism, the 1990s began by presenting a rather different policy environment. Consistent economic growth since 1987 had set the scene for 'Vision 2020', which was launched in 1991. Its broad appeal boosted the Mahathir government's popularity, returning it to power with a landslide victory in the 1995 elections (*New Straits Times*, 27 April 1996). The economic policies of the 1990s were not fundamentally different from those of the 1980s, but there was a shift towards subtler forms of hegemony based on positive, populist messages and a 'feel-good factor' promoted using slick media campaigns. 'Vision 2020' promised a new nation-building project – the achievement of 'fully developed nation', 'developed' not only in the economic sense, but also socially and culturally, envisioning a new multicultural 'Malaysian race ... united in full and fair partnership'. This optimistic and forward-looking national scenario was complemented by the emerging regional discourses of 'New Asia', 'Asian Renaissance' and 'Pacific Century'.

Malaysian think tanks became active in developing and popularizing these new frames of reference, adopting a more politically and culturally liberal language. 'Civil society' and a 'new era in politics' were represented by a new generation of young, media-friendly politicians with a less ethnically nationalist and more global, cosmopolitan outlook. The 1990s media boom gave broadcast and print media a more upfront role in the construction of a new hegemonic vision of 'Malaysia Boleh!' ('Malaysia can do it!'), a modernist and technocratic but distinctively 'Asian' vision deploying both Islamic and East Asian cultural references.

IKIM: a modernist Islamic vision

Influenced by, and responding to, the 'Vision 2020', the think tanks of the 1990s were created not just to influence policy 'insiders', but also to shape broader public opinion. Mahathir's attempts to domesticate the power of Islam reached a peak with the establishment of IKIM, a prestigious, government-funded Islamic research institute. IKIM's domestic role was to promote a Malaysian identity that was modern, technocratic and multicultural, yet assertive of Islam's centrality. It adopted a moderate and pro-capitalist stance, emphasizing the need for the 'image-correction of Islam' (*Asiaweek*, 15 September 1993). It promotes a moderate and acceptable face for Islam domestically and internationally, making extensive use of the government-dominated national print and broadcast media, with dedicated columns and broadcast slots allocated to its activities and views.

IKIM describes itself as not 'an Islamic institute based on religious knowledge' but a 'policy-oriented group, looking at policy from an Islamic point of view' (interview with IKIM director-general, 22 March 1995). Its research agenda reflects the search for complementarities between Islam and the Mahathirist vision of technocratic economic development. IKIM has two distinct audiences: an international scholarly audience and the Malaysian general public. The former sits within a context of Malaysia's push to position itself as a key Islamic player in the 'knowledge economy', anticipating a future 'global shift' in the Islamic world towards the 'New Asia'. IKIM has links to scholarly organizations like the International Institute of Islamic Thought (IIIT) in Washington, DC, and similar institutes in Britain, Turkey, Australia and Japan. It has participated in high-profile interfaith dialogues such as the 1994 'Parliament of World Religions' and it has advised the European Union and Scandinavian government on policy regarding Muslim minorities and the promotion of religious tolerance.

IKIM is an impressive illustration of the Mahathir administration's ability to harness Islam to its programme of modernization. Its high-profile premises showed the willingness of government to devote significant resources to develop Islamic ideas that could play a strategic part in the mainstream development vision of the 1990s.

The IKD: the Anwar connection

The IKD was established by the founder of the Muslim Youth Movement (Angkatan Belia Islam Malaysia) and former deputy prime minister, Anwar Ibrahim, in 1985, with Anwar's speech-writer and fellow activist, Kamaruddin Jaafar, as chairman. The IKD was set up as an activist institution, geared towards training youth and workers in leadership skills and citizenship. The IKD can be seen as part of a wider 'family' of Islamic reformist organizations connected to Anwar and ABIM, which is one of the largest NGOs in the country, with some 60,000 active members.

The reformist Islamic tradition articulates concerns about the inadequacies of secular models of economic development, aspiring towards a modernist Islamic model of holistic human development (*pembinaan insan*). It emphasizes the 'spiritual, moral and ethical considerations, on which religious belief and principles of development are based' (IKD, 1995). The IKD places great emphasis on the concept of *budaya ilmu* or 'knowledge culture'. Their approach favours a more 'organically intellectual' than technocratic view. A participative ethos is reflected in its training activities, targeting middle-level public servants, junior managers, workers and students.

Anwar's ascendancy to the post of deputy prime minister in 1993 led the IKD to develop a higher profile. Between 1994 and 1997, it gained visibility as a 'respectable research organization' (interview with IKD director, June 1995), able to co-operate and compete with the established mainstream think tanks, but with particular research and policy strengths in the areas of Islamic, youth and cultural policy, which were specific political strengths for Anwar. By the mid-1990s, the IKD had gained prominence on the bustling national seminar circuit, sponsoring a major national seminar on voluntarism in collaboration with the Ministry of Youth and Sports, and hosting a flamboyant conference on the intellectual legacy of José Rizal, the Filipino nationalist. The latter was part of a series of activities to develop the theme of 'Asian Renaissance', a platform that could position Anwar as a key intellectual with broadly 'Asian' as well as specifically Islamic intellectual credentials. Reflecting a higher level of influence, the Rizal conference was attended by regional heads of state, diplomats and politicians, as well as scholars.

The IKD evolved a hybrid model of intellectual participation that was part academic institution, part mainstream political think tank and part non-mainstream Islamic activist organization. It has strong connections to the Malaysian Youth Council (Majlis Belia Malaysia), which provides access to a large and important section of the public, representing thirty-seven large NGOs with around two million members. The IKD continued to develop these links throughout the 1990s, delivering youth training and civic education programmes, reaching out to a wide section of mainly young Malay Muslims, and building bridges with a diversity of other youth groups.

There were interesting similarities between the IDS and the IKD during the early and mid-1990s, since both think tanks illustrated the politics of co-optation, bringing together the dominant policy mainstream and alternative paradigms. These think tanks formed a bridge between the NGO–grass-roots constellation (associated with civil society) and the technocratic/authoritarian mainstream (associated with state power and dominant political figures). Both institutions originated outside the centre of power, and retained their linkages to non-governmental organizations involved in grass-roots activities. They moved towards the mainstream of political power following the capture of state power in the IDS case and the political rise of Anwar in the case of the IKD.

Anwar Ibrahim was tipped to succeed Mahathir until the former was sacked in 1998. His rise had been viewed optimistically by some NGOs and activists, who hoped that he could reform Malaysian politics 'from within' and bring civil society back into the political system if he could succeed Mahathir. His political platform of 'civil society' and youth, and his background as a social justice activist and founder of Malaysia's leading Islamic NGO, indicated that he might bring a new style of leadership. However, in September 1998, Anwar became a victim of 'a high-level conspiracy' when he was arrested, held without charge under the Internal Security Act and seriously assaulted by the Inspector-General of Police (Amnesty International, 1998). There was public uproar when a photograph was published showing his injuries. He was subsequently accused of sexual offences and abuse of power. After a deeply flawed and sensational trial, deemed 'unfair' by Amnesty International (1999), he was sentenced to six years in prison for abuse of power. His appeals were rejected and in 2000 he was sentenced to an additional nine years' imprisonment.

Mahathir appeared to have acted to forestall a leadership challenge from Anwar. In removing Anwar and dealing with the ensuing public outcry, Mahathir's government resorted to 'measures including the misuse of law, state institutions and the courts, the ill-treatment of detainees to coerce confessions, and the erosion of the right to a fair trial' (Amnesty International, 2000). The Anwar saga catalysed a mass public reaction. Public rallies were held, calling for Mahathir's removal, democratization and *'reformasi'* (government reform), and a new opposition party, the National Justice Party (Keadilan), was formed, led by Anwar's wife, Wan Azizah.

Following Anwar's removal from government, the IKD reverted to a non-governmental approach, focusing on civil society, democratization and *reformasi* issues. It established a Political Education Unit, targeting student and youth groups as potential agents for democratic change, and running seminars and workshops on political understanding and human rights. The Anwar affair and rise of the *reformasi* movement have sharpened the divisions between Mahathir's government and an emerging civil society. The IKD's links to both Anwar and civil society mean that it forms advocacy coalitions with human rights NGOs, the *reformasi* movement, opposition parties and campaigns against restrictive or punitive legislation like the Internal Security Act and other human rights abuses, especially cases of police brutality against public protesters and prisoners.

Conclusion: Malaysian think tanks, governance and the democratic deficit in the 'New Asia'

The emergence of Malaysian think tanks in the 1980s coincided with Mahathir's reforms, which improved bureaucratic efficiency and deepened government–business linkages, but continued to rely on, and increase, authoritarian forms of control. Malaysian think tanks partly reflect the wider processes of global consensus-building along neo-liberal lines, but in an Asian variant that is more interventionist and reliant on authoritarian rather than democratic forms. The 'New Asia' and 'Asian

Values' discourses were elite-driven, and tended to be conservative and authoritarian. Consensus was valued, but its proponents were willing to meet, or forestall, dissent with coercive and even arbitrary power.

Think tanks such as ISIS, MIER and IKIM emerged to service the political and technocratic needs of the Mahathir administration, but other institutions reflect the salience of internal political struggles and competition as well as the emergence of alternative and challenging positions to the Mahathir regime. The consolidation in the 1990s of a Mahathir/Anwar 'dream team' led to the co-option of alternatives such as Islamic ideas or 'People Development'. This co-option process broadened the intellectual hegemony of the government, allowing it to project a more populist vision. During this 'vision' period, 'hybrid' think tanks such as the IDS and the IKD were able to retain some elements of their distinctive, non-elite, civil society connections and capitalize on the NGO boom or 'associational revolution' of the 1990s (see Yamamoto, 1995). While the influential mainstream think tanks like ISIS played a key 'envisioning' role, hybrid think tanks seemed better placed to build genuine synergies between government and the much-neglected civil society sector, since they were already attempting to reconcile governmental and non-governmental conceptions of development. Although NGOs like the TWN found some common ground with Mahathir during the 1990s when both were advocating a 'Southern' perspective on development issues, NGOs are more likely to retain critical distance from domestic government, while having relatively little influence over it. However, the TWN has gained a particularly important international profile since the 1990s as a NGO think tank that can argue the case for the 'South' in important areas of global development policy, such as the WTO, intellectual property rights, the environment and biosafety.

The 1997 Asian crisis highlighted the difficulty of harmonizing governmental and non-governmental approaches. As the government–civil society relationship is increasingly replaced by conflict and repression, think tanks inevitably have to choose between toeing the mainstream government line and allying with NGOs, human rights movements, opposition parties and more resistant and alternative agendas.

From the technocratic perspective, the demand for strategic expertise is likely to continue to grow, especially in areas such as human resource development, future-oriented industrialization, the 'knowledge economy' and sustainable development. Think tanks' policies, ideas and plans may serve the interests of existing 'distributional coalitions' or help to consolidate new ones associated with specific emerging policy areas. Newcomers will seek to achieve a balance between competition and collaboration with the larger and more established institutions.

The social agenda of the 1990s started to address questions about the quality of life, ethical development and multiculturalism, but this has taken a back seat to accommodate the exigencies of economic crisis, recovery and its political fallout. As new policy areas develop, think tanks can be expected to play the roles not just of experts but also of partisans and visionaries.

The greatest challenge for Malaysian think tanks as visionaries and partisans is probably that of democratization and human rights. In contradiction to the comparative studies that suggest a positive correlation between economic development and democracy (such as Lipset, 1960; Moore, 1996), the Malaysian case shows that democracy can decrease in quality as economic 'development' accelerates. The government relies increasingly on coercive legalism, 'the use of legally constituted laws and amendments to laws to ensure authoritarian rule over citizens' (Saravanamuttu, 2002: 4). Authoritarianism has become more obvious and the government has come to rely on extreme and bizarre measures to maintain power in the face of crisis and challenge (International Bar Association *et al.*, 2000; Saravanamuttu, 2002). The 1990s presented opportunities for Malaysian society to evolve towards a more inclusive and sustainable society worthy of the 'Asian Renaissance' label, with greater emphasis on civil society and a creative approach to endogenous and alternative views of development. These hopes have receded as the Asian Crisis has turned into political crisis, political crisis has led to arbitrary power and this, in turn, has led to systemic injustice and a worsening human rights record.

Appendix: Malaysian think tanks

Think tank	Established Date	Established By	Staff	Location	Main funding sources	Policy focus
Centre for Policy Research (CPR)	1974	University of Science Malaysia	9	Penang	University research and development funds, contract research	Social policy, rural and regional development
Institute for Strategic and International Studies (ISIS)	1983	Mahathir Cabinet	70	Kuala Lumpur	Government endowment, contract research, international organizations	All areas of national development policy, 'second-track' diplomacy
Third World Network (TWN)	1984	Consumers' Association of Penang, partner NGO	n.a.	Penang	International organizations	Global development policy: trade issues, intellectual property, biosafety
Institute for Development Studies (IDS)	1985	Sabah state government	66	Kota Kinabalu	State government grants, contract research, international organizations	State development policy, rural and regional development
Institute for Policy Studies (Institut Kajian Dasar, IKD)	1985	Anwar Ibrahim	20	Kuala Lumpur	Private sector sponsorship, seminars and conferences, international organizations	Social policy: youth, culture, education and labour policy; political education
Malaysian Institute for Economic Research (MIER)	1986	Council on Malaysian Invisible Trade (COMIT)	32	Kuala Lumpur	Government and private sector endowments, contract research, membership, international organizations	Economic research and forecasting
Institute of Strategic Analysis and Policy Research (INSAP)	1989	MCA	15–20[a]	Kuala Lumpur	MCA Secretariat	Economic policy, Chinese business
Malaysia Institute of Islamic Understanding (IKIM)	1992	Mahathir cabinet	30	Kuala Lumpur	Government endowment, contract research, international organizations	Islamic affairs
Malaysian Strategic Research Centre (MSRC)	1993	Najib Razak	8	Kuala Lumpur	Razak Foundation, international organizations	Strategic issues, defence, labour policy
Sarawak Development Institute (SDI)	1995	Sarawak state government	12	Kuching	State government grant, international organizations, private sector donations	State development policy
Centre for Intellectual Promotion and Technological Advancement (CIPTA)	2000	n.a.	n.a.	Kuala Lumpur	n.a.	Science and technology policy

[a]Honorary members only. n.a. = information not available.

12 Miguel Braun, Antonio Cicioni and Nicolas J. Ducote

Think tanks in developing countries: lessons from Argentina

Civil society, and non-profit organizations in particular, have expanded rapidly in Argentina since the return of democracy in 1983. The military dictatorship of 1976–83 systematically suppressed political and civil liberties and thus thwarted the development of these organizations. Since then, new organizations of various sorts, including political parties, local and international ecological organizations, human rights groups, private universities, faith-based organizations, research centres and think tanks, have emerged and flourished. This makes Argentina an interesting case study for the growth and evolution of think tanks and their influence in the policy process.

In this chapter we concentrate not only on research and advocacy organizations oriented towards influencing policy decisions, but also on research bodies that implement policy jointly with government. The chapter is organized as follows. First we present an operational definition of think tanks in Argentina. Next we discuss the evolution and current situation of think tanks. In the following section we define the concept of the policy implementation think tank and argue that it could play an important role in developing the country's policy-making. We go on to present a case study that illustrates our points, and finally to conclude that despite recent financial and economic strains, the prospects for think tanks remain favourable.

Think tanks in Argentina

The number of non-profit organizations in Argentina skyrocketed during the 1980s, as it did in many other Latin American countries, following the transition from an authoritarian to a democratic political system that took place during that decade. Years of military regimes weakened the fabric of civil society and made it difficult for groups of volunteers to associate to form civic organizations, particularly to organize around political or policy issues. With the return to democracy in 1983, it was possible for Argentines to start organizing and giving shape to a third sector again. The roots of civil organization go back to 1853, when the drafters of the Argentine Constitution first recognized the right of citizens 'to form associations for useful purposes'. This right to associate in voluntary organizations was ratified and its importance highlighted in Article 14 of the revised constitutional text of 1994. Today, with over 36 million inhabitants, Argentina has approximately 5000 organizations that fall into the NGO category. Over 80 per cent of these have been created since the late 1980s, with a dramatic increase in the number and resources of non-profit organizations throughout the 1990s.

Many non-profit public policy research or advocacy organizations came into existence in this period of time, particularly as the policy role of political parties and government agencies lagged behind the demands imposed by the significant transformation of Argentina's economy during the last decade. This void was filled by organizations aiming to lobby policy-makers to take their positions into account and thus affect the decision-making processes at different levels of government. Some of these organizations focus on specific issues (for example, the Asociación Conciencia on responsible citizenship, and Poder Ciudadano working on transparency), while others – such as the Centro de Estudios para el Desarrollo Institucional (CEDI), the research branch of the Fundación Gobierno y Sociedad (FGS) – have broader agendas of economic and political reform. What they all have in common is their intent to bridge the gap between the demands of certain groups of civil society and the work of policy-makers.

However, the term 'think tank' is extremely elusive and elastic. One of the causes of difficulty in characterizing the term is the heterogeneity of patterns of organizations that share a common objective: a link with public policies – even though these policies may comprise a broad set of subjects (Salamon and Anheier, 1992). This difficulty is particularly serious in Argentina, where a history of authoritarianism and suppression of civil society associations has led to a unique development of the third sector. Only with the return of democracy in 1983 could civil society develop freely. Since then, several new think tanks have been created. Furthermore, some pre-existing organizations, such as the academic-oriented (Facultad Latinoamericana de Ciencias Sociales (FLACSO)) have adopted think tank-like characteristics as the state has become more pluralist and receptive to civil society influences.

The particular nature of the Argentine case leads us to choose a broad definition of 'think tanks', based principally on the role that an organization assumes rather than the particular structure that it adopts. We define think tanks as organizations that undertake analysis of scientific or technical characteristics related to public policies, and that follow certain criteria related to the publicity of their work. We will also analyse organizations that centre their activity on advocacy rather than research, but still play a key role in the policy process.

The evolution of think tanks in Argentina: history and classification

In this section we classify think tanks in Argentina into four categories: (1) private research centres, (2) political party foundations, (3) attorney's NGOs and (4) policy implementation think tanks. These organizations emerged in three waves: first, those that were created before the restoration of democracy in 1983; secondly, those that appeared during the first two democratic governments (before the state reform driven by Carlos Menem); and thirdly, those founded since the mid-1990s. The different political realities existing when the think tanks appeared were not only the cause of their creation, but also influenced their functioning and the kind of relationship they established with the state.

The first wave of think tanks in Argentina was clearly shaped by the authoritarian and corporatist character of the state during the period 1966–83. This explains both the form and activities that were common to these organizations. The institutional model adopted was the *private research centre* (see Levy, 1996). The relationship with the state was virtually none because of the risks involved in working with an authoritarian government. As Schmitter argues more generally:

> Although a third sector can coexist with state-led corporatism, it would then lack pluralist features such as true privateness, spontaneous creation and growth, multiple organizations, autonomy from government, voluntary association, diverse founders and authorities, interinstitutional competition, and system decentralization. Instead [private research centres] would be dependent on an architect state, which would create or at least carefully license, regulate, coordinate, control, and subsidize. (1974: 93–4)

Private research centres, such as the Fundación de Investigaciones Económicas Latinoamericanas (FIEL), established in 1964, isolated themselves to maintain autonomy from the state (which had expelled researchers from the universities). On 26 June 1966, Ongania's military government authorized the police to enter the University of Buenos Aires, with the goal of eliminating political opposition. Faculty and students were expelled, in what came to be known as the tragic 'Night of the Long Clubs'. Consequently (and as noted more generally of Latin American think tanks – see Sherwood Truitt, 2000: 53), these institutes were mostly of a traditional academic character somewhat distant from policy-making concerns.

With the return of democracy, a period of pluralization took place.

However, many of the corporatist aspects of the state did not disappear, among them the prevalence of state-owned enterprises, government-mediated labour negotiations, and widespread regulation of economic activity. Therefore, the think tanks moulded by authoritarian governments collaborated with the new government but not through direct institutional engagement or policy partnership. Instead, many think tank researchers formed the basis for the technical cadre of the state. Among them we may mention Dante Caputo and Felipe Sola from the Centro de Investigaciones Sociales sobre el Estado (CISEA); Domingo Cavallo, Humberto Petrei and Aldo Dadone from the Fundación Mediterránea; Roque Fernandez and Carlos Rodriguez from the Centro de Estudios Macroeconomicos de Argentina (CEMA), Ricardo Lopez Murphy and Daniel Artana from FIEL, Jose Luis Machinea from the Fundación Argentina para el Desarrollo con Equidad (FADE) and Oscar Oszlak from the Centro de Estudios de Estado y Sociedad (CEDES). Many of these researchers became ministers, secretaries and advisors in the new democratic government, following a 'revolving door' model that is common in the United States.

In addition, the return of democracy permitted a second wave of think tanks to emerge: *political party foundations* and what Thompson (1994) calls *attorney's NGOs*. Both of these groups are a byproduct of democracy, pluralization and a change in the way citizens relate to political parties. Foundations related to political parties are a direct consequence of the retrenchment of mass politics and the laws that govern political party and campaign finance. As these laws impose restrictions on sources of financing for politics, they create incentives to open foundations, which sometimes also work as think tanks, to channel financing to a particular politician and not to a party. For example, CEDES is close to the Radical Party (Sherwood Truitt, 2000: 530).

Attorney's NGOs are devoted mostly to fostering democracy via advocacy work. They are called attorney's NGOs because, according to Thompson, they 'do not produce research, do not advise government agencies, do not generate basic information nor do they train human resources for key decision positions. However, they do exert pressure when policy decisions are taken' (1994: 4). Their existence would be impossible without a democratic government, and they are strengthened as people learn to live in a democratic system. For example, the Asociación Conciencia was founded in 1982 and engages mostly in issue campaigning in favour of democratic institutions and policies upholding republican governance. It currently works in fourteen provinces and has thirty-one offices throughout the country.

Finally, with the pluralization and the retrenchment of the state from its traditional functions, a third wave of think tanks is emerging: *policy implementation think tanks*. Since 1983, several processes that affected the relationship between the state and civil society have begun to develop. As mentioned before, democracy brought about a pluralization of society and the state that strengthened civil society. The reforms carried out by Carlos Menem's government in the 1990s led to a consolidation of a free market economy, as well as a redefinition of the role of the state. These changes fostered the creation of implementation think tanks. The failure of the state in the implementation of public policy, and its subsequent retrenchment from its traditional public service functions, opened a new opportunity for NGOs that worked in public policy. Furthermore, the pluralization of the state gave the opportunity for these newly created think tanks to work with different governments on implementation projects. Their proclivity for teaming up with local or national government agencies for the delivery as well as conceptualization of policy distinguishes them from the older, more academic-style think tanks. Indeed, they might be described as 'think-and-do tanks' (Stone, 1996b). Founded in 2000, the Centre for the Implementation of Public Policies Promoting Equity and Growth (CIPPEC) works closely across party lines with leaders in academia, business and the media to build action-oriented coalitions that aim to improve government outcomes. Likewise, the Grupo Sophia, another implementation-oriented think tank founded in 1995, brings together a group of young leaders with a vocation for public service. The group finances and develops a wide variety of projects related to public policy and public affairs, working in conjunction with academia, the private sector and government.

Table 12.1 presents a selection of the most important think tanks in the four organizational categories we describe, together with their year of foundation. Whilst only twenty-eight are listed here, the number of think tanks active in Argentina today is closer to fifty (Thompson, 1994), although it is difficult to categorize organizations precisely as think tanks according to our criteria.

In sum, think tanks created during the first wave concentrated mainly on research of issues at the national level. This is a consequence of both their origin – they were created by researchers who could not work in the public universities – and the difficulty of working on policy advocacy or implementation under a dictatorship, together with the lower prevalence of decentralization of policy under the military. Consequently, most Argentine think tanks focus on national-level policy issues and most are based in the capital city. Their client group varies, but is mainly composed of the state, private donors, international organizations such as the Inter-American Development Bank, and interest groups that finance research. Many think tanks like FIEL also find it necessary to sell services such as monthly economic reports as a way to finance their operations.

The second wave was quite heterogeneous. New research groups appeared, together with foundations linked to political parties and

Table 12.1 Classification of think tanks in Argentina by organizational form

Private research centres	Political party foundations	Attorney's NGOs	Implementation think tanks
Instituto de Desarrollo Económico y Social (IDES) (1960)	Fundación Andina (1984)	Asoción Conciencia (1982)	Grupo Sophia (1995)
Fundación de Investigaciones Económicas Latinoamericanas (FIEL) (1964)	Fundación del Sur (1987)	Centro de Estudios Legales y Sociales (CELS) (1985)	Innova (1999)
Centro de Estudios e Investigaciones Laborales (CEIL) (1971)	Siglo XXI (1987)	Poder Ciudadano (1989)	Centro de Implementación de Politicas para la Equidad y el Crecimento (CIPPEC) (2000)
Facultad Latinoamericana de Ciencias Sociales (FLACSO) (1972)	Fundación Karakachoff (1989)		
Centro de Estudios de Estado y Sociedad (CEDES) (1975)			
Centro de Investigaciones Sociales sobre el Estado (CISEA) (1975)	Fundación Centro de Estudios para el Cambio Estructural (CECE) (1990)		
Centro de Estudios Macroeconomicos de Argentina (CEMA) (1976)	Fundación Argentina para la Libertad de la Información (FUALI) (1992)		
Fundación Mediterranea (1977)	Fundación Argentina para el Desarrollo con Equidad (FADE) (1997)		
Fundación de Investigaciones para el Desarrollo (FIDE) (1978)	Fundación Creer y Crecer (2001)		
Fundación Libertad (1988)			
Centro Interdisciplinario para el Estudio de Políticas Públicas (CIEPP) (1989)			
Fundación Capital (1993)			
Centro de Estudios para el Desarrollo Institucional (CEDI) (1997)			
Grupo FÉNIX (2001)			

Note: All think tank names are followed by date of establishment.

attorney's NGOs. These organizations specialized mainly in advocacy and research focused on the national agenda, mainly with the goal of strengthening civil society and democratic values. The third wave of think tanks that is currently appearing works in implementation, at both the national and local levels of government. A more open and pluralistic media, the retrenchment of the state from its traditional functions, and decentralization of functions to local governments contribute to this focus. We argue in the next section that this third wave is producing a type of think tank that can play an increasingly important role in policy-making, especially in developing countries. Indeed, this category could be applied to the Sabah-based IDS (see chapter 11 in this volume).

Policy implementation think tanks

In Figure 12.1, we classify the main Argentine think tanks along the axes of orientation and level of operation. On the vertical axis we classify think tanks in respect of what proportion of their resources is allocated to conducting research or engaging in the implementation of projects and policies. On the horizontal axis, we classify them in respect of the extent to which their focus is on national or regional policy-making. The trend in recent years has been for think tank growth to occur mainly in the top two quadrants.

Figure 12.1 Research versus implementation orientation of Argentine think tanks

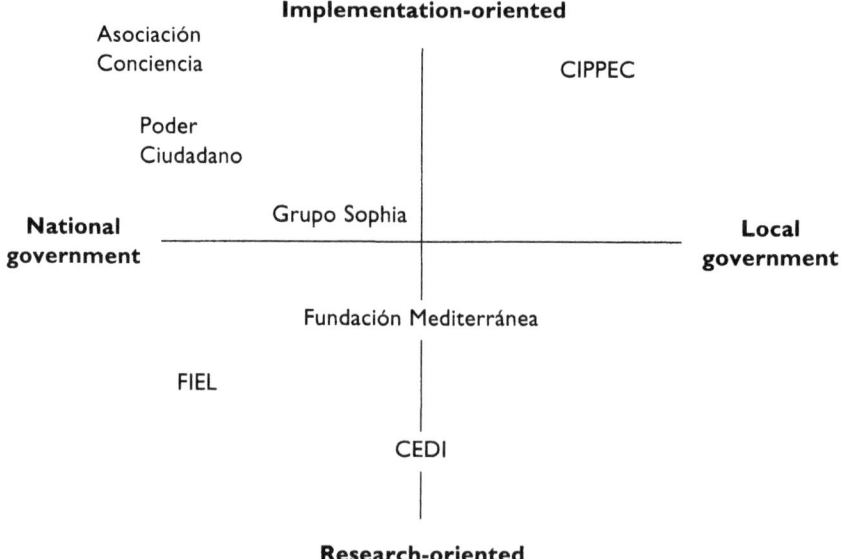

We have stated that think tanks are generally considered to be organizations that attempt to influence policy by producing ideas applied to policy problems through high-quality research, and then trying to convince policy-makers to implement these ideas. In an article on think tanks, William Dunn (1996: 1) argued that

> One of the main functions of think tanks is to conduct policy analyses which offer creative, insightful and even counterintuitive solutions for complex problems of great public importance. Nevertheless, think tanks are unlikely to earn a reputation for excellence unless they concentrate on alternative solutions to a problem – rather than the supposed certainty that a single policy will solve that problem – and judiciously employ a strategy of multiple advocacy in reaching policy recommendations. Think tanks must develop specific strategies of contingent policy communication to guide the preparation of policy documents and oral briefings. After all, the mission of think tanks is to improve public policy by maximizing the likelihood that policy analyses will be used to solve real-world problems.

We argue that think tanks that invest resources in actual micro-policy formulation and implementation – especially in developing countries – have a higher likelihood of influencing policy, and can become relevant and positive actors in policy-making.

We have suggested that the main think tanks and advocacy groups in Argentina can play an important role in the formulation of policy and in increasing public awareness on certain policy issues, such as the importance of civic participation, corruption and the environment. However, the third sector can be an even more *active participant* in the policy process rather than only a *policy informant*. In particular, a policy implementation think tank could contribute to improving the quality of policies pursued and the effectiveness with which they are implemented, especially at the provincial and municipal level.

A policy implementation think tank involved in micro-policy formulation actively lobbies the different levels of government to promote the implementation of these policies. Accordingly, these think tanks are more likely to be encountered in local and regional policy domains. This type of organization also attempts to bridge the gap between research and policy-making that exists especially in developing countries. In these countries, state capacity – especially at the local level – is lower than in developed countries, and bureaucrats are less willing or able to implement the ideas put forward by research institutions. This means that the caveat often placed on developed country think tanks regarding not getting involved with actual policy implementation is counterbalanced by the added benefit of doing so.

A policy implementation think tank is different from a typical think tank in that its emphasis is not on producing and publishing research. Rather, the resources of the organization are mainly devoted to helping different levels of government implement better policies. This can be done in two ways: either by providing technical assistance and consulting services or by conducting advocacy campaigns to mobilize voters for a cause, so as to give incentives to politicians to implement the desired changes. The relevant question now is whether such an organization can play a relevant and positive role in developing country policy-making. In addition to the traditional contributions made by think tanks, it can:

1 *articulate the efforts of domestic and international think tanks and research centres*, making ideas available to policy-makers and facilitating processes of cross-national and cross-regional policy learning (Dolowitz and Marsh, 2000). This is relevant in developing countries, because the bureaucracy often lacks the political motivation or the ability to understand and implement the recommendations of think tanks. Thus, an organization that concentrates on working with the different levels of government, providing technical assistance and consulting services, can contribute to overcoming these difficulties.
2 *contribute much-needed human capital at the local level of government*. In many developing countries, there are simply not enough qualified people to fill the necessary positions in each province or municipality. Thus, a think tank that works on policy implementation at the local level of government can take advantage of economies of scale arising from the replication of projects in different regions.
3 *help reform-minded policy-makers implement their programmes more effectively*. In many cases, honest, competent politicians are elected to local office. If these politicians are successful in implementing a reform agenda, and are recognized by their electorate, the national press or other opinion formers, it can generate a demonstration effect across jurisdictions, again promoting policy learning and improving policy-making throughout the country.

The synergies between the different activities give this type of organization the potential to become a role model for think tanks throughout the region. Traditional think tanks are not suited to this purpose, because their resources are mostly dedicated to research and publication. Thus, despite the high standard of their academic product, their ideas often do not reach the relevant policy-maker, or are not implemented due to a lack of political will, technical expertise or voter pressure.

A case from Argentina

In this section we discuss how a policy implementation think tank can be a key factor in facilitating the introduction of innovative policies, by analysing the implementation of charter schools in the province of San

Luis, Argentina. One of the authors of this paper, Antonio Cicioni, was co-ordinator of this project, as part of the FGS team hired by the province in 1999.

Argentina has over 40,000 primary and secondary schools. The 23 provinces and the autonomous city of Buenos Aires manage public schools, and regulate the system of private schools, which 24 per cent of the country's children attend. Provinces vary greatly in size, ranging from Buenos Aires, with 13,782 schools, to Tierra del Fuego, with only 109. In some provinces, a large share of students attend private schools (46 per cent in the case of Buenos Aires), while in others this share is almost insignificant (for example, Chaco, Neuquén and Formosa with less than 9 per cent) (Dirección General Red Federal de Información, 2000).

The Federal Law of Education of 1993 introduced a new institutional arrangement for education, decentralizing most responsibilities to the provinces, making them the main actors in defining and implementing policies for elementary schooling. This posed a difficult challenge for most provinces, given that historically they had not considered education their exclusive responsibility. Under the new rules, they found themselves virtually alone in facing the many and complicated interests that the different stakeholders have in shaping education policy. Furthermore, the economic stability that Argentina experienced following the introduction of a Currency Board in 1991 made rational planning of government actions feasible again. In particular, it allowed greater deliberation in the allocation of public resources. Finally, the traditionally weak state capacity of provincial governments was seriously challenged by the incorporation of hundreds of new schools, further complicating the situation of their long-neglected bureaucracies.

A few years after the conclusion of the decentralization process, it is clear that some provinces are adjusting better than others to the new situation. Some have shown themselves much more willing than others to innovate in the sensitive area of education. The small province of San Luis is probably the best example among the innovators.

San Luis has one of the smallest educational systems in the country. The Ministry of Education manages 362 schools, and there are about 47 private schools (Dirección General Red Federal de Información, 2000). At least one third of public institutions are very small rural schools with up to three teachers. San Luis has also enjoyed political stability and increased prosperity since the return to democracy in 1983. However, education policy has been very unstable. The government has made several attempts to implement major systemic changes. For example, between 1983 and 2000 it passed a provincial law of education, created and then eliminated a Ministry of Education, organized a congress of educators to discuss and agree on a provincial educational policy, and created new administrative regions, among other reforms. However, these efforts could not avoid permanent conflict with teachers' unions. Education ministers lasted on average less than two years. Furthermore, when a national standardized test was taken for the first time in 1993, it showed that the performance of San Luis schools was dismal. The same occurred with the second evaluation, taken in 1994. Once again, the governor sacked the minister, and offered the position to Héctor Torino, a young politician from a small town in the interior of the province. Torino has achieved what seemed impossible: surviving as a minister. He resigned after being in charge for four years but was able to implement reforms which are unique in Argentina.

In November 1998, Antonio Cicioni, while working for FGS, visited San Luis to evaluate the reforms made to the regulations for becoming a school principal or a system supervisor. As in the rest of Argentina, the procedures to attain those positions were heavily regulated by the Teacher's Statute from 1960 – Law N 2886. San Luis eliminated the old rules, and allowed a new influx of educators into public schools. During the interview, the minister invited the FGS to help integrate his management team at the ministry. The FGS responded by proposing to implement charter schools in San Luis. Although Torino did not know about the charter schools movement in the United States (see, for example, Hassel, 1995; Nathan, 1996; Manno, 1997), he was acquainted with independent schools in Britain. The legislation that gave the legal background for the San Luis charter schools was inspired by the American charter schools legislation. Although there was no direct support from US think tanks, FGS staff had established informal contacts with these organizations and gathered relevant information from them.

A team of five FGS staff moved to San Luis in February 1999, staying until January 2,000. By then, the first five charter schools in Argentina had opened their doors, with more than 2000 students registered (more than 2 per cent of the total number of students in San Luis), and more than 200 educators hired. Furthermore, conditions were set for the opening of three new schools in March 2001. The result was that when the 2001 term ended, the charter schools register reached 4,500 students (equivalent to half of the students from the private schools) with 247 teachers and 27 managers.

These charter schools are self-managed schools funded by the government. They are public schools, so they are not allowed to select or discriminate their student population in any arbitrary way, and they cannot charge students any kind of fee. Funds are paid monthly to the not-for-profit corporations ('educational associations') that run the schools, according to the number of students they have. The per-student allocation varies according to the location of the school, and the type and level of education (see Roitter and González Bombal, 2000). In the case of San Luis, the educational associations are awarded a five-year government contract, which can be extended if the school proves it has been able to improve the quality of education. The idea was to create better schools without spending more funds than allocated to state-run public schools. If charter schools are well implemented, it is possible to offer those who cannot afford an expensive private education the opportunity to attend a better, mission-focused school. In short, an effective charter school programme can create effective schools where the government fails to do so.

The experience of implementing charter schools in San Luis led us to identify at least four key elements necessary to implement an effective charter schools programme. First, the legislation that allows the creation of charter schools must be adequate, since small differences in the regulations can imply big differences in the policy outcome. Second, it is essential to be able to select the winning projects exclusively on the basis of merit criteria. Third, it is important to give interested educators assistance in how to create a charter school, particularly for those who have not been involved previously in the creation of a privately run school. Finally, it is fundamental to establish an effective auditing system once the schools exist, especially regarding the administration of public funds. In these processes, the FGS played a key role as a 'policy transfer entrepreneur' (Dolowitz and Marsh, 2000: 345). In other words, they acted as intermediaries between the scholarly community and the policy domain, importing and modifying ideas about charter schools for implementation in Argentina.

In this charter schools programme, hiring an independent think tank was essential to guarantee the correct implementation of these four elements. The FGS was an independent external organization. However, the FGS team worked very closely with the education minister in the implementation of the project. In some situations, the team 'used' its independence as a way to push the agenda. In other cases, it practically acted as an official voice of executive power. Below, we detail three examples of how this was put into practice and show how a think tank can help governments effectively introduce innovative public policies.

1 *The prestige factor*: that the team was part of a prestigious Buenos Aires organization was useful for the local government's strategy, which stressed that experienced professionals were in charge of developing key aspects of the programme. However, this same strategy eventually led to the accusation from some local groups of this being a 'foreign' project. Consequently, this element was discarded for the public 'selling' of the project in the local community, and this tactic was limited to different contexts, such as other provincial governments, foreign academics or the media.

2 *The independence factor*: that the FGS was an external organization

operating with a high degree of autonomy for developing the project allowed it to guarantee non-interference from government in some key aspects of the implementation process. For example, it was possible to establish an evaluation committee that was completely independent of the Ministry of Education. It also permitted the team to talk to opposition parties or groups, and to educators not identified with the provincial government, from a different perspective, less influenced by suspicion than if it had been part of the ministry. Finally, the Ministry of Education allowed the team to take charge, from 2000 onwards, of the auditing programme for the schools. This is a task where independence of criteria and action is essential in attaining the goals of transparency and effective use of public funds. The auditing is undertaken by another Buenos Aires policy implementation think tank, CIPPEC.

3 *The flexibility factor*: provincial bureaucracies in Argentina are very rigid organizations that have tight restrictions on action. For the FGS, being an external organization with its own funding and hiring capabilities was essential to retain the necessary flexibility to perform all its responsibilities. In stark contrast to the different sections of the ministry, the team could allocate its resources according to the project's short-term needs, in a process that had several changes from one month to the next. Both the ministry and state-run schools are severely limited in their ability to do this, because of the numerous restrictions and rules that affect the use of financial resources and hiring of personnel.

Had the government lacked the political vision and courage to carry on with a policy that has so many powerful enemies, it would not have been possible to develop the San Luis charter schools project successfully. At the same time, it was crucial that a think tank had a key role in the process as an entrepreneur and implementer. First, the idea of creating charter schools was brought by a think tank to the government of San Luis. Second, it was a responsibility of the team that went to live in San Luis to do all the economic and legal studies necessary to design the law – they even wrote the legal instruments used. The FGS presented the projects in dozens of meetings, with members of the legislature, opposition groups, and many schools all over the province. The team was in charge of assisting the educators that came from all over Argentina to analyse the possibility of creating a charter school in San Luis. Finally, the team gathered a prestigious evaluation committee, and then worked with the winning groups to organize the beginning of their projects. These tasks and many others could be performed thanks to the autonomy that the team had and, at the same time, the strong support given by the minister of education. It was a useful mixture of politicians convinced by the need for reform, and professionals dedicated to the countless details that allow any reform to be implemented, and introduced in San Luis the first self-governing public schools of Argentina.

This experience reveals the real potential for policy impact when a think tank gets involved in the micro-design of policy and allocates resources to push for the implementation of policy. We believe that this experience can be the basis of many other similar successes developed by other think tanks. Indeed, there is some secondary literature on the role of think tanks in micro-policy research and their roles in aiding the implementation of privatization policies in Western as well as Central and Eastern Europe (James, 2000) or in building local public–private partnerships in Sub-Saharan Africa (Johnson, 2000: 476). More recently, the 'Bridging Research and Policy' project of the GDN has been harnessing the lessons learnt by think tanks world-wide in translating ideas into policy practice (see www.gdnet.org).

Conclusion

One of the questions that arises after the crisis that broke out in Argentina in December 2001 is what will happen with think tanks in general and implementation think tanks in particular. Will it have for the latter a similar effect to that the return of democracy had for research centres, that is, as a possibility to increase their influence on public policy?

The crisis that led to the resignation of three presidents in less than a month presents both opportunities and risks. One possible interpretation of the crisis is that it represents the failure of think tanks as a primary source of policy analysis and as incubators for the technical cadre for appointments in government office. Mediterránea and CEMA during Menem's government and FADE, FIEL and again Mediterránea during De la Rua's government were directly linked with many of the market-oriented reforms of the 1990s. Their involvement could also be interpreted as a failure of research centre academics in the implementation of policies and ideas in a complex political environment and regulated by relatively rigid state bureaucratic institutions. This could lead to a loss of credibility of traditional private research centres. In this sense, it is worthwhile for think tanks to begin working on implementation at subnational or municipal levels, as this task can serve as a training ground for later policy implementation at higher government levels, and provides the necessary network of contacts to 'sell' good ideas in policy circles.

Another challenge for think tanks in the crisis is in helping to maintain financial sustainability. The heavy budget cuts that the state is carrying out, together with the reduction in private financing due to the economic recession, directly affect think tanks' potential domestic income. Therefore, the crisis is making think tanks more dependent on international funding. Considering the peso depreciation and the renewed interest in Argentina in the international community, it is possible that this source of funding will at least partially offset domestic losses.

These problems have clearly affected traditional research centres of the first wave. Furthermore, the current problem of legitimacy facing traditional political parties will affect the political foundations of the second wave. On the other hand, there is an opportunity for think tanks to expand their role from research into more active policy implementation. In the current context, political parties and the government are suspected of corruption and mismanagement. Therefore, there is a role for think tanks to provide some legitimacy, as representatives of civil society, to the government.

This opportunity for think tanks is strengthened by the increased mobilization and participation of citizens in politics as a response to the financial and political crisis. This mobilization, in the form of convening public assemblies and organizing civic protests, has not ended and can be channelled into other forms of participation. An interesting example of the possibilities that civic participation presents is the demand that many public assemblies in Buenos Aires are making to implement a participatory budget process. At the time of writing, NGOs and think tanks were working to articulate these demands into specific policy action in the city of Buenos Aires.

Overall, it is unclear whether think tanks will be strengthened or harmed by the current crisis. Financial constraints and a possible loss of the credibility of traditional think tanks may be counterbalanced by increased citizen participation, an enhanced relative legitimacy of newer organizations and heightened interest in the international community. We believe that these conditions favour new organizations that focus on policy implementation. To sum up, this chapter contributes to clarifying the actual and potential role of non-profits in developing countries in general and Argentina in particular. Furthermore, we hope that this chapter serves as a call for action. The best test for our ideas would be if policy implementation think tanks were to crop up in different countries, and seek an increasingly proactive role in the policy process.

Part IV

The Anglo-American tradition

13 Donald E. Abelson

The business of ideas: the think tank industry in the USA

As the tragic events of September 11, 2001 began to unfold, network executives and journalists in the United States scrambled to find policy experts who were capable of answering two critical questions: why were two of America's greatest symbols of economic and military prowess – the World Trade Center and the Pentagon – attacked? Who ultimately was responsible for orchestrating and co-ordinating these heinous acts? Not surprisingly, journalists quickly flipped through their rolodexes to locate foreign policy and terrorism experts at dozens of American think tanks. Their frantic search quickly paid off. Indeed, even before the initial shock of what had transpired sunk in, policy experts from some of America's leading think tanks began to appear on the major television networks to share their insights. Over the next several weeks and months, the visibility of think tank scholars in the media continued to increase.

The willingness of think tanks to participate in the media frenzy surrounding September 11 came as no surprise to scholars who have studied their increasingly active involvement in the policy-making process. Since think tanks are in the business of developing, repackaging and marketing ideas to policy-makers and the public, they could hardly pass up an opportunity to comment on one of the most tragic days in American history. Gaining access to the media however, is only one of the many strategies think tanks rely on to shape public opinion and public policy.

The purpose of this chapter is not simply to describe what activities think tanks in the United States engage in, or to speculate on how much or little influence directors of think tanks or disinterested observers believe these institutions have. Rather, the purpose here is two-fold: to examine and explore the evolution and proliferation of American think tanks and to highlight the extent to which they have become involved in the policy-making process.

In the first section of this chapter, a brief history of the origin and evolution of think tanks will be provided. The purpose of documenting the history of think tanks is to trace the emergence of four generations or waves of think tanks in the United States. Comparing think tanks created in the first decades of the 1900s such as the Brookings Institution, the CFR and the Hoover Institution to those established during and after World War II, including the AEI and the Heritage Foundation, one can observe the transformation of think tanks from non-partisan research institutions to avowedly ideological organizations committed to influencing Washington's political agenda. Once this has been done, the discussion will shift to the various factors that have contributed to the proliferation of both domestic and foreign affairs think tanks in the United States. In the next section, the many channels think tanks rely on to shape and mould public opinion and public policy will be discussed. Finally, some consideration will be paid to the many difficulties scholars encounter in trying to assess the impact of think tanks. The think tank industry in the United States continues to grow, but unlike the high-tech or energy sector, whose balance sheets are greatly influenced by the laws of supply and demand, there are few tangible indicators we can rely on to determine the relative success or failure of think tanks.

The emergence of American think tanks: a brief history

Chronicling the origin and evolution of the estimated 1,600 think tanks competing for power and prestige at the local, state and national level in the United States (Hellebust, 1996; Abelson, 2002) is far beyond the scope of this chapter. However, it is not necessary to document the mandate, research agenda and outreach activities of hundreds of think tanks to identify their principal function in the policy-making process. A more manageable approach is to identify, as Kent Weaver (1989: 563–78) and James McGann (1995; McGann and Weaver, 2000: 1–36) among others have done, the key motivations and institutional characteristics or traits associated with each major wave of think tank growth.

The first generation of policy research institutions

Since there is no consensus as to what think tanks are or how they differ from the hundreds of other organizations in the United States that share an interest in studying and making recommendations on public policy (Wallace, 1994), it is not surprising that scholars have been unable to agree on when the first think tank in the United States was created. While some maintain that organizations engaged in policy analysis initially emerged in the early 1900s, others contend that the seeds of contemporary think tanks were planted well before the end of the nineteenth century (Dickson, 1971; Smith, 1991). However, there is some consensus that it was during the first two decades of the twentieth century that the true impact of think tanks as policy research institutions began to be felt. Five think tanks in particular left a lasting impression on the formulation and implementation of public policy prior to and in the aftermath of World War I. They were the Russell Sage Foundation (1907), the CEIP (1910), the Institute for Government Research (1916, which merged with the Institute of Economics and the Robert Brookings Graduate School of Economics and Government to form the Brookings Institution in 1927), the Hoover Institution on War, Revolution and Peace (1919) and the CFR (1921).

These organizations were 'rooted in the social sciences and supported by private individuals and foundations [and were seen] as part of a larger effort to bring the expertise of scholars and managers to bear on the economic and social problems of this period' (McGann, 1992: 733). Developing their own areas of expertise in an environment insulated from the partisan interests of board members and from the vicissitudes of American politics, each of these organizations dedicated itself to the advancement of knowledge. This is not to suggest that think tanks created during the Progressive era should be regarded as the sole guardians of the public interest, devoid of any political motivations. Rather, it appears that several institutes created during this period assigned a higher priority to providing government officials with policy expertise than to lobbying members of Congress and the Executive or appeasing influential donors. The Hoover Institution's pioneering research on the causes and consequences of twentieth-century warfare, the Brookings Institution's contribution to the creation of a national budget system, and the CFR's War and Peace Studies Project stand as testaments to the vital contribution early research institutions made to assisting government leaders in charting a course for America's future. Many of these institutes continue to contribute in significant ways to educating policy-makers. Several scholars from the Brookings Institution, for instance, have through their publications and media commentary helped enlighten policy-makers about the many domestic and foreign obstacles America needs to overcome to combat global terrorism effectively. The Hoover Institution and the CFR have also played important roles in informing high-level policy-makers about other critical policy issues, such as a National Missile Defense, an initiative which the George W. Bush administration is actively pursuing despite ongoing concerns from America's European allies.

While these institutions attracted policy experts committed to a wide range of political beliefs, the organizations themselves were rarely transformed into ideological battlefields. Individual scholars at times overtly supported or opposed governmental policies, but their primary goal and that of their institutions was not to impose their political agenda on policy-makers, but to improve and help rationalize the decision-making process.

By engaging in policy research instead of political advocacy, early twentieth-century think tanks helped foster close and lasting ties to policy-makers. The willingness of philanthropic organizations such as the Carnegie Corporation and the Ford and Rockefeller Foundations to support many of these research institutions also contributed to a more stable and permanent link between policy experts and government (Berman, 1983; Nielsen, 1989). Providing research institutions with the financial security of million-dollar endowments allowed think tanks such as the Brookings Institution, the Hoover Institution and the CEIP to devote more of their time and resources to studying the long-term implications of particular governmental policies. It is a luxury few contemporary think tanks and government departments enjoy. Moreover, since these institutions did not solicit and rarely received government funding, they could comment on and critique government policy without jeopardizing their financial future. Indeed, unlike the vast majority of think tanks which depend on corporate, government and individual donations to survive, policy research institutions supported by generous endowments are less vulnerable to the partisan pressures of donors. Philanthropic foundations can refuse and have refused to renew grants to research institutions, but endowments normally remain in place indefinitely (Abelson, 2002: 65–7).

The major distinguishing characteristic of most think tanks created during this period was, and for the most part is, their commitment to scholarly research. The Brookings Institution and the Hoover Institution, which, next to RAND (formerly the Rand Corporation) and the Urban Institute, are the largest think tanks in the United States, function, in Kent Weaver's words (1989: 566), much like 'universities without students'. They hold conferences, seminars and workshops, maintain close ties to the academic community and require their scholars to publish articles and books. Moreover, they identify and pursue long-term research programmes and allocate the majority of their funding to this purpose. Their preferred target audience is policy-makers, but their voluminous research findings tend to attract more attention in the scholarly community.

The Brookings Institution, like many other policy research institutions created in recent decades, may encounter difficulties in convincing policy-makers to absorb information contained in their often weighty studies on issues ranging from reforming health care to pursuing closer economic relations with Russia (Newsom, 1996: 153–6). However, when government departments and agencies provide millions of dollars to think tanks for their research and analysis, policy-makers and bureaucrats are more inclined to digest their findings. This may in part explain why studies released by government contract research institutions such as RAND tend to generate considerable attention in Washington's policy-making circles.

As the following section will illustrate, the major difference between first-generation think tanks and those that emerged in the immediate post-World War II era was the principal source of their funding.

The second generation of government contract research institutions

Following World War II, government contract research institutions emerged in the United States largely in response to growing international and domestic pressures on American policy-makers. Acknowledging the invaluable contribution defence scientists made during the war, the Truman administration recognized the enormous benefits that could be derived from continuing to fund private and university-based research and development centres. By tapping into the expertise of engineers, physicists, biologists, statisticians and social scientists, policy-makers hoped to meet the many new challenges they inherited as the United States assumed the role of a hegemonic power after the war. It was in this environment that the idea for creating RAND (for research and analysis) was born.

Chartered in 1948, RAND's principal client in the immediate postwar years was the Department of Defense. Using systems analysis, game theory and various simulation exercises, RAND scientists began to 'think about the unthinkable'. Faced with the prospects of a nuclear exchange, RAND devoted much of its resources to advising the Air Force on how best to defend the United States against enemy attacks (Kaplan, 1985).

In addition to making several important contributions to strengthening America's nuclear deterrent, RAND also served as a prototype for other research and development organizations, including the Hudson Institute and the domestic-policy-oriented Urban Institute, an organization, inspired by President Lyndon Johnson (Abelson, 2002). Hired by federal and state government departments and agencies and by private companies to conduct research on issues ranging from the safe removal of toxic waste to the technical feasibility of installing a space-based defence system, RAND, the Hudson Institute and the Urban Institute have assumed a prominent role in the policy-making process.

The extent to which think tanks depend on federal funding varies considerably, yet the continued dependence of some of them on government contracts makes them highly vulnerable to political and budgetary pressures. As a result, although research and development organizations perform the same function as first-generation think tanks, their reliance on government grants and contracts may create the perception, rightly or wrongly, that their policy advice is slanted.

Since many of America's leading economists and scientists were employed at prominent universities or independent research centres after the war, it is not surprising that Washington was willing to provide these institutions with generous funding in exchange for their expertise. Yet, while research and development organizations were able to rely on their contractual relations with government departments and high-level officials to establish strong ties to political leaders, the policy-making community did not become dominated by federally funded research institutions in the post-World War II era. Although a handful of government contractors such as RAND and the Urban Institute became key players in the political arena during the 1950s and 1960s, by the mid to late 1970s, Capitol Hill was inundated with a small but vocal group of highly aggressive and ideologically driven institutes commonly referred to as advocacy think tanks.

The third generation of political advocacy think tanks

Breaking with the traditions established by Robert Brookings, Andrew Carnegie and founders of other early twentieth-century think tanks who were determined to insulate their scholars from partisan politics, several organizations often described as 'advocacy think tanks', because of their ideologically derived policy agendas, have consciously avoided erecting a barrier between policy research and political advocacy. Rather than promoting scholarly inquiry as a means to serve the public interest better, advocacy think tanks such as the Heritage Foundation and the Institute for Policy Studies have come to resemble interest groups and political action committees by pressuring decision-makers to implement policies compatible with their ideological beliefs and those shared by their generous benefactors (Abelson, 2002). No longer content to observe domestic and foreign affairs from the comfort of their book-lined offices, advocacy think tanks have made a concerted effort to become part of the political process.

Unlike traditional policy research institutions, advocacy think tanks are not driven by an intense desire to advance scholarly research. On the contrary, their primary motivation is to engage in political advocacy (Abelson, 1995). In short, they do not covet attention in the scholarly community, but are deeply committed to influencing public policy. As Heritage's president, Edwin Feulner, points out, 'our role is trying to influence the Washington public policy community ... most specifically the Hill, secondly the executive branch, thirdly the national news media' (McCombs, 1993).

Although think tanks, as non-profit, tax-exempt organizations, are prohibited by the Internal Revenue Service from influencing specific legislation, many advocacy think tanks have made a concerted effort to do so. As a director at a major policy institute stated, '[think tanks] are tax-exempt cowboys defying the sheriff with their political manipulations. They don't want to stimulate public dialogue, they're out to impose their own monologue' (Linden, 1987).

Through various governmental and non-governmental channels, advocacy think tanks have attracted considerable attention in the political arena. Moreover, as a result of the meteoric success of the Heritage Foundation, the quintessential advocacy think tank, dozens of other institutes determined to leave their ideological imprint on Washington have entered the policy-making community.

The fourth generation of vanity and candidate-based think tanks

Vanity or candidate-based think tanks (Landers, 1986) perform similar functions to those of advocacy think tanks, but rarely possess an extensive institutional infrastructure. Indeed, unlike the AEI and the Heritage Foundation, which employ between 100 and 200 people and have annual budgets exceeding $10 million and $40 million respectively, vanity think tanks tend to be more modest in scope. They are established by political leaders and aspiring office holders to lend intellectual credibility to their political platforms, a function no longer performed adequately by mainstream political parties (Gellner, 1995). Vanity think tanks may generate new ideas for candidates or simply reinforce and legitimate preconceived policy beliefs. Like many advocacy think tanks, these organizations place little emphasis on scholarly research. Vanity think tanks are also established to circumvent spending limits imposed on presidential candidates by federal campaign finance laws (Chisolm, 1990). Examples of vanity or candidate-based think tanks are Ross Perot's organization, United We Stand; the Progress and Freedom Foundation, which was the ideological inspiration for the former speaker of the House, Newt Gingrich's, Contract with America (or 'Contract on America', as several Democrats claim); and former Senator Bob Dole's short-lived institute, Better America (Melton, 1995).

Vanity think tanks are the latest generation of public policy institutes in the United States, but it is unlikely they will be the last. Think tanks exhibiting a combination of characteristics common to the various types of institutions discussed in this section will in all likelihood join the hundreds of thinks tanks competing for recognition in the policy-making community. At the very least, existing think tanks will modify their institutional behaviour to meet new demands and challenges in the political arena.

Explaining the growth of American think tanks

In the first half of the twentieth century, policy-makers did not require a directory to contact experts at various policy research institutions. After all, between 1907 and 1950, fewer than two dozen think tanks existed in

Table 13.1 Selected profile of American think tanks

Think tank	Location	Date established	Staff	Budget category, 1999/2000 ($millions)
Russell Sage Foundation	New York, NY	1907	31 S	2–5
Carnegie Endowment for International Peace (CEIP)	Washington, DC	1910	39 FTR, 43 S	Over 10
Brookings Institution	Washington, DC	1916	79 FTR, 161 S	Over 20
Hoover Institution on War, Revolution and Peace	Stanford, CA	1919	80 FTR, 20 PTR, 130 S	Over 20
Twentieth Century Fund	New York, NY	1919	33 FTR, 1 PTR, 2 S	2–5
National Bureau of Economic Research (NBER)	Cambridge, MA	1920	500 PTR, 45 S	2–5
Council on Foreign Relations (CFR)	New York, NY	1921	100 FTR and PTR, 100 S	Over 20
American Enterprise Institute for Public Policy Research (AEI)	Washington, DC	1943	100 FTR, 65 S	Over 10
RAND	Santa Monica, CA	1948	543 FTR, 80 PTR, 453 S	Over 100
Foreign Policy Research Institute (FPRI)	Philadelphia, PA	1955	7 FTR, 13 PTR, 5 S	1–2
Hudson Institute	Indianapolis, IN	1961	54 FTR, 10 PTR, 13 S	Over 10
Center for Strategic and International Studies (CSIS)	Washington, DC	1962	50 FTR, 10 PTR, 62 S	Over 10
Institute for Policy Studies (IPS)	Washington, DC	1963	16 FTR, 3 PTR, 4 S	1–2
Urban Institute	Washington, DC	1968	212 FTR, 33 PTR, 134 S	Over 10

The think tank industry in the USA

Center for Defense Information (CDI)	Washington, DC	1972	15 FTR 4 S	1–2
Institute for Contemporary Studies (ICS)	San Francisco, CA	1972	8 FTR and S	Under 1
Heritage Foundation	Washington, DC	1973	134 FTR, 46 S	Over 40
Worldwatch Institute	Washington, DC	1974	14 FTR, 16 S	2–5
Ethics and Public Policy Center	Washington, DC	1976	5 FTR, 10 PTR, 5 S	1–2
Rockford Institute	Rockford, IL	1976	4 FTR, 3 S	1–2
CATO Institute	Washington, DC	1977	42 FTR and PTR, 43 S	10–20
Northeast-Midwest Institute	Washington, DC	1977	11 FTR, 2 PTR, 5 S	2–3
Manhattan Institute for Policy Research	New York, NY	1978	25 FTR, 15 S	Over 5
Carter Center	Atlanta, GA	1982	35 FTR, 150 S	Over 10
Citizens for a Sound Economy Foundation (CSE)	Washington, DC	1984	98 FTR, 2 PTR, 10 S	Over 20
United States Institute of Peace (USIP)	Washington, DC	1984	50 FTR, PTR and S	Over 10
Economic Policy Institute (EPI)	Washington, DC	1986	18 FTR, 20 S	2–5
Progressive Policy Institute (PPI)	Washington, DC	1989	17 FTR, 3 S	1–2
Empower America	Washington, DC	1993	10 FTR, 25 S	5–10
Progress and Freedom Foundation	Washington, DC	1993	4 FTR, 5 PTR	2–5
Nixon Center for Peace and Freedom	Washington, DC	1994	7 FTR, 3 S	n.a.

Source: Several sources were used to compile this data, including personal correspondence and institute web sites. Additional information was obtained from Lynn Hellebust (1996).
Note: FTR = Full-time researchers; PTR = Part-time researchers; S = Support staff.

the United States. However, by the early 1980s, think tanks had become a virtual cottage industry. Over one hundred think tanks had been established in Washington, DC, and several hundred more were created throughout the United States (listed in chronological order in Table 13.1). But why did such a massive proliferation of think tanks take place following World War II? A number of possible explanations are worth exploring.

First, as a result of casting aside its isolationist shell to assume the global responsibilities of a hegemonic power after World War II, the United States had to rely increasingly on policy experts for advice on how to conduct its foreign relations. The demand for foreign policy expertise contributed to the creation of several institutes, including RAND (1948), the Foreign Policy Research Institute (FPRI, 1955), the Institute for Defense Analysis (1956) and the CSIS (1962).

Second, the impact of the anti-war and civil rights movements in awakening the public conscience to political and social turmoil at home and abroad also appeared to contribute to the proliferation of think tanks. Not unlike interest groups mobilizing popular support against the Vietnam war, many so-called 'liberal' think tanks, including, although by no means limited to, the IPS, were created to provide scholars with an opportunity to challenge many of the underlying motivations of American domestic and foreign policy (Muravchik, 1987).

Similarly, during the late 1960s and early 1970s, as several conservative academics were becoming increasingly disillusioned with what they considered to be a growing liberal bias among the faculty at American universities, a growing demand for autonomous research institutions emerged. Accordingly, the Institute for Contemporary Studies (ICS, 1972), the Heritage Foundation (1973) and the CATO Institute (1977) were founded to allow conservative academics to pursue their research interests in a more congenial environment. The growth of conservative, neo-conservative and liberal think tanks during this period clearly reflected a breakdown in consensus in the foreign policy-making establishment over America's role in world affairs (Ehrman, 1995).

Fourth, generous corporate financing and tax exemptions for non-profit organizations provided an impetus for policy entrepreneurs, political leaders and aspiring office holders to create think tanks (Chisolm, 1990). By establishing private think tanks as non-profit organizations and employing sophisticated direct mailing techniques, founders of third- and fourth-generation think tanks could encourage corporations, philanthropic foundations and private citizens to contribute thousands of dollars to support and advance their institution's particular ideological and political perspectives on domestic and foreign policy issues.

The tremendous growth in the number of think tanks in the United States can also be attributed to the declining role and importance of political parties in providing members of Congress and the Executive with sound policy advice. As Kent Weaver (1989: 570) of the Brookings Institution points out, 'weak and relatively non-ideological parties have enhanced think tanks' role in several ways. The most important effect of the U.S. party system is that parties have not themselves taken a major role in policy development by establishing sizeable policy research arms of their own. Think tanks have helped fill this void.' Unlike in Germany, where political parties have created their own political foundations to conduct policy research, or in Canada and in the United Kingdom, where members of Parliament are bound by strong party unity, decision-makers in the White House and on Capitol Hill are not required to follow a defined set of party principles. As a result, they can and often do actively solicit policy expertise from think tanks and other institutions capable of providing policy-relevant, though not necessarily empirically sound, advice. Many presidents have turned to think tanks for policy expertise and for ideological validation (Abelson and Carberry, 1997). In fact, as noted, dozens of members from think tanks have served in high-level positions in recent administrations. In their attempts to fill the ideological void left by political parties, third- and fourth-generation think tanks have also inundated members of Congress and the bureaucracy with their policy recommendations. Indeed, the willingness of the policy-makers to rely on contract research institutions and consultants for advice, on issues ranging from the economic implications of deregulating the airline industry to the utility or futility of developing and deploying a national missile defence system, has resulted in the creation of dozens of think tanks.

The highly decentralized and fragmented nature of the American political system should also be taken into consideration in explaining the proliferation of think tanks. In a system based on separate branches sharing powers, and one in which politicians are not constrained by the philosophical goals of political parties, think tanks are provided with multiple channels, not to mention unlimited opportunities, to convey their ideas to several hundred policy-makers (Abelson, 2000). The opposite situation exists, for instance, in Canada, where political power is not widely dispersed, but formally concentrated in the cabinet (see Lindquist, chapter 16 in this volume).

The booming think tank industry in the United States following World War II not only altered the complexion of the policy-making community but, more importantly, fundamentally changed the relationship between policy experts and policy-makers. In an environment where think tanks had to compete aggressively to promote their ideas, their priorities began to change. As new generations of think tanks emerged, they realized that developing effective marketing techniques to enhance their status in the policy-making community, rather than providing decision-makers with sound and impartial advice, had to become their main priority. In the following section, the various strategies all generations of think tanks employ to influence the direction of American politics will be discussed.

Competing in the market place of ideas: the public and private influence of think tanks

In observing the increasingly crowded think tank industry in the United States, several scholars and journalists have stated, usually without foundation, that think tanks exercise considerable influence in the political arena. Particularly in the months and weeks leading up to presidential campaigns, think tanks, especially those that have established close ties to candidates, are frequently portrayed as the architects of new and sometimes innovative ideas. Indeed, we are left with the impression that think tanks are largely responsible for shaping the political and economic agenda of incoming administrations. Unfortunately, in their efforts to monitor the behaviour of these organizations, few scholars (Higgott and Stone, 1994; Abelson, 2002) have attempted to explain how think tanks operationalize influence, or at the very least how they seek to achieve it.

Although it is difficult to accurately assess how much or little influence think tanks wield in the policy-making process, it is none the less possible to make informed judgements about the nature of their influence. A useful point of departure is to examine how they attempt to exercise both public and private influence in the United States. By making this distinction, scholars can at least begin to think more critically about the methodological problems that must be addressed in studying the influence of think tanks in American politics.

Public influence

Though once portrayed as elite organizations composed of scholars pursuing research in relative isolation, think tanks have become increasingly visible in the political arena. Many contemporary think tanks have descended from the ivory tower to assume an active role in American politics. To this end, several contemporary think tanks have employed a wide range of strategies to shape and mould public opinion and public policy. While some of these strategies are concealed from the public, many can be easily identified. In fact, to varying degrees, think tanks employ some or all of the following strategies to influence public attitudes and beliefs.

- Holding open public forums and conferences to discuss various domestic and foreign policy issues. Many of these forums are televised and available to viewers through satellite television. This strategy is part of the educational function some think tanks perform.

The think tank industry in the USA

- Encouraging scholars to give public lectures and addresses at universities, rotary clubs and other organizations.
- Testifying before committees and subcommittees of Congress. Several experts from think tanks are frequently called upon to give testimony. Their remarks and written reports become part of the official public record.
- Enhancing their media exposure by submitting op-ed (opposite the editorial page) articles to major American newspapers. Some think tanks have hired ghost writers to submit articles for particular scholars. Members of think tanks also appear frequently on network newscasts, political talk shows and radio programmes to discuss the implications of various domestic and foreign policy issues. Some think tanks have even built their own radio and television studios (Abelson, 1992, 2002).
- Publishing opinion magazines, newsletters, policy briefs and journals that have wide distribution. For instance, the CFR and the CEIP publish *Foreign Affairs* and *Foreign Policy* respectively. Moreover, several think tanks, including the Brookings Institution, the AEI and the CATO Institute, to name a few, publish a variety of opinion magazines.
- Selling audio tapes to the public which summarize key policy issues. The Heritage Foundation, for instance, sells monthly briefing tapes to interested listeners. In his endorsement of this product, which appeared regularly in Heritage's opinion magazine, *Policy Review* (a publication now produced by the Hoover Institution), the speaker of the House, Newt Gingrich, stated, 'A monthly dose of conservative common sense. You'll wonder how you ever got along without it.'
- Creating home pages on the internet. This is a new medium that think tanks representing various ideological views are relying on to reach thousands of internet users. Several think tanks, including the Brookings Institution, the CATO Institute, the Heritage Foundation, the CFR, the Hoover Institution and the Progressive Policy Institute (PPI), have created home pages. By 'going on line', think tanks have provided the public with an opportunity to find out information on their ongoing research programmes, staff and institutional resources. Some think tanks also include recent speeches and reports. Others have even gone so far as to advise people on how to find jobs in Washington.
- Targeting the public during annual fund-raising campaigns. In exchange for sizeable donations, some think tanks will allow members to join exclusive clubs which will provide them with access to key policy-makers.

Private influence

The many channels that think tanks rely on to exercise public influence are relatively easy to observe and document. However, it is often difficult to closely monitor how think tanks seek to influence policy-makers in the corridors of power. The following list provides some examples of how think tanks and scholars affiliated with them have attempted to exercise private influence. These instances include the following.

- Accepting Cabinet, sub-Cabinet or bureaucratic positions in administrations. Some think tanks, including the Heritage Foundation, monitor job vacancies in the bureaucracy and try to fill them with individuals who share their political and ideological views. Writing letters of reference on behalf of colleagues being considered for high-level positions is also frequently done.
- Serving on policy task forces and transition teams during presidential elections or simply as advisors to presidential candidates. During the controversial 2000 presidential election in the US, several scholars from the Hoover Institution, the AEI and the CSIS, to name a few, advised the Texas governor, George W. Bush, on a host of issues. Following the election, many of these people, including Lawrence Lindsey from the AEI and Condoleeza Rice, a fellow at the Hoover Institution, joined the new administration. Think tank scholars are also often invited to serve on various presidential advisory boards.
- Maintaining liaison offices with the House of Representatives and the Senate. This allows think tanks to establish close ties to policy-makers and to provide them with current analyses of major domestic and foreign policy issues. It also allows think tanks to discuss various legislative bills with congressional aides. The creation of the Congressional Policy Advisory Board has also provided think tank scholars with an opportunity to gain even closer access to members of Congress.
- Inviting selected policy-makers to participate in conferences, seminars and workshops and to head fund-raising campaigns.
- Offering former policy-makers positions at think tanks. Several think tanks have become retirement homes for important policy-makers. Their presence helps to enhance the prestige of institutes. It may also help to generate funding from philanthropic and private donors.
- Inviting bureaucrats to work at think tanks on a limited-term basis. For instance, the Diplomat in Residence Program overseen by the State Department has resulted in several ambassadors accepting research positions at think tanks.
- Preparing studies and policy briefs for policy-makers. This is the main function of research programmes at several advocacy think tanks.
- Developing specialized programmes for key policy-makers. The CSIS's

Transition project in 1988, to advise the president-elect on how to govern a new administration, is an example.
- Maintaining direct correspondence with policy-makers.

Although this list is by no means exhaustive, it does provide some insight into how think tanks attempt to assert private influence. Having said this, two central questions remain. What are some of the major problems in assessing influence? How can scholars properly assess the impact of think tanks in the policy-making process?

Conclusion: do think tanks really matter?

While it is not difficult to observe the many channels that think tanks in the United States rely on to exercise policy influence, determining how influential they are at different stages of policy-making remains problematic. To assess how much or little influence think tanks have, several methodological barriers must be overcome. One of the major obstacles scholars studying these institutions have to confront is how to measure policy influence. Should it be measured by recording media citations, appearances before legislative committees, number of publications produced in a given year and the number of staff appointed to high-level positions in the government? Or are there other tangible and intangible indicators that should be considered? Moreover, do some indicators provide a more accurate measurement of policy influence than others?

Although data on each of these indicators may provide insight into the amount of exposure think tanks and their staff generate, it cannot confirm how much or little influence policy institutes have in shaping public opinion and the policy preferences and choices of policy-makers. For instance, several think tanks keep track of how often their organizations are referred to in the media and the number of times their staff are called to testify before legislative committees. But what conclusions can be drawn from this data? Not surprisingly, think tanks that register the most media citations and appearances before committees naturally conclude that they are the most influential in the policy-making process. Scholars and journalists studying these institutions must, however, be a bit more circumspect. Data on media citations may tell us which institutes are effective at making the news. Yet such information tells us little about whether their views have helped shape, reinforce, clarify or change the minds of policy-makers and the public. Scholars cannot even conclude that policy-makers or members of the general public are familiar with what certain think tanks have stated in the media. Similarly, when think tanks testify before legislative committees, we cannot be certain that their statements have made a difference in how policy-makers approached particular policy issues. Other indicators, such as the number of publications think tanks produce or how many of their staff receive high-level appointments, may tell scholars even less about the institutes' influence in policy-making.

In addition to considering how to measure policy influence, or if in fact it can be measured at all, scholars must overcome several other obstacles in evaluating the impact of think tanks. Scholars must, for instance, determine how to isolate the views of think tanks from those of dozens of other individuals and governmental and non-governmental organizations that actively seek to influence public policy. As the policy-making community becomes increasingly congested, tracing the origin of an idea to a particular individual or organization gives rise to its own set of problems.

For some students of public policy, examining the various organizations and individuals that coalesce around particular policy issues offers a useful point of departure (Heclo, 1978). By studying the interaction between policy-makers and representatives from NGOs in specific policy communities, some important insights can be drawn. In addition to identifying the organizations and individuals most actively involved in discussing a particular policy concern with government officials, scholars can, through interviews and surveys, determine which views generated the most attention. However, unless policy-makers admit that their policy decisions were based primarily on recommendations from a particular individual or organization (something they are rarely inclined to do), it is difficult to determine how much influence participants in the policy process have had.

Since it is unlikely that these and other methodological obstacles will be overcome, it may be more appropriate to discuss the relevance of think tanks in the policy-making process than to speculate about how much policy influence they wield. In other words, rather than trying to state categorically that, on the basis of a handful of indicators, some think tanks are more influential than others, scholars should determine whether, when and under what conditions think tanks can contribute and have contributed to specific public policy discussions and to the broader policy-making environment. At the very least, scholars and journalists studying these institutions should acknowledge that, given the tremendous diversity of the think tank community in the United States, all think tanks do not possess the resources, expertise or desire to become embroiled in every policy debate. Scholars should also acknowledge that think tanks vary in terms of the priority they assign to becoming involved at different stages of the policy-making process. As a result, while some think tanks may play a more active role in discussing the implications of a specific government policy with the media, others may try to convey their views to policy-makers through less visible channels.

The growth of think tanks in the United States and their active involvement in American politics has compelled social scientists to think more critically about the institutes' role and function in the policy-making process. Scholars have also been forced to reflect on the implications of the politicization of policy expertise. Yet to date, few scholars have paid close attention to how think tanks seek to influence the political agenda. Even less attention has focused on the extent to which think tanks have left an indelible mark on public policy. To address these and other deficiencies in the available literature, this chapter has explored, among other things, how think tanks attempt to wield public and private influence. In the process, some preliminary suggestions on how to study the influence of American think tanks have been made. Think tanks have become permanent fixtures in the policy-making process. Future researchers must now determine the most effective methods to evaluate their performance.

14 Andrew Denham and Mark Garnett

A 'hollowed-out' tradition? British think tanks in the twenty-first century

British think tanks have a long history, and their numbers are increasing rapidly. Yet they have still to be accorded the scholarly attention that they deserve. Coverage is almost entirely confined to the media, which means that their claims to influence tend to pass without challenge. The aim of this chapter is to suggest a more sceptical approach to British think tanks, but also to offer some general ideas for future research which might clarify their role.

Briefly, the main political factors which have influenced the development of think tanks in Britain are key elements of what is commonly described as the 'Westminster Model': (1) a permanent civil service that has not relied heavily on external sources of policy advice; (2) strong and relatively cohesive political parties, with an adversarial model of party competition (under a 'first past the post' electoral system); (3) executive dominance vis-à-vis the legislature; and (4) the absence (until very recently) of devolved national and regional assemblies. An additional (cultural) factor is the relatively weak British tradition of individual and corporate private philanthropy, at least in respect of independent policy research. Finally, Britain has a broadsheet press with an insatiable appetite for stories based on the 'research findings' of any organization which can plausibly be described as a think tank.

These factors provide both opportunities and constraints for think tanks. Clearly the institutional and cultural context in Britain has worked against the development of any think tanks of comparable size to the most prominent groups in the US. However, the recent sharp increase in the number of bodies which either claim the status of think tanks or have the name bestowed upon them by media commentators might indicate a change in one or more of the factors listed above.

Recently there has been a lively debate over the continuing relevance of the Westminster Model, and it has also been claimed that the British state has been 'hollowed out' (see, for example, Rhodes, 1997; Marsh, Smith and Richards, 2001; Richards and Smith, 2002). Developments in the world of think tanks can offer an interesting and original perspective on these debates, but this provides an agenda for future research. For our present purpose we have concentrated on the influence of the media, which seems to offer the most satisfactory explanation for the sudden proliferation of British think tanks, and for the behaviour of the new bodies.

The British think tank tradition

Table 14.1 lists the best-known British think tanks by date of origin and provides basic information about each institute. It excludes those organizations whose primary focus is on foreign policy and/or the EU, which are discussed elsewhere in this book. As Table 14.1 shows, British think tanks are typically small organizations, and most of them operate with relatively modest resources. The table also confirms that 'think tanks' have a long history in Britain. Indeed, given that bodies such as the Scottish Council Foundation (1997), the Institute of Welsh Affairs (1987) and Democratic Dialogue ('Northern Ireland's first think tank', 1995) are of recent provenance, it would be more accurate to say that the British political tradition has given rise to a 'very English succession of "think tanks"' (Harrison 1993: 73).

In Britain, the term 'think tank' first gained currency after 1971, when the government of Edward Heath established the Central Policy Review Staff (CPRS) to conduct strategic research within Whitehall. But more familiar examples of the genre – relatively organized groups, concerned either to bring about specific policy changes or to engineer a more general

Table 14.1 Selection of British think tanks

Think tank	Date established	Staff	Budget (£million)
Fabian Society	1884	8	0.5
Policy Studies Institute (PSI, formerly Political and Economic Planning (PEP))	1931	35	2.2
National Institute for Economic and Social Research (NIESR)	1938	54	2.0
Institute of Economic Affairs (IEA)	1957	12	1.2
Institute for Fiscal Studies (IFS)	1969	37	2.4
Centre for Policy Studies (CPS)	1974	4	0.4
Adam Smith Institute (ASI)	1977	7	0.4
New Economics Foundation (NEF)	1987	45	1.9
Institute for Public Policy Research (IPPR)	1988	46	2.0
Social Market Foundation (SMF)	1989	9	0.5
Demos	1993	15	0.7
Politeia	1995	2	0.25

shift in the 'climate of opinion' – can be traced back to the nineteenth century. The 'Philosophic Radicals' identified closely with the ideas of Jeremy Bentham. As well as enthusiastic campaigners such as Francis Place and the dynamic civil servant Edwin Chadwick, they also boasted supporters in the House of Commons. They compensated for their lack of numbers with vigorous research and relentless campaigning through their journal, the *Westminster Review*. While the influence of the Philosophic Radicals can be exaggerated, it is apparent in much of the social and political legislation of the period (Dicey, 1905: 181).

The most notable work of the Philosophic Radicals was done when the Industrial Revolution was producing new social pressures, government was taking on a more active role, and the prestige of 'science' had reached new heights. Later in the century, the roots of the Fabian Society (1884) are discernible in the years of economic depression which succeeded the mid-Victorian boom. As in the early years of the century, this was a period when orthodox ideas were being challenged and when the electoral franchise was being reformed to embrace the (male) working class (McBriar, 1966; MacKenzie and MacKenzie, 1977). Like the Philosophic Radicals, the early Fabians backed their arguments with detailed empirical evidence and attempted to 'permeate' the political establishment rather than seek election to Parliament (Harrison, 1993).

Fabians such as George Bernard Shaw and Beatrice Webb were skilled self-publicists and some historians have sought to debunk their more extravagant claims (see Hobsbawm, 1964; Thompson, 1967). This reaction is understandable, but can be taken too far. If not directly responsible for laying the foundations of the welfare state, the Webbs arguably provided at least some of the bricks and mortar; and Sidney Webb famously helped to draft the Labour Party's original constitution. Yet, for most of the past fifty years, the Fabian Society's place in the formal institutional arrangements within the Labour Party has been 'definitely peripheral' (Callaghan, 1996: 39, 42). In the run-up to the 1997 general election, the Society's membership increased and it seemingly returned to favour, but very much as an adjunct to the party rather than a source of independent thinking. This impression was reinforced when, in November 2001, the Fabians followed 'New' Labour in removing Sidney Webb's commitment to public ownership from their aims and values (*Guardian*, 19 November 2001).

A second 'wave' of British think tanks emerged in the inter-war period. In February 1931, a new periodical, the *Weekend Review*, published 'A National Plan for Great Britain' by its assistant editor, Max Nicholson. The article appeared at a time when a number of active spirits were disillusioned with the major political parties. The article inspired the creation of a research organization known as Political and Economic Planning (PEP). In the 1930s, PEP produced reports on specific industries, and its work on housing, health and social services anticipated the postwar welfare state.

During the 1950s and 1960s, PEP continued to press its ideas on government. Budd (1978: 86) has argued that PEP's report on 'Growth in the British Economy' (1960) closely anticipated the approach of the National Economic Development Council set up in the following year, and that of the later Department of Economic Affairs. PEP's report on 'Racial Discrimination' (1967) also strengthened the case for a new Race Relations Act (Rose *et al.*, 1969). In 1978, PEP was superseded by the Policy Studies Institute (PSI), following a merger with the Centre for Studies in Social Policy (CSSP). Now affiliated to the University of Westminster, PSI continues to produce thoroughly researched publications on a range of subjects. It prefers to characterize itself as a research institute, rather than a 'think tank'.

Another notable research organization to emerge in the 1930s was the National Institute of Economic and Social Research (NIESR). In 1931, Sir Josiah Stamp was appointed by Ramsay MacDonald to the Labour government's Economic Advisory Council. The subsequent obstruction of that group by the Treasury reinforced Stamp's belief in the need for a body outside government to act as a source of expert economic advice. Stamp's original hope for a British equivalent to the American Brookings Institution was never realized. But the NIESR has undoubtedly influenced economic policy in Britain since World War II, at least when governments have been open-minded enough to heed the 'objective' forecasts of outsiders, rather than following ideological blueprints or distorting the economy for political gain.

The distinction between 'first' and 'second' wave think tanks is more than a matter of chronology. The latter bodies arose after Britain became a mass democracy, and they reflected disillusionment with parliamentary politics rather than enthusiasm about the new possibilities being opened up by the prospect of mass education and the expansion of the franchise. Their work was not 'value-free' – it fell within the broad framework of the 'Keynesian consensus'. But ideological advocacy was far less important to them than the presentation of detailed evidence to support their views. Preferring to jog ministerial elbows rather than browbeat governments, they were respected by decision-makers without themselves forming a part of 'policy networks' in any formal sense.

The third wave: New Right think tanks

By contrast with the second wave, most commentators would accept that (with the partial exception of the (more 'academic' and earlier founded) Institute of Economic Affairs (IEA), the New Right groups that came to prominence in the late 1970s are best described as ideological 'advocacy tanks' (Weaver, 1989). Like their predecessors, they emerged in response to a perceived crisis. The IEA (1957) was founded at a time when, despite the emphasis on 'freedom' in their party propaganda, in practice the Conservative governments of Churchill and Eden proved no more sympathetic to economic liberalism than the opposition Labour and Liberal Parties. Thus the IEA (like PEP before it) had party-political independence thrust upon it by the circumstances of its foundation.

The Centre for Policy Studies (CPS, 1974) and the ASI (1977) belong in the same 'wave' as the IEA because they were responding to the same problem: the alleged failure of the 'Keynesian' approach in arresting and reversing Britain's relative economic decline. The main difference is that the CPS and the ASI were established after the 1973–74 oil shock – a crisis in the developed world that provoked a search for alternatives to Keynesian economic management. Unlike the IEA, the CPS has always enjoyed very intimate links with the Conservative Party and its donors cannot claim tax relief through charitable status. The ASI's long-serving president, Madsen Pirie, has described its contributors as 'policy engineers', who seek to provide 'practical' ideas, in contrast to the more abstract fare offered by the IEA (Pirie, 1988; Denham, 1996). To support this claim to a market niche, the ASI has been conspicuously more aggressive than other New Right think tanks in proclaiming its influence over policy, as opposed to the less tangible achievement of affecting 'the climate of opinion'.

The pursuit of influence was very important for both the first- and second-wave organizations, but for the third it became an obsession. But it is difficult to assess the extent to which the New Right bodies really fulfilled their objectives. An avowedly ideological prime minister was a new phenomenon in British politics, and anyone who shared Margaret Thatcher's general outlook was bound to win publicity from the media, whether she listened to them or not. Even the cheer-leaders of the think tanks are inconsistent on the subject of influence. Richard Cockett claims that the free market groups 'did as much intellectually to convert a generation of "opinion-formers" and politicians to a new set of ideas as the Fabians had done with a former generation at the turn of the century' (Cockett, 1994: 5). Yet while Hywel Williams has written that under think tank influence the Conservative Party 'acquired a taste for half-digested intellectualism', Cockett himself allows that the ideas promulgated by the New Right 'never captured the hearts, let alone the minds, of more than a small minority of Conservative MPs, even during the heyday of Thatcherism in the mid-1980s' (Williams, 1998: 4; Cockett, 1994: 325). Nor, for that matter, does the free market message appear to have trickled down to a stubbornly non-Thatcherite electorate (Crewe, 1988).

By their nature, think tanks are elite organizations, and the first- and second-wave groups were more interested in persuading political elites than in converting the general public. Even so, it remains an ironic coincidence that the economic liberals who set out to convince the intellectual community as a whole 'succeeded' only because the Westminster Model concentrates so much power at the centre. But when the Cabinet papers for the period are released it seems unlikely that any direct think tank influence will be proved; indeed, case studies of key 'Thatcherite' innovations like the Community Charge, or 'Poll Tax', already suggest that the 'policy engineers' have exaggerated their role (Butler, Adonis and Travers, 1994). In other cases the think tanks responded to a general policy agenda to which the government was already committed, rather than shaping it themselves.

If the New Right think tanks failed to influence the wider 'climate of opinion', and cannot prove that they directly shaped policy during the 1980s, what is left for them to claim? Are commentators merely guilty of an 'intellectualist fallacy' – attributing influence to intellectuals because, as intellectuals themselves, they have a vested interest in doing so? Just as the British think tank tradition is well established, so too is the argument, furnished with impressive historical research and documentary evidence, that the role of ideas and intellectuals in British politics is relatively modest (MacDonagh, 1958; Roberts, 1959; Thomas, 1979). As Dahrendorf (1995: 40) has shrewdly observed, 'we do not like the complexity of real history. The authors of ideas prefer to think that they are directly responsible for realities which correspond to their speeches and writings, and the rest love simple causal explanations, not to say conspiracy theories.'

There remain two respects – closely related, but distinct – in which the third-wave think tanks really do seem to have played a noteworthy role in recent British politics. Instead of the slippery term 'climate of opinion' we should examine the concept of ideological fellowship. They provided an institutional setting for like-minded individualists, which probably helped to convince Thatcher that her views enjoyed the support of enthusiastic and well-informed people outside Whitehall and Westminster.

The second respect in which the third-wave think tanks could claim influence is through recruitment. With the increasing 'professionalization' of politics, a background in think tanks became a useful platform for a career in Parliament. This is a trend which reached full maturity with the fourth wave; of the New Right think tanks, the CPS was easily the most fertile source of recruits, because of its close relationship with the Conservatives. John Redwood and David Willetts are the most prominent examples of politicians whose careers have advanced in this way.

Beyond the New Right: the fourth wave

Whether or not the New Right bodies made a crucial difference to British politics in the 1980s, the public profile of the third-wave groups under Thatcher undoubtedly helped to inspire a spirit of emulation among people who dissented from the rigid Anglo-American free market model. This provides a contextual basis for the identification of a fourth wave of British think tanks. For example, the Institute for Public Policy Research (IPPR, 1988) was set up as Labour's answer to the CPS and ASI. From the outset the IPPR represented something of a mid-way point between second-wave think tanks like PSI and the Thatcherite bodies; it has a much more polemical edge than the former groups, but lacks the ideological certainties of the latter. Its first major project, the Borrie Commission on social justice, suggested that in spite of its partisan orientation the working methods of the IPPR would resemble those of the PSI and the NIESR. But while the Commission provided a detailed blueprint for the renewal of social democracy, it coincided with a period when the Labour leadership was reviewing its core principles. The lesson for the IPPR was that if were to compete with other fourth-wave groups, it would have to work in a way which would allow it to respond more flexibly to a rapidly changing political context.

The Social Market Foundation (SMF, 1989) was founded by Lord Keynes' biographer Robert (later Lord) Skidelsky and Lord Kilmarnock. Originally associated with the Social Democratic Party (SDP), the SMF has been independent since that party lost its separate existence. At the time of its foundation the term 'social market' could mean almost anything; in continental usage it implied a mix of free market economics and 'communitarian' social philosophy, but Sir Keith Joseph hijacked the term in the mid-1970s and other senior Conservatives were using the phrase even before the disappearance of the SDP. Like the IPPR, the SMF was young enough, and sufficiently adaptable, to survive the disappearance of its original *raison d'être*.

Demos (1993) could be described as the first 'postmodern' think tank. Instead of pursuing any of the traditional postwar ideological agendas, it reflected the breakdown of belief. Its staff were young and, while its founder Geoff Mulgan was close to senior figures in 'New' Labour, it sought to attract support for its ideas across the political spectrum rather than from any one political party. Like the ASI, Demos was adept at winning media coverage. A typical example was a front-page *Daily Mail* article in July 1998 on a Demos plan to strip the queen of her few remaining constitutional powers. This was a subject close to Demos' heart; at the time of the Queen's Golden Jubilee in 2001 it advised her to abdicate.

Whatever their origins, then, the chief characteristic of fourth-wave British think tanks is a refusal to be confined by traditional ideologies.

Lord Hattersley has pointed out the irony that 'policy research has increased as disagreements about policy have diminished' (Hattersley, 2001). This distinguishes the outlook of the fourth wave from first- and third-wave bodies, which saw themselves as crusaders on behalf of certain principles. However, the fourth wave's methods have more in common with the third-wave think tanks like the ASI, in their determination to win headlines by focusing on 'topical' issues. Unlike think tanks of the first and second waves, these youthful organizations recognize that painstaking research designed to force neglected issues onto the political agenda is far less fruitful for their purposes than the (hasty) production of ideas on subjects that were already widely discussed. Whatever the private beliefs of think tank authors, the fierce competition for press attention has dictated that their published suggestions should challenge prevailing orthodoxies, without being entirely outlandish. It might be impossible to 'prove' direct influence over policy, and the 'climate of opinion' is difficult even to define. But no one can dispute the black-and-white evidence of a newspaper article; and if such pieces describe the think tank in question as 'influential', so much the better.

Think tanks and the decline of ideology

In the early days of 'New' Labour government, it seemed that the think tank with the flimsiest ideological attire would outstrip the others. Hardly a week went by without a media mention of Demos. Yet there were political dangers in the back-of-an-envelope radicalism it purveyed. For example, the 1998 attack on the queen's powers was attractive to the *Daily Mail* because that newspaper could claim that its thinking was supported by some senior 'New' Labour figures. But the Blair government was gripped by a fear of negative media coverage, and had no desire for outspoken friends who could offer hostages to its foes. Even before the furore over the queen, the *Guardian* claimed that Demos' 'love affair with New Labour seems to be on the rocks' (30 June 1998). For some key staff members, the 'affair' has been consummated by the offer of posts in government (Geoff Mulgan, for example, became head of the Number 10 Policy Unit). But the organization they have left has lost vitality as well as its proximity to ministerial ears.

The fate of Demos presented fourth-wave think tanks with a stark choice. They could win headlines through bold independent thinking, or enjoy a reputation for backstairs influence at the cost of shedding any iconoclastic thoughts and of having their brightest (and 'safest') staff poached by government. Rather than discrediting think tanks entirely, the eclipse of Demos left a vacancy at the top because Tony Blair was still anxious to have sympathetic intellectuals in his entourage. Having been temporarily eclipsed by Demos, IPPR was now the obvious candidate. In 1998 it acquired a new director, Matthew Taylor, who combined energy, charisma and excellent connections. He had been 'New' Labour's policy director, and contributed to the 1997 manifesto.

Yet even for a skilful operator like Taylor, running 'the government's preferred think tank' has been problematic at times. In March 2001 he joked that he had jeopardized his chances of a peerage after criticizing Blair's 'Third Way'. The government, he felt, had adopted 'a politics of accommodation' (Beckett, 2001). Yet if the IPPR was damned for outflanking Labour on the left, it also courted media criticism through its own 'accommodation' with the free market. Just after the 2001 general election, an IPPR commission on public–private partnerships in the National Health Service (NHS) provoked a stern editorial rebuke from the *Guardian*, which accused the Institute of 'behaving as if it were taking orders from [Labour Party Headquarters]' (26 June 2001).

A year after the election, the IPPR was once again in the news for the wrong reasons. This time, a reporter from the *Guardian*'s stablemate, the *Observer*, posed as a representative of a US company keen to sponsor some research. When the reporter asked about the possibility of gaining access to government ministers, an IPPR fund-raiser confirmed that it was usual for donors to attend such meetings. In fact, such gatherings are highly characteristic of the IPPR; typically, instead of conducting research itself, it assembles people with suitable qualifications – and, more importantly, eye-catching job titles – to deliberate on a topical issue. It is highly convenient for ministers to attend such fora, which give leading 'experts' on a given subject the impression that their views are being taken seriously.

Matthew Taylor rejected any imputation that the IPPR was offering access in return for cash, arguing that meetings with ministers were opportunities 'to focus on progressive policy solutions, not to lobby' (*Observer*, 30 June 2002). Significantly, other think tanks rushed to confirm that their own research conclusions were never dictated by their sponsors. Yet to the untrained eye the fact that many 'New' Labour sponsors also gave money to the IPPR seemed to be more than a coincidence. The *Observer* continued to explore the tangled relationship between think tanks, corporate interests and government ministers. In October 2002 it revealed that the Institute of Directors had asked the IPPR not to publish the findings of a business survey that it had commissioned (*Observer*, 27 October 2002).

The allegations of 'cash for access' underline the new problems faced by the fourth-wave think tanks. Their third-wave predecessors were widely criticized, but only stern ideological opponents could accuse them of reaching conclusions for venal motives. Bodies like the IEA, the CPS and the ASI existed precisely because their founders and supporters were not open-minded; readers knew what to expect as soon as they learned the subject matter of each new pamphlet. Impatient with the idea that government is 'the art of the possible', these bodies were more likely than not to accuse their ministerial allies of inadequate commitment to the faith that burned within them. In the run-up to the 1997 general election it looked as if the IPPR might emulate that role, acting as a 'guardian of the social-democratic conscience' for 'New' Labour. But this would have meant that a body set up as an 'insider' organization would have been pushed away by a party which was already notorious for its 'crony culture'. At a time when the old ideologies were breaking down, the IPPR had every reason to feel that a think tank which clung even to a broad principled position was likely to lose relevance, as well as influence.

The recent history of the SMF offers an alternative model for fourth-wave think tanks. It would be unfair to suggest that the Foundation has ceased to be a think tank at all. It continues to publish on a range of issues. Yet its own publicity reveals a clear shift of emphasis, away from 'thinking' and towards 'hosting'. In 2000 an SMF statement of objectives and achievements identified its 'intellectual task' as 'to reconsider the meaning of a "social market economy" in a world where the factors of production are increasingly mobile'. The statement refers to 'the relationship and tension between the market system and the social order'. This is all very laudable; but these questions have been central to the British debate on the 'social market' since the 1970s and evidently they are no closer to resolution. Even if the SMF traded in philosophical ambiguity, it was at least compatible in that sense with the government, which continued to wrestle with the elusive 'Third Way'.

One useful spin-off from the SMF's fence-sitting position is its ability to provide a platform for senior politicians of all parties without the event looking too incongruous. The Foundation's newsletter for spring 2002 claimed that 'There could be no clearer proof that the SMF is now at the very centre of political life in this country than Gordon Brown's decision to explain the philosophy behind his Budget in a speech here shortly before his announcements in the Commons.' More accurately, Brown's choice of venue only 'proved' that the SMF was an attractive venue for a seasoned politician who recognizes the advantages of being pictured speaking in front of the logo of a 'high-brow' organization. Clare Short and David Blunkett are other ministers who have appreciated this photo-opportunity. Significantly, in the same newsletter, 'Events', including more ministerial speeches, feature ahead of 'Publications'. No doubt all this is very attractive for prospective sponsors of a body which styles itself as 'Britain's number one think tank'. But the impression remains that publicity has become an end in itself for the SMF; and it seems ironic that the document should close with the quotation 'enough words, time for action'.

Think tanks and the rise of apathy

At the time of writing (November 2002), the pecking order among think tanks is very different from the situation in the mid-1980s. The third wave has been receding since Thatcher's downfall; as Hywel Williams has written, under John Major the think tanks 'picked up the signals from Downing Street that their services were not wanted' (Williams, 1998: 8). Although it remains very active, the IEA is generally overlooked by a media which now has little time for ideological certainties of left or right. There has been little change, though, in the attention accorded to think tanks as a genre. Their output is valued by broadsheet newspaper editors, hard pressed to fill their columns with eye-catching stories.

After four distinct 'waves' of think tanks, Britain now has more of these bodies than ever before. Orthodox pluralist theory would suggest that Britain is indeed becoming a mature democracy, with numerous competing groups struggling to win attention for their views, backed by at least a modicum of empirical evidence. But it is possible to reach a very different conclusion. At best, the sheer volume of output from the different groups can only sow confusion even among obsessive 'policy wonks' among the audience. The *Guardian*'s Catherine Bennett has been even more outspoken, writing that

> Once you add [to the work of the Performance and Innovation Unit – see later] the product of all the other think tanks – Demos, Civitas, the Centre for Policy Studies, Localis, Policy Exchange, Reform, the Adam Smith Institute, N[ew] L[ocal] G[overnment] N[etwork], Politeia, the Foreign Policy Centre, the Social Affairs Unit, Catalyst, the Fabian Society, the Social Market Foundation, the racy new Do Tank and others too numerous to list, you are forced to think the unthinkable: who needs them? (Bennett, 2002)

On this view, whatever might have happened to Britain's democratic institutions, the think tank tradition has been 'hollowed out'. One might conclude that the media is most to blame. It is certainly ironic that some broadsheet commentators are now turning against the monster created in large part by their own industry. Yet even if think tank personnel hanker after an ideal world in which the race for publicity is won by the brightest minds with the sharpest literary style, they do seem willing participants in the existing game.

It is a common public complaint that politicians are 'out of touch' – that they cannot comprehend the concerns of 'ordinary' people because British political life is a cocoon which insulates Westminster from 'real life'. 'New' Labour's most significant contribution to the rise of apathy is arguably its over-reliance on unelected 'special advisors' – a trend which it has not invented, but certainly augmented. Think tank personnel are obvious recruits to government, and again 'New' Labour has only extended the practice of its Thatcherite predecessors. Yet while it was understandable that Thatcher should wish to bring fellow-believers into government, for obvious reasons one cannot associate 'New' Labour with 'ideological fellowship'. At their worst, the current breed of apparatchiks seem to act as comfort-blankets for ministers who have discarded their former idealism.

Recently the chief contribution of think tanks has been to foster the impression that power in Britain is concentrated within a charmed circle, where policy wonks rub shoulders with politicians and businesspeople in a kind of corporatism without the trade unions. The third-wave think tanks included their fair share of eager recruits straight from university. But Thatcher's backroom boys also included people with experience of life outside the Westminster village, such as John Hoskyns and Alfred Sherman. It might be argued that their experience was highly misleading, and thus hazardous in so far as they were allowed to influence policy. But to those who value democracy, the fourth-wave recruits are dangerous whether they exert influence or not. The existence of people who have never worked outside the policy sphere at or near the centre of things lends support to the impression of increasing distance between the government and the governed. Some might argue that the civil service is open to the same charges, and to the extent that senior officials have been forced to move away from the traditional ethos of the service such criticisms are well founded. But while the bureaucracy has yet to capitulate entirely, and still has the potential to offer advice from a contrasting perspective, Matthew Taylor's throwaway line about his lost peerage underlines the serious point that today's think tankers can hope for advancement only to the extent that they are prepared to echo their masters' voices.

Conclusion: the wave of the future?

The argument suggests that one can distinguish four 'waves' of British think tanks. The first predated mass democracy, and consisted of enthusiasts who wanted a more active government to be informed by 'experts'. These specialists were ideologues who thought that a more 'scientific' approach to policy on the part of government and advisors would present new voters with a clear choice – between the 'stupid' parties, and those that knew what they were talking about.

The second-wave think tanks, unlike the first, were not primarily motivated by ideology, although their work was not value free. Their mission was to accumulate evidence; and although they hoped to guide policy-makers towards definite conclusions, they thought that they were addressing themselves to politicians of all parties who shared their 'empirical' outlook. The dividing line between this second wave and its predecessor was the fact that bodies like the PSI and the NIESR were never polemicists; they consciously addressed themselves to a specialist audience, and would have had difficulty accommodating a Shaw or even John Stuart Mill.

In its sense of ideological purpose, the third wave of British think tanks represented a return to the roots of the tradition in Britain. But it clearly also represented a new departure, because while the Philosophic Radicals and the Fabians had struck a reasonable balance between research and advocacy, the output of the New Right think tanks was openly (sometimes extravagantly) polemical.

It is difficult to draw a clear distinction between some third-wave bodies, like the ASI, and their successors of the fourth wave. But those bodies which were founded after the beginning of the Thatcher premiership tended to be drawn (whether they liked it or not) into a battle for newspaper headlines which their predecessors had not seen as their primary purpose.

Although well-written (and even persuasive) material can emanate from this source, the fourth wave as a general phenomenon raises awkward questions for pluralist theory. The charge of elitism can be levelled at the representatives of previous 'waves', but at least they were motivated by the hope that their findings would be educative, either for policy-makers or for the public at large. Even on a charitable view, this urge seems lacking in the fourth-wave bodies, perhaps reflecting a more 'realistic' assessment of the attention span of the average citizen (or minister).

The general trend of British think tank decline is illustrated in Table 14.2. Obviously this is a rough and ready guide, in which the rating of each 'wave' is based on an overall judgement of more than one body. But if one accepts that the characteristic virtue of bodies which deserve the name 'think tank' is to provide interested parties with well-researched material on subjects which may or may not be of immediate concern, the second wave provided something like an ideal balance between research and advocacy. The first wave comes close; but while ideological advocacy is perfectly compatible with a healthy democratic system, it is far from

Table 14.2 Categories of British think tanks

Wave	Empirical research	Ideological advocacy
First	Strong	Strong
Second	Strong	Moderate
Third	Moderate	Strong
Fourth	Weak/Moderate	Weak

being the exclusive preserve of think tanks and unless kept within bounds it can adulterate research conclusions. On this basis, it might be thought that the third wave marks a nadir from which the British think tank tradition has since recovered. But while the weak ideological commitment of the fourth-wave bodies might be welcome if it was married to intensive research, in practice it seems that without some kind of 'road map' of principle, think tanks are all too likely to seek the most attractive route, regardless of the destination.

There are good reasons for thinking that the process of 'hollowing out' is irreversible, because the emergence of the fourth wave merely reflects more general structural and ideological developments. Some commentators have claimed that the Westminster Model is now outdated, and that the British policy arena has become more 'diverse, fragmented, complex and decentralised' (Richards and Smith, 2002: 6). This implies that the number of access points allowing outside bodies to influence decision-makers has increased. There is no space here to rehearse the arguments in detail, but the present discussion suggests that it is dangerous to underestimate the resilience of the Westminster Model. As we have seen, the centre can fight back by absorbing 'outsiders' into its own ranks. A less subtle weapon is the current tendency of Whitehall to foster think tanks, linked to one department or several, like the Social Exclusion Unit (1997) and the Performance and Innovation Unit (1998). At the same time, ad hoc 'task forces', like the committee established to study Potentially Hazardous Near-Earth Objects (2000), have been set up; if this particular phenomenon had been thought worthy of examination in the early 1970s it would have been entrusted to Heath's CPRS. This development shores up the government's position at the centre of the policy web; if it chooses, it can still commission work from arm's-length groups like the IPPR, but only on the explicit assumption that their findings will be disowned if they cause any embarrassment.

It could be argued that such attempts to control the channels of communication to ministers are symptomatic of a beleaguered government machine. But even if the new Whitehall bodies are part of a conscious 'fight-back' by the centre, there is good reason to suppose that it will succeed. The privileged status (and greater resources) of such groups puts outside bodies at a considerable disadvantage, in an increasingly frenzied battle for attention.

The nature of the fourth wave also suggests that the British polity has entered a postmodern era in which all belief is in constant flux. On this view, it is perfectly understandable (if not commendable) that a socialist like Clare Short should choose to speak before an SMF backdrop. Finally, the proliferation of fourth-wave think tanks has accentuated one of the fundamental constraints facing all such bodies in Britain. Unless they are backed by well-resourced and generous patrons, British think tanks start work on shoestring budgets. Even if they hope eventually to establish a reputation for long-term research, they are sure to feel pressure to produce immediate 'results' – that is, newspaper headlines. The obvious danger is that they will attract funding only from sponsors who want more of the same. The quest for short-term 'sensations' will tend to become a habit, particularly because the pool of available funding is not large, and so many other organizations can bid against them. There is good evidence to suggest that the media now associates think tanks with a craving for publicity at any cost. In 2002 an organization calling itself 'Migration Watch UK' claimed that 2 million immigrants would 'swamp' Britain over the next decade. The group, whose motives were fairly transparent, had previously tried to cause a splash by talking of 1 million over 5 years. When no one took much notice, they merely doubled the number and the time-frame. Even the first 'finding' had been based on a wilful distortion of Home Office figures, but the *Daily Mail* and the *Sun* continued to describe Migration Watch UK as a 'think tank'.

Despite the devaluation of the think tank currency, it is also possible to be more optimistic. The survival of earlier 'waves' into the 'postmodern' period is a reason to hope that think tanks in the future will be more than just a picturesque venue for a speech, a source of misleading headlines, or a channel for fresh-faced recruits to the party machines. Recent work published under the old Fabian rubric is a case in point. Even more encouraging, perhaps, is the media prominence of the Institute for Fiscal Studies (IFS, 1969). Newspaper coverage of the Institute's forensic examination of public finances tends to rise in election years, and to some extent it does compete for column inches with the rest of the discredited band. But at worst the IFS is a second-wave think tank masquerading as a member of the fourth. It overlaps to a considerable extent with the NIESR; but it tends to be more energetic in its attempts to bring truly independent economic judgements to the attention of the general public.

On balance, looking back over their long history, British think tanks have probably been an asset to an educated democracy. The balance struck by the IFS seems about right; it wins headlines because of its sober research, not simply because it courts politicians and journalists – the same kind of people, from similar backgrounds, as its own staff members. Given the ability of the IFS and a revitalized Fabian Society to compete with the fourth-wave think tanks without stooping to their level, it is reasonable to hope that the continuing history of British think tanks might prove to be cyclical, and not one of progressive decline from an inter-war peak.

15 Ian Marsh and Diane Stone

Australian think tanks

Since the 1970s, there has been gradual growth in the number of Australian think tanks. This development has been complemented by greater public and political awareness of their activities. However, the development of think tanks in Australia is less extensive than in the other countries discussed in this volume. There are a number of contributing factors including the federal structure of government, taxation laws, an underdeveloped philanthropic culture, and the strength of the policy-analytic capacity of the Australian state. The supposed 'anti-intellectualism' of Australian society (see Stokes, 1994: 10) may be a contributing factor. Nevertheless, a handful of policy institutes have gained public prominence and some influence in advancing their ideological perspectives. In particular, the rise of the so-called New Right think tanks with their discourse of economic rationalism (that is, a market liberal policy agenda) has paralleled that of the British New Right think tanks. More generally, the growth of think tanks in difficult conditions testifies to the tenacity of Australian intellectual life.

The Australian think tank scene

The development of independent institutes in Australia has not been on the scale witnessed in North America, Asia or Europe. Only three institutes established before or just after World War II are still operating: the Institute of Public Affairs (IPA), the AIIA and the Committee for the Economic Development of Australia (CEDA). The oldest still in existence – the AIIA – emerged in 1933. It was designed as a non-partisan institute to stimulate interest in and promote understanding of international affairs. While the AIIA has played a prominent role in Australian intellectual life concerning foreign affairs, the organization has not adapted well to a changing environment and other think tanks have emerged as competitors (Stone, 1996a).

The IPA was established in 1943 with overt political motivations and a clear link to a political party – the nascent Liberal Party of Australia. By the 1970s the Institute began to drift, and it was only revitalized in the 1980s through the proactive leadership of Rod Kemp (subsequently a Liberal Party Senator). Yet recessionary conditions and other institutional factors made it difficult for the organization to grow. For example, attempts to spin off a new organization devoted to foreign and defence policy issues – the Pacific Security Research Institute in Sydney, with Owen Harries (then co-editor of the *National Interest* in the USA) as the president – failed. Similarly, the conservative Council on the National Interest, set up in the mid-1980s, closed after two years. It was unable to retain staff or attract funding.

CEDA is most closely associated with business interests but, like the AIIA, presents itself as an apolitical and independent forum for research and debate. It acts as a 'communications bridge' among private and public decision-making elites to facilitate an improved and co-ordinated approach to economic development (da Silva, 2002). The Australian Fabians, established in 1947, did not have the public prominence or intellectual and other resources of their British counterparts, but continues to organize policy thinking and publication.

As in Great Britain, from the mid-1970s, a 'second wave' of New Right think tanks were established. The Centre for Independent Studies (CIS) was created in 1976 and most closely resembles the IEA in London, with a scholarly rather than activist focus. A number of loose club-like sub-organizations, focused on specific issues, have been spawned around the neo-liberal group. The first of these, the H.R. Nicholls Society, was founded in 1986 to promote deregulation of the industrial relations system. It gained notoriety and ongoing media attention when the former prime minister, Bob Hawke, referred to the organization as a group of 'political troglodytes and economic lunatics'. Although established at later dates, two other groups have formed to champion a conservative viewpoint on social and economic issues: the Bennelong Society (1999), which opposes Aboriginal self-determination and the concept of white 'guilt'; and the Lavoisier Society (2000), which opposes the Kyoto protocol. The Tasman Institute, based in Victoria, was established in the second wave. It was an influential member of the 'New Right' group until it was privatized as a commercial consultancy in 1998. The Australian Institute of Public Policy (AIPP) was founded in 1982 by a former Liberal Party federal politician, John Hyde, to promote the principles of the free market and individual liberty. Located in Western Australia, the AIPP had a local rather than national character. It never acquired an image of stability – despite efforts to expand through a branch office in Canberra – and experienced constant difficulty in retaining both people of talent on low salaries and membership loyalty. In 1991, the AIPP amalgamated with the IPA. Finally, the Sydney Institute, founded in 1989, grew from what was by then the moribund New South Wales branch of the IPA. Positioning itself as a mainstream public affairs forum devoted to opposing extremism, the Sydney Institute is less ideologically identifiable. It operates more as a policy discussion forum described as a 'talk tank' rather than a 'think tank'. By comparison, CIS is more of a publications-oriented 'ink tank'.

Again, in tandem with British developments, the perceived impact of the New Right think tanks provoked a third wave of centre-left organizations. Originally created as a training organization in 1979, the Evatt Foundation was transformed in the late 1980s into a public interest group to promote the ideals of the labour movement. The Sydney based WETtank (an acronym for Women's Economic Think Tank) was established in 1992. It is a very small organization, reliant upon the personal drive of its director, Eva Cox, and supporters within the women's movement. Launched in 1994, the Australia Institute is a prominent Canberra-based think tank with a 'progressive' orientation.

A number of diverse organizations have been established in the late 1990s. The first was the Australian Business Foundation (ABF), constituted as an independent industry policy research organization by one of the major employer associations, Australian Business. The ABF has an independent board and independent funding. Its purpose is to explore new approaches to economic strategy. The Foundation's first major report, *The High Road or the Low Road*, published in 1997, proved particularly influential in establishing the case for a more proactive role for the state in industry policy, especially in emerging 'knowledge economy' areas. The Institute for Private Enterprise (IPE), established by Des Moore, a former Treasury official with links to other New Right institutes, in February 1996, advocates a reduction in the role of government. Like WETtank, it revolves around the personal energy of its founder.

In 1997, a new business-funded think tank was launched by the Australian prime minister to promote research on and links with Asia. Known as the AustralAsia Centre, this body is linked with the prestigious US-based Asia Society but is yet to develop think tank-like features. However, the Foundation for Development Cooperation (FDC) has acquired think tank features since its establishment in 1990. It concentrates on sustainable development and poverty issues in the Asia-Pacific, has a good relationship with AusAid (the Australian agency for development assistance and a key donor), and is part of the GDN (see Stone, chapter 1 in this volume).

In 2000, government funding led to the establishment of two new think tanks associated with the major political parties: the Menzies Research Centre, attached to the Liberal party, and the Chifley Research Centre, linked to Labor. In addition, two other centre-left think tanks have been established: the Brisbane Institute and the Whitlam Institute. The Brisbane Institute was established as an independent organization in 1999 but with support from the University of Queensland, government and private interests. It has been closely associated with the efforts of the Queensland government to development that state's industrial future with a research and conference programme. For example, it has focused on the potential and implications of biotechnology as well as on urban and transportation issues. Its founding director, Peter Botsman, had formerly acted as director of the Evatt Foundation. Subsequently, in 2001, he became founding director of the second new think tank, the Whitlam Institute. This was established partly as a library to house the papers of the former prime minister, Gough Whitlam, and partly to promote 'Third Way' approaches. Its focus is on urban, education, transport and communication issues as well as reconciliation and the promotion of a republic. This institute joins together two centres established earlier in the 1990s as repositories for prime ministerial papers: the Hawke Collection at the University of South Australia and the Chifley Centre at Curtin University in Western Australia. Although these later organizations sponsor occasional speaker programmes, they are primarily academic institutions. By contrast, the Whitlam Institute was conceived as a think tank. More recently, the government has established a quasi-independent think tank, the Australian Strategic Policy Institute (ASPI), funded wholly by the state. Chaired by Robert O'Neill, the governing board includes former politicians from both major parties. Its mission is to research, and promote discussion of, defence issues.

Think tanks are not the only manifestation of the increasing salience of private policy advice. The Australian government has promoted academic input into policy (Marsh, 1995a). University centres have proliferated, some with a strong policy focus. Individual academics have been incorporated into the policy process, invited to write reports, appointed to government agencies or to sit on committees of inquiry. Furthermore, during the 1980s a number of new consultancy companies emerged, most especially Access Economics, initially staffed by six former Treasury personnel. Finally, a number of pressure groups have boosted their policy analytic capacity, notably the Business Council of Australia and the Australian Council on Social Services (ACOSS). These groups are 'moving beyond old-style lobbying functions and adopting more sophisticated roles in the public policy process' (Bell, 1995: 26).

In general, and as Table 15.1. demonstrates, Australian think tanks are not large organizations, and cannot be equated with the leading American and British establishments. Nor are they as well funded. A 1994 review of think tanks found that twenty independent Australian institutes collectively spent A$20 million (Marsh, 1995b: 11). This compares poorly with the resources of university-based centres and, especially, nineteen government policy research institutes with expenditures totalling A$89 million (Marsh, 1995b: 9).

Table 15.1 Selected Australian think tanks

Think tank	Date established	Location	Expenditure (A$)	Personnel
Australian Institute of International Affairs (AIIA)	1933	State capitals	300,000	3 FT 5 PT plus volunteer
Australian Strategic Policy Institute	2001	Canberra	2.5 million	17–20 FT
Australian Collaboration	2000	Melbourne	30,000	1 FT, plus researchers
Australia Institute	1994	Canberra	450,000	5
Brisbane Institute	1999	Brisbane	1 million	12
Committee for the Economic Development of Australia (CEDA)	1960	5 state offices	3,984,000	28 across all states
Centre for Independent Studies (CIS)	1976	Sydney	1.3 million	21 PT and FT plus 14 research fellows
Chifley Research Centre	2000	Canberra		
Evatt Foundation	1979	Sydney		7 FT & PT; adjunct
Foundation for Development Cooperation (FDC)	1990	Brisbane	914,000	4FT and 2 PT
Institute of Public Affairs (IPA)	1943	Melbourne	700,000	12 FT equivalent
Menzies Research Centre	1996			
Sydney Institute	1989	Sydney	884,000	6 FT
WETtank	1992	Sydney	n.a.	No paid staff
Whitlam Institute	2001		500,000	3

Note: Data is for 2001 unless indicated otherwise. FT = Full-time; PT = part-time.

Think tank funding has been closely linked to the economic cycle. For example, cost cutting at the IPA involved relocation from a central highrise office building in Melbourne to the fringes of the business district. Another response to a more straitened financial environment has been amalgamation. This was one cause of the merger between the AIPP and the IPA, noted earlier. Another major problem that the smaller policy institutes confront is the lack of a career structure for their research scholars, particularly as think tanks operate with a small core of executive staff. In most Australian think tanks, salaries do not exceed those found in the private sector or universities. Think tanks cannot guarantee an employment base allowing for predictable careers. It is easier to attract visitors who have a secure base of employment elsewhere, and ex-politicians or bureaucrats seeking a pre-retirement post. However, it is difficult to attract middle-level people to make a long-term commitment. Instead, Australian think tanks have always relied upon the support of academics.

The typical Australian institute has a small staff and commissions academics or experts to write on topics. The advantage of the network organization is that management can draw upon a wider pool of expertise. At the same time, a wide range of viewpoints can be encompassed. Networking potentially curtails the problem of an institute running out of new ideas and is an efficient strategy for small institutes with limited resources. Indeed, the New Right think tanks have been important as organizational foci for networks linking previously isolated individuals in a broad, if not united, liberal movement from 1975 onwards (Kemp, 1988).

Public and philanthropic funding

As in Canada, not all Australian institutes have charitable status. Indeed, the Australian tax system undermines more extensive development of think tanks. The AIIA, the Australia Institute, the Tasman Institute, CEDA and the CIS are categorized as charitable or public educational institutions on some or all of their activities. 'Approved research institutes', including the AIIA, the CIS, the Australia Institute and the Evatt Foundation, are also exempt from tax, whilst the gifts or subscriptions of donors are tax deductible for the individual. But tax exemption is quite difficult to acquire. Furthermore, in Australia, there is a poorly developed culture of philanthropy. Additionally, much private philanthropy has concentrated on social and welfare provision. As one director of the AIIA lamented, 'it is much harder to get Australians and Australian institutions to give to a cause that has an intellectual appeal than to one that has an emotional appeal' (Millar, 1976: 15). The state is the dominant source of funding for research through universities, departmental research bureaux and scientific laboratories. However, government reorganization and funding cutbacks since the election of the Howard government in 1996 have reduced both the analytic capacities of the state and the absolute volume of funds devoted to political and public policy activity.

Since the 1980s, Australian business has been more willing to fund independent research, but not on the scale of their American or European counterparts. Nevertheless, sections of the Australian business community consistently pay high membership fees to CEDA. This organization has successfully marketed a package of selective benefits for subscribers. The establishment of the ABF is another sign of business interest.

Party competition and think tanks

The roles of political parties have undergone substantial change in recent years and this has had considerable impact on the 'political opportunity structure' facing think tanks (McAdam, McCarthy and Zald, 1996). Think tanks potentially have greater impact on large parties with weak discipline that act more like electoral coalitions. They may also have greater impact on catch-all parties, as these seek to identify and attract particular sectional constituencies or interests, or on policy environments that are porous and conflictual, as occurs in the United States. None of these conditions prevails in Australia. Strategic policy-making is dominated by major party elites and by the central bureaucracy (notably the departments of Treasury and of the prime minister). Think tanks can become influential with individual party leaders or parliamentarians with strong policy interests. But direct influence requires the cultivation of key individuals or the development of indirect channels through the media or powerful pressure groups.

The problem of achieving direct influence on the major parties is compounded by recent trends affecting their positioning, funding and roles. Australia's major parties – the Australian Labor Party (ALP), the Liberal Party of Australia (LPA) and its coalition partner, the National Party – exhibit many of the characteristics of Peter Mair's 'cartel parties' (1997). Parties of this kind depend heavily on state funding and state resources (such as staff, postage, email and copying entitlements and other special allowances). These are channelled directly to the party leadership and parliamentarians, thus reducing party organizational influence. Further, the party organizations have become primarily promotional and electioneering machines. Their policy roles have atrophied. The party in government has access to the policy resources of the public service, and in recent years, parties in opposition have been preoccupied with gaining tactical electoral advantage, not major policy development. Indeed, since

1983, both major parties have broadly adopted the neo-liberal policy agenda. Labor's third electoral defeat in 2001 occasioned a rethinking on policy and organizational roles that may create more opportunities for influence – although the 'New Right' think tanks have long-standing and strong links to a number of senior Labor figures.

The political parties have yet to develop any close affinity with independent research organizations. The Labor Party has severed its formal links with the Evatt Foundation and established a new 'shell' think tank (or what Denham and Garnett, in chapter 14 of this volume, refer to as a 'hollowed-out' think tank), the Chifley Centre, to take over the public subsidy to political party research organizations. Funding under the auspices of the Chifley Centre was the base for Labor's major policy development exercise prior to the 2001 election. This involved the development of the so-called 'Knowledge Nation' programme. However, organizational co-ordination and support was provided by full-time party staff. The Liberal Party body, the Menzies Research Centre, has not hitherto had a high profile on any issue. However, it has recently acquired a new and politically ambitious chair, Malcolm Turnbull, who has already used this organization as a springboard for developing his public profile (*Sydney Morning Herald*, 15 July 2001: 1). But there are no parallels to the kind of relationships that the PPI or EPI enjoy with the Democratic Party in the USA. The links of the Liberals to the IPA and the CIS, and of Labor to any of the centre-left think tanks, are weaker than the relationship of the Conservative Party to the CPS, or the Labour Party to the IPPR, in Britain.

Despite its broad affinity with the ALP, the Evatt Foundation was never able to cultivate much favour at either the state or federal levels in Australia. From 1993 until Labor's defeat in 1996, Evatt convened quarterly meetings of sympathetic organizations (such as the Women's Electoral Lobby and ACOSS) to discuss the emerging policy agenda (Sawer and Jupp, 1996). Yet Evatt had very limited access to the Federal Labor government, which was largely dominated by Treasury thinking and neo-liberal perspectives on the role of the state. The general ethos of Evatt research did not reflect the economic beliefs and political values of the party's power brokers. Prime ministers Hawke and Keating were more likely to consult their own advisors within the party than those outside it (Watson, 2002). The distance between the party and this organization was reflected in the decision to create the shell Chifley Centre as a home for the public subsidy that was withdrawn from Evatt. Additionally, the factional system of the ALP fragments the party into contending sets of policy preferences. It is difficult for any of the centre-left think tanks to address the party as a whole, whereas identification with a faction can lead to marginalization. With the defeat of the ALP in the 2001 federal election, it remains to be seen whether any reassessment of party policies will be conducted in conjunction with the two 'progressive' think tanks. Much depends on the proclivities of party leaders. The pressures on the new leadership, Simon Crean and Jenny Macklin, may induce more openness to the centre-left think tanks. For the immediate future, the leadership is preoccupied with proposals to reduce formal union influence in party deliberations. Nevertheless, think tanks will continue to serve as a platform for politicians, and politicians will request these organizations to provide policy advice and briefings. For example, following Labor's most recent electoral defeat, the Australia Institute has been called upon by its left faction to organize briefings on a variety of social, economic and environmental issues.

Architecture of the state

State- or provincial-level governments provide yet another arena in which think tanks can operate. This is not the case in Australia. For the older institutes, such as the AIIA and the IPA, a federal branch structure was an important feature at the time of establishment in building a strong membership and support base. However, there are significant disadvantages of decentralization. Resources are spread thinly over several distant offices. It is instructive that the new Australian think tanks have concentrated their activity in one city, usually Sydney or Melbourne, or more recently Brisbane.

It is a commonly stated argument that parliamentary systems are closed to think tanks (Oliver, 1993). The decline of Parliament and concentration of power in the prime minister, Cabinet and bureaucracy supposedly insulates policy-making from outside influences. An entrenched, career public service with considerable control over information also acts as a gatekeeper to policy-making. Furthermore, the privacy of the advisory relationship between ministers and senior public servants enshrined in the principle of collective ministerial responsibility is symptomatic of a more cohesive and co-ordinated decision-making structure than in the American system, where there is a separation of powers. In Australia, the Department of Prime Minister and Cabinet has 'become something of a prime-ministerial think tank', while the rising influence and rapidly increasing numbers of ministerial 'minders' or advisors in the upper echelons of political policy-making have occluded the search for external advice (Jarman and Kouzmin, 1993: 507–9). Think tanks are further constrained by the absence of conduits into government for the exchange of information and personnel.

Another important factor retarding the development of Australian think tanks is the analytic strength of research bureaus within government and Parliament. For example, the Parliamentary Research Service (comparable to, but much smaller than, the US Congressional Research Service) provides Senators and Members of Parliament with 'analysis and advice on current and prospective issues, policies, legislation and programs' and other services. With a budget of A$20 million in 2001, and a staff of 102, the Service has resources at its disposal that far exceed those of the independent think tanks. The development of policy research bureaux inside the Australian public service during the 1970s and 1980s has helped to meet greater government demand for policy analysis. The Productivity Commission provides a particularly notable example. With a budget of A$23 million and a staff of 195, this organization conducts public inquiries on reference from the government on key economic strategy issues. This embraces both the case for sustaining protection or subsidies (for example for the auto, textile or pharmaceutical sectors) and more esoteric subjects, such as the funding and role of charitable organizations or the implications of growing state-government dependence on gambling taxes. Other think tanks within government include the Australian Bureau of Agricultural and Resource Economics and the National Office of the Information Economy. The growth of internal government research bureaux has been a more notable trend in Australia than the growth of private think tanks (Jarman and Kouzmin, 1993; Marsh, 1995), but this was reversed after the election of the New Right Howard government in 1996. As part of general public service retrenchment, research organizations such as the Australian Manufacturing Council, the Economic Planning Advisory Council and the Bureau of Industry Economics were disbanded. Analytic capacity in the Departments of Prime Minister and Cabinet, Finance, and Employment, Education and Training have, however, been developed.

The Australian parliamentary system is not impervious to think tanks. Parliamentarians, party officials and bureaucrats participate in think tank functions. Some are think tank members and others independently seek advice and information. Additionally, Commissions of Inquiry and the circulation of 'discussion papers' provide opportunities for policy research institutes to make submissions and contribute to public debate. The revived committee system in the Australian Parliaments potentially represents a limited source of demand for think tank research and analysis (Marsh, 1980). The Australian Senate, which acts as a house of review, has shown a greater proclivity for drawing on external sources of advice.

As discussed through the remainder of this chapter, think tanks are symptomatic of the importance of ideas in fashioning the national political conversation and ultimately public policy. But executive dominance of policy-making, a closed bureaucratic culture and a weak Parliament create a difficult environment for immediate think tank influence. Rather than having decisive impact on policy development or political influence on politicians or legislation, think tanks have played a greater role in shaping the climate of opinion and in establishing the terms of debate.

The impact of Australian think tanks

As discussed in the introduction to this volume, power based on knowledge is notoriously difficult to examine and measure. Accordingly, the following analysis commences with three standard hypotheses concerning think tanks and the policy process. Think tanks supposedly introduce 'greater rationality' (Dror, 1984), perform an 'enlightenment' function (Weiss, 1990), and offer 'alternative views' to enhance the democratic functioning of policy debate (Parsons, 1995: 167). More abstractly, the literature on institutions identifies, as one of their key roles, the seeding and dissemination of (in Douglass North's phrase) 'ideas, choice sets and motives' (North, 1992). Think tanks are potential critical agents in specific dimensions of such processes. For reasons outlined below, Australian think tanks rarely achieve these ambitions. Instead, it is more appropriate to consider think tanks as strategic organizations for policy entrepreneurship and networking.

Theoretically, think tanks can make the policy process more rational or comprehensive, in the sense that their analysis provides additional insights for decision-makers, allowing them to address a wider range of possible policy alternatives. Such a perspective assumes, first, that think tanks are designed to produce unbiased recommendations on the basis of full investigation of an issue or problem. It also assumes that, secondly, think tanks can directly communicate research results to government and, thirdly, government incorporates such analysis into its deliberations. An almost ritual theme in Australian policy discourse since the 1970s has been the need to improve the policy process given the pressures on Cabinet, ministerial overload and other institutional constraints that limit the comprehensive discussion of long-term issues and priorities. A concern has been to broaden perspectives within government and the nature of inputs to decision-making. Although think tanks represent an additional advisory system to counter bureaucratic bias within the system, in-house advisors in government ministries continue to provide the bulk of policy advice. Politicians and bureaucrats do not call upon private policy institutes in any systematic fashion.

The less ambitious claims of 'enlightenment' and proffering 'alternative views' are more realistic assessments of think tank contributions to policy. The former involves giving decision-makers the illumination of the best available knowledge and social scientific research. This approach assumes that social science has impact at the broader level of opinion and worldview through a longer-term percolation of ideas into public policy (Weiss,

1990: 101). The market-liberal institutes in Australia, for example, have collectively championed the economic rationalist agenda and tried to set the frame of discourse for key public servants and media commentators. The CIS was created to challenge Keynesian policy perspectives and government intervention (Kemp, 1988: 344–8). In conjunction with the IPA, and the various specialized offshoots mentioned earlier, these institutes were policy entrepreneurs in the 'liberal policy network', informing some of the ideas of the 'dries' (that is, free market advocates and libertarians) in the Liberal Party (Kelly, 1992). In particular, these institutes pioneered policies such as deregulation and privatization, labour market reform and trade liberalization, and were able to provide decision-makers in federal and state governments with policy blueprints, economic arguments and political justifications to legitimate the adoption of such ideas. The impact of these think tanks was to shift the centre of political debate and dislodge the ideological hegemony of the Keynesian regulators (Sawer, 2002).

Advocacy of the premises of free market and limited government intervention has been undertaken with two related aims. Firstly, these think tanks have facilitated a more regularized interaction between leading political figures from the major parties, market liberal economists and other scholars through their research projects, conferences and seminars. Secondly, through these interactions, think tanks have sought to inform the policy agendas of both major parties. Importantly, think tanks do not operate alone but as part of a coalition of intellectual, material and partisan interests. Economic rationalism was not only espoused by the think tanks but also had a significant following within the Canberra bureaucracy, particularly in the Treasury, in government advisory bodies concerned with economic affairs (such as the Productivity Commission), in backbench parliamentary groups such as the libertarian 'modest members' society, and among academics from the universities and other 'dries' (see Keating, 2000; Argy, 2003). Think tanks and others were provided with opportunities to entrench their discourse of economic liberalism as the dominant policy paradigm from the 1970s onwards, as decision-makers sought new interpretative frameworks to comprehend the recessionary conditions and economic malaise of the Australian economy, and as the federal Labor Government of 1983–96 sought to distance itself from what was then seen as the problematic economic legacy of the Whitlam era.

The 'enlightenment' model of understanding think tank influence does not adequately address the political dimensions of how these organizations attempt to create the intellectual conditions for problem-solving by weakening prevailing policy orthodoxy. Think tanks have not relied on the inherent persuasiveness of ideas but enhanced ideational appeal through advocacy, outreach and dissemination of analyses. 'Enlightenment' presumes that knowledge trickles incrementally into public understanding. However, think tanks can hasten this process of opinion mobilization as policy entrepreneurs within policy networks. As already noted, the New Right think tanks have long-standing informal links with leading members of the major parties in Australia. They have cultivated relations with and between conservative business leaders and academics. The Evatt Foundation tried to build a constituency based primarily on the labour movement, but lost influence in step with the broader decline of trade union power. WETtank draws its base from the women's movement, which links it to a much broader coalition of groups and activists (Sawer and Groves, 1994). By contrast, the AIIA is not concerned with political mobilization, as its mandate prevents it from expressing a political viewpoint. It is restricted to an enlightenment function.

The new think tanks have been far more successful in gaining political attention and media coverage, partly as a consequence of their advocacy of specific and ideologically informed policy agendas. The market-liberal think tanks – the CIS and the IPA – are less engaged in enlightenment than in persuasion and popularizing a market-liberal policy agenda. They have a clear set of principles, which inform their analysis and guide their policy recommendations. In seeking to entrench the discourse of the market within policy frameworks, think tank knowledge and intellectual activity are politicized. Although direct support for political parties or legislation is eschewed by think tanks, the language employed and the frameworks of analysis often lead to conclusions that are of partisan advantage. For the new breed of Australian institutes to be educational and apolitical in the style of the AIIA is contradictory, since the investigation of policy and recommendation of a course of action or series of options are intrinsically political.

The enlightenment model does not give adequate attention to the characteristics of the policy process, which give some ideas more influence than others (see Yankelovitch, 1992; also Richardson, 2000). The decline of the policy role of the major party organizations is one development that has changed the dynamics of the national political conversation. Others include the emergence of a broadened and more contested policy agenda. This has resulted from both external and domestic developments. Externally, economic globalization has created a new context for state economic strategies. Domestically, the new social movements have successfully extended the political agenda to include a variety of new issues such as the environment, women's, indigenous, ethnic, gay and lesbian rights. These varied developments are synthesized into issues, agendas and programmes through the political system, which is the familiar two-party adversarial system. Despite the 'environmental' developments mentioned above, this formal architecture of power has remained unchanged for nearly a century.

In this context, the media, both electronic and print, has become much more influential, as gatekeeper and protagonist in the national political conversation (Katz, 1998). The think tanks have been alive to the opportunities thus created. They have used the media, both directly and via opinion-forming columnists, to project their discourses. Journalists are more frequently approaching think tanks for information and as a source of expert opinion. Some think tanks have been able to capitalize on this interest. The CIS commissions columns from its specialist advisors and then offers these free to national, regional and specialist media (da Silva, 2002). The director of the Sydney Institute has an influential weekly column in the major metropolitan dailies of Sydney and Melbourne. In addition, he occupies a weekly opinion slot on national current affairs radio. Many other think tank fellows regularly feature in the newspapers as a source of commentary. For example, the Australia Institute is adept at offering stories to fill the quiet news spots on Sunday evening for Monday morning newspaper dissemination. Indeed Peter Botsman, the director of the Whitlam Institute, has long claimed that 'the Right has become institutionalised in the media' (Hughes, 1992). Certainly, the free market think tanks treat the media as an important channel to public opinion, whilst journalists have a fruitful relationship in acquiring easy access to information and informed commentary. While links with the media are necessary, the extent of interaction varies considerably from institute to institute. CEDA keeps journalists at arm's length and does not encourage punditry. Similarly, the AIIA cannot provide the polemical point of view often sought by journalists.

Although economic rationalists have been influential in entrenching a new language of policy debate, these circumstances do not help explain the role of other think tanks with less ideological sway. WETtank articulates a feminist policy discourse that does not have wide acceptance in policy circles. Yet this think tank is not ineffectual or hopelessly marginalized. Instead, it resists patriarchal assumptions in policy and provides intellectual support for feminist redefinition of the role of women in society and the economy as part of the broader women's movement. Notwithstanding its minuscule resources, WETtank instigated a major media splash in 1998 when it convened a women's tax forum to consider the implications of a proposed goods and services tax (Warhurst, Brown, and Higgins, 2000).

Furthermore, influence need not be construed only in terms of direct policy impact. The AIIA, for example, is more concerned to promote wider understanding of international affairs in the community and serve its membership. The CIS has brought to Australia a number of renowned international scholars, such as James Buchanan and Milton Friedman, for its public lecture series. The Sydney Institute regularly holds public lectures on Australian literature and the arts. These organizations perform a subtler social and cultural role, such as contributing to the body of knowledge of and about Australia that does not have direct policy relevance.

The final claim regarding the role of think tanks in the policy process is that they provide alternative points of view and are a 'manifestation of pluralism at work in a modern information society' (Parsons, 1996: 167). Providing alternative analysis to that of government and articulating diverse viewpoints, think tanks potentially act as a counterbalance to the dominance of bureaucratic advice.

Yet this only occurs if political and bureaucratic audiences are open to alternative perspectives. There is some evidence of this occurring in an ad hoc manner. Politicians and bureaucrats have attended conferences, been members of and made speeches at the functions of bodies such as the AIIA, the CIS, the Brisbane and Sydney Institutes and the IPA. At the establishment of a new think tank such as the AustralAsia Centre, or the opening of new premises, politicians cluster to applaud think tank contributions to public debate, or at the very least to take advantage of a photo-opportunity. Think tanks often act as service organizations for government, organizing conferences or seminars and lectures by visiting international speakers. For example, the AIIA occasionally plays an unofficial role in the informal diplomacy of the Department of Foreign Affairs and Trade (Stone, 1996a). CEDA plays a quasi-public role in collecting and passing on information to decision-makers, responds to requests for information about business opinion on policy options, and helps explain public policy decisions to its members. Before its privatization, the Tasman Institute undertook contract research for the Victoria State government. In short, governments and politicians 'use' think tanks. This does not necessarily entail the politicization of think tanks by government. Australian governments have not pressured these bodies to toe a political line, although it is possible (and not unknown) for think tank reports or analyses to be used to legitimate political or bureaucratic decisions. Indeed, a few institutes – WETtank, the IPA and the CIS – refuse to accept or apply for government grants.

A tour of the web sites of Australian think tanks in August 2002 revealed a common set of claims among think tanks that their research, contribution to public discussion and alternative policy advice enhance the democratic functioning of society. The IPA 'seeks to promote the general interest rather than sectional ones', the CIS 'encourages debate' through 'independent research', while the ABF is 'challenging conventional wisdom and doctrinaire thinking'. The Brisbane Institute portrays itself as an 'ideas marketplace'. In this regard, the 'competition in ideas' between various institutes reflects the pluralist position that diverse, non-governmental voices highlight new ideas and present possible policy alternatives to decision-makers who might not otherwise receive full information. Certainly the Australia Institute considers it provides 'a better balance' to economic rationalist thinking. Policy research institutes provide a democratic fillip in broadening the agenda. Similarly, think tanks perform a useful 'watchdog' role in observing government, watching for instances of waste, inefficiency, corruption or poor policy implementation.

However, such a role is limited. Most policy institutes are run by an intellectual elite, speak to a small, politically educated audience, and have small memberships or none at all. They often claim to act in the public interest. Yet the majority of the citizenry is a passive recipient of pronouncements that trickle down from experts in think tanks via the media. As some journalists have observed, the Australian think tank is 'full of bias' (Bone, 2000), operates with 'a guiding philosophy, a set of beliefs it wishes to foist on the community' (Dusevic, 1990: 2) and is 'largely unaccountable' (da Silva, 2002). The pluralist 'marketplace of ideas' is not one of open competition. Think tanks use the expertise and credentials of their staff to claim superior input to public debate on the basis of the knowledge they encompass. Though the use of technical and theoretical language, think tanks are just as likely to mystify policy debate and make it inaccessible to the ordinary person who lacks professional standing (Jones, 1993: 267). The 'cult of the expert' can undermine the educative and critical functions often presumed to be the *raison d'être* of think tanks. They do not necessarily represent a democratization of opinion but can further entrench the position of intellectual elites.

Conclusion

In the broad scheme of Australian politics, think tanks are small and relatively unimportant organizations. In Australia, think tanks have not consolidated as a strong policy advice industry as in the USA. They are on the margins not only of bureaucracy but also of the political parties. To gain greater political, policy and intellectual credibility, Australian think tanks need regularized channels of access to decision-makers. This is unlikely with existing institutional constraints: a restrictive taxation system, minimal corporate philanthropy, the strength of party political policy advice and the structural dominance of (quasi-) bureaucratic analysis, for which there appears to be a political preference.

Nevertheless, a number of think tanks are acting strategically as policy entrepreneurs to spread new ideas and ways of thinking about policy problems. The 'New Right' group has been particularly effective in this role over the past couple of decades. It remains to be seen whether the more recently established centre-left organizations can play a similar role for a political system (and perhaps a community) increasingly in search of alternatives to neo-liberal orthodoxy. At one level, think tanks target decision-makers and attempt to educate actors within policy networks. At another, broader level, they are engaged in the longer-term enterprise of societal influence on the climate of opinion via mediums such as the media, educational establishments and interest groups. Australian think tanks are sufficiently numerous to represent a new institutional dimension to policy debates. They are also worthy of scholarly attention in that their policy entrepreneurship and networking strategies distribute policy advice and intellectual arguments within the political system in such a way as to give some actors, who favour a particular world-view or policy paradigm, more power and intellectual credibility than others.

16 Evert A. Lindquist

Three decades of Canadian think tanks: evolving institutions, conditions and strategies

Canadian think tanks are a relatively young group of organizations, having only started to emerge in the early 1970s. In some cases, Canadian think tanks and their leaders have acquired something close to celebrity status; their leaders and senior staff appear frequently on television and comment regularly in the print media. Think tank leaders and senior analysts are important elements of elite networks, sometimes injecting expertise into the policy-making process and public debate, and sometimes interpreting policy research and developments to the public. For example, several think tanks have hosted public conferences and other events for the federal government as part of national consultation exercises during the 1990s (Russell, 1993; Lindquist, 1994b; Abelson, 2002). These and other think tank events are often televised on the Canadian Parliamentary Channel, providing additional public exposure. However, despite the prominence of think tanks, most policy elites and citizens know relatively little about how they attempt to exercise influence, and how they manage to survive.

This chapter attempts to explain the character and distinctive features of Canadian think tanks both as a collectivity and as individual organizations. It also provides readers with a sense of how the environment of think tanks has changed since the early 1970s and how this has influenced their activities. It does not attempt to assess the effectiveness of Canadian think tanks, provide detailed historical accounts of think tanks, or set out a conceptual framework to compare and assess their outputs, which would require considerably more space (see Lindquist, 1989, 1994a; Abelson, 2002). However, I pose questions that should prove useful for reflecting on the experience of think tanks in Canada and other jurisdictions. Accordingly, this chapter has four parts and a conclusion: first, it provides an overview of the size and structure of social and economic policy institutes; second, it outlines think tank diversity in size and structure; third, it discusses how the Canadian political, economic and institutional environment constrains and promotes their development;

and, fourth, it addresses some contemporary issues facing think tanks, such as the emergence of a new generation of 'virtual' institutes.

Three decades of think tanks in Canada: a synopsis

Most accounts of how modern Canadian think tanks emerged begin with the Ritchie report (Lindquist, 1989; Abelson, 2002). In late 1968, Ronald Ritchie was directed by the Canadian government to consider the feasibility of creating an independent policy institute. He surveyed the status of policy research in Canada and compared this with arrangements in other countries. Ritchie acknowledged that royal commissions, task forces, government councils, universities and several non-profit organizations undertook activities relevant to public policy analysis, but he concluded there was insufficient multidisciplinary and policy-oriented research in Canada. His report, submitted in 1969 (Ritchie, 1971), led to the creation of the Institute for Research on Public Policy (IRPP). But, even as the IRPP was established during the early 1970s, the institutional landscape quickly began to change.

Four established organizations underwent significant transitions that produced part of the first wave of Canadian policy institutes. Until 1971, the Canadian Welfare Council functioned as a peak interest association, housing three national associations in the social services field, two divisions on ageing and family and child welfare, and a small research branch. Mounting internal tensions led to its transformation into a social policy institute by having independence granted to the associations and its being renamed the Canadian Council on Social Development (CCSD). In 1954, the New York-based Conference Board established a small Montreal office to serve companies with interests in Canada with studies on economics, personnel administration and business practices, with its membership and staff growing steadily. In 1971, under a new president, its offices moved to Ottawa, and the Canadian branch grew rapidly, transforming into a more autonomous research operation anchored by a short-term economic forecasting model, and improved meeting and information services for members. The C.D. Howe Institute was formed following a merger of the Private Planning Association of Canada and a foundation, becoming a centre for short-term economic policy analysis, and continuing to serve three private sector councils. Finally, the profile of the Canadian Tax Foundation (CTF), founded in 1946 to conduct and sponsor research on taxation, increased significantly during the early 1970s due to the national debate stimulated by the Royal Commission on Taxation on the economic and social policy objectives of the tax code.

In the early 1970s, three new policy institutes were established. In 1972, the IRPP was created by the federal government to become

Canada's equivalent of the Brookings Institution. The plan was to secure a hefty endowment with contributions from the federal government, provincial governments and private sector donors. In 1973, the Canada West Foundation (CWF) was established in Calgary to focus more on the role of the West in the Confederation. A year later, the Fraser Institute was established in Vancouver to conduct research, to educate Canadians about the viability of market solutions to policy problems, and to draw attention to the growing and allegedly counterproductive presence of government in the economy.

A second wave of institutes arrived in the late 1970s and early 1980s. The Canadian Institute for Economic Policy (CIEP) was formed in 1979 by Walter Gordon, a former finance minister, to sponsor a five-year research programme revolving around the themes of economic nationalism. In 1980, the Canadian Centre for Policy Alternatives (CCPA) was established by supporters of the union movement and social democratic principles to counter the influence of the Fraser Institute. Finally, following the defeat of the Progressive Conservative government in early 1980, some party loyalists sought to create an institute dedicated to conservative principles in the analysis of economic, social and international issues. However, the National Foundation for Public Policy Development soon foundered because of shifting party priorities.

Several more institutes emerged. In 1987, the Public Policy Forum was established to improve the performance of the Canadian government and its public service, to expand the constituency for public service reform in the private sector, and to foster greater understanding across the business, labour, academic and public service sectors. In 1990, the Institute on Governance developed a niche in drawing on Canadian expertise to advise governments in developing nations to manage public services and train executives better, serving as broker for Canadian agencies seeking to assist such governments, and sponsoring seminars and providing advisory services for Canadian policy-makers. In 1992, the Caledon Institute for Social Policy was created in Ottawa, with the financial support of the Maytree Foundation, to enable Ken Battle (a former executive director of the federal government's National Council of Welfare) to undertake policy research and advocacy without the distractions and constraints of serving a government council. In 1994, the Canadian Policy Research Networks Inc. was formed by Judith Maxwell, the former head of the Economic Council of Canada, to sponsor longer-term, interdisciplinary policy research programmes on social and economic policy issues, and to lever research capabilities from across Canada.

In the early 1990s, several think tanks underwent significant transformations. The IRPP's new president consolidated operations in Montreal, adopting a structure similar to the Howe Institute, but focused on different issues. The CCSD floundered as the federal government cut grants and contributions, sold its building in Ottawa, and restructured so that it could survive with research contracts. In 1993, the Conference Board of Canada absorbed the Niagara Institute, which was dedicated to organizing conferences for many different clients, developing new techniques for improving the dynamics of such events. Finally, the Public Policy Forum established a separately funded, autonomous Public Management Research Centre in 1995 to commission research on private sector approaches to management and on comparative practice in public management.

At the time of writing, in 2002, there is certainly no shortage of Canadian think tanks. To date, no census on think tanks has been attempted for Canada, but 100 non-profit policy think tanks may exist. This chapter addresses only think tanks with relatively broad policy interests and does not account for the many working in particular sectors on specific subject matters.

The diversity of Canadian think tanks

It should be evident that Canadian think tanks vary considerably in terms of mandate and ideological orientation. But equally important sources of variation involve financial resources, as shown in Table 16.1 (think tanks are listed in ascending order of size of revenue), and their respective portfolios of activities.

The best place to begin is by reviewing some figures that indicate revenue flows and staff complements. Some think tanks – such as the Caledon Institute for Social Policy – are quite small and rely on anywhere from four to five staff. The majority of think tanks range in revenue between CAN$1.4 million and CAN$5 million, and employ between 14 and 35 staff. In terms of both its annual budget and staff complement, however, the Conference Board of Canada continues to dwarf the others: its 2000 revenues exceeded CAN$26 million and it employed just over 200 people, rivalling major US research institutions.

Canadian think tanks vary with respect to the inquiries they undertake. When observers conjure up images of 'typical' think tanks, they probably envisage a critical mass of in-house staff who, in collaboration with a larger network of researchers and supporters, produce a variety of research studies, short-term policy analyses, newsletters, seminars and conferences. This image applies to several think tanks – the CCSD, the CCPA, the Fraser Institute, the Howe Institute and the IRPP come to mind – but it does not account for their full diversity. Consider the following examples.

Table 16.1 Selected Canadian policy think tanks

Think tank	Date established	Location	2000 revenues (CAN$)	2000 staff (full-time equivalent)
Caledon Institute for Social Policy	1992	Ottawa	1,126,953	4.2
Canada West Foundation (CWF)	1973	Calgary	1,462,658	14.0
C.D. Howe Institute	1973	Toronto	1,853,222	17.0
Canadian Council on Social Development (CCSD)	1971	Ottawa	1,855,153	31.0
Institute on Governance	1990	Ottawa	1,935,113	15.0
Institute for Research on Public Policy (IRPP)	1972	Montreal	2,292,000	16.5
Canadian Centre for Philanthropy	1981	Toronto	2,641,701	30.0
Public Policy Forum	1987	Ottawa	2,688,657	21.0
Canadian Policy Research Networks (CPRN)	1994	Ottawa	2,802,630	24.0
Canadian Centre for Policy Alternatives (CCPA)	1980	Ottawa	3,000,000	17.0
Fraser Institute	1974	Vancouver	4,690,544	35.0
Canadian Tax Foundation (CTF)	1946	Toronto	5,000,000	28.0
Conference Board of Canada	1954	Ottawa	26,109,000	201.0

Note: These figures were obtained from the annual reports of think tanks and from telephone interviews. In some cases, the financial year of think tanks did not correspond to the calendar year, and in those cases figures were chosen from the financial year that overlapped most with the calendar year. The author thanks Tatiana Roberston for preparing this table.

- The CIEP focused almost exclusively on producing research and, over five years, published over thirty monographs by contracting to outsiders, usually academics. Responsibility for managing the institute was also contracted out.
- The Public Policy Forum, which organizes round tables, search conferences and other events to explore medium-term issues, generally seeks to be a catalyst for learning and for reforming the public sector, often through private–public partnerships.
- With approximately 200 staff, the Conference Board regularly sponsors an impressive number of conferences and other meetings (250) and scores of leadership programmes, and issues 150 research reports of one kind or another.

- The CTF sponsors several annual conferences showcasing research papers and analyses of recent tax developments. It supports academics and others to conduct extensive research, often published in the *Canadian Tax Paper* series or its scholarly journal, and it has a superb research library. Staff produce important reference volumes on national, provincial and municipal finances. The CTF has many features similar to organized research units at a major research university.

The key point is that there are many different 'social technologies' employed by Canadian think tanks to achieve the objectives of their supporters and leaders. Some think tanks are managed more like conglomerates. This may be achieved either by locating programmes in different cities, or by giving programmes considerable autonomy. Consider the following examples.

- Until the late 1980s, the IRPP had a rolling set of five or six broad programmes or 'mini-institutes' on specific themes. Each had a director, obtained funding from separate sources, and was located in a different city across Canada.
- The Conference Board had fourteen 'knowledge areas' in 2000, each encompassing from a few to several distinct councils, research centres and fora which meet regularly. Councils and centres are supported by a separate membership fee structure and have advisory councils.
- The CPRN established several networks of researchers across Canada who work in different institutional environments. Each has a director and one or more research fellows (depending on the funding streams) who may not reside at the head office.

Despite this diversity, it is possible to discern some patterns. First, very few institutes generate their own data. Only the Conference Board is heavily involved in producing data not available from other sources. It produces national and provincial economic forecasts; surveys of business investment, consumer spending, and now corporate donation intentions; regular reports on a variety of corporate practices; and various 'outlook' documents. Some institutes, such as the CCSD and the Fraser Institute, 'mine' and repackage existing data available from Statistics Canada, putting it in a more accessible format for members of the public, or in the case of the CTF, making it available as a valuable library resource. The CPRN has essentially utilized 'focus group' methodology or 'dialogues' to produce nuanced data on citizen preferences on complex issues, and this informs its recommendations.

Second, policy research tends not to be conducted by institute staff; such work is usually undertaken by outsiders (again, the Conference Board is an exception). There are good reasons for this practice. Institute staff are often hired as generalists who can dabble in many policy areas and attend to the day-to-day demands of managing contracted research projects and the publication programme, organizing conferences and fora, meeting the demands of members, seeking funding opportunities and responding to requests from the media. Moreover, some experts may be too expensive or unavailable to work on a full-time basis, so it makes sense to contract out the responsibility for undertaking major research projects.

Finally, policy analysis tends to be more closely held, since it may be provocative and have implications for an institute's image. Some think tanks, such as the Conference Board, avoid producing policy prescriptions (though they seek to influence policy debates by supplying new information), while others indicate that recommendations in studies do not represent the 'official' position of the think tank and its directors. Conversely, think tanks that regularly produce prescriptive policy analyses typically ensure that such work is undertaken by staff or trusted outsiders.

Evolving environments for Canadian think tanks

In the period since the first Canadian think tanks emerged, significant changes have occurred in their broader policy and institutional environments. The trajectory of the welfare state, as well as public confidence in government leadership, has changed markedly, which, in turn, have affected the 'market' for think tank outputs.

During the 1960s and early 1970s, the federal government and its programmes grew rapidly, inspired by activist US governments, an interest in building capacity to comprehend and solve social and economic problems, and a belief that solutions could be found. Policy planning, analysis and evaluation units proliferated in federal departments and central agencies, as well as arm's-length advisory organizations – the Economic Council of Canada (1963), the Science Council of Canada (1966) and the National Council of Welfare (1969) – intended to marry policy research capabilities with the promise of consensus. Not unrelated was the drive to create the IRPP and the emergence of the CCSD, the latter relying heavily on federal funding during the late 1960s and early 1970s. It was in this context that think tanks critical of government policies – the Fraser Institute, the Howe Institute and the CWF – emerged, relying primarily on private sector support. In short, economic and government growth created a relative abundance of funds, which, combined with general confidence in the social sciences and policy analysis, supported the emergence of think tanks. Yet these early think tanks did not challenge government bureaucracies or influence policy debates, largely because they were young, fledgling organizations.

A national mood of optimism was shaken by events during the rest of the 1970s and the 1980s. Like many other Western industrialized nations, Canada grappled with two energy shocks and the severe recession of the early 1980s, leading to declining confidence in economic policy. Federal policy-makers added to the mixture the highly regionally divisive National Energy Program of the 1980s, a failed attempt to reform the tax code, and a bruising, but ultimately successful, initiative to import the equivalent of the Canadian constitution from the United Kingdom in 1982. Government political leaders and their public service advisors steadily lost credibility with the public and interest groups; the capability and wisdom of governments to remedy social and economic problems were increasingly questioned. The growing sense of malaise provided fertile ground for several new institutes – the CCPA, the CIEP, and the NFPPD – and provided increasingly receptive audiences for the Fraser Institute and the Howe Institute.

As the 1980s unfolded, the sense of malaise deepened. Despite worsening national finances, even a Conservative government could not take strong measures to reduce deficits and to restructure important programmes because it did not have sufficiently strong public support. One strategic response was 'managerialism': during the late 1980s, the government announced a succession of expenditure restraint measures, launched internal searches for efficiencies in government operations, and undertook piecemeal efforts to modify existing programmes. The government did negotiate a Canada–US free trade agreement and announced significant tax policy reforms following considerable public debate. Finally, there were sustained attempts to mollify Quebec following its objections to the 1982 Canadian Constitution Act. Think tanks were prominent players in the free trade, tax reform and constitutional debates, receiving grants and contributions to undertake studies and host conferences and seminars, probing the economic and social implications of various options, and providing media commentary.

These constitutional deliberations diverted the governments from grappling with the poor state of federal and provincial finances, and the need to rethink many programmes and policy regimes, even though the Howe Institute and the Fraser Institute continually sought to draw attention to these problems. Constitutional matters were set aside until after 1992, when Canadian governments started taking concerted steps to balance budgets and initiate debt repayment programmes in the context of public worry about the deficit and of growing resistance to tax increases. Policy-makers made difficult and long overdue decisions about how programmes should be reshaped or continue, and the role of government. At the federal level, ministers and senior officials concluded that the policy capacity of the public service had declined as a result of managerialism, which downplayed policy and used scarce resources to preserve existing programmes, and because a Conservative government, distrustful of bureaucratic policy advice, strengthened the policy capabilities of ministerial offices and sought external advice from consultants and lobbyists. In late 1993, a new Liberal government sought to rely more heavily on the public service for policy advice, but many departments could not fully meet the challenge (Government of Canada, 1995; Bakvis, 2002). In the late 1990s, in what came to be know as the 'post-deficit environment', the government anchored the Policy Research Initiative, which was designed to link policy capabilities across the public service and to strengthen linkages with think tanks and universities, with a Policy Research Secretariat. Conferences, collaborative research projects, a web site, awards and a journal on policy research were launched. There soon followed significant increases in funding for the federal granting councils for the social sciences, engineering and sciences, and health sciences, as well as the Canada Research Chair programme.

These developments created interesting cross-pressures for Canadian think tanks during the 1990s and beyond. On the one hand, the drive to review and restructure federal programmes, the federal public service and federal–provincial arrangements in all sectors led to the demise of several prominent government research bodies (the Economic Council of Canada, the Science Council of Canada and the Law Reform Commission of Canada) and a significant reduction in unencumbered funding for outside bodies. On the other hand, policy-makers had to rely more heavily on outside organizations to assist with policy research and analysis, and the organization of conferences and seminars. In short, a healthy 'public market' developed for the provision of 'policy inquiry' services at the expense of sustaining grants (Pierre, 1995; Halligan, 1995).

The concept of 'market' implies competition, and Canadian think tanks have been exposed to increasing competition since the early 1970s. One source has been the emergence of more generalist and specialist think tanks. There has also been a dramatic increase in the number of universities and, more importantly, in the number of specialized research units, many of which have a decided policy orientation. Indeed, several governments have not only funded 'centres of excellence', often linking researchers located at several universities, but, more recently, 'reinvested' in national granting councils and 2,000 Canada Research Chairs at universities across the country. The number of business, labour and other associations, not to mention the proliferation of special interest groups, involved in policy debates has greatly expanded, and these often support or sponsor policy research and analysis. Finally, there has been an explosion in the number of integrated and 'boutique' government-relations and policy consulting firms (such as Ekos Research and the Sussex Circle). Some government departments have increasingly relied on these firms for advice on policy and restructuring, and sometimes to manage projects. In some cases, consulting firms seek to distinguish themselves by generating 'public' policy research outputs. For example, KPMG Canada created a Centre for Governance Foundation, and Kaufman, Thomas and Associates established a Centre for Collaborative Government (see www.crossingboundaries.ca for more details).

Funding remains a critical issue for all Canadian think tanks, particularly for sustained projects that explore medium- to longer-term issues. For think tanks that rely on government support, the shift to service contracts means they can divert less funding towards building new intellectual capital, since many contracts are awarded on a competitive basis, and they can be undercut by other organizations not interested in deepening their research competence. The funds available for policy research are largely channelled through the Social Sciences and Humanities Research Council and specialized department granting programmes; it is difficult for think tanks to tap into this stream of funds, since they target university professors, and peer review defers to disciplinary standards and scholarly output as opposed to policy relevance. In some cases, the Council has experimented with jointly sponsored programmes with government and other partners with more elastic standards. Unlike the case in the US, there is relatively limited support in Canada from private foundations for policy research (there are fewer foundations, they tend to be quite small, and they have tended not to support policy research), and the competition to secure foundation funding for the non-profit sector is intense. In short, the funding base for most Canadian think tanks remains tenuous and even the most successful ones struggle to retain members and to secure support for important research topics.

Evolving images of Canadian think tanks: thematic reflections

This section examines some intriguing recent developments and issues for Canadian think tanks, which also constitute a prism for examining their past activities. What follows should not be interpreted as a complete list of the most compelling management challenges for think tank leaders. Several enduring issues could be added to the list, particularly the critical role of leaders in ensuring organizational success, the uneasy relationship between values and inquiry, and measurement of the relevance and impact of think tank activities.

Think tanks as virtual networks: new or old idea?

The first annual report of the CPRN billed it as a 'virtual' institute, a think tank 'without walls' in the information age. The CPRN is a transformed remnant of the Economic Council of Canada.[1] Its founding president, the former Economic Council chair, established a small head office with several networks looping out across Canada, connected by email, fax machines and telephones. But is CPRN really a 'virtual' think tank, and does this constitute an innovation?

If 'virtual' means a think tank 'without walls', or not having many primary contributors working inside the organization, then there have been several such Canadian think tanks. The first was the CIEP, which contracted out the research and management responsibilities to outsiders, maintaining a smaller head office than the CPRN. During the 1980s, the IRPP ran a *de facto* network of institutes guided by an elaborate governance framework; more recently it has relied on outside directors to commission and edit series of studies. Others, like the Howe Institute, rely on academics to contribute research monographs and analyses on a regular basis. Finally, the Fraser Institute and the Institute on Governance depict, as one of their core functions, the nurturing of international networks of practitioners and scholars. One strategy for developing Canadian think tanks is to eschew building a significant 'in-house' research capacity.

The other interpretation of 'virtual' is a reliance on the internet and web sites as research and communication tools, reducing the need for non-professional support staff. However, all think tanks have established home pages or web sites.[2] So, if the CPRN is not unique as a surfing think tank, in what ways is it a rare experiment in Canada?

The following discussion focuses on two important qualities because they are *not* – in combination – a defining feature of Canadian think tanks. The first is the CPRN's objective of securing funding for research projects with two- or three-year time horizons. To raise the necessary funds, its president must build a consortium of funders, including government departments at the federal level, provincial counterparts, private foundations and other sources. But other think tanks – such as the Howe Institute and the IRPP – have supported research programmes resulting in a steady stream of studies over two years or more. The CPRN's ambition was to develop an *interdisciplinary* network of researchers to produce genuinely interdisciplinary insights, something few think tanks ever accomplish (Lindquist, 1989). The CPRN realized that unless it could mobilize significant resources – say, CAN$500,000 over two years for a group of scholars with diverse backgrounds working on a modest project – it would be impossible to create an 'in-house' critical mass for undertaking interdisciplinary policy research. The alternative was to tap into an equally diverse group of scholars who reside in their home institutions, to articulate clear research objectives, and then to encourage scholars to work across disciplinary boundaries.

Securing a web presence is commonplace for think tanks; indeed, in contrast to even five years ago, it is hard to imagine that modern think tanks would not have a state-of-the-art web site. However, some think tanks use web technologies in a more proactive manner than others. For example, the CPRN and the North–South Institute regularly distribute newsletters and notices of new studies and presentations by staff, conveying a sense of dynamism and accessibility. Others are increasingly using web sites as archives providing ready access to published studies, proceedings of events and annual reports. Finally, web technologies make it easier for 'public' and 'private' distinctions to be made; organizations like the Howe Institute and the Conference Board provide members'-only access to certain services and information, thus providing an incentive for individuals or firms to become members.

Technologies for 'thinking the unthinkable': think tanks and deliberation

On 30 October 1995, the citizens of the province of Quebec voted in a referendum on whether to give a mandate to the Parti Quebecois government to negotiate sovereignty or independence from Canada. The vote was very close, a slim 'No' against granting the government such a mandate, but the country was shaken to the core. Several think tanks played important roles in alerting the public and experts alike in the 'rest of Canada' to consider possible scenarios and their implications for Canada and Quebec seriously, regardless of the outcome of the vote (see Gibson, 1994; Robson, 1995; Vander Ploeg and Elton, 1994, 1995). The federal government, either due to miscalculation or because its leaders believed the government should not be seen to be seriously considering and therefore endorsing various options, did not stimulate a debate outside Quebec. Think tank contributions were thus useful and timely, though several research centres at universities and independent researchers made similar contributions.

These contributions are interesting because Canadian think tanks were involved, in varying degree, in thinking more systematically about different futures, the quintessential think tank function. But most think tanks have not acquired a reputation or solid track record for doing so. Although they have worried about the future and advocated proposals for new policy or institutional frameworks, they have tended not to develop scenarios and examine them in a detailed manner, showing how they might unfold along dimensions of concern to citizens and policy-makers. Too often Canadian think tanks have simply decried one unacceptable future and advocated a single solution as a response. Indeed, they were slow to develop new social technologies to assist policy-makers and citizens in grappling with complex problems and to propose possible solutions (Lindquist, 1989, 1993a), but this has started to change.

The IRPP began making progress on this front as early as 1990. The

Governance Program supported a two-year 'participatory action research' project that brought together several senior federal officials (with funding from their departments) to listen to a series of experts, probe the trends and implications of the emerging 'information society', and write a final report (Rosell *et al.*, 1992). The second phase focused more on scenario-building methods to assist senior officials, political leaders and citizens to chart courses in a rapidly changing social and economic environment. The IRPP dropped the project not long after its move to Montreal, but it continued under the Meridian International Institute, based in the San Francisco Bay Area (Rosell, 1999). In recent years, the Howe Institute has sponsored analysis on policy issues that will often explore issues by means of scenarios and sensitivity analysis around key variables.

More recently, and in different ways, Canadian think tanks are attempting to assist governments to listen better to, and facilitate, the deliberations of citizens. The CPRN Family Network reviewed studies and opinion polling on Canadian values, and then commissioned twenty-five discussion groups to determine which values are changing and which are not. The next phase consisted of launching a 'public dialogue project' in partnership with several organizations across the country to engage more citizens in deliberative processes; a 'dialogue kit' was created to assist small groups in diverse settings (Peters, 1995) and has recently been applied to deal with thorny debates over the future of the health system (Maxwell, *et al.* 2002). The CCPA has worked with several organizations to commission studies and then, through a deliberative process, develop an 'alternative budget' for the Minister of Finance. The Institute on Governance has sought support to further work on deliberative polling and other processes. The Niagara Institute (now an arm of the Conference Board of Canada) experimented with technology that permits workshop or search conference participants to rapidly indicate their ranking of options as well as their strength of preferences. As noted, the CWF has often held town-hall and citizen meetings related to its long-standing interest in the reform of the Canadian Parliament, particularly the Senate, and other constitutional matters. Finally, the IRPP continues to publish *Policy Options*, a magazine which provides a forum for experts on special thematic issues.

Encouraging more speculative *and* disciplined thinking by elites and citizens should be a primary concern of think tanks. Focusing on deliberative techniques and processes should not be their only 'line of business', although some institutes and foundations may begin specializing in this area, as in the US. Policy analysis and research, as well as promoting networking among experts and policy-makers, will probably continue to be the most significant contributions of Canadian think tanks, but the recent interest in citizen deliberations remains exciting terrain.

Should think tanks dance with the devil?

Many think tanks have long been reluctant to 'dance with the devil' by providing services for government. Nevertheless, others have assisted governments with major research studies, hosting public consultations, publishing the proceedings of meetings, co-ordinating the coming and going of foreign delegations investigating certain issues, delivering programmes, and providing assistance to help potential or newly elected governments deal with transitions (Lindquist, 1993b). The proportion of a particular think tank's rolling portfolio of activities that such activities constitute may range from very small to significant. Via such activity, think tank leaders and staff expand networks, obtain glimpses into the policy-making process, acquire information and intelligence to position them better to secure grants, and increase the relevance of the work they publish.

The key issue is whether or not the benefits of taking up such activities, even if consistent with the mandates of think tanks, outweigh the costs. Leaders must predict whether working for governments serves to increase or diminish the credibility or reputation of the think tank, and whether taking on contracts will create a dependency relationship that may, perhaps in the future, compromise its independence. For smaller think tanks, the administrative challenges associated with meeting contract obligations can be all-consuming, and the net proceeds may not be sufficiently large to support deepening work-in-progress or moving into new lines of inquiry. For larger think tanks this presents less of a problem. However, there may not be many alternatives for think tank leaders, who cannot rely on securing grants available to university researchers from government funding councils or from foundations, unless they receive support from an enlightened individual or organization with deep pockets and similar interests.

If think tanks choose to 'dance with the devil', they must identify projects that build up organizational capital and credibility. This suggests that think tanks must search for projects that are almost proprietary, and negotiate contracts that deepen or broaden their expertise. Think tanks should pursue ideas that are truly innovative, at least in the settings in which they are applied. Even if think tanks retain non-profit or charitable status, they must act like for-profit entities, if only because these latter now constitute an important source of competition. Increasingly, however, funders – whether governments, private firms or foundations – expect think tanks to demonstrate the effectiveness of their projects. There are growing demands for reporting on performance, and, despite the thorny methodological issues this raises, particularly given the unpredictable and complex dynamics of policy-making processes, several think tanks attempt to respond to these demands in annual reports and other assessments.

'Getting caught by the wave': think tanks as emergent policy organizations

Implicit in my discussion is a model of think tanks led by entrepreneurs identifying new policy, process or service niches. But this belies the experience of some of Canada's earliest think tanks. During the late 1960s and early 1970s, the Canadian Welfare Council was transformed into the CCSD because of the dramatic increase in government social spending, and the profile of the CTF was enhanced due to increased interest in tax policy. In both cases the ascendancy of a policy problem or domain transformed existing institutions into policy think tanks. At the risk of misusing a phrase developed for another context, rather than 'waiting for the wave' (Flanagan, 1995) some leaders suddenly find themselves 'in the midst of a big wave'. However, if such organizations are to take full advantage of the opportunity, they must be led by shrewd people who will identify niches compatible with the existing fabric of the organization while, at the same time, developing new capabilities to take up other niches.

The question is which organizations – not currently viewed as think tanks – are about to be engulfed by a wave, and may potentially be transformed. Such a development may not necessarily mean an organization starts prescribing policy but may make it relevant as a knowledge producer, like the Conference Board. The most dramatic changes in motion – and ones that are likely to endure in Canada – are the restructuring and downsizing of governments, and the increasing pressure to have 'public services' delivered, if not both financed and delivered, by the non-profit and voluntary sectors.

If this reasoning is correct, organizations like the Canadian Centre for Philanthropy, the Coalition of National Voluntary Organizations and the Institute of Public Administration of Canada – to name only a few possibilities – may assume more important roles and develop higher profiles outside their normal networks. Such transformations may happen not because leaders are the first to divine the possibilities, but rather because members insist that the organization deal more effectively with their needs. Such a path is more likely to occur in 'membership' organizations, but as the experience of the CCSD suggests, it may be a difficult transition to manage. However, if existing organizations cannot fulfil the needs of members, then pressure to establish new entities to provide think tank functions will mount.

Conclusion

This chapter has shown the ideological and structural diversity of Canadian think tanks by reviewing the activities and evolution of several economic and social policy institutes. They resist easy categorization; it is difficult to generalize about think tank practices, structure and change. Think tanks in Canada continue to be small when compared to prominent US think tanks (with the exception of the Conference Board), but resemble the vast majority of smaller think tanks in the US and other countries.

The broader policy and institutional environment in which think tanks work has changed dramatically: we have witnessed a dramatic shift from a growing, if troubled, welfare state and national economy to cash-strapped governments trying to placate an increasingly disgruntled and fractious public in the context of fundamental economic restructuring. This, in turn, has led to the restructuring of governance in Canada at the constitutional, policy and administrative levels. These changes and pressures have produced an increase in the number of think tanks, and more opportunities and exposure for their outputs and staff in the media. However, this should not be construed as arguing that Canadian think tanks regularly influence policy debates and policy-making – that kind of assessment requires a detailed case study. Even more importantly, the opportunities afforded by widespread change have not necessarily led to a better endowed or more financially secure group of organizations; financing remains a critical contingency for think tank leaders. Membership fees remain important for them, but governments now tend to provide project-specific funding (for those think tanks that received such support) rather than sustaining grants, and foundations have started to fund policy research and think tanks. Many would argue that such insecurity and project-based funding increase their ingenuity.

At stake is whether governments, corporations, non-profit sector organizations and individual citizens will support organizations dedicated to exploring issues and educating the public on policy matters. Think tanks are not simply competing with each other for funding support from the private sector and the public sector; they are now competing with university, non-profit and consulting entities in almost every niche of policy inquiry and deliberative practice. The federal government made a strong statement by funding 2,000 Canada Research Chairs at universities across the country; not one was allocated to a think tank, which suggests that governments believe fundamental research obtains in university settings. Think tanks cannot wait for public sector and private sector leaders to become more enlightened in this regard; they must persuade their own leaders of the value of policy inquiry, and to support talented leaders, analysts, researchers and facilitators by means of partnerships that spread costs and risk.

There can be no one model to guide such strategic and institutional development, since think tanks vary enormously in normative and substantive aspirations and how they engage members. Despite the bewildering possibilities, a time of fundamental social, economic and political change augurs greater support of think tanks in general in order to help comprehend rapidly changing environments; to assist in the search for new ways for policy-makers, experts, interest groups and citizens to comprehend shifting environments; to deliberate; to identify plausible scenarios and alternative courses of action; and to involve and groom a new generation of policy analysts and leaders. Sponsoring new think tanks may not fully respond to the challenge: a critical issue remains that of the level of funding required for truly innovative insights and perspectives to emerge from think tanks.

Notes

1 The Economic Council had a larger organization that had well over 100 full-time employees and representation from many sectors of the economy. The Council produced annual reviews of the economy and undertook a rolling portfolio of about five or six fundamental research projects that often lasted three years, producing consensus reports and many background studies. The CPRN emerged, in part, as a reaction to the cumbersome qualities of these arrangements, and, in part, to continue with the objective of undertaking definitive research projects.
2 The CWF is perhaps most innovative in this regard. In late 1994, not only did the CWF make its publications, notices and various lines of data available on line, but it helped to establish 'free net' services in the Calgary area, advised other communities on how to create such capabilities, and established a network among experts across Canada to exchange information and discuss social policy alternatives (CWF, 1995).

William Wallace

Afterword:
soft power, global agendas

All governments operate within the bounds of the conventional wisdom of their elites. Exceptionally, dictatorial regimes may jump from one set of operating ideas to another, at the whim of an all-powerful leader. Weak states without well-established structures of administration and law may lack a community of understanding among elites about the purposes and priorities of government, or about its appropriate role in the economy or society. Elsewhere, governing ideas and the vocabulary that encapsulates them constitute the shared discourse of political, administrative, judicial, economic and media elites: derived from shared historical understandings, and from shared education, and maintained through shared media and through the commonly understood limits to acceptable alternative ideas.

Government cannot operate if policy-makers stop to consider first principles. Time is short, multiple issues press for attention. Policy-makers therefore 'satisfice', as Herbert Simon (1955) put it, by relying on stereotypes and standard operating assumptions as short cuts to categorization and decision. Such stereotypical assumptions may become sufficiently well accepted to be almost unquestioned by all 'practical men', impatient with the 'academic' alternatives put forward by would-be advisors; but such practical men, as John Maynard Keynes reminded us, are unknowingly the slaves of long-dead economists. In the day-to-day operation of modern government, in democratic and authoritarian systems alike, governing ideas change only incrementally. Only under conditions of crisis are governments open to radical change. New governments coming into power may bring in new ideas, nurtured in the enforced leisure of opposition; once in office, attitudes and assumptions change only incrementally.

Think tanks, as the many case studies in this volume have shown, operate on the boundaries of the conventional wisdom. They operate in a wide variety of different ways, well illustrated in previous chapters. Some place emphasis on high-quality research, others on easily digestible policy briefings; others use conferences and seminars to communicate their message and to build networks of like-minded thinkers. They also operate at different distances from government, as has been made clear: within the government machine but outside the 'line departments', funded by government but formally autonomous, partly funded by government, even entirely independent in financial terms. Whatever their position along this spectrum, however, all depend upon access to political elites in and around government, or to counter-elites which operate within the accepted boundaries of the political system, and exert significant influence within it. Authoritarian regimes, as we have seen, find it useful to give think tanks some licence to disseminate ideas from abroad, and to speculate about reform, leaving think tank staff to balance carefully on the line between acceptable criticism and intellectual subversion. The 'second-track diplomacy' that Asian governments, both democratic and authoritarian, conduct through co-operation among government-supported think tanks provides a classic example of this licensed (but limited) dissent. Democratic regimes have no formal sanctions over these sources of expert criticism and radical alternatives, beyond the withdrawal of government funding. Yet democratic elites in stable political systems share assumptions about 'sound' and 'unsound' ideas, and think tankers who gain a reputation for being unsound lose the attention of their target audiences.

While academics often pride themselves on their detachment from immediate policy problems, therefore, think tanks pursue a strategy of semi-detachment: maintaining a certain distance from day-to-day policy-making, but keeping close enough to attract the attention of policy-makers to their longer-term perspectives and alternative analyses. They have to behave as if they are 'establishment intellectuals' (to use Ming-Chen Shai's description, in chapter 9 of this volume, of the staff of Chinese research institutes). Their self-conscious role is to offer additional expertise, and alternative ideas, to those in power without diverging too far from what is acceptable. In democratic and in authoritarian regimes, these licensed advisors to the powerful attempt to calculate carefully where the shifting boundaries of the acceptable are, while the bravest – or most foolhardy – test whether they can shift the boundaries further without provoking outrage and suffering loss of access.

The social democratic consensus of the 1950s and 1960s, across the developed democracies of the OECD, provided a framework within which 'non-partisan' think tanks could operate. They were able to command the respect of leaders from opposing parties who shared broad assumptions about market economies modified by active state intervention and underpinned by social welfare systems. Marxist and free market groups, outside this consensus, busily organized conferences and published tracts, but remained relatively unsuccessful in capturing the attention of the established media or of 'respectable' political opinion. It was the breakdown of the postwar consensus that followed from the recession of the early 1970s, and from taxpayer resistance to the rising costs of welfare, that provided free market groups with a more sympathetic audience, and with a rapid increase in financial support. Right-wing political leaders looking for alternative policies welcomed entrepreneurial intellectuals who wished to persuade them to champion an alternative set of economic and social assumptions: willing buyers thus met willing sellers in this market of ideas.

From the 1970s, centrist and centre-left political leaders defended the postwar consensus against this coalition of intellectuals and politicians, continuing therefore to feel comfortable with established networks of consensual think tanks, and creating a demand for intellectual innovators of their own only when the right had begun to establish an intellectual hegemony of its own, most of all in the USA and Britain, New Zealand and Australia. The growing complexity of government within advanced democracies, and the eruption of such new fields for policy as global warming and the ethics (and costs) of medical advances, fuelled the proliferation of specialist think tanks in the 1980s and 1990s. It was, however, the declining deference of both political elites and publics to professional experts, in the last decade of the twentieth century, that set the context for the 'fourth generation' of think tanks, offering new packages of concepts rather than carefully researched analyses of the limits of the possible.

International linkages, national constraints

The country chapters in this volume have illustrated the diversity of think tank operations and structures across political systems. They have, however, also shown that waves of think tank development have been visible in the ocean of global political ideas. Emulation and imitation have carried models developed in the industrial democracies and socialist-authoritarian states across other continents. Different political cultures, different levels of available resources in terms of finance and expertise, and above all different patterns of government and politics have, however, made for distinctive adaptations of the models imitated.

The growth of think tanks in different political systems across the world has been shaped by foreign example, and by foreign intellectual and financial assistance, as successive chapters have made clear. The prestige of German scientific institutes, as well as of British and French 'academies', was reflected in the Russian Academy of Science: from which, after the Russian revolution and World War II, a range of institutes across the socialist world developed. The social science institutes within these academies were state-funded, but allowed a degree of licence, and a higher degree of access to foreign publications and travel. In the Western democracies, as chapters 1, 2 and 13 note, domestic think tanks have developed from early American models, and foreign policy think tanks from the intellectual frustrations and ideals of British and American attachés at the 1919 Versailles peace conference. The Rockefeller Foundation in the 1930s and 1950s, and the Ford Foundation over half a century, helped to spread this American model across the developed democracies and into the developing world through the financial support they provided for struggling think tanks with limited domestic support. After 1989, American and German foundations actively supported the growth of independent institutes – for economic analysis, foreign policy, social development – across the former socialist states of CEE.

The CSIS was modelled on the IISS, which had been founded on the initiative of the British Council of Churches and a number of concerned academics. But the general direction of influence has been from the world's most open market for political and intellectual ideas – the United States – to other states, substantially assisted by the financial power of US foundations and the culture of private support for public bodies within the USA. The ISS itself succeeded by becoming the *International* Institute for Strategic Studies (IISS), attracting a substantial proportion of American funds and staff, and successfully competing with US bodies in the American-dominated epistemic community of defence experts. The debate in Britain in the 1970s over strengthening institutional capacity for domestic policy analysis outside government revolved around the concept of a 'British Brookings', as chapter 14 notes.

It has, however, proved impossible to replicate the particular patterns of Washington's public–private policy debate within the very different constraints of other national political systems. No other democratic political system has institutionalized the exchange of elites and counter-elites on the scale of Washington, with the think tank community serving as the main base for oppositional intellectuals awaiting the return of their party to power. The strength of the French state and of its permanent civil service, and the institutionalized hierarchy of the French educational system, provides a far smaller pool of acceptable expert participants in the policy debate. Postwar Germany, as Martin Thunert notes in chapter 5, institutionalized diversity of policy advice by providing substantial state funding for party foundations; but the weight of the democratic consensus, and of political inhibitions about venturing into left- or right-wing radicalism, has nevertheless limited the range of elite debate. In states where armed forces set limits to democratic politics, or where violence is on the fringes of political life, expert challenges to the conventional wisdom are dangerous. Two policy advisors associated with programmes for economic reform in Italy have been assassinated in the 1990s. In openly authoritarian regimes there are policy institutes which serve the same ostensible functions as their counterparts in Washington, London

Afterword

and Berlin; but the circumstances to which they have to adapt necessarily means that they take great care not to challenge the preferences of the powerful too openly.

Given this transnational flow of influence and emulation, it is paradoxical that there have as yet been so few successful attempts to create international think tanks not primarily rooted in one political system. The IPR, which flourished under American sponsorship and financial support in the 1930s, was an early effort to build a forum through which policy intellectuals from different countries could exchange ideas. The suspicion that attaches to such elite exchanges between authoritative people from often mutually hostile states, behind closed doors, was, however, evident in post-1949 McCarthyite allegations that the IPR had served as a front for communist sympathizers. The Trilateral Commission, also under American leadership and with American foundations providing financial support, similarly attempted to provide a forum for elite exchange, and for the preparation and publication of joint policy papers, that might narrow the gap in policy assumptions between Japan, Western Europe and the United States. It, too, became a target for suspicion among anti-capitalist groups, as representing a conspiracy among national elites. The WEF (as Diane Stone notes in chapter 3) has, perhaps, most clearly succeeded in providing a forum for elite interchange on a global scale. It has the advantage of being managed from neutral Switzerland, and largely self-funded from the subscriptions of multinational companies. It has brought together political leaders from North and South America, Europe, Asia and Africa to mix with business leaders, think tankers, academics and journalists. It is an opportunity for multi-track official and unofficial diplomacy in a relatively visible setting, with intellectuals setting out their wares for the politically and economically powerful to consider.

Some American-based think tanks have 'internationalized' their activities to a degree. The RAND Corporation has expanded its consultancy operations across Europe and the Mediterranean. The Aspen Institute has developed affiliates in Germany and Italy, formally autonomous but with the same blend of conferences, workshops and reports. The IISS, in turn, established an office in Washington in 2000, and initiated an annual conference on Asian security in co-operation with governments and think tanks in east and southeast Asia. As yet, these remain exceptional; most think tanks remain embedded in national political systems and political cultures, in spite of the strong trends towards global communications and global social and economic interaction in recent decades.

However, a small number of think tanks, such as SIPRI in Stockholm, or Transparency International in Berlin, have succeeded in establishing themselves as effectively international. They address themselves to issues of relevance to a wide number of governments (arms control, democratic institutions, corruption) and attract funding from a wide range of private and public sources. The rapid development of bodies like the International Crisis Group – based in Brussels but with offices and teams sent out to areas in conflict in several continents, and with a management and supervisory board that are highly multinational – might indicate that a global space for policy research and dissemination is at last developing.

Chapter 4 describes the hesitant development of think tanks in Brussels, where the concentration of European institutions, both EU and NATO, should in principle provide a focus around which think tanks might cluster. Brussels has, after all, accumulated a significant population of law firms, European company headquarters, consultancies and lobbies. Heidi Ullrich notes, however, that Brussels policy institutes have so far proved fragile and financially squeezed. Much policy-related research and debate on Europe-wide issues is conducted from centres in Paris and London, Berlin, Munich and Florence, reflecting the dispersal of European political elites and the weak authority of the Brussels institutions. Networks of national think tanks operate in foreign policy, economic analysis, defence and EU issues, ensuring that their output will feed directly into different domestic debates. In the 1980s some foreign policy institutes experimented with publishing joint reports in multiple languages, in order to gain maximum access within different national capitals (Kaiser *et al.*, 1980, 1983). By the end of the 1990s, however, English had become an acceptable lingua franca for Europe's policy elites. Yet it was remarkable how little intellectual interchange there was among policy advisors or independent institutes across national boundaries in the years after the Berlin Wall came down. The transformation of European order was perceived, and discussed, largely within the distinctive assumptions and memories of each national context (Niblett and Wallace, 2001). Only American reconceptualizations of Europe's regional order, its relationship to the former Soviet Union and to other 'civilizations', commanded attention – and provoked debate – across the territorial and linguistic boundaries that still divided Western Europe.

Think tanks and the projection of 'soft' power

The imbalance of prestige, of intellectual authority, of financial weight and autonomy between the Western democracies and the rest of the world is reflected in the pattern of think tank development and in the flow of ideas through them. The United States remains, as chapter after chapter has indicated, the superpower of policy research: the prime exporter of concepts and intellectual frameworks, the most important source of transnational funding, the model that others take as their point of reference in the post-Cold War world. It is this intellectual 'soft power' that leaves the USA 'bound to lead' global political and economic order, as Joseph Nye (1990) has put it. Even during periods of American self-doubt and economic weakness, Nye persuasively argues, the ability of American policy institutions and intellectuals to set the international agenda – even to define the terms within which that agenda is agreed – give its policy-makers built-in advantages in multilateral diplomacy.

A scattering of institutes in Europe command global attention, as noted above, and a number of European conferences – most of all the Davos World Economic Forum – command global prestige. Beyond the transatlantic area, however, there are only regional networks and national institutes that aim to adapt policy concepts flowing from the West to local audiences. The visitor to Moscow or to Beijing, in the 1980s and 1990s, might have been struck by how deep and how detailed was the familiarity of researchers in policy institutes with Western publications and the European and American policy debate. In Washington, in contrast, only a small number of country specialists followed Russian or Chinese policy debates in detail.

One significant exception to this flow has been the development of 'second-track' diplomacy among east and southeast Asian states. As noted in chapters 2 and 9, this is a method of informal negotiation of the acceptable boundaries of policy change that neither commits the sponsoring governments nor entirely escapes their control (Kraft, 2000). Even here, however, attempts to define distinctive Asian values and to agree on autonomous approaches to regional co-operation have met with limited success. Many of the participants in such exercises, after all, have been partly trained in American universities and are unavoidably influenced by the predominance of American expertise in economic, social and international discourse.

The growth of global intellectual networks – what many in this volume have referred to as epistemic communities – has depended on the spread of shared intellectual assumptions and shared definitions of scientific understanding and expertise. Here the American universities' prestige, institutional and financial strength, and openness to foreign students have played an important role, reinforced further by the dominance of the English language in scientific and academic exchange. When economists from across the world gather, their community revolves around those teaching in the top American universities, and those who have at some point studied with them. A period at Princeton, Chicago or MIT enhances the reputation of an ambitious Indian economist. The schools of public policy at Harvard, Princeton, Johns Hopkins, Columbia and Syracuse, and the Fletcher School of Law and Diplomacy, train policy-makers and policy advisors from around the world. Reintegration of China into international diplomacy and the global economy has been accompanied, and assisted, by a rising flow of Chinese students to the United States.

There are some fields – environmental science, perhaps, studies of migration – in which the quality of European expertise, and the reputation of European research, may still contest the primacy of intellectual leadership that central European universities and research centres lost to North America in the 1930s and 1940s. In most fields of policy research, however, American publications circulate most widely, and American concepts shape the debate. Across Europe, for example, students of foreign policy read the CFR journal *Foreign Affairs*, and take the arguments they find there as a starting point for their own work (Huntington, 1993); no European policy review attracts similar attention.

The flow of ideas through intergovernmental organizations is similarly shaped by the predominance of American universities and the strength of American policy institutes – reinforced by the predominance of US military power and the strength of the American economy. The 'Washington consensus' on international economic and financial policies, much criticized in recent years, had been formally shaped within the IMF and the World Bank. Informally, however, it had grown out of the dominant paradigm among the world's leading academic departments of economics – all of them, from the 1960s onwards, within the United States – attracting faculty from other continents, and educating economists who went on to staff finance ministries and central banks across the world. Diane Stone, in chapter 3, notes the efforts the World Bank has made to develop a network of institutes beyond the developed world. This was partly to encourage more expert and authoritative challenges to the predominant consensus of the Washington institutions; but that in itself was a Washington initiative, with Joseph Stiglitz and others attempting to promote alternative views. The Paris-based OECD is in some ways a think tank disguised as an intergovernmental organization: operating through expert groups and seminars, bringing together officials and outside advisors, and publishing well-researched reports. For its European and East Asian members the OECD thus provides an institutional forum within which to moderate, even on occasion to contest, American conventional wisdom on economic and social policy, to which think tanks from these countries contribute. It is a multilateral framework within which to attempt to set an agenda for global public policy for heads of government to discuss, within the Group of Seven (now G-8) international economic summits, in particular, that is not overwhelmingly shaped by North American assumptions.

Is there a global 'public space'?

Policy debates, as argued in the opening paragraphs of this chapter, take place within established communities of policy-makers and advisors.

Outsiders who wish to influence such debates need to adapt their style and language to those with which such communities are familiar. But first, they need to gain access to the media through which these elites communicate, so that their ideas can be heard. For that they need politically or economically influential sponsors; they need to be in the right place, with the right education and experience to get their ideas across.

All these are easiest to acquire within the close-knit framework of a national society and political system. National elites have emerged from a process of education and socialization that equips them with common reference points and understandings. They move through political, intellectual and economic institutions that provide a focus for debate. They communicate through national media, watching the same television news and comment programmes, listening to the same radio discussions, scanning the same newspapers and journals. The communications revolution, the globalization of the international economy, the internationalization of education, and the expansion of international organizations and of associated international conferences and regulatory frameworks have begun to build the skeleton of a thin global policy community (Reinicke, 1998). Its weak focal points are in New York and Washington, Geneva and Paris; its members scan *The Economist,* the *Financial Times, International Herald Tribune* and *Wall Street Journal,* and cast an eye at BBC World and CNN. They meet in Aspen, at Davos, and through a wide range of regional conferences and bilateral meetings. Subgroups of this global policy community have their own journals and paper series, and now also web sites and web networks, their own specialist conferences and centres – fora for expert exchanges through which their consensus on problems to address and how to address them gradually evolves.

They communicate in English, with American concepts – and American intellectuals, and meeting places – playing a major role in the intellectual interchange. Yet part of the success of American soft power has been to encourage sufficient diffusion of policy expertise and of the think tank model for autonomous Asian and European networks to have developed, interacting partly to contain the dominance of American ideas on the global agenda. Asian second-track diplomacy and European networks of think tanks and academics have grown up under the shadow of American intellectual hegemony. They constitute, with their North American (and South American) counterparts, the shadowy outlines of a global public space, which is likely to take clearer shape as communications grow ever closer, markets more integrated, and local conflicts more a matter for global concern.

Diane Stone

Appendix: think tanks and their web sites

Wherever possible, this appendix lists the following for the think tanks and policy research institutes addressed in the preceding chapters: acronym, full title, country where based or where network is co-ordinated, and web address. Omitted are institutes now defunct or moribund (like Maroc 2020) and many of the looser clubs and hybrid associations (like Solidarité Moderne and République Moderne) found in France. In a couple of instances, only an email address is available. Many Chinese institutes do not have web-site addresses; the appendix to chapter 9 provides more detail on these. The entries are listed alphabetically by acronym, where available, or otherwise by full name. As a rule, where an institute's web site gives an English-language name, the institute is listed in English here but the original-language acronym is retained. Some institutes are known only by their original-language name or acronym (such as the French, Italian and Argentinian institutes or the German Öko Institute and Stiftungen). A few are best known by their location rather than formal name (such as the Clingendael Institute, also known as the Netherlands Institute of International Relations), and are listed accordingly here. Where feasible, English-language versions of web sites are given.

ABF	Australia Business Foundation, Australia, www.abfoundation.gov.au
	Academica Sinica, Taiwan, www.sinica.edu.tw
ADELS	Association pour la Démocratie et l'Education Locale et Sociale, France, www.adels.org
AEI	American Enterprise Institute for Public Policy Research, USA, www.aei.org
	Agroconsult, Hungary, www.gak.hu/mbc/ac_alap.html
AIIA	Australian Institute of International Affairs, Australia, www.aiia.asn.au
AILES	Autogestion Initiative Locale et Économie Sociale, France, www.globenet.org/horizon-local/ailes
AKNF	African Knowledge Networks Forum, Ethiopia, www.unsia.org/aknf ERF
	Albanian Centre for Economic Research, Albania, Email: ceralb@adanet.com.al
	American Academy, Germany, www.americanacademy.de
	Archivio Disarmo, Italy, www.archiviodisarmo.it
AREL	Agenzia di Ricerca e Legislazione, Italy, www.arel.it
ARES	Action pour le Renouveau Socialiste, France, n.a.
	Asahi Bank Research Institute Co., Ltd, Japan, www.asahibank-research.com

ASEAN-ISIS	Association of South East Asian Nations – Institutes of Strategic and International Studies, Regional, www.aseanisis.org
ASI	Adam Smith Institute, United Kingdom, www.adamsmith.org
	Asian Society, USA, http://asiasociety.org/
	Asociación Conciencia, Argentina, www.conciencia.org
	Aspen Institute Berlin, Germany, www.aspenberlin.org
ASPI	Australian Strategic Policy Institute, Australia, www.aspi.org.au
ASU-UNI	Small Business Institute, Germany, www.unternehmerinstitut.de
	Atlas Economic Research Foundation, USA, www.atlasusa.org/australasia
	AustralAsia Centre, Australia, www.asiasociety.org/worldwide/
	Australia Institute, Australia, www.tai.org.au
	Australian Fabian Society, Australia, www.fabian.org.au
	Baden-Württemberg Academy for Technology Assessment, Germany, www.ta-akademie.de
	Bennelong Society, Australia, www.bennelong.com.au
	BerlinPolis, Germany, www.berlinpolis.de
	Bertelsmann Stiftung, Germany, www.stiftung.bertelsmann.de
BICC	Bonn International Center for Conversion, Germany, www.bicc.de
BIOSt	Federal Institute for Russian, East European and International Studies, Germany, www.biost.de
BITS	Berlin Institute for Transatlantic Security, Germany, www.bits.de
	Brisbane Institute, Australia, www.brisinst.org.au
	Brookings Institution, USA, www.brook.edu
	Burda Academy for the Third Millennium, Germany, www.burda.de
	Caledon Institute for Social Policy, Canada, www.caledoninst.org
	Canadian Centre for Philanthropy, Canada, www.ccp.ca
CAP	Centre for Applied Policy Research, Germany, www.cap.uni-muenchen.de
	Carter Center, USA, www.cartercenter.org
CAS	Center for American Studies, China, www.fudan.edu.cn/big5/research/7zhongxin/usa.html
CASE	Centre for Economic and Social Research, Poland, www.case.com.pl
CASS	Chinese Academy of Social Science, China, www.cass.net.cn
	Catalyst, United Kingdom, www.catalyst-trust.co.uk
	CATO Institute, USA, www.cato.org
CCPA	Canadian Centre for Policy Alternatives, Canada, www.policyalternatives.ca
CCSD	Canadian Council on Social Development, Cananda, www.ccsd.ca
	C.D. Howe Institute, Canada, www.cdhowe.org
CDI	Center for Defense Information, USA, www.cdi.org
CDI	China Development Institute, China, www.cdi.com.cn
CECE	Fundación Centro de Estudios para el Cambio Estructural, Argentina, www.cece.org.ar
CEDA	Committee for the Economic Development of Australia, Australia, www.ceda.com.au
CEDES	Centro de Estudios de Estado y Sociedad, Argentina, www.cedes.org
CEDI	Centro de Estudios para el Desarrollo Institucional, Argentina, www.fgys.org
CEIL	Centro de Estudios e Investigaciones Laborales, Argentina, www.ceil-piette.setcip.gov.ar
CEIP	Carnegie Endowment for International Peace, USA, www.ceip.org
CELS	Centro de Estudios Legales y Sociales, Argentina, www.cels.org.ar
CEMA	Centro de Estudios Macroeconomicos de Argentina, Argentina, www.cema.edu.ar
CeMiSS	Centro Militare di Studi Strategici, Italy, www.starfarm.it/casd

Appendix

Censis	Centro Studi Investimenti Sociali, Italy, www.censis.it/censis/indexf.html
	Central Economic and Mathematical Institute, Russia, www.ras.ru
	Centre for Liberal Strategies, Bulgaria, www.cls-sofia.org
	Centre for Political Technologies, Russia, www.cpt.ru
	Centre for the Study of Democracy, Bulgaria, www.csd.bg
CEPR	Centre for Economic Policy Research, United Kingdom, www.cepr.org
CEPS	Centre for European Policy Studies, Belgium, www.ceps.be
CER	Centre for European Reform, United Kingdom, www.cer.org.uk
CER	Centre for European Research, Italy, n.a.
CES	Center for Economic Studies, Germany, www.cesifo.de
CFR	Council on Foreign Relations, USA, www.cfr.org
CGIAR	Consultative Group on International Agricultural Research, USA, www.cgiar.org
	Chifley Research Centre, Australia, www.chifley.org.au/index.php
CIEP	Canadian Institute for Economic Policy, Canada, n.a.
CIEPP	Centro Interdisciplinario para el Estudio de Políticas Públicas, Argentina, www.ciepp.com.ar
CIIA	Canadian Institute on International Affairs, Canada, www.ciia.org
CIPPEC	Centre for the Implementation of Public Policies Promoting Equity and Growth, Argentina, www.cippec.org,
CIPTA	Centre for Intellectual Promotion and Technological Advancement, Malaysia, www.cipta.com.my
CIS	Centre for Independent Studies, Australia, www.cis.org.au
CISEA	Centro de Investigaciones Sociales sobre el Estado, Argentina
	Citoyens 60, France, www.clubcitoyens.org
	Civitas, United Kingdom, www.civitas.org.uk
	Clingendael Institute, Netherlands, www.clingendael.nl
	Club of Rome, Germany, www.cluboffrome.org
CNRS	Centre National de la Recherche Scientifique, France, www.cnrs.fr
	Conference Board, Canada, www.conferenceboard.ca
	Conference Board, USA, www.conference-board.org
	Convaincre, France, www.partiblanc.fr/convaincre.htm
CPR	Centre for Policy Research, Malaysia, www.usm.my/cpr/index.html
CPRN	Canadian Policy Research Networks, Canada, www.policyalternatives.ca
CPS	Centre for Policy Studies, United Kingdom, www.cps.org.uk
CSA	Conseil Scientifique de l'Audio-visuel, France, www.csa.fr
CSE	Citizens for a Sound Economy Foundation, USA, www.cse.org
CSIS	Center for Strategic and International Studies, USA, www.csis.org
CTF	Canadian Tax Foundation, Canada, www.ctf.ca
CWF	Canada West Foundation, Canada, www.cwf.ca
	Daiwa Institute of Research, Ltd., Japan, www.dir.co.jp
	Democratic Dialogue, United Kingdom, www.democraticdialogue.org
	Démocratie 2000, France, accessible via www.regioncentre.com
	Demos, United Kingdom, www.demos.co.uk
	Dentsu Institute for Human Studies, Japan, www.dihs.dentsu.co.jp/english
	Deutschland Denken, Germany, www.deutschland-denken.de
DGAP	German Council on Foreign Relations, Germany, www.dgap.org
DIW	German Institute for Economic Research, Germany, www.diw-berlin.de
DRC	Development Research Centre, China, www.drc.gov.cn
DÜI	German Overseas Institute, Germany, www.duei.de
EI	European Institute, at the London School of Economics, United Kingdom, www.lse.ac.uk/depts/european
EIPA	European Institute of Public Administration, Netherlands, www.eipa.nl

ELIAMEP	Hellenic Foundation for European and Foreign Policy, Greece, www.eliamep.gr
	Empower America, USA, www.empower.org,
ENEPRI	European Network of Economic Policy Research Institutes, Belgium, www.enepri.org
EPC	European Policy Centre, Belgium, www.theepc.be
EPF	European Policy Forum, United Kingdom, www.epfltd.org
EPI	Economic Policy Institute, USA, www.epinet.org
ERF	Economic Research Forum, Egypt, www.erf.org.eg
	Ethics and Public Policy Center, USA, www.eppc.org
EUISS	European Union Institute for Security Studies, France, www.iss-eu.org
	EuroMeSCo, Spain, www.euromed.net/information-notes/EuroMescofr.html
	Euronet, www.uta.fi/laitokset/tyoelama/euronet.html
	Evatt Foundation, Australia, evatt.labor.net.au
	Evian Group, Switzerland, www.eviangroup.org
	Fabian Society, United Kingdom, www.fabian-society.org.uk
FADE	Fundación Argentina para el Desarrollo con Equidad, Argentina, Email: fade@arnet.com
FAW	Research Institute for Applied Knowledge Processing, Germany, www.faw.uni-ulm.de
FDC	Foundation for Development Cooperation, Australia, www.fdc.org.au
	Federal Trust for Education and Research, United Kingdom, www.cix.co.uk/~fedtrust
FES	Friedreich Ebert Stiftung, Germany, www.fes.de
FIDE	Fundación de Investigaciones para el Desarrollo, Argentina, www.fidefund.com.ar
FIEL	Foundation for Latin American Economic Research, Argentina, www.geocities.com/~fielargentina
FLACSO	Facultad Latinoamericana de Ciencias Sociales, Argentina, www.flacso.org.ar
FNS	Friedrich Naumann Foundation, Germany, www.fnst.de
	Fondazione Agnelli, Italy, www.fga.it
	Fondazione Einaudi, Italy, www.fondazioneeinaudi.it
	Fondazione di Ricerca di Istituto Carlo Cattaneo, Italy, www.cattaneo.org
	Fondazione Rosselli, Italy, www.fondazionerosselli.it
	Foundation for Economic Education, Poland, no website
	Foundation ItalianiEuropei, Italy, www.ItalianiEuropei.it
	Foundation Lech Walesa Institute, Poland, www.ilw.org.pl/english/otfund.html
	Foundation for Market Economics (Frankfurter Institute), Germany, www.stiftung-marktwirtschaft.de
FPC	Foreign Policy Centre, United Kingdom, www.fpc.org.uk
FPRI	Foreign Policy Research Institute, USA, www.fpri.org
	Fraser Institute, Canada, www.fraserinstitute.ca
	Freedom House, Hungary, www.ngonet.org
	Friends of Europe, Belgium, www.friendsofeurope.org
FUALI	Fundación Argentina para la Libertad de la Información, Argentina, n.a.
	Fuji Research Institute Corporation, Japan, www.fuji-ric.co.jp/english/profile
	Fujitsu Research Institute, Japan, www.fri.fujitsu.com
	Fundación Andina, Argentina, www.fundacionandina.org.ar
	Fundación Capital, Argentina, www.fcapital.com.ar/fcapital
	Fundación Creer y Crecer, Argentina, www.creerycrecer.org.ar

Appendix

	Fundación Karakachoff, Argentina, www.futena.org
	Fundación Libertad, Argentina, www.libertad.org.ar
	Fundación Mediterránea, Argentina, www.ieral.org
	Fundación del Sur, Argentina, www.fundasur.org.ar
	FuturX (Society for (Inter-)Generational Justice), Germany, www.futurx.de
GCF	Global Contract Foundation, Germany, www.weltvertrag.de
GDN	Global Development Network, USA, www.gdnet.org
GIME	Gdansk Institute for Market Economics, Poland, www.pfcg.org.pl
	Global ThinkNet, Japan, www.jcie.or.jp/thinknet/index.html
GPA	Group of Policy Advisors (European Commission), Belgium, europa.eu.int/comm/cdp/index_en.htm
GRECE	Groupement de Recherche et d'Étude sur la Civilisation Éuropéenne, France, grece.hypermart.net
	Groupe d'Etudes Politiques Européennes, Belgium, www.tepsa.be/html/GEPE.htm
	Grupo FÉNIX, Argentina, www.econ.uba.ar/www/planfenix/principal/fenix.htm
	Grupo Sophia, Argentina, www.gruposophia.org.ar
	Heinrich Böll Foundation, Germany, www.boell.de
	Herbert Quandt Foundation, Germany, www.herbertquandtstiftung.com
	Heritage Foundation, USA, www.heritage.org
	Hitachi Research Institute, Japan, www.hitachi-hri.com
	Hoover Institution on War, Revolution and Peace, USA, www.hoover.stanford.edu
	H.R. Nicholls Society, Australia, www.hrnicholls.com.au
HSFK/PRIF	Peace Research Institute Frankfurt, Germany, www.hsfk.de and www.prif.org
HSS	Hanns Seidel Foundation, Germany, www.hss.de
	Hudson Institute, USA, www.hudson.org
HWWA	Hamburg Institute of International Economics, Germany, www.hwwa.de
IAI	Istituto Affari Internazionali, Italy, www.iai.it
ICEG	International Center for Economic Growth, USA, www.iceg.org
ICS	Institute for Contemporary Studies, USA, www.icspress.com
IDA	Institute for Defense Analyses, USA, www.ida.org/index.html
	Ideazione, Italy, www.ideazione.com
IDES	Instituto de Desarrollo Económico y Social, Argentina, www.ides.org.ar
IDS	Institute of Development Studies, Sabah, Malaysia, www.ids.org.my
IEA	Institute of Economic Affairs, United Kingdom, www.iea.org.uk
IEEP	Institute for European Environmental Policy, United Kingdom, www.ieep.org.uk
IEP	Institute for European Politics, Germany, www.iep-berlin.de
IFO	Institute for Economic Research, Germany, www.ifo.de
IFRI	Institut Français des Relations Internationales, France, www.ifri.org
IFS	Institute for Fiscal Studies, United Kingdom, www.ifs.org.uk
IFSH	Institute for Peace Research and Security Policy, Germany, www.core-hamburg.de/
IfW	Kiel Institute for World Economics, Germany, www.uni-kiel.de/IfW
IIE	Institute for International Economics, USA, www.iie.com
IISS	International Institute for Strategic Studies, United Kingdom, www.iiss.org
IKD	Institut Kajian Dasar, Malaysia, www.ikdasar.tripod.com
IKIM	Malaysia Institute of Islamic Understanding, Malaysia, www.ikim.gov.my
	Il Mulino, Italy, www.mulino.it
IMEMO	Institute of the World Economy and International Relations, Russia, n.a.

INED	Institute National d'Études Demographique, France, www.ined.fr
INEF	Institute for Development and Peace, Germany, www.inef.de
	Innova, Argentina, www.grupo-innova.org.ar
INSAP	Institute of Strategic Analysis and Policy Research, Malaysia, www.mca.org.my/accomplishment/a_agenda.asp
INSEE	Institut National de Statistiques et d'Études Economiques, France, www.insee.fr
	Institute for International Policy Studies, Japan, www.kosonippon.org/info
	Institute on Governance, Canada, www.iog.ca
	Institute of International Relations, Taiwan, http://iir.nccu.edu.tw/
	Institute for Market Economics, Bulgaria, www.ime-bg.org
	Institute for National Policy Research, Taiwan, www.inpr.org.tw
	Institute of Public Administration Canada, Canada, www.ryerson.ca/~ipactor/menu.htm
	Institute for Public Affairs, Slovakia, www.ivo.sk/english.asp
	Institute of Welsh Affairs, United Kingdom, www.iwa.org.uk
	Instituto Juan March de Estudios e Investigaciones, Spain, www.march.es/portada_e.html
	International Crisis Group, http://www.crisisweb.org/
	International Development Center of Japan, Japan, www.idcj.or.jp
IPA	Institute of Public Affairs, Australia, www.ipa.org.au
IPE	Institute for Private Enterprise, Australia, www.ipe.net.au
IPPR	Institute for Public Policy Research, United Kingdom, www.ippr.org.uk
IPS	Institute for Policy Studies, USA, www.ips-dc.org
IRPP	Institute for Research on Public Policy, Canada, www.irpp.org
IRS	Istituto per la Ricerca Sociale, Italy, www.irs-online.it
ISA	Institute for Strategic Analysis, Germany, www.isa-ev.de
ISEAS	Institute of South East Asian Studies, Singapore, www.iseap.edu.sp
ISI	Fraunhofer Institute for Systems and Innovation Research, Germany, www.isi.fhg.de
ISIS	Institute of Strategic and International Studies, Malaysia, www.jaring.my/isis
ISKAN	Institute for the Study of the USA and Canada, Russia, n.a.
ISPI	Istituto di Politica Internazionale, Italy, www.ispinet.it
ISPI	Istituto per gli Studi di Politica Internazionale, Italy, www.ispionline.it
IWEP	Institute of World Economics and Politics, China, www.iwep.org.cn/english
IWG	Institute for Economics and Society, Germany, www.iwg-bonn.de
IZT	Institute for Future Studies and Technology Assessment, Germany, www.izt.de
	Japan Initiative, Japan, www.kosonippon.org/info
	Japan Research Institute, Japan, www.jri.co.jp
JCIE	Japan Center for International Exchange, Japan, www.jcie.or.jp
KAS	Konrad Adenauer Stiftung, Germany, www.kas.de
KIIS	Kansai Institute of Information Systems, Japan, www.kiis.or.jp
	Koerber Foundation, Germany, www.stiftung.koerber.de
LACEA	Latin American and Caribbean Economic Association, USA, www.lacea.org
	Lavoisier Society, Australia, www.lavoisier.com.au
	Lebanese Center for Policy Studies, Lebanon, www.lcps-lebanon.org
	Liberal, Italy, www.liberalfondazione.it
	Limes, Italy, www.limesonline.com
	Localis, United Kingdom, www.localis.org.uk
LTCB	Long Term Credit Bank Research Institute, Japan, n.a.
	Ludwig Erhard Foundation, Germany, www.ludwig-erhard-stiftung.de

Appendix

	Manhattan Institute for Policy Research, USA, www.manhattan-institute.org
	Max Planck Institute for the Study of Societies, Germany, www.mpi-fg-koeln.mpg.de
	Menzies Research Centre, Australia, www.mrcltd.org.au
	Meridian International Institute, USA, www.meridianinternational.org
	MicroMega, Italy, www.micromega.manipulite.it
MIER	Malaysian Institute of Economic Research, Malaysia, www.mier.org.my
	Mitsubishi Research Institute, Japan, www.mri.co.jp/top.html
	Mont Pelerin Society, n.a., www.montpelerin.org
MSRC	Malaysian Strategic Research Centre, Malaysia, n.a.
MZES	Mannheim Centre for European Social Research, Germany www.mzes.uni-mannheim.de/mzes2_e.html
NBER	National Bureau of Economic Research, USA, www.nber.harvard.edu
NBI	Oswald von Nell-Breuning Institute for Business Ethics, Germany, www.st-georgen.uni-frankfurt.de/nbi
NEF	New Economics Foundation, United Kingdom, www.neweconomics.org
	New Local Government Network, United Kingdom, www.nlgn.org.uk
	Niagara Institute, Canada, www.niagrainstitute.com
NIESR	National Institute for Economic and Social Research, United Kingdom, www.niesr.ac.uk
NIRA	National Institute for Research Advancement, Japan, www.nira.go.jp
	Nikko Research Center, Ltd, Japan, www.nrc-net.co.jp
	Nixon Center for Peace and Freedom, USA, www.nixoncenter.org
	NLI Research Institute, Japan, www.nli-research.co.jp
	Nomisma, Italy, www.nomisma.it
	Northeast-Midwest Institute, USA, www.nemw.org
	North–South Institute, Canada, www.nsi-ins.ca
	Notre Europe, France, www.notre-europe.asso.fr
ODI	Overseas Development Institute, United Kingdom, www.odi.org.uk
	Öko Institute, Germany, www.oeko.de
	Open Society Foundation Sofia, Bulgaria, www.osf.bg
OSI	Open Society Institute, USA and Hungary, www.soros.org *and* www.osi.hu
PIK	Potsdam Institute for Climate Research, Germany, www.pik-potsdam.de
	Poder Ciudadano, Argentina, www.ciudadano.org.ar
	Policy Exchange, United Kingdom, www.policyexchange.org.uk
	Politeia, United Kingdom, www.politeia.co.uk
PPI	Progressive Policy Institute, USA, www.dlcppi.org
PRIO	Peace Research Institute Oslo, Norway, www.prio.no
	Prognos Group, Switzerland, www.prognos.ch/ehtml
	Progress and Freedom Foundation, USA, www.pff.org
	Prometeia, Italy, www.prometeia.it
PSI	Policy Studies Institute, United Kingdom, www.psi.org.uk
	Public Policy Forum, Canada, www.forumpp.ca
RAND	Research and Development, USA, www.rand.org
	Research Center of Taiwan, Hong Kong and Macao, China, www.ruc.edu.cn
	Research Institute of Economy, Trade and Industry, Japan, www.rieti.go.jp/jp
RIIA	Royal Institute of International Affairs, United Kingdom, www.riia.org
	Rockford Institute, USA, www.rockfordinstitute.org
	Rosa Luxemburg Foundation, Germany, www.rosaluxemburgstiftung.de
RSC	Robert Schuman Centre, at the European University Institute, Italy, www.iue.it/rsc
	Russell Sage Foundation, USA, www.epn.org/sage.html

RWI	Rhine-Westphalia Institute for Economic Research, Germany, www.rwi-essen.de
SAIIA	South African Institute of International Affairs, South Africa, www.wits.ac.za
	Sakura Institute of Research, Inc., Japan, n.a.
	Sanwa Research Institute & Consulting Corporation, Japan, www.ufji.co.jp
	Scottish Council Foundation, United Kingdom, www.scottishpolicynet.org.uk
SDI	Sarawak Development Institute, Malaysia, www.sdi.com.my
SFZ	Bureau for Future Studies, Germany, www.sfz.de
SHIP	Schleswig-Holstein Institute for Peace Research, Germany, www.schiff.uni-kiel.de
	Siglo XXI, Argentina, www.fas21.org.ar
SIIS	Shanghai Institute for International Studies, China, www.siis.org.cn/english
SIPRI	Stockholm International Peace Research Institute, Sweden, www.sipri.se
SISERA	Secretariat for Institutional Support for Economic Research in Africa, Senegal, www.idrc.ca/research/xsisera_e.html
SMF	Social Market Foundation, United Kingdom, www.smf.co.uk,
SRZG	Foundation for the Rights of Future Generations, Germany, www.srzg.de
STB	Sumitomo Trust Bank Research Institute, Japan, www.stbri.co.jp
	Sumitomo-Life Research Institute, Inc., Japan, http://homepage1.nifty.com/slri/
SVR	Council of Economic Experts, Germany, www.sachverstaendigenrat-wirtschaft.de
SWP	German Institute for International and Security Affairs, Germany, www.swp-berlin.org
	Sydney Institute, Australia, www.syndeyins.org.au
SZW	Weikersheim Study Centre, Germany, www.studienzentrum-weikersheim.de
	Taiwan Research, China, www.ygi.edu.cn
	Tasman Institute (defunct), now Tasman Economics, Australia, www.tasman.com.au
TEPSA	Trans European Policy Studies Association, Belgien, www.tepsa.be
	Thyssen Foundation, Germany, www.fritz-thyssen-stiftung.de
TIER	Taiwan Institute of Economic Research, Taiwan, www.tier.org.tw
TNI	TransNational Institute, Netherlands, www.tni.org
	Tokyo Foundation, Japan, www.tkfd.or.jp
	Trilateral Commission, USA, www.trilateral.org
	Twentieth Century Fund, USA, www.epn.org/tcf.html
	21st Century Public Policy Institute, Japan, www.21ppi.org
TWN	Third World Network, Malaysia, www.twnside.org.sg
	Urban Institute, USA, www.urban.org
USIP	United States Institute of Peace, USA, www.usip.org
WEF	World Economic Forum, Switzerland, www.weforum.org
WETtank	Women's Economic Think Tank, Australia, http://216.92.140.78/hostedpages/wettank/wettankindex.htm
	Whitlam Institute, Australia, www.whitlam.org.au
	World Watch Institute, USA, www.worldwatch.org
WRI	World Resources Institute, USA, www.wri.org
WSI	Institute for Economic and Social Research, Germany, www.wsi.de
	Wuppertal Institute for Climate, Environment and Energy, Germany, www.wupperinst.org/sites/home1.html
WZB	Social Science Center Berlin (for Social Research), Germany, www.wz-berlin.de
ZEF	Centre for Development Research, Germany, www.zef.de
ZEI	Centre for European Integration Research, Germany, www.zei.de
ZEW	Centre for European Economic Research, Germany, www.zew.de

Bibliography

Abelson, D.E. (1992) 'A New Channel of Influence: American Think Tanks and the News Media', *Queen's Quarterly* 99(4): 849–72.
Abelson, D.E. (1995) 'From Policy Research to Political Advocacy: The Changing Role of Think Tanks in American Politics', *Canadian Review of American Studies*, 25 (1): 93–126.
Abelson, D.E. (1996) *American Think Tanks and their Role in US Foreign Policy*, New York, St Martin's Press.
Abelson, D.E. (2000) 'Do Think Tanks Matter? Opportunities, Constraints and Incentives for Think Tanks in Canada and the United States', *Global Society*, 14 (2): 213–36.
Abelson, D.E. (2002) *Do Think Tanks Matter? Assessing the Impact of Public Policy Institutes*, Montreal, McGill-Queen's University Press.
Abelson, D.E. and C.M. Carberry (1997) 'Policy Experts in Presidential Campaigns: A Model of Think Tank Recruitment', *Presidential Studies Quarterly*, 27 (4): 679–97.
Addison, P. (1977) *The Road to 1945: British Politics and the Second World War*, London, Quartet.
Akami, T. (2002) 'Between the State and Global Civil Society: Non-Official Experts and their Networks in the Asia-Pacific, 1925–45', *Global Networks: A Journal of Transnational Affairs*, 2(1): 65–81.
Almeida, P. and S.C.M. Wong (1991) 'Globalization, Governance and Think Tanks: Malaysia's Experience Thus Far', in J.W. Langford and K. Lorne Brownsey (eds), *Think Tanks and Governance in the Asia-Pacific Region*, Halifax, Nova Scotia, Institute for Public Research and Policy.
Alpert, I. and A. Markusen (1980) 'Think Tanks and Capitalist Policy', in G.W. Domhoff (ed.), *Power Structure Research*, Beverley Hills and London, Sage.
Amato, G. and M.L. Salvadori (eds) (1990) *Europa Conviene?*, Bari and Rome: Laterza.
Amnesty International (1998) 'Malaysia: A Crossroads for Human Rights and the Rule of Law?', AI INDEX: ASA 28/19/98.
Amnesty International (1999) 'Malaysia: Anwar Verdict: A Door has Opened that Cannot be Closed', AI INDEX: ASA 28/02/99.
Amnesty International (2000) 'Malaysia: Sodomy Verdicts – A Major setback for human rights', AI INDEX: ASA 28/009/2000.

Anon. (1991) 'Think Tanks', *Free China Review*, 14(2): 30–5.
Ansari, A.A. (1977) 'The Legal Structure and Attendant Problems of the Sabah Foundation', Kuala Lumpur, unpublished paper submitted to the University of Malaya.
Antonenko, O. (1996) 'New Russian Analytical Centers and their Role in Political Decision-Making', CSIA Occasional Paper: Strengthening Democratic Institutions, John F. Kennedy School of Government, Harvard University.
Arbatov, G. (1992) *The System*, New York, Times Books.
Argy, F. (2003) *Where to Australian Egalitarianism?*, Sydney, Allen and Unwin.
Askiah Adam (1995) 'Think Tanks: Any Political Thoughts?', *New Sunday Times*, 12 March.
Augelli, E. and C.N. Murphy (1988) *America's Quest for Supremacy and the Third World: A Gramscian Analysis*, London, Pinter.
Bakvis, H. (2002) 'Rebuilding Policy Capacity in the Era of the Fiscal Dividend', *Governance*, 13(1): 71–103.
Barker, R. (1996) 'Political Ideas since 1945, or How Long was the Twentieth Century?', *Contemporary British History*, 10(1): 2–19.
Barnett, D.A. (1985) *The Making of Foreign Policy in China: Structure and Process*, Boulder, CO, Westview Press.
Barry, N. (1989) 'Ideas and Interests: The Problem Reconsidered', in A. Gamble, M. Olson, N. Barry, A. Seldon, M. Hartwell and A. Melnyk, *Ideas, Interests and Consequences*, London, IEA.
Beckett, A. (2001) 'Dulling Down', *Guardian*, 5 March.
Behn, R.D. (2001) *Rethinking Democratic Accountability*, Washington, DC, Brookings Institution.
Bell, S. (1995) 'Between Market and State: The Role of Australian Business Associations in Public Policy', *Comparative Politics*, 28(1): 25–53.
Bellucci, P. and M. Bull (2002) *Italian Politics: The Return of Berlusconi*, New York, Berghahn.
Bennett, C. (2002), 'Think Tanks? No Thanks', *Guardian*, 18 July.
Berman, E.H. (1983) *The Influence of the Carnegie, Ford and Rockefeller Foundations on American Foreign Policy*, Albany, NY, State University of New York Press.
Bone, P. (2000) 'Why Think Tanks are Full of Bias', *Age*, 12 October: 12.
Bonnic, M. and Y. Chevrier (1991) 'The Intellectual and the State: Social Dynamics of Intellectual Autonomy During the Post-Mao Era', *China Quarterly*, 127(3): 569–93.
Bosco, A. and C. Navari, eds (1994) *Chatham House and British Foreign Policy*, London, Lothian Foundation Press.
Bostock, A.L. (1984) *A Short History of the South African Institute of International Affairs 1934–1984*, Braamfontein, SAIIA.
Boulden, J. (1999) 'Independent Policy Research and the Canadian Foreign Policy Community', *International Journal*, 65(4): 625–47.
Braun, D. and A. Busch, eds (2000) *Public Policy and Political Ideas*, Cheltenham, Edward Elgar.
Brook, T. (1997) 'Auto-Organization in Chinese Society', in T. Brook and B. Michael Frolic (eds), *Civil Society in China*, London: M.E. Sharpe.

Bruckner, S. (1996) 'Policy Research Centres in Russia: Tottering Towards an Uncertain Future', *NIRA Review*, Summer.
Brown, L.D. (1991) 'Bridging Organizations and Sustainable Development', *Human Relations*, 44(8): 807–31.
Budd, A. (1978) *The Politics of Economic Planning*, London, Fontana.
Bufacchi, V. and S. Burgess (2001) *Italy since 1989: Events and Interpretations*, 2nd edn, Basingstoke, Palgrave.
Butler, D., A. Adonis and T. Travers (1994) *Failure in British Government: The Politics of the Poll Tax*, Oxford, Oxford University Press.
Callaghan, J. (1996) 'The Fabian Society since 1945', *Contemporary British History*, 10(2): 35–50.
Campbell, J. (1998) 'Institutional Analysis and the Role of Ideas in Political Economy', *Theory and Society*, 27: 377–409.
Capano, G. and M. Giuliani, (2001) 'Governing without Surviving? An Italian paradox: Law-Making in Italy, 1987–2001', *Journal of Legislative Studies*, 7(4): 13–36.
CEIP (Carnegie Endowment for International Peace) (1953) *Institutes of International Affairs*, New York, CEIP.
Chadwin, M.L. (1968) *The Hawks of World War II*, Chapel Hill, NC, University of North Carolina Press.
Cheung, T.M. (1987) 'The Impact of Research Institutes in the Post-Mao Period of Peking's Foreign Policy-Making', *Issues and Studies*, 23(7): 68–85.
Chin, J.K. (2000) 'Think Tanks and Policy Community in Hong Kong', *NIRA Review*, Summer.
Chisolm, L.B. (1990) 'Sinking the Think Tanks Upstream: The Use and Misuse of Tax Exemption Law to Address the Use and Misuse of Tax-Exempt Organizations by Politicians', *University of Pittsburgh Law Review*, 51 (3): 577–640.
Christie, K. and D. Roy (2001) *The Politics of Human Rights in East Asia*, London, Pluto Press.
Clough, M. (1994) 'Grass-Roots Policymaking: Say Good-Bye to the "Wise Men"', *Foreign Affairs*, 73(1): 2–7.
Cockett, R. (1994) *Thinking the Unthinkable: Think-Tanks and the Economic Counter-Revolution 1931–1983*, London, HarperCollins.
Coleman, W. and A. Perl (1999) 'Internationalized Policy Environments and Policy Network Analysis', *Political Studies*, 47: 691–709.
Commission for a New Asia (1994) *Towards a New Asia: A Report of the Commission for a New Asia*, Kuala Lumpur, ISIS.
Conference Board of Canada (2000) *Annual Report 2000*, Ottawa, Conference Board of Canada, web site: www.conferenceboard.ca/pdfs/ar.00-e.pdf.
Crewe, I. (1988) 'Has the Electorate become Thatcherite?', in R. Skidelsky (ed.), *Thatcherism*, London, Chatto and Windus.
Critchlow, D.T. (1985) *The Brookings Institution, 1916–52: Expertise and the Public Interest in A Democratic Society*, Dekalb, Northern Illinois Press.
CWF (Canada West Foundation) (1995) *Annual Report 1994*, Calgary, Canada West Foundation.
Dahrendorf, R. (1995) *LSE: A History of the London School of Economics and Political Science, 1895–1995*, Oxford, Oxford University Press.

da Silva, W. (2002) 'Agents of Influence', *Australian Financial Review*, 28 June: 22–40.
Day, A. (2000) 'Think Tanks in Western Europe', in J.G. McGann and R.K. Weaver (eds), *Think Tanks and Civil Societies: Catalysts for Ideas and Actions*, London and New Brunswick, NJ, Transaction Publishers.
Della Loggia, E. and A. Panebianco (2002) 'Il bipolarismo: una sfida per "il Mulino"', *Il Mulino*, 51(3). Available at: www.mulino.it/ilmulino/sd/discussioni/index.html.
Della Porta, D. (1996) 'The System of Corrupt Exchange in Local Government', in S. Gundle and S. Parker (eds), *The New Italian Republic: From the Fall of the Berlin Wall to Berlusconi*, London, Routledge.
Delors, J. and the Committee for the Study of Economic and Monetary Union (1989) *Report on Economic and Monetary Union in the European Community: Committee for the Study of Economic and Monetary Union*, Luxembourg, Office for Official Publications of the European Communities.
Denham, A. (1996) *Think-Tanks of the New Right*, Aldershot, Dartmouth.
Dente, B. and G. Regonini (1987) 'Politics and Policies in Italy', in P. Lange and M. Regini (eds), *State, Market, and Social Regulation*, Cambridge, Cambridge University Press.
Dente, B. (ed.) (1995) *Riformare la pubblica amministrazione*, Turin, Fondazione Agnelli.
Desai, R. (1994) 'Second-Hand Dealers in Ideas: Think Tanks and Thatcherite Hegemony', *New Left Review*, 203: 27–64.
Dicey, A.V. (1905) *Lectures on the Relation between Law and Public Opinion in England during the Nineteenth Century*, London, Macmillan.
Dickson, P. (1971) *Think Tanks*, New York, Atheneum.
Dirección General Red Federal de Información (2000) *Relevamiento Anual 2000*, Buenos Aires Dirección General Red Federal de Información.
Dobell, P.C. and R. Willmott (1977–78) 'John Holmes', *International Journal*, 33(1): 104–14.
Dolowitz, D. and D. Marsh (2000) 'Learning from Abroad: The Role of Policy Transfer in Contemporary Policy-Making', *Governance*, 13(1): 5–24.
Domhoff, W.G. (1983) *Who Rules America Now? A View for the '80s*, Englewood Cliffs, NJ, Prentice Hall.
Drake, W. and K. Nicolaidis (1992) 'Ideas, Interests, and Institutionalization: "Trade in Services" and the Uruguay Round', *International Organization*, 46(1): 37–100.
Dror, Y. (1984) 'Required Breakthroughs in Think Tanks', *Policy Sciences*, 16: 199–225.
Dudley, G. and J. Richardson (1996) 'Why does Policy Change over Time? Adversarial Policy Communities, Alternative Policy Arenas, and British Trunk Roads Policy 1945–95', in *Journal of European Public Policy*, 3(1): 63–83.
Dunn, W.N. (1996) 'A Look inside Think Tanks', *Economic Reform Today*, 3, www.cipe.org/ert/e21/dunE21.html.
Duranton-Crabol, A.M. (1988) *Visages de la nouvelle droite: Le GRECE et son histoire*, Paris, Presses de la Fondation Nationale des Sciences Politiques.
Dusevic, T. (1990) 'The Idea Factories', *Australian Financial Review*, 25 May: 1–3.

Dye, T.R. (1978) 'Oligarchic tendencies in national policy making: the role of private planning organisations', *Journal of Politics*, 40: 309–31.
Dyson, K. and K. Featherstone (1999) *The Road to Maastricht: Negotiating Economic and Monetary Union*, Oxford, Oxford University Press.
Economic Reform Today (1996) 'Shedding Light on the Gray Sector: Poland's Gdansk Institute for Market Economics', 3: 15–16.
The Economist (1988) 'The Darkest Hour is Before the Dawn', *The Economist*, 17 October: 86.
The Economist (2000) 'The European University Institute. Director of the Robert Schumann Centre' 22–8 January: 10.
EDI (Economic Development Institute) (1998) 'Capacity Building for Knowledge Institutions', Global Development Network Initiative, Washington, DC, Economic Development Institute.
Edwards, M. (2002) 'Public Sector Governance: Future Issues for Australia', *Australian Journal of Public Administration*, 61(2): 51–62.
Ehrman, J. (1995) *The Rise of Neo-Conservatism: Intellectuals and Foreign Affairs 1945–1994*, New Haven, CT, Yale University Press.
EUI (European University Institute), Robert Schuman Centre (1999) 'Self-Assessment Report 1993–1999' Doc. IUE 45/99 (CR2), Florence, EUI.
Federal Court of Audit (1996) 'Die Präsidentin des Bundesrechnungshofes als Bundesbeauftragte für Wirtschaftlichkeit in der Verwaltung: Gutachten über die Koordinierung der Aktivitäten im Bereich Ostforschung' ('President of the Federal Court of Audit: Report on the Coordination and Rationalisation of Federally Funded Research into Eastern and International Studies'), Bonn, internal unpublished report.
Ferdinand, P. (1991) *Communist Regimes in Comparative Perspective: The Evolution of the Soviet, Chinese and Yugoslav Models*, Hemel Hempstead, Harvester Wheatsheaf.
Fischer, F. (1993) 'Policy Discourse and the Politics of Washington Think Tanks', in F. Fischer and J. Forester (eds), *The Argumentative Turn in Policy Analysis and Planning*, London, UCL Press.
Flanagan, T. (1995) *Waiting for the Wave: The Reform Party and Preston Manning*, Toronto, Stoddart.
Fondazione Giovanni Agnelli (1996) *Programmi*, Turin, Fondazione Giovanni Agnelli.
Forsyth, W.D. (1974) 'The Pre-War Melbourne Group of the AIIA: Some Personal Recollections', *Australian Outlook*, 28(1): 44–9.
Fowler, R.M. (1977–78) 'Editor's Introduction', *International Journal*, 33(1): 1–4.
Freedom House Directory, accessed via www.ngonet.org/ttd2idx.htm.
Gaffney, J. (1988) 'French Socialism and the Fifth Republic', *West European Politics*, 11(3): 42–56.
Gaffney, J. (1991) 'Political Think Tanks in the UK and Ministerial Cabinets in France', *West European Politics*, 14(1): 1–17.
Gellner, W. (1995) '"Political Think-Tanks" and their Markets in the U.S. Institutional Setting', *Presidential Studies Quarterly*, Summer: 497–510.
Gibson, G. (1994) *Plan B: The Future of the Rest of Canada*, Vancouver, Fraser Institute.
Gilbert, M. (1994) *The Italian Revolution: The End of Politics, Italian Style?*,

Boulder, CO, and Oxford, Westview Press.
Gill, S. (1990) *American Hegemony and the Trilateral Commission*, Cambridge, Cambridge University Press.
Gill, B. and J. Mulvenon (2002) 'Chinese Military-Related Think Tanks and Research Institutions', *China Quarterly*, 171 (September): 617–24.
Giuliani, M. and C.M. Radaelli (1999) 'Italian Political Science and the European Union', *Journal of European Public Policy*, 6(3): 517–24.
Glaser, B.S. and P.C. Saunders (2002) 'Chinese Civilian Foreign Policy Research Institutes: Evolving Roles and Increasing Influence', *China Quarterly*, 171 (September): 559–74.
Goldman, M. (1981) *China's Intellectuals: Advice and Dissent*, Cambridge, MA, Harvard University Press.
Goldman, M. (1999) 'The Emergence of Politically Independent Intellectuals', in M. Goldman and R. MacFarquhar (eds), *The Paradox of China's Post-Mao Reforms*, Cambridge, MA, Harvard University Press.
Goldman, M. and T. Cheek (1987) 'Introduction: Uncertain Change', in M. Goldman, T. Cheek and C.L. Hamrin (eds), *China's Intellectuals and the State: In Search of a New Relationship*, London, Havard University Press.
Goldman, M., T. Cheek and C.L. Hamrin, eds (1987) *China's Intellectuals and the State: In Search of a New Relationship*, London, Harvard University Press.
Gomez, E.T. (1990) *Politics in Business: Umno's Corporate Investments*, Kuala Lumpur, Forum.
Gomez, E.T. (1994) *Political Business: Corporate Involvement of Malaysian Political Parties*, Townsville, James Cook University of North Queensland.
Gomez, E.T. and K.S. Jomo (1997) *Malaysia's Political Economy: Politics, Patronage and Profits*, Cambridge, Cambridge University Press.
Goodwin, C. and M. Nacht, eds (1995) *Beyond Government: Extending the Public Policy Debate in Emerging Democracies*, Boulder, CO, Westview Press.
Gorham, W. (1998) *The Urban Institute: 30 Years of Service*, Annual Report, Washington, DC, Urban Institute.
Government of Canada (1995) 'Strengthening Our Policy Capacity – Report', Task Force on Strengthening the Policy Capacity of the Federal Government, mimeo, 3 April.
Gramsci, A. (1971) *Selections from the Prison Notebooks of Antonio Gramsci*, eds Q. Hoare and G. Nowell-Smith, London, Lawrence and Wishart.
Greathed, E.D. (1969) 'Antecedents and Origins of the Canadian Institute of International Affairs', in H.L. Dyck and H.P. Crosby (eds), *Empire and Nations*, Toronto, University of Toronto Press.
Grose, P. (1996) *Continuing the Inquiry: The Council on Foreign Relations from 1921 to 1996*, New York, CFR.
Guo Ruihua, ed. (1996) *Zhong gong dui tai gong zuo zu zhi ti xi gai lun (The General Issues of CCP's Work and Organizational Systems toward Taiwan)*, Taipei, Ministry of Justice.
Haas, P. (1992a) 'Introduction: Epistemic Communities and International Policy Organisation', *International Organization*, 46(1): 187–224.
Haas, P. ed. (1992b) 'Knowledge, Power, and International Policy Coordination', *International Organization*, 46(1): 1–35.

Hall, P.A. (1990) 'Policy Paradigms, Experts, and the State: The Case of Macroeconomic Policy-Making in Britain', in S. Brooks and A-G. Gagnon (eds), *Social Scientists, Policy and the State*, New York, Praeger.

Hall, S. (1988) *The Hard Road to Renewal: Thatcherism and the Crisis of the Left*, London, Verso.

Halligan, J. (1995) 'Policy Advice and the Public Service', in B.G. Peters and D. Savoie (eds), *Governance in a Changing Environment*, Montreal and Kingston, McGill-Queen's University Press and the Canadian Centre for Management Development.

Halpern, N.P. (1992) 'Information Flows and Policy Coordination in the Chinese Bureaucracy', in K.G. Lieberthal and D.M. Lampton (eds), *Bureaucracy, Politics and Decision Making in Post-Mao China*, Berkeley and Los Angeles, University of California Press.

Harrison, R. (1993) 'The Fabians: Aspects of a Very English Socialism', in I. Hampsher-Monk (ed.), *Defending Politics: Bernard Crick and Pluralism*, London, British Academic Press.

Hassel, B. (1995) *The Charter School Idea: Elements of an Effective Charter School Program*; Taubmann Center, Kennedy School of Government, Cambridge, MA: Harvard University.

Hattersley, R. (2001) 'The Apostasy of the Think Tanks', *Guardian*, 20 August.

Headquarters for the Administrative Reform of the Central Government (2001) *Central Government Reform of Japan*, Tokyo, Headquarters for the Administrative Reform of the Central Government of Japan.

Heclo, H. (1978) 'Issue Networks and the Executive Establishment', in A. King (ed.), *The New American Political System*, Washington, DC, American Enterprise Institute for Public Policy Research.

Hellebust, L., ed. (1996) *Think Tank Directory: A Guide to Nonprofit Public Policy Research Organizations*, Kansas, Government Research Service.

Higgott, R. and D. Stone (1994) 'The Limits of Influence: Foreign Policy Think Tanks in Britain and the USA', *Review of International Studies*, 20(1): 15–34.

Hilderbrand, R.C. (1990) *Dumbarton Oaks: The Origins of the United Nations and the Search for Postwar Security*, Chapel Hill, NC, University of North Carolina Press.

Himmelstein, J.L. (1990) *To the Right: The Transformation of American Conservatism*, Berkeley, University of California Press.

Hobsbawm, E. (1964) *Labouring Men: Studies in the History of Labour*, London, Weidenfeld and Nicolson.

Hooper, P.F., ed. (1995) *Remembering the Institute of Pacific Relations: The Memoirs of William L. Holland*, Tokyo, Ryukei Shyosha.

Hough, J. and M. Fainsod (1979) *How the Soviet Union is Governed*, Cambridge, MA, Harvard University Press.

Hughes, G. (1992) 'The Minds that Shape Australia', *Weekend Australian Review*, 4–5 July: 3.

Huntington, S. (1993) 'The Clash of Civilizations?', *Foreign Affairs*, 72(3): 22–49.

Huntington, S. (1996) *The Clash of Civilizations and the Remaking of World Order*, New York, Simon and Schuster.

International Bar Association, ICJ Center for the Independence of Judges and Lawyers, Commonwealth Lawyers' Association and Union Internationale des

Avocats (2000) *Justice in Jeopardy: Malaysia 2000*, Report of a Mission on Behalf of the International Bar Association, the ICJ Centre for the Independence of Judges and Lawyers, the Commonwealth Lawyers' Association, Union Internationale des Avocats.
IKD (Institut Kajian Dasar) (1995) *Buletin IKD*, 2(1).
Inglis, A. (1977–78) 'The Institute and the Department', *International Journal*, 33(1): 88–103.
INPR (Institute for National Policy Research) (1998) *Brief Introduction of INPR*, Taipei, INPR.
Iokibe, M. (1999) 'Japan's Civil Society: An Historical Overview', in T. Yamamoto (ed.), *Deciding the Public Good: Governance and Civil Society in Japan*, Tokyo, Japan Center for International Exchange.
James, E. (1987) 'The Nonprofit Sector in Comparative Perspective', in W. Powell (ed.), *The Non Profit Sector: A Research Handbook*, New Haven, CT, Yale University Press.
James, S. (2000) 'Influencing Government Policymaking', in D. Stone (ed.), *Banking on Knowledge: The Genesis of the Global Development Network*, London, Routledge.
Jarman, A. and A. Kouzmin (1993) 'Public Sector Think Tanks in Inter-Agency Policy Making: Designing Enhanced Governance Capacity', *Canadian Public Administration*, 36(4): 499–529.
Jayasuriya, K. (1994) 'Singapore: The Politics of Regional Definition', *Pacific Review*, 7(4): 411–20.
JCIE (Japan Center for International Exchange) (2000) *Directory of Research Institutions/China*, Tokyo, Japan Center for International Exchange.
Jobert, B., ed. (1994) *Le Tournant Néo-Libéral en Europe*, Paris, L'Harmattan.
Johnson, E.C. (1996a) 'Central Europe's Think Tanks: A Voice for Reform', *Economic Reform Today*, 3: 9–14.
Johnson, E.C. (1996b) 'How Think Tanks Improve Public Policy', *Economic Reform Today*, 3: 34–8.
Johnson, E. (1997) *Improving Public Policy in the Middle East and North Africa: Institution Building for Think Tanks*, Washington, DC, Center for International Private Enterprise.
Johnson, E. (2000) 'Think Tanks in Sub-Saharan Africa', in J.G. McGann and R.K. Weaver (eds), *Think Tanks and Civil Societies: Catalysts for Ideas and Action*, London and New Brunswick, NJ, Transaction Publishers.
Jomo, K.S. (1994) *U-Turn: Malaysian Economic Development Policies after 1990*, Townsville, James Cook University of North Queensland.
Jones, E. (1993) 'Economic Language, Propaganda and Dissent', in S. Rees, G. Rodley and F. Stilwell (eds), *Beyond the Market: Alternatives to Economic Rationalism*, Sydney, Pluto Press.
Kaiser, K., T. de Montorial, C. Merlini and W. Wallace (1980) *Western Security: What has Changed? What Should be Done?*, London, Royal Institute of International Affairs
Kaiser, K., T. de Montorial, C. Merlini and W. Wallace (1983) *The European Community: Progress or Decline?*, London, Royal Institute of International Affairs.
Kaplan, F. (1985) *The Wizards of Armageddon*, New York, Simon and Schuster.

Katz, E. (1998) 'Mass Media and Participatory Democracy', in T. Inoguchi, E. Newman and J. Keane (eds), *The Changing Nature of Democracy*, Tokyo, United Nations University Press.
Keating, M. (2000) 'The Pressures for Change', in G. Davis and M. Keating (eds), *The Future of Governance*, Sydney, Allen and Unwin.
Kelly, P. (1992), *The End of Certainty*, Sydney, Allen and Unwin.
Kemp, D. (1988) 'Liberalism and Conservatism in Australia since 1944', in B. Head and J. Walter (eds), *Intellectual Movements and Australian Society*, Melbourne, Oxford University Press.
Kendle, J.E. (1975) *The Round Table Movement and Imperial Union*, Toronto, Toronto University Press.
Kennedy, P. (1988) *The Rise and Fall of the Great Powers*, London, Fontana.
Keohane, R.O. and J.S. Nye (1998) 'Power and Interdependence in the Information Age', *Foreign Affairs*, 77(5): 81–94.
KFPE (2001) *Enhancing Research Capacity in Developing and Transition Countries*, Berne, Swiss Commission for Research Partnerships with Developing Countries (KFPE).
Khoo, B.T. (1995) *Paradoxes of Mahathirism*, Kuala Lumpur, Oxford University Press.
Kimball, J. (2000) 'From Dependency to the Market: The Uncertain Future for Think Tanks in Central and Eastern Europe', in J.G. McGann and R.K. Weaver (eds), *Think Tanks and Civil Societies: Catalysts for Ideas and Action*, London and New Brunswick, NJ, Transaction Publishers.
Kingdon, J. (1984) *Agendas, Alternatives and Public Policies*, 1st edn, Boston, Little Brown.
Kingdon, J. (1995) *Agendas, Alternatives and Public Policies*, 2nd edn, New York, HarperCollins (1st edn, 1984, Boston, Little, Brown).
King-Hall, S. (1937) *Chatham House: A Brief Account of the Origins, Purposes and Methods of the Royal Institute of International Affairs*, London, Royal Institute of International Affairs.
Kislov, A. (1996) Interview at Institute of Peace Research/IMEMO, Moscow, July.
Kitingan, J. (1987) *People Development: A New Direction*, Sabah Foundation Policy Paper 1/87, Kota Kinabalu, Sabah Foundation.
Klaiber, K.-P. (1996) 'Zielvorgabe: Aktualität, Praxisnähe und Durchsetzbarkeit', *Internationale Politik*, 9 (September): 51, 63–4.
Kraft, H. (2000) 'Track Two Diplomacy in Southeast Asia', *Security Dialogue*, 31(3): 343–56.
Krastev, I. (2000a) 'The Liberal Estate: Reflections on the Politics of Think Tanks in Central and Eastern Europe', in J.G. McGann and R.K. Weaver (eds), *Think Tanks and Civil Societies: Catalysts for Ideas and Action*, London and New Brunswick, NJ, Transaction Publishers.
Krastev, I. (2000b) 'Think Tanks: Making and Faking Influence', in D. Stone (ed.), *Banking on Knowledge: The Genesis of the Global Development Network*, London, Routledge.
Landers, R.K. (1986) 'Think-Tanks: The New Partisans?', *Congressional Quarterly*, 1 (23): 455–72.
Langford, J.W. and K.L. Brownsey (1991) 'Introduction: Think Tanks and Modern Governance', in J.W. Langford and K.L. Brownsey (eds), *Think Tanks*

and Governance in the Asia-Pacific Region, Halifax, Novia Scotia, Institute for Research on Public Policy.
Lavin, D. (1995) *From Empire to International Commonwealth: A Biography of Lionel Curtis*, Oxford, Clarendon Press.
Legge, J.D. (1999) *Australian Outlook: A History of the Australian Institute of International Affairs*, Sydney, Allen and Unwin.
Levy, D. (1996) *Building the Third Sector: Latin America's Private Research Centers and Nonprofit Development*, Pittsburg, University of Pittsburgh Press.
Linden, P. (1987) 'Powerhouses of Policy', *Town and Country*, January: 99–179.
Lindquist, E. (1989) 'Behind the Myth of Think Tanks: The Organization and Relevance of Canadian Policy Institutes', doctoral thesis, Berkeley, University of California.
Lindquist, E.A. (1993a) 'Think tanks or Clubs? Assessing the Influence and Roles of Canadian Policy Institutes', *Canadian Public Administration*, 36(4): 547–79.
Lindquist E.A. (1993b) 'Transition Teams and Government Succession: Focusing on the Essentials', in D.J. Savoie (ed.), *Taking Power: Managing Government Transitions*, Toronto, Institute of Public Administration of Canada.
Lindquist, E.A. (1994a) 'Balancing Relevance and Integrity: Think Tanks and Canada's Asia-Pacific Policy Community', in S. Brooks and A.-G. Gagnon (eds), *The Political Influence of Ideas: Policy Communities and the Social Sciences*, New York, Praeger.
Lindquist, E.A. (1994b) 'Citizens, Experts and Budgets: Evaluating Ottawa's Emerging Budget Process', in S.D. Phillips (ed.), *How Ottawa Spends 1994–5: Making Change*, Ottawa, Carleton University Press.
Link, A.S. and R.L. McCormick (1983) *Progressivism*, Arlington Heights, IL, Harlan Davidson.
Lipset, S.M. (1960) *Political Man*, New York, Doubleday.
Liu Zhifeng, ed. (1996) *Ping 'di san zhi yan jing kan zhong guo': jie shi zhong guo (Comment on 'The Third Eye on China': Explaining China)*, Hong Kong, Ming Pao.
Loh, K.W.F. (1992) 'Modernisation, Cultural Revival and Counter-Hegemony: The Kadazans of Sabah in the 1980s', in J. Kahn and F. Loh (eds), *Fragmented Vision: Culture and Politics in Contemporary Malaysia*, Sydney, Allen and Unwin.
Loh, K.W.F. (1996) 'A "New Sabah" and the Spell of Development: Resolving Federal–State Relations in Malaysia', *South East Asia Research*, 4(1): 63–83.
Lucarelli, S. and R. Menotti, eds (2002a) *Studi internazionali: I luoghi del sapere in Italia*, Rome: Edizioni Associate.
Lucarelli, S. and R. Menotti (2002b) 'No-Constructivists' Land: IR in Italy in the 1990s', *Journal of International Relations and Development*, 5(2): 114–42.
Luo, Z. (1991) 'The Globalization Challenge and the Role of Think Tanks in China', in J.W. Langford and K.L. Brownsey (eds), *Think Tanks and Governance in the Asia-Pacific Region*, Halifax, Nova Scotia, Institute for Research on Public Policy.
MacDonagh, O. (1958) 'The Nineteenth-Century Revolution in Government: A Reappraisal', *Historical Journal*, 1(1): 52–67.
MacKenzie, N. and J. MacKenzie (1977) *The First Fabians*, London, Weidenfeld and Nicolson.

Bibliography

Mair, P. (1997) *Party System Change*, Oxford, Oxford University Press.
Malaysian Business Council, Centre for Economic Research and Services (1991) 'Malaysia: The Way Forward', text of speech given to the Malaysian Business Council, 28 February.
Manaev, O. (2000) 'Think Tanks in Independent Belarus: Catalysts for Social Transformation', in D. Stone (ed.), *Banking on Knowledge*, London, Routledge.
Manno, B.V. (1997) *What Do We Know about Charter Schools?*, Taubmann Center, Kennedy School of Government, Cambridge, MA, Harvard University.
Mansourov, V. (1996) Interview in Institute of Sociological Studies, Moscow, July.
Marsh, D. and R.A.W. Rhodes, eds (1992) *Implementing Thatcherite Policies: Audit of an Era*, Buckingham, Open University Press.
Marsh, D., M.J. Smith and D. Richards (2001) *Changing Patterns of Governance: Reinventing Whitehall*, Basingstoke, Palgrave.
Marsh, I. (1980) *An Australian Think Tank?*, Sydney, NSW, New South Wales University Press.
Marsh, I. (1995a) *Beyond the Two Party System: Political Representation, Economic Competitiveness and Australian Politics*, Melbourne, Cambridge University Press.
Marsh, I. (1995b) 'The Development and Impact of Australia's "Think Tanks"', CEDA Information Paper No. 43, February, Melbourne and Sydney, CEDA.
Marwick, A. (1964), 'Middle Opinion in the Thirties: Planning, Progress and Political Agreement', *English Historical Review*, 79: 285–98.
Mathews, J.T. (1996) 'Creating an Independent Institute for Policy Research on Global Issues: The World Resources Institute', in J. Telgarsky and M. Ueno (eds), *Think Tanks in a Democratic Society: An Alternative Voice*, Washington, DC, Urban Institute.
Maxwell, J., K. Jackson, B. Legowski, S. Rosell and D. Yankelovich *et al.* (2002) *Report on Citizens' Dialogue on the Future of Health Care in Canada*, Canadian Policy Research Networks, web site: www.cprn.com/cprn.html.
McAdam, D.J., McCarthy, J. D. and M. Zald (1996) *Comparative Perspectives on Social Movements: Political Opportunities, Mobilising Structures and Cultural Framings*, New York, Cambridge University Press.
McBriar, A. (1966) *Fabian Socialism and English Politics 1884–1918*, Cambridge, Cambridge University Press.
McCombs, P. (1983) 'Building a Heritage in the War of Ideas', *Washington Post*, 3 October.
McGann, J.G. (1992) 'Academics to Ideologues: A Brief History of the Public Policy Research Industry', *PS: Political Science and Politics*, December: 733–40.
McGann, J.G. (1995) *The Competition for Scholars, Dollars and Influence in the Public Policy Research Industry*, Lanham, MD, University Press of America.
McGann, J.G. and R.K. Weaver, eds (2000) *Think Tanks and Civil Societies: Catalysts for Ideas and Action*, London and New Brunswick, NJ, Transaction Publishers.
Means, G. (1991) *Malaysian Politics: The Second Generation*, Singapore, Oxford University Press.

Mehmet, O. (1988) *Development in Malaysia: Poverty, Wealth and Trusteeship*, Kuala Lumpur, Institute of Social Analysis.

Melton, R.H. (1995) 'Closing of Dole's Think Tank Raises Questions About Fundraising', *Washington Post*, 18 June: 8.

Mesežnikov, G. (2001), 'Role of Think Tanks in Social Transformation Process', accessed at www.ivo.sk, 20/3/2002.

Mielke, G. (1999) 'Sozialwissenschaftliche Beratung in den Staatskanzleien', *Forschungsjournal Neue Soziale Bewegungen*, 12(3): 40–8.

Millar, T.B. (1976) 'The Role of the Institute', *Australian Outlook*, 30(1): 3–15.

Millar, T.B. (1977–78) 'Commonwealth Institutes of International Affairs', *International Journal*, 33(1): 5–27.

Moody, P. (1977) *Opposition and Dissent in Contemporary China*, Stanford, CA, Hoover Institute.

Moore, C. and S. Heffer, eds (1989) *Tory Seer*, London, Hamish Hamilton.

Moore, M. (1996) 'Is Democracy Rooted in Material Prosperity?', in R. Luckham and G. White (eds), *Democratization in the South: The Jagged Wave*, Manchester, Manchester University Press.

Muravchik, J. (1987) 'The Think Tank of the Left', *New York Times Magazine*, 27 April: 46.

Muta, S. and M. Noda (1995) 'Status of Research Institutions in China: A Trend Report', in T. Yamamoto (ed.), *Emerging Civil Society in the Asia Pacific Community*, Tokyo and Singapore, Japan Center for International Exchange and the Institute of Southeast Asian Studies.

Nathan, J. (1996) *Charter Schools: Creating Hope and Opportunity for American Education*, Jossey Bass.

Naughton, B. (2002) 'China's Economic Think Tanks: Their Changing Role in the 1990s', *China Quarterly*, 171(September): 625–34.

Nelson, D.N (1984) 'Charisma, Control, and Coercion: The Dilemma of Communist Leadership', *Comparative Politics*, 17(1).

Newsom, D.D. (1996) *The Public Dimension of Foreign Policy*, Bloomington, IN, Indiana University Press.

Niblett, R. and W. Wallace, eds (2001) *Rethinking European Order: West European Responses, 1989–1997*, London, Palgrave.

Nielsen, W.A. (1989) *The Golden Donors: A New Anatomy of the Great Foundations*, New York, Dutton.

NIRA (National Institute for Research Advancement) (1996) *1996 NIRA's World Directory of Think Tanks*, Tokyo, NIRA.

NIRA (National Institute for Research Advancement) (2001) *Sinku Tanku Nenpo 2001*, Tokyo, NIRA.

NIRA (National Institute for Research Advancement) (2002) *2002 World Directory of Think Tanks*, Tokyo, NIRA.

Noda, M. (1995) 'Research Institutions in Malaysia', in T. Yamamoto (ed.), *Emerging Civil Society in the Asia-Pacific Community*, Singapore and Tokyo, Institute for Southeast Asian Studies and Japan Centre for International Exchange.

Noguchi, Y. (1995) *1940 Nen Taisei*, Tokyo, Toyo-Keizai Shimposha.

North, D. (1992) *Institutions, Institutional Change and Economic Performance*, New York, Cambridge University Press.

Bibliography

Nye, J.P. (1990) *Bound to Lead: The Changing Nature of American Power*, New York, Perseus Books.

ODC (Overseas Development Council) (1999) 'Dialogue with Think Tanks: A Report of a Meeting with the United Nations Secretary General', 4–5 May, United Nations Headquarters, New York.

Oliver, S. (1993) 'Lobby Groups, Think Tanks, the Universities and Media', *Canberra Bulletin of Public Administration*, 75 (December): 134–7.

Olson, W.C. and A.J.R. Groom (1991) *International Relations Then and Now*, London, Routledge.

Open Society Institute (2001) *Open Society Institute Related Public Policy Centers*, Activity Report, June, Budapest, OSI.

Oshio, T. (2002) 'Outlook for Japan's Aging Society', *Journal of Japanese Trade and Industry*, May/June.

Page, D. (1977–78) 'The Institute's "Popular Arm": The League of Nations Society in Canada', *International Journal*, 33(1): 28–65.

Parmar, I. (1994) 'Chatham House, the Foreign Policy Process, and the Making of the Anglo-American Alliance', in A. Bosco and C. Navari (eds), *Chatham House and British Foreign Policy*, London, Lothian Foundation Press.

Parmar, I. (1999a) 'Mobilizing America for an Internationalist Foreign Policy: The Role of the Council on Foreign Relations', *Studies in American Political Development*, 13(2): 337–73.

Parmar, I. (1999b) 'The Carnegie Corporation and the Mobilisation of Opinion during the United States' Rise to Globalism, 1939–1945', *Minerva*, 37: 355–78.

Parmar, I. (2000) 'Engineering Consent: The Carnegie Endowment for International Peace and the Mobilisation of American Public Opinion, 1939–1945', *Review of International Studies*, 26: 35–48.

Parmar, I. (2002a) 'American Foundations and the Development of International Knowledge Networks', *Global Networks*, 2(1): 13–30.

Parmar, I. (2002b) 'Anglo-American Elites in the Interwar Years: Idealism and Power in the Intellectual Roots of Chatham House and the Council on Foreign Relations', *International Relations*, 16(1): 53–75.

Parsons, W. (1996) *Public Policy: An Introduction to the Theory and Practice of Policy Analysis*, Aldershot, Edward Elgar.

Peschek, J.S. (1987) *Policy Planning Organizations: Elite Agendas and America's Rightward Turn*, Philadelphia, Temple University Press.

Peters, S. (1995) *Exploring Canadian Values: Foundations for Well-Being*, Ottawa, Canadian Policy Research Networks.

Pierre, J. (1995) 'The Marketization of the State: Citizens, Consumers, and the Emergence of the Public Market', in B.G. Peters and D.J. Savoie (eds), *Governance in a Changing Environment*, Montreal and Kingston, McGill-Queen's University Press and Canadian Centre for Management Development.

Pirie, M. (1988) *Micropolitics: The Creation of Successful Policy*, Aldershot, Wildwood House.

Polsby, N. (1983) 'Tanks but no Tanks', *Public Opinion*, April/May: 14–16, 58–9.

Prospecta (1992) *Ideologie e prassi delle relazioni industriali prossime venture*, 2 volumes, typescript, Milan.

Quigley, K.F.F. (1995) 'Think Tanks in Newly Democratic Eastern Europe', in J. Telgarsky and M. Ueno (eds), *Think Tanks in a Democratic Society: An Alternative Voice*, Washington, DC, Urban Institute.
Quigley, K.F.F. (1997) *For Democracy's Sake: Foundations and Democracy Assistance in Central Europe*, Washington, DC, Woodrow Wilson Center Press.
Radaelli, C. (1995) 'The Role of Knowledge in the Policy Process', *Journal of European Public Policy*, 2(2): 159–83.
Radaelli, C.M. (2002) 'The Italian State and the Euro: Institutions, Discourse, and Policy Regimes', in K. Dyson (ed.), *The European State and the Euro*, Oxford, Oxford University Press.
Radaelli, C.M. and A.P. Martini (1998) 'Think Tanks, Advocacy Coalitions and Policy Change: The Italian Case', in D. Stone, M. Garnett and A. Denham (eds), *Think Tanks Across Nations*, Manchester, Manchester University Press.
Reford, R.W. (1976) 'Canada and the World: The Work of the Canadian Institute of International Affairs', *Canadian Business Review*, 3 (Winter).
Regonini, G. and M. Giuliani (1994) 'Italie: au-delà d'une démocratie consensuelle?', in B. Jobert (ed.), *Le Tournant néo-libéral en Europe*, Paris: L'Harmattan.
Reid, E. (1989) *Radical Mandarin: The Memoirs of Escott Reid*, Toronto, Toronto University Press.
Reinicke, W. (1998) *Global Public Policy: Governing without Government*, Washington, DC, Brookings Institution.
Reinicke, W.H. (2001) 'Walking the Talk: Global Public Policy in Action', in *Global Public Policies and Programs: Implications for Financing and Evaluation*, proceedings from a World Bank Workshop, Washington DC, World Bank.
Rhodes, M. and M. Bull, eds (1997) *Crisis and Transition in Italian Politics*, London, Frank Cass.
Rhodes, R.A.W. (1997), *Understanding Governance: Policy Networks, Governance, Reflexivity and Accountability*, Buckingham, Open University Press.
Ricci, D. (1993) *The Transformation of American Politics: The New Washington and the Rise of American Politics*, New Haven, CT, Yale University Press.
Richards, D. and M.J. Smith (2002) *Governance and Public Policy in the United Kingdom*, Oxford, Oxford University Press.
Richardson, J. (2000) 'Government, Interest Groups and Policy Change', *Political Studies*, 48(5): 1007–25.
RIIA (Royal Institute of International Affairs) (1946) *The Future of Chatham House*, London, RIIA.
Ritchie, R.S. (1971) *An Institute for Research on Public Policy: A Study and Recommendations*, Ottawa, Information Canada.
Rix, A., ed. (1988) *Intermittent Diplomat: The Japan and Batavia Diaries of W. Macmahon Ball*, Melbourne, Melbourne University Press.
Roberts, D. (1959) 'Jeremy Bentham and the Victorian Administrative State', *Victorian Studies*, 2(3):193–210.
Roberts, P. (2001) 'Underpinning the Anglo-American Alliance: The Council on Foreign Relations and Britain between the Wars', in J. Hollowell (ed.), *Twentieth-Century Anglo-American Relations*, Basingstoke, Palgrave.

Bibliography

Robson, W.B.P. (1995) 'Change for a Buck? The Canadian Dollar after Secession', *Commentary*, 68 (March).
Roitter, M. and I. González Bombal, eds (2000) *Estudios sobre el Sector sin Fines de Lucro en Argentina*, IV Encuentro Iberoamericano del Tercer Sector, Buenos Aires.
Rose, E.J.B., N. Deakin, M. Abrams, V. Jackson, M. Peston, A.H. Vanags, B. Cohen, J. Gaitskell and P. Ward (1969), *Colour and Citizenship*, London, Oxford University Press for the Institute of Race Relations.
Rosell, S.A. (1999) *Renewing Governance: Governing by Learning in the Information Age*, Toronto, Oxford University Press.
Rosell, S.A. et al. (1993) *Governing in an Information Society*, Montreal, Institute for Research on Public Policy.
Russell, P.H. (1993) *Constitutional Odyssey: Can Canadians Become a Sovereign People?*, 2nd edn, Toronto, University of Toronto Press.
Sabatier, P.A. (1993) 'Policy Change over a Decade or More', in P.A. Sabatier and H.C. Jenkins-Smith, (eds), *Policy Change and Learning: An Advocacy Coalition Approach*, Boulder, CO, Westview Press.
Sabatier, P.A., ed. (1999) *Theories of the Policy Process*, Boulder, CO, Westview Press.
Sabatier, P.A. and H.C. Jenkins-Smith, eds (1993) *Policy Change and Learning: An Advocacy Coalition Approach*, Boulder, CO, Westview Press.
Salamon, L. and H. Anheier (1992) 'In Search of the Nonprofit Sector II: The Problem of Classification', *Voluntas*, 3(3): 267–309.
Saravanamuttu, J. (2002) 'Report on Human Rights in Malaysia', *Aliran Online*, www.malaysia.net/aliran/hr/js.html.
Sartori, G. (1976) *Parties and Party Systems*, Cambridge, Cambridge University Press.
Sawer, M. (2002) *Waltzing Matilda: Feminism and Social Liberalism in Australia*, Melbourne, Melbourne University Press.
Sawer, M. and A. Groves (1994) 'The Women's Lobby: Networks, Coalition Building and the Women of Middle Australia', *Australian Journal of Political Science*, (29)3: 443–59.
Sawer, M. and J. Jupp (1996) 'The Two Way Street: Government Shaping of Community Based Advocacy', *Australian Journal of Public Administration*, 55(4): 82–100.
Schmitter, P. (1974) 'Still the Century of Corporatism?', in F. Pike and T. Stritch (eds), *The New Corporatism*, Paris, University of Notre Dame Press.
Seck, D. and Philips, C.P. (forthcoming) *Adjusting Structural Adjustment: Best Practices in Policy Research in Africa*.
Shambaugh, D. (1987) 'China's National Security Research Bureaucracy', *China Quarterly*, 110(2): 276–304.
Sherrington, P. (2000) 'Shaping the Policy Agenda: Think Tank Activity in the European Union', *Global Society*, 14(2): 173–89.
Sherwood Truitt, N. (2000) 'Think Tanks in Latin America', in J.G. McGann and R.K. Weaver (eds), *Think Tanks and Civil Societies: Catalysts for Ideas and Action*, London and New Brunswick, NJ, Transaction Publishers.
Shimokobe, A., ed. (1996) *Seisaku Keisei No Soshutu*, Tokyo, Dai-ichi Shori.
Shimotomai, N. (1990) 'Perestroika, Glasnost and Society', in T. Hasegawa and

A. Pravda (eds), *Perestroika: Soviet Domestic and Foreign Policies*, London, Sage.
Shoup, L. and W. Minter (1977) *Imperial Brain Trust: The Council on Foreign Relations and United States Foreign Policy*, New York, Monthly Review Press.
Simon, H. (1955)'A Behavioral Model of Rational Choice', *Quarterly Journal of Economics*, 69: 99–118.
Sinclair, T.J. (2000) 'Reinventing Authority: Embedded Knowledge Networks and the New Global Finance', *Environment and Planning C: Government and Policy*, 18: 487–502.
Smith, J.A. (1991) *The Idea Brokers: Think Tanks and the Rise of the New Policy Elite*, New York, Free Press.
Soward, F.H. (1977–78), 'Inside a Canadian Triangle: The University, the CIIA, and the Department of External Affairs. A Personal Record', *International Journal*, 33(1): 66–87.
Stefanic, J. and R. Delgado (1996) *No Mercy: How Conservative Think Tanks and Foundations Changed America's Social Agenda*, Philadelphia, PA., Temple University Press.
Stokes, G. (1994) 'Australian Political Thought: Editorial Introduction', in G. Stokes (ed.), *Australian Political Ideas*, Sydney, University of New South Wales Press.
Stone, D. (1996a) 'A Think Tank in Evolution or Decline? The Australian Institute of International Affairs in Comparative Perspective', *Australian Journal of International Affairs*, 50(2): 117–36.
Stone, D. (1996b) *Capturing the Political Imagination: Think Tanks and the Policy Process*, London and Portland, Frank Cass.
Stone, D. (2000a) 'Private Authority, Scholarly Legitimacy and Political credibility', in R. Higgot, G. Underhill and A. Bieler (eds), *Non-State Actors and Authority in the Global System*, London, Routledge.
Stone, D. (2000b) 'Introduction to the Symposium: The Changing Think Tank Landscape', *Global Society*, 14(2): 149–52.
Stone, D. (2000c) 'Think Tank Transnationalism and Non-Profit Analysis, Advice and Advocacy', *Global Society*, 14(2): 153–72.
Stone, D. (ed.) (2000d) *Banking on Knowledge: The Genesis of the Global Development Network*, London, Routledge.
Stone, D. (2001) 'The Policy Research Knowledge Elite and Global Policy Processes', in D. Josselin and W. Wallace (eds), *Non-State Actors in World Politics*, Basingstoke, Palgrave.
Stone, D. (2002) 'Global Knowledge and Advocacy Networks', *Global Networks*, 2(1): 1–11.
Struyk, R. (1999) *Reconstructive Critics: Think Tanks in Post-Soviet Bloc Democracies*, Washington, DC, Urban Institute Press.
Struyk, R. (2000) 'Think Tanks in the Former Soviet Union', in J.G. McGann and R.K. Weaver (eds), *Think Tanks and Civil Societies: Catalysts for Ideas and Action*, London and New Brunswick, NJ, Transaction Publishers.
Struyk, R.J. (2002) 'Transnational Think Tank Networks: Purpose, Membership and Cohesion', *Global Networks*, 2(1): 83–90.
Struyk, R.J., M. Ueno and T. Suzuki (1993) *A Japanese Think Tank*, Washington, DC, Urban Institute.

Suzuki, T. and M. Ueno (1993) *Sekai No Sinku Tanku*, Tokyo, Saimaru Shuppankai.
Swaine, M.D (1996) *The Role of the Chinese Military in National Security Policymaking*, Santa Monica, Rand.
Taguieff, P.A. (1994) *Sur la Nouvelle Droite*, Paris, Descartes.
Tanner, M.S. (2002) 'Changing Windows on a Changing China: The Evolving "Think Tank" System and the Case of the Public Security Sector, *China Quarterly*, 171 (September): 559–74.
Telgarsky, J. and M. Ueno, eds (1996) *Think Tanks in a Democratic Society*, Washington, DC, Urban Institute.
Thomas, W. (1979) *The Philosophic Radicals: Nine Studies in Theory and Practice 1817–1841*, Oxford, Clarendon Press.
Thompson, A. (1994) 'Think Tanks en la Argentina, Conocimiento, instituciones y política', Buenos Aires, CEDES.
Thompson, P. (1967) *Socialists, Liberals and Labour: The Struggle for London, 1885–1914*, London, Routledge and Kegan Paul.
Thorne, C. (1978) 'Chatham House, Whitehall and Far Eastern Issues: 1941–45', *International Affairs*, 54(1): 1–29.
Thunert, M.W. (2001) 'Germany', in R.K. Weaver and P. Stares (eds), *Guidance for Governance: Comparing Alternative Sources of Policy Advice*, Tokyo and New York: Japan Center for International Exchange.
Ueno, M., ed. (1993) *Seisak Keisei to Nihongata Sinku Tanku*, Tokyo, Toyo-Keizai Shimposha.
Ueno, M. (2000) 'Northeast Asian Think Tanks', in J.G. McGann and R.K. Weaver (eds), *Think Tanks and Civil Societies: Catalysts for Ideas and Action*, London and New Brunswick, NJ, Transaction Publishers.
Ullrich, H. (2001) 'The Impact of Policy Networks in the GATT Uruguay Round: The Case of the US–EC Agricultural Negotiations', unpublished thesis, LSE.
Van der Ploeg, C. and D. Elton (1994) *The Quebec Question: A Roadmap of the PQ Agenda and the Questions for Canada*, Calgary, Canada West Foundation.
Van der Ploeg, C. and D. Elton (1995) 'Suppose the "Yes" Side Wins: Are We Ready?', Calgary, Canada West Foundation, January.
Wala, M. (1994) *The Council on Foreign Relations and American Foreign Policy in the Early Cold War*, Oxford, Berghahn Books.
Wallace, W. (1990) 'Chatham House at 70: To the 1990s and Beyond', *World Today*, 46 (5): 75–7.
Wallace, W. (1994) 'Between Two Worlds: Think Tanks and Foreign Policy', in C. Hill and P. Beshoff (eds), *Two Worlds of International Relations: Academics, Practitioners and the Trade in Ideas*, London, Routledge.
Warhurst, J., J. Brown and R. Higgins (2000) 'Tax Groupings: The Group Politics of Taxation Reform', in M. Simms and J. Warhurst (eds), *Howards Agenda: The 1998 Australian Election*, Brisbane, University of Queensland Press.
Watson, D. (2002) *Memoirs of A Bleeding Heart*, Sydney, Random House.
Weaver, R.K. (1989) 'The Changing World of Think Tanks', *PS: Political Science and Politics*, September: 563–78.
Weaver, R.K. and B.A. Rockman (1993) 'Assessing the Effects of Institutions', in R.K. Weaver and B.A. Rockman (eds), *Do Institutions Matter? Government*

Capabilities in the United States and Abroad, Washington, DC, Brookings Institution.

Weaver, R.K. and P. Stares (2001) *Guidance for Governance*, Tokyo, Japan Center for International Exchange.

Weilemann, P.R. (2000) 'Experiences of a Multidimensional Think Tank: The Konrad Adenauer Stiftung', in J. McGann and R.K.Weaver (eds), *Think Tanks and Civil Societies*, New Brunswick, NJ, Transaction Publishers.

Weiss, C.H. (1979) 'The Many Meanings of Research Utilisation', *Public Administration Review*, 39(5): 426–31.

Weiss, C.H. (1990) 'The Uneasy Partnership Endures: Social Science and Government', in S. Brooks and A.-G. Gagnon (eds), *Social Scientists, Policy and the State*, New York, Praeger.

Weiss, C.H. (1992) *Organizations for Policy Analysis*, Newbury Park, Sage.

Weiss, L. (1995) 'Governed Interdependence: Rethinking the Government–Business Relationship in East Asia', *Pacific Review*, 8(4): 589–616.

Williams, H. (1998) *Guilty Men: Conservative Decline and Fall 1992–1997*, London, Aurum Press.

Williams, P. (2001) 'Intellectuals and the End of Apartheid: Critical Security Studies and the South African Transition', unpublished PhD dissertation, University of Wales, Aberystwyth.

Woods, L.T. (1999) 'Canada and the Institute of Pacific Relations: Lessons from an Earlier Voyage', *Canadian Foreign Policy*, 6 (2): 119–38.

World Bank (1993) *The East Asian Miracle*, Oxford, Oxford University Press.

Wong, D. (1995) 'Regionalism in the Asia-Pacific – A Response', *Pacific Review*, 8(4): 683–8.

Wu, G. (1997) *Zhao Ziyang yu zheng zhi gai ge (Political Reform under Zhao Ziyang)*, Hong Kong, Pacific Century Institute.

Wu, J. (1994) 'The Growing Influence of Think Tanks in Shanghai', *NIRA Review*, Autumn.

Xu, M. (1996) 'Xin zi you zhu yi de kun jing' ('The Dilemma of Neo-Liberalism'), in Liu Zhifeng (ed.), *Ping 'di san zhi yan jing kan zhong guo': jie shi zhong guo (Comment on 'The Third Eye on China': Explaining China)*, Hong Kong, Ming Pao.

Yamamoto, T., ed. (1995) *Emerging Civil Society in the Asia-Pacific Community*, Singapore and Tokyo, Institute for Southeast Asian Studies and Japan Centre for International Exchange.

Yankelovitch, D. (1992) *Coming to Public Judgement*, New York, Syracuse University Press.

Yee, A. (1996) 'The Causal Effects of Ideas on Policies', *International Organization*, 50(1): 69–108.

Zhao, Q. (1996) *Interpreting Chinese Foreign Policy: The Micro–Macro Linkage Approach*, Hong Kong, Oxford University Press.

Index

academic, 200, 235, 250
  alternative/academic flight, 133, 281
  think tanks, 72–6, 85, 87, 199, 217–18
academics, 53, 63, 92, 99, 170, 177, 182, 190, 202, 211, 224, 250, 259, 268, 274, 282
accountability, lack of, 172–3, 262
active participant, 205, 212
administrative reform, 100, 175
adversarial coalitions, 99
advocacy, 4, 42, 43, 44, 50, 85, 128, 137, 200, 201, 202, 204, 205, 206, 235, 244, 258, 266
  coalitions, 2, 13, 62, 64, 97–103
  think tank, 33, 72, 76–8, 81, 85, 93, 198, 199, 200, 201, 202, 204, 205, 220–1, 236–7
agenda setting, 67, 85, 109, 110, 259, 289
agora, 34
  global, 41, 48–9
American intellectual hegemony, 287, 289
Anglo-American
  co-operation, 25, 31
  model (or Anglo-Saxon model), 2, 10, 40, 107
anti-communism, Liberal, 25
apathy, 242–3
Asian values, 143, 173, 180, 191, 194–5, 287
Asia Pacific Economic Cooperation (APEC), 36
Association of South East Asian Nations (ASEAN), 37, 43, 186
associations, 53, 109, 110, 199
Australian Institute of International Affairs (AIIA), 25, 27, 28, 32, 247, 252, 255, 259, 260
authoritarian political system, 10, 171, 172, 177, 180, 184, 191, 194–6, 198, 199, 201, 202, 180, 281, 282
autonomy *see* independence

bipolarism, 94, 96
Bretton Woods System, 23
bridging research and policy, 185–7, 205
British Broadcasting Corporation (BBC), 36
Brookings Institution, 10, 107, 117, 216, 217, 218, 227, 266, 284
bureaucracy, 6, 7, 8, 151, 184, 185, 257, 262
  developing countries, 206
  Japan, 169, 171, 172, 173, 174;
    imperial institutional structures, 170
  Soviet, 122–6, 136
  see also think tanks, relationship to the state
bureaucratic institutions, 211
bureaucrats, 14, 63, 166, 171, 172, 205
business sector, 1, 7, 10, 15, 164, 167, 169, 174, 202, 184, 187, 216, 219, 224, 248, 249, 253, 259, 266, 270, 277, 279

cabinets, 106, 110, 111, 113–17
Canadian Institute of International Affairs, 25, 32
Canadian International Development Agency, 35, 181
'cash for access', 240
catalyst, 52, 67, 268
censorship, 122, 123, 170, 182
Central News Network (CNN), 36
charitable organisations *see* non-profit organizations
Chatham House (Royal Institute for International Affairs), 19–33, 21–4, 58

Chinese Communist Party, 141, 146, 147, 150, 151
Christian Democrats, 77, 79, 93, 96, 97, 101, 102, 115
civil and political liberties *see* human rights
civil service, 53, 63, 96, 110, 232, 243
civil society, 1, 37, 46–50, 53, 59, 107, 121, 128, 131, 133, 136, 142, 143, 146, 149, 180, 189, 191, 193, 198, 199, 202, 204, 212
climate of opinion, 66, 234, 236, 237, 239
Cold War, 89, 94, 95, 103, 169, 171
communism, 113, 121–37, 168, 172
Communist Party, 94, 102, 121, 122, 168
Conservatism, 174, 236, 237, 266, 271, 272
consultancy, 206, 272, 285
consulting firms, 272, 273, 279
contract research, 76, 91, 270, 274
  corporate commissioned, 71, 131, 187
  government commissioned, 71, 166, 181, 185–7, 218–20, 225, 270, 277
convergence, 8, 137
co-option, 24, 174
corporatism, 31
Council on Foreign Relations, 19–33, 21–4, 216, 217
cross-coalition learning, 102, 103
Cultural Revolution, 146

decentralization, 204, 207, 225
decision-making, 13, 56, 62, 217
deliberative techniques, 276, 280
democracy and democratization, 121, 127, 130, 131, 136, 137, 163, 164, 166, 168–77, 198, 199, 201, 204, 207, 235, 242, 243, 281–4
  Western-style, 164, 168, 171
demonopolization, 136
development, 189, 195
  studies, 179–96, 249, 250
  transnational, 34
devolution, 232
diplomacy
  informal, 43, 197
  multilateral, 287
  private, 63
  second track, 186, 282, 284, 287, 289
  unofficial, 19, 29–31, 285
discourse coalitions, 13, 14, 184
dissemination of ideas, 25, 30, 89, 101, 122, 125, 131, 282
  control of ideas, 122, 125
diversification, 131, 133
Dolowitz, David and Marsh, David, 206, 209

Dror, Y., 142, 257

Economic and Monetary Union (EMU), 45, 56, 98
economic
  co-operation, 125, 168
  crises, 271
  decline/uncertainty, 129, 134, 135, 236
  development, 8, 48, 74, 90, 127, 165, 166
  growth, 168, 169, 174; global, 35, 37, 163
  stagnation, 177
economies of scale, 206
economists, 1, 65, 92, 102, 163, 167, 169, 287
electoral reform, 98, 100
elite opinion, 13, 262
elitism/elites, 10, 12, 20, 21, 22, 26, 27, 29, 108, 136, 179, 186, 226, 237, 244, 262, 276, 281, 283, 284, 286, 289
  transnational, 33
enlightenment, 12, 126, 257, 257, 258–9, 279
environmental issues, 198, 205, 259, 283
epistemic communities, 2, 10, 62, 63–4, 65, 106, 117, 136, 287
  politicisation, 135
Euro (the), 90, 96, 97
Euro-American co-operation, 25
European Commission, 55, 101
European Council, 55
European Institutes of International Affairs, 24–6, 32
European integration, 67, 80, 91, 95, 96, 101
European policy *see* policy-making role, European
European studies, 56, 60, 61, 91, 96
European Union (EU), 6, 10, 13, 36, 41, 45, 51–68, 131, 134, 192, 286
  Brussels-based think tanks, 53, 54, 56–7, 286
  Cellule de prospective, 53, 55
  Group of Economic Analysis, 55
  impact on policy-making process *see* influence, on policy-making; policy-making
  internal think tanks, 53, 54, 55
  member-state EU orientated think tanks, 53, 54, 57–60
  networks, 55, 57, 60, 61–2, 63, 97
  university-based European research institutes, 53, 54, 60–1
evaluation research (or programmes), 63, 90, 97, 166, 172, 176

Index

exclusion, 137
executive dominance (or power), 209, 232, 256
ex-politicians (or ex-policy makers), 80, 228
expertise, 2, 7, 15, 64, 65, 66, 110, 117, 195, 225

Fabian Society, 234, 246
feasibility studies, 97
federalism, 6, 71, 74, 81, 100, 126, 132, 181, 187–9, 247, 255, 271
financial
  institutions, 165, 166
  sustainability, 80–1, 167, 211, 212, 252, 266, 267, 273, 274, 279, 280
  viability, 135, 252
flexibility, 210, 237
foreign policy *see* policy-making role
for-profit institutions, 165, 166, 277
forum, 67, 103, 240, 269, 270, 285, 288
foundations, 1, 6, 11, 15 34, 79, 277
  business-related, 47, 273, 284
  philanthropic, 3, 41, 218, 284
  political party, 44, 201, 225, 248, 249
  Western, 44, 129, 131, 284, 285
four modernizations, 146, 147
Freedom House, 128–30, 133, 134
fundraising, 274, 277, 286
  Western, 129, 134–5

glasnost (openness), 10, 125
globalism, 23, 24, 31
globalization, 7, 33, 35, 37, 38, 116, 259, 289
global policy community, 289
Gorbachev, Mikhail, 124–5, 126
governance, 13, 34, 40, 49
  global, 38, 48
  principles of, 168
government agencies, 199
government reform, 6
  Japan, 175–7
Gramscian approaches, 12, 13, 31–3
Greenpeace, 44
guanxi, 148, 153

Haas, Peter, 13, 106
hegemony, 12, 31, 44, 119, 142, 224, 258
Heritage Foundation, 107, 216, 220, 221, 224, 227, 228
human rights, 91, 129, 163, 182, 196, 198
  freedom of speech, 5, 166, 171

ideas, 3, 13, 15, 257, 258, 261
  battle of, 217, 261
  brokerage or diffusion of, 38, 44–5, 262, 289
  marketing of, 211, 215, 262
  market place of, 12, 226, 261, 262
  see also media
ideological
  controls (or monism), 142, 136
  ideological fellowship, 237, 243
  ideological positioning, 92, 93
ideology, 4, 12, 93, 109, 110, 112, 119, 142, 151, 172
independence, 3, 5, 66, 124, 129, 130, 135, 164, 166, 178, 200, 209, 210, 265, 266, 267, 269, 281
  compromised, 23, 24, 165, 277
  constrained, 25, 122–4, 126, 134, 135, 141–53, 194, 243, 284
  financial, 4, 58, 71, 80, 89, 125, 128, 131, 145, 181, 218, 219, 240, 272
  organisational, 90, 125, 128, 209, 238
  party-political, 235, 236
  scholarly, 4, 58, 89, 125, 128, 239, 246
influence
  on funding, 91, 92
  limits of, 10, 11, 57, 67, 126, 229–31, 239, 241
  methodological question of, 15–10, 257–62, 229–31, 269, 277
  on policy-making, 51, 55, 62, 65–7, 98, 99, 132–135, 205, 211, 228–9, 236, 239, 270, 271, 289
  source of, 19, 28, 65
  on subject areas, 57, 91, 230
  transnational, 38, 50, 285
ink tank, 249
innovation, 277
insiders, 13, 100
instability
  economic, 134, 135
  political, 134, 135
Institutes of International Affairs, 19ff
  dominion institutes, 21, 24, 25, 26ff, 32
  leaders *see* think tanks, leaders
instituteniki, 123
institutional design, 100
institutionalization, 137
inter-war period, 234
intellectuals, 237, 239, 285
  establishment, 141–53, 145–8, 282
intellectual roots, 26, 27, 244
interest groups, 3, 8, 14, 35, 42, 109
intergovernmental organisations, 288
internationalisation, 91, 103, 289
internationalism, 31
international organisations, 10, 15, 202, 289
isomorphism, 41

'ivory tower' syndrome, 92, 175

Johnson, Erik, 6, 127, 128, 133

Keynesianism, 9, 74, 137, 235, 236, 258, 281
Kimball, J., 127, 128, 130, 133–5
kitchen cabinets, 82
knowledge, 13
  economy, 192, 195
  global, 19
  networks, 10, 37, 47
  and power, 127, 263
  utilisation, 47, 103
Krastev, Ivan, 1, 4, 8, 127, 137

Labour Party, 234, 238
leadership programmes, 175, 268
legitimacy, 43, 44, 66, 95, 97, 212
Liberal Democrats, 168, 169, 171, 173
liberal intellectuals, 136, 137, 258
liberal internationalism, 19, 25, 32
liberalism, 44, 171–2, 248, 254
liberalization, 124, 136, 190
libertarianism, 8, 258
lobbying, 3, 53, 205, 217, 240, 250
local government, 135, 166, 175, 204, 206, 242

managerialism, 271
market economy, 136, 152, 164, 174, 282
  free, 202, 282
marketization, of think tanks, 136
Marxism, 13, 114, 168, 282
  Leninism, 121, 137
McGann, James, 1, 2, 5, 106, 127, 128, 216
media, 3, 12, 14, 15
  blame, 242
  demand, 8, 215, 232, 236, 260, 270
  growth, 128, 260
  influence of, 233
  leaders, 202
  pluralistic, 153, 204
  and public communication, 84, 191, 215, 225, 227, 229, 260
  visibility, 94, 191, 215, 225, 227, 229, 239, 244, 245, 247, 264, 279, 289
membership (of think tanks), 25–6, 37, 43, 278
Mercado Común del Sur (Mercosur), 36
military dictatorship *see* authoritarian political system

national identity, 170, 179, 191
nationalism, 20, 137, 169, 182, 192
national security, 163, 166, 168

networking, 14, 41, 252, 263, 276
networks, 13, 14, 100, 252, 273, 283
  coherence of, 38
  formation of, 12, 98, 99, 125
  management of, 252
  regional, 97, 287, 289; *see also* European Union
  transnational, 12, 38, 39, 286, 287
New Labour, 238, 239, 240, 241, 242
New Liberalism, 20
new partisans, 93
New Right, 9, 12, 118, 119, 235–8, 244, 248, 256, 259, 262
Night of the Long Clubs, 200
non-governmental organizations, 12, 15, 32, 38, 39, 41, 42, 44, 45, 48–9, 53, 63, 78, 83, 130, 135, 174, 181, 189, 193–4, 198, 199, 212
non-partisan relationship, 33, 216, 282
non-profit
  activities, 175
  organizations, 75, 76, 106, 164, 166, 174–5, 198, 199, 207, 277, 279
  sector, 273, 278, 279
non-state actors, 1, 34, 37, 48–9, 52, 87
North Atlantic Treaty Organisation (NATO), 134, 286
novoe politicheskoe mishlenie (new political thinking), 125

objectivity, 4, 32
opinion-formers, 236
Organisation for Economic Co-operation and Development (OECD), 1, 6, 39, 282, 288
Organisation of Petroleum Exporting Countries (OPEC), 35
overseas education, 148, 152, 153, 287

paradigm, 101, 258, 288
  Keynesian, 9
  shift, 11, 126, 189
parliamentary politics, 235
partnership, Public/private, 211, 240, 268
paternalism, 170, 171
patron–client relations, 92, 123, 142
patronage, 13, 37, 38, 48, 123, 146, 148
perestroika (restructuring), 10, 125, 127
personal contacts/connections, 132, 133, 143, 147, 166
philanthropy, 5, 25, 232, 247, 252
Philosophic Radicals, 234, 244
pluralism, 31, 32, 125, 136, 171, 172, 174, 177, 179, 199, 200, 261
pluralisation, 142, 174, 200, 201, 202
policy
  actors, 59, 61, 63, 64
  advisors, 286–8

Index

analysis, 1, 34, 44, 172, 173, 175, 176, 177, 178, 199, 211, 270, 272, 276
analysts, 176, 177, 280
change, 233
clubs, 90, 93, 94, 97
coalition *see* networks
communities, 13, 34, 35, 38, 62, 63, 133
engineers, 236, 237
entrepreneurs, 14, 62, 64–5, 75, 78, 179, 181, 224, 258, 262, 263, 278, 283
implementation, 7, 85, 198, 202, 204–206, 206–11, 212
implementation think tank *see* think-and-do-tank
informant, 205
innovation, 275
learning, 103, 268; cross-national and cross-regional, 206
makers, 199, 215, 221, 225, 228, 272, 275, 276, 280, 281, 287, 288; educating, 133, 206, 217
making, 172, 201, 217, 218, 220, 221, 229, 255, 256, 277; monopolized, 169
making role, 13, 89, 127, 135, 141, 142, 146, 148, 163, 164, 166, 167, 198, 204, 243, 264; developing countries, 206, 206–11; economic, 101, 102, 103, 123, 124, 131, 135, 165, 235; European, 51–68, 233 (*see also* influence); exaggerated, 234, 237; foreign, 27, 28, 31, 32, 92, 93, 94, 96, 123, 233; multi-level, 52, 61, 62; national and/or regional, 204, 234, 235; Soviet, 122, 123, 125, 126
network, 13, 37, 38, 41, 45, 48, 235, 245
orientated learning, 64
paradigms, 87, 99
process, 141
relevance, 84, 85, 87, 88
research, 166, 175, 176, 177, 178, 218, 239, 244, 264–6, 269, 272, 286, 288
solutions, progressive, 240
transfer, 38, 206
transfer entrepreneur, 209, 210
web *see* policy, network
political
clubs, 111–16
corruption, 95, 96, 98, 100, 169–70, 172, 174, 185, 205, 212
culture, 5, 143
environment, 171
leadership, 171

parties, 2, 7, 10, 14, 57, 72, 77–80, 83, 85, 86, 90, 98, 108, 109, 111–13, 117, 120, 125, 131, 164, 198, 199, 200, 201, 202, 225, 232, 248, 249, 253, 254, 258
reforms, 169, 194, 199
transparency, 164
will, lack of, 206
politicians, 63, 206
politicisation of research, 87, 88, 135
postcommunism, 121–37
presidentialism, 111
presidential
politics, 111, 112, 132
systems, 6, 132
prestige, 209, 210, 286, 287
private sector *see* business sector
professionalization of politics, 237
proliferation, 128, 129, 131, 147, 148, 190, 221–6, 272, 283
public
debate, 67, 90, 142
education, 4, 28, 29, 126, 128, 205, 235
funding, 90
interest, 174
opinion, 3; cynical, 173, 174, 177; listening to, 276; mobilising, 28, 29; shaping, 126, 237, 257
see also media
private, 172, 174, 275, 284
sector, 167, 268
sphere (or fora), 123, 125; *see also* forum; global, 192, 288, 289 (*see also* agora)

RAND, 3, 36, 73, 218, 219, 224, 285
RAND-Europe, 76
rationalization, 103
regulatory impact analysis, 97
Republicanism, 111
research brokerage, 266
'revolving door', 30, 8, 82, 143, 181, 201, 228, 237, 239, 242, 243, 244
Round Table, 21, 268
Russian Revolution, 283

Sabatier, 13, 99
self-evaluation, Lack of, 172–3, 231
semi-detachment, 282
services, organizational and technical, 44
Smith, James, 2, 216
Social Democrats, 266
socialism, 20, 113, 115, 116, 172
Socialist Party, 97, 102, 168
social market economy, 238, 241
soft power, 286, 287, 289
Solidarity movement, 133, 134
state, (the)

authoritarian *see* authoritarian
  political system
 developmental, 180
 postcommunist, 121–37
 statization of society, 143
 welfare state, 234, 235, 270
statism, 31
status quo, 170
strategic research, 233
Struyk, Raymond, 1, 127, 128, 130, 134, 135, 165, 177

talk tank, 249
technical expertise, 206
terrorism, 92, 163, 215
Thatcherism, 236, 244
Thatcherite, 243
think-and-do-tank, 200, 201, 202, 205, 206–11, 242
think tanks
 academic, 72–76, 92, 97; *see also* academic; academics; universities
 bureaucracy, 82, 145, 151, 153, 185, 185, 256, 258; *see also* bureaucracy; think tanks, relationship to the state
 capacity-building, 151, 178, 206
 competition among, 84–6, 225, 243–6, 272, 279
 competition with other institutions, 279
 corporate interests, 240, 244; *see also* business sector
 decline thereof, 244
 definitions and typologies, 2–5, 72, 80–3, 106–10, 199
 development of, 5–10, 34ff, 41, 78
 directors, 56, 59, 143, 147, 148, 155–62, 249, 250, 260, 269
 diversity, 267–70, 278, 279, 281, 283
 elitism *see* elitism
 European Union *see* European Union
 evaluation of, 87–8
 financial autonomy *see* independence
 foreign policy *see* policy-making
 freedom of expression, 149–51, 153
 government funding, 71, 73
 international organisations, 84, 186, 189
 leaders, 23, 25, 88, 143–4, 148, 254, 264, 273, 277
 political participation in, 78, 80, 87
 political parties *see* political, parties
 proliferation of *see* proliferation
 relationship to the state, 71–6, 82, 83, 87, 105, 106, 108, 110, 111, 118, 120, 143, 144, 147, 149–53, 180–6, 188, 200, 202, 209, 219, 228–9, 272, 277–9, 281
 reputation of, 153, 181
 social movements, 259
 staffing, 71, 73, 74, 81–3, 107, 108, 181, 219, 252
 tax laws, 220, 224, 236, 247, 252
 transnationalisation, 12, 34ff, 37, 39, 49–50
 waves of development, 9, 35, 71, 72, 180–2, 184, 200–4, 216–1, 233–46, 247–52, 265–7, 283
 Western-style, 8, 145, 178
third sector organizations, growth of, 36, 199
Third Way, 240, 241
trade unions, 14, 90, 124, 259
traditional ideologies, free from, 238
transnational actors, 15
Treaty on European Union (TEU), also known as Maastricht Treaty, 97, 98, 101, 102

United Nations (UN), 6, 8, 10, 23, 27, 30, 43, 45
universities, 7, 224, 258, 272, 275, 279
 relations with think tanks, 73–5, 227, 252, 253, 272, 279
universities without students, 3, 91, 130, 218
USAID, 15, 35

vanity think tanks, 221
violence, 284
virtual institute, 265, 273
voter pressure, 206

Weaver, Kent, 1–3, 5, 6, 106, 127, 128, 216, 218, 225, 236
web sites, 105, 227, 274, 275, 291–8
web technologies, 275
Weiss, Carol, 12, 187, 257
Westernisation, 48, 287
Westminster Model, 232, 237, 245
World Bank, 6, 10, 23, 46, 47, 186, 288
World Economic Forum (WEF), 36, 285, 287, 289
World War I, 21
World War II, 22–4, 27, 28, 29, 31, 168, 169, 170, 216, 219, 220, 224, 225, 283–1

EU authorised representative for GPSR:
Easy Access System Europe, Mustamäe tee 50,
10621 Tallinn, Estonia
gpsr.requests@easproject.com